THE MAG[...]
AND OTHER
NINETEENTH-CENTURY
PLAYS

DRAMA

£9

10/24

AN

THE MAGISTRATE

AND OTHER NINETEENTH-CENTURY PLAYS

EDITED BY

MICHAEL R. BOOTH

OXFORD UNIVERSITY PRESS

LONDON   OXFORD   NEW YORK

1974

Oxford University Press

OXFORD LONDON NEW YORK
GLASGOW TORONTO MELBOURNE WELLINGTON
CAPE TOWN IBADAN NAIROBI DAR ES SALAAM LUSAKA ADDIS ABABA
DELHI BOMBAY CALCUTTA MADRAS KARACHI LAHORE DACCA
KUALA LUMPUR SINGAPORE HONG KONG TOKYO

ISBN 0 19 881336 8

*Selection and editorial material © Oxford University Press
1974*

The texts of the plays are reprinted from English Plays of
the Nineteenth Century *edited by Michael R. Booth*, vols.
*i–iv (Oxford: Clarendon Press, 1969 and 1973), © Oxford
University Press 1969 and 1973*

*Printed in Great Britain
at the University Press, Oxford
by Vivian Ridler
Printer to the University*

CONTENTS

ACKNOWLEDGEMENTS

―――

ACKNOWLEDGEMENTS are due to Samuel French Ltd. for permission to reprint *The Magistrate* by Arthur Wing Pinero, and to Mrs. Dorinda Maxse for permission to reprint *Mrs. Dane's Defence* by Henry Arthur Jones.

INTRODUCTION

AMONG historians of the drama and theatre, at universities, and to a lesser degree in the professional theatre, the reputation of nineteenth-century English drama—aside from the always popular Shaw and Wilde—is slowly but certainly raising itself from that abyss of darkness at whose uttermost depths it has lived, condemned by academic proscription and theatrical contempt, so furtively and so long. Such a progress toward the light must be welcomed, not only by its advocates but also by all those concerned to see critical fair play and interested in an intrinsically fascinating period of dramatic and theatrical history.

There is, indeed, no need to be apologetic about it: one can advance and substantiate considerable claims for the nineteenth-century drama. Before the middle-class take over of the theatre was completed towards the end of the century, or possibly a few years later, that drama offered for the last time in English history entertainment for all classes of society, a truly popular drama in both senses of the word. From the meanest penny gaff in Whitechapel to the Rubens Room in Windsor Castle, and from the lowest street urchin to the monarch of the land, the English enjoyed theatre in confusingly multifarious forms. Then as now, its very popularity and lack of intellectuality made it the object of intellectual middle-class attack. At a time when English-speaking theatre has become a middle-class minority entertainment catering to a maximum potential audience of about 2 per cent of the population of Britain and North America, we should value nineteenth-century drama for the universality of its appeal. And today, when popular cultures are the focus of much academic study, there is no reason why the popular aspects of nineteenth-century drama and theatre should not command respectful attention.

Two principal charges against nineteenth-century drama have been that it was divorced from literature and therefore inconsequential and trivial; furthermore, since it was written purely for the 'theatre' (a naughty pejorative in some academic circles), it was separated from the real world around it and bore little or no relation to the serious concerns of life and thought. The first charge is true in the sense that except for Bulwer-Lytton the important poets and novelists of the century were not fortunate in the theatre, their efforts varying from occasional successes, often caused by ingenious staging or skilful adaptation by other hands, such as Coleridge's *Remorse* (1813) and Tennyson's *Becket* (1893), to utter disasters or rejection by managers. In fact, one of the troubles with early nineteenth-century tragedy is that it was *too* conscious of literature and anxious to emulate dead Elizabethan modes of playwriting, looking to a past age for themes and styles rather than to its own times, a period plenteously endowed with dramatic substance. The relationship between the stage and the novel was very close, and although the novelists did not on the whole establish reputations as dramatists, their novels—from Ann Radcliffe through Scott and Dickens to Mrs. Henry Wood, Ouida, and Anthony Hope—were continuously adapted for stage perform-ance. Not only that: all the major tendencies of nineteenth-century drama can be found in the novel—a strong emphasis on narrative and moral line, a great deal of sensation, shining virtue, and dark-hued vice; romantic passion, and a romantic landscape (in the earlier period); eccentric native humour; domestic idealism, domestic bliss, and domestic agony; senti-ment and pathos, a fondness for the happy ending; a more than cursory examination of themes relating to wealth (inherited and newly acquired), commerce, class conflict, industrial strife, the urban environment, social problems and social protest. Nobody has accused the nineteenth-century novel of being divorced from contemporary life and thought, and if nineteenth-century drama deals with this material—as indeed it does—then the second charge cannot be sustained. When it is recalled that playwrights were effectively prevented by the absolute power of the Examiner of Plays from dealing seriously with sex, religion, and politics, it is remarkable how much they reflected and commented on the life of their times; the fact that they were writing mainly for audiences seeking entertainment at a popular and non-intellectual level makes this achievement not insignificant.

As the century progressed, the social context of drama

became more specifically delineated, and technological developments in the theatre enabled managers, carpenters, and scene-painters to make elaborate attempts at verisimilitude and the realistic reproduction of a particular social environment. The drama was thus able to find settings suitable to its thematic concern with the two nations of rich and poor in contemporary London, and the result is the first metropolitan and environmental drama in England. The metropolis fascinated Victorian dramatists and audiences (and novelists, one need hardly add), and a deliberate artistic and thematic use of London as an image of existence, a moral symbol, and a strikingly visual and richly human presentation of the realities of its daily living, originates in the theatre with the Victorian stage. The theme of lost innocence, of a vanished rural heritage, of a dimly remembered and already mythicized Garden of Eden, as expressed by the purely symbolic world of the village of melodrama, is very strong in the theatre from the 1820s. That innocence is tainted and lost in the dark world of London, a world of moral squalor and physical and mental suffering, as well as a spectacle of life. Hundreds of nineteenth-century plays deal with this theme, and scores of them, like *The Heart of London* (1830), *The Streets of London* (1864), *The Poor of London* (1864), *Lost in London* (1867), *The Dark Deeds of London* (1882), and *The Great World of London* (1898), name that City of Dreadful Night in their titles. These plays teem with the life and people of the streets, of the homeless poor, of the cheap lodging-houses, the taverns, the gambling dens, and the cold pavement beneath the arches of Waterloo Bridge; on a different social level the rich villa in Regent's Park, the splendidly appointed fashionable drawing-room, the elegant resorts of the wealthy, and the characters appropriate to such settings are material for the same dramatists and frequently for the same plays. Business life, commercial ambition in the City, financial intrigue, the sudden bankruptcy and the plunge from riches to poverty are also prominent themes; authors like Dion Boucicault and Tom Taylor dramatized this material and showed the effects on character and domestic life of involvement with business and speculation. Again, these themes are of major importance and deal with essential structures of nineteenth-century life and thought.

The strong tide of the domestic that engulfed Victorian art forms also flowed over the drama, a drama which in both its melodramatic and comic components dealt extensively with the humble home as well as with various kinds of middle-class domestic existence. In this drama the English theatre gets its first substantial emphasis on domestic themes, both comic and tragic, its first substantial exposure to suffering on the level of home and hearth, daily living, and ordinary family life. Well before Ibsen, English dramatists in both the East End and the West End theatres were exploring stresses, tensions, conflicts, and discords against the detailed background of a domestic environment. Before Ibsen, too, characters in domestic drama were trying to free themselves from the weight of the past and to live with the inexorable consequences of their own acts; indeed, their struggle to do so—like Bob Brierly's in Taylor's *The Ticket-of-Leave Man* (1863) or Mathias's in Leopold Lewis's *The Bells* (1871)—constitutes the core of the drama. More simplistically, the hero of temperance melodrama and the female sinner of domestic melodrama face a similar struggle. Unlike Ibsen, the nineteenth-century English dramatist usually avoided a tragic termination to these domestic agonies and the often violent or pathetic effort to escape the determinism of the past, but the raw material is basically the same nevertheless.

The breakdown of the remarkably homogeneous and predominantly middle-class audience of the established eighteenth-century playhouse, and its replacement in the nineteenth century by a variety of audiences drawn from several class levels, meant the inclusion, especially in plays written for theatres catering to the working and lower-middle class, of characters drawn from the lower social strata—these characters being employed, not merely for low comedy, but also and more importantly for serious, pathetic, moral, and tragic or potentially tragic purposes. With a drama of this kind went an appropriate vocation and an appropriate habitat. Thus it is in nineteenth-century drama that we see the first serious treatment of the working class in the English theatre, and the first attempt to locate drama entirely in the environment of working-class life. On the comic level, usage can be significantly different from the earlier employment of servants and other characters from humble walks of life in plays whose important concerns were carried on by their masters and mistresses. Early and mid-Victorian farce, for example, is sometimes exclusively concerned with journeymen, tailors, laundresses, maids of all work, milkmen, hairdressers, waiters, chemists' assistants, commercial travellers, and the like.

A relevance to contemporary life can hardly be found in the more respected closet tragedies of the Romantic and Victorian poets, but it is abundantly apparent in the melodrama, comedy, farce, and pantomime—extremely lively and flourishing forms—that are *persona non grata* with those very critics who deplore the lack of significance in nineteenth-century drama. One of the most perceptive observers of the early Victorian theatre was Richard Hengist Horne, who, despite his advocacy of a drama of ideal art and his rejection of social reality and contemporary life as fit subjects for the stage, recognized that these forms represented the true taste of the age. 'The most legitimate, because the most genuine offspring of the age, is that Drama which catches the manners as they rise and embodies the characteristics of the time. . . . Whatever the amount of their ability, the truly dramatic, as far as it exists on the modern stage at all, will be found in those comparatively neglected writers of the minor drama.[1]

The most important and the newest form of this 'minor drama'—a term applied before 1843 to the 'illegitimate' drama performed at theatres other than Drury Lane, Covent Garden, and the Haymarket—was the melodrama. It too, with all its crudities, fantasies, and dramatized dream-world of ideal love, justice, courage, and virtue, was not only thoroughly representative of its age but also socially and politically more advanced than other forms of nineteenth-century theatre. In times of war it evolved the mythic character of the heroic British tar, who in plays like Douglas Jerrold's *Black-Eyed Susan* (1829) and J. T. Haines's *My Poll and My Partner Joe* (1835) became a national symbol of dauntless maritime prowess, with all the essential virtues of a sea-going John Bull. For a century military and nautical melodrama fought the major land and sea battles of British history, and long before Imperialism was a conscious political doctrine the Union Jack waved triumphantly over a battalion of militantly expansionist and

[1] *A New Spirit of the Age* (London, 1844), ii. 90, 94.

imperialist melodramas. The form developed as a separate dramatic entity in the 1790s, both at Drury Lane and Covent Garden and in spectacle dumbshow at transpontine theatres like the Royal Circus. Strongly influenced by the English Gothic novel and a few years later by the political idealism of the plays of Goethe and Schiller and the sensational, post-Revolutionary Parisian melodramas of Pixérécourt and his followers, melodrama was a popular branch of the Romantic movement. Especially Romantic was the Gothic melodrama, which antedated the fully blown nautical melodrama by a generation. At first primarily a means of eliciting suspense and terror from situations involving cloisters, castles, forests, dungeons, wild heaths, brooding despots, robber chieftains, pale apparitions, fleeing heroines, and persecuted heroes of noble but mysterious birth, the Gothic melodrama slowly took a more domestic turn, either substituting or adding a range of settings and characters that includes the humble cottage where virtue and poverty dwell, the honest woodsman or peasant, and the old father whose peace is menaced by the designs of the abductor-villain upon his lovely and innocent daughter. Very early in the nineteenth century the character stereotypes of melodrama—hero, heroine, villain, good old man and woman, comic man and woman, and eccentric character role—were complete; also fully evolved were the standard plot devices, the machinery of coincidence and sensation, the extensive musical accompaniment, the spectacular physical effects, and (with rare exceptions) the inexorability of poetic justice, the rewards of virtue and love, and the downfall of villainy.

The Miller and His Men (1813) was the foremost and, for nearly a century, both in the live theatre and in children's toy theatres, the most popular example of Gothic melodrama; it also well expressed the tendency to mitigate, with some degree of domestic tenderness and the softer virtues, the gloomy severity of earlier Gothicism. In the character of Karl, it illustrated the comic element essential to nearly all melodrama. A sudden switch from the darkest violence or the most heart-rending pathos to the extremes of farce was a common melodramatic technique, and demonstrates the emotional and situational eclecticism of the genre. Somewhat sophisticated, at times more socially elevated, and greatly extended in subject matter over the years, melodrama nevertheless preserved almost unchanged its unshakeable dogmas and moral verities until its final disintegration after the First World War. Change indeed it could not, without ceasing to be melodrama. What appears at first an utterly confusing and anarchic dramatic sprawl turns out upon closer inspection to be a highly ordered form operating by fixed principles and moral absolutes codified into rigid and immutable dramatic laws.

One of the most interesting aspects of melodrama is its social radicalism, sometimes expressed in vague rhetorical generalities, but frequently—as in *The Factory Lad* (1832)—located in a specific social context. Melodrama was indeed the chief social protest drama of the century. It protested about drink, homelessness, poverty, the poor laws, the game laws, naval discipline and press-gangs, slavery, attitudes to ex-convicts, and a wide range of social injustices. Its political sentiments, though necessarily expressed with caution, could be militant. In plays such as *The Factory Girl* (1832), *The Factory Strike* (1838), *The Factory Boy* (1840), *The Labour Question* (1861), *The Long Strike* (1866), *Free Labour* (1870), *The Miners' Strike* (1875), *The Foreman of the Works* (1886), *Work and Wages* (1890), and many others of the same description, melodrama concerned itself, albeit sensationally—but that is its nature—with fundamental questions of profit-making, working conditions, automation, the morality of the strike, and industrial discontent, coming down more often on the side of man than of master. In treating the industrial theme it even anticipated the novel: *The Factory Lad* antedates Frances Trollope's *Michael Armstrong, the Factory Boy* (1840), Disraeli's *Sybil* (1845) and Mrs. Gaskell's *Mary Barton* (1848).

Considering its social emphasis in an age increasingly conscious of class, the amount of latent or actual class conflict in melodrama is hardly surprising: the oppression of the virtuous peasant by the villainous aristocrat or landowner, the seducing squire's pursuit of the village heroine, the employer's harsh treatment of his employee, and the antipathy between owner and worker—all this is evidence of the social responsiveness of melodrama to its period, and engrossing material for the social historian interested in popular attitudes to class, attitudes whose variations depended in part upon the geographical location of particular theatres in working-class districts or in the middle-class West End.

The great merit of *The Factory Lad* is that it forcefully expresses radical sentiment through domestic means: the intense sufferings of the Allen family are set against a larger national theme of some importance. This domestication of the tragic is a sign of the direction that major nineteenth-century art forms, especially painting, the novel, and the drama, were to take. In the 1830s Bulwer-Lytton called on playwrights to be modern and dramatize 'tales of a house-hold nature, that find their echo in the heart of the people—the materials of the village tragedy, awakening an interest common to us all; intense yet homely, actual—earnest—the pathos and passion of every-day life.'[1] Probably without knowing it, he was describing not only *The Factory Lad* but also the popular domestic and village melodrama which had been flourishing for some years. *The Factory Lad*, with its exceptional unhappy ending and lack of comic relief, is indeed a domestic 'village tragedy' of considerable power and advanced social consciousness. Unlike *The Miller and His Men*, there is nothing romantic and escapist in *The Factory Lad*, and little in the way of fantasy, except for a nightmare image of repressive social and economic force, for an audience to take shelter in; the play is closer to tragedy than melodrama. Social protest melodramas took less account of dreams than other kinds.

With the beginning of the Victorian period proper, the older and now exhausted legitimate tragedy found itself entirely irrelevant to the nineteenth century. In plays like Westland Marston's *The Patrician's Daughter* (1842) and Browning's *A Blot in the 'Scutcheon* (1843), legitimate tragedy could only deal weakly and vaguely with contemporary themes. Gradually it compromised with popular melodrama and evolved into the 'drama': an elevated melodrama, in prose or verse, sometimes with literary pretensions and a historical setting—as in the dramas of Sheridan Knowles and Bulwer-Lytton—but with basically the same machinery of coincidence, sensation, character stereotype, and the happy ending that marks the earlier melodrama. In fact, after about 1850 it is generally difficult and profitless to distinguish between 'drama' and 'melodrama',

---

[1] *England and the English*, 2nd edn. (London, 1833), ii. 145.

except in the neighbourhood working- and lower middle-class theatres outside the West End; elsewhere the strongly melo-dramatic 'drama' became middle-class and even fashionable in its settings and characters, thus reflecting the changing nature of nineteenth-century audiences.

The Corsican Brothers (1852) admirably reflects these develop-ments.[1] It contains hero (a double one), heroine, villain, comic relief, sensational incident, elaborate settings, mood-reinforcing musical accompaniment, rhetoric, and a firm sense of poetic justice—all these being standard elements of melodrama. Yet at the same time it is middle-class and fashionable in significant aspects of content; its hero (or heroes) and villain are polished gentlemen, and it was produced by Charles Kean, a favourite of Queen Victoria and an actor-manager much concerned with respectability and social status. Boucicault himself was to make a greater reputation in Irish dramas like The Colleen Bawn (1860), Arrah-na-Pogue (1864), and The Shaughraun (1875),[2] and became one of the cleverest practitioners of the Victorian 'drama'.

The three- or four-act drama, developing through the work of Boucicault, Tom Taylor,[3] and a host of lesser dramatists in the fifties, sixties, and seventies, attained heights of upper middle-class elegance in the 1880s and 1890s, as well as a much greater sophistication of theme, character, and dialogue than Boucicault or Taylor could command. But one remains aware of its melodramatic ancestry. A play like Mrs. Dane's Defence (1900) is a long way from The Factory Lad, but its author, Henry Arthur Jones, had also collaborated in one of the most famous melodramas of the century in The Silver King (1882) and displayed a great fondness for melodramatic devices and character types in later serious dramas like Saints and Sinners (1884), The Dancing Girl (1891), and The Masqueraders (1894). These and other dramas by Jones are odd mixtures of ambitious and experimental theme material and conventional melodrama.

---

[1] It has the added distinction of possessing the most important of nineteenth-century stage ghosts, the last great representative of a long and illustrious English dramatic tradition.

[2] In 1852 he already had a reputation as the author of the comedy London Assurance (1841), which long remained a stock play.

[3] Best known for a long-running London crime drama, The Ticket-of-Leave Man (1863).

The best serious drama of the nineties was alive with new ideas but frequently timid in their expression. A combination of innovation and social conservatism also characterizes the work of Jones's contemporary Arthur Wing Pinero, whose *The Second Mrs. Tanqueray* (1893) is by far his boldest venture before the Edwardian period. Both dramatists were concerned to make their work acceptable to a middle-class audience interested in new ideas but living, at least publicly, by strict moral and social standards. Problems posed could be difficult and even unpleasant, but their solutions (or non-solutions) had to be socially palatable. Thus the unfortunate Mrs. Dane (a direct descendant of melodrama's woman with a past), like Paula Tanqueray, cannot be rehabilitated, and must be sacrificed to the implacable gods of a harsh social morality, gods whom Jones wholeheartedly worshipped. That she possessed the sympathy of the audience in her plight was morally irrelevant.

Like much of the 'drama' of the last half of the nineteenth century—which nevertheless coexisted with straight melo-drama, virtually unchanged at the popular theatres—the comedy of the entire century was exclusively a middle-class preserve. Like that drama also, comedy could deal in an intensely melo-dramatic way with serious matters, matters not commonly thought of as the province of comedy. *John Bull* (1803) and its fellows established a basic pattern of comedy that endured for generations: the idealizing of the domestic and of family ties (notably, as in *John Bull*, the father-daughter relationship); the presentation of eccentric character and low comedy; situations of pathos and potential disaster; the sentimental presentation of rural virtue; heroes, heroines, and semi-villains; a stern morality; and a glorification of goodness wherever it was to be found. A catholic pattern, certainly, and one given primarily to the provision of an extravagant variety of entertainment rather than careful plotting and economy of technique.

The Victorians inherited this earlier comic material, refined it somewhat, and made their own distinctive contributions. They could not be said to have invented class consciousness on the stage, since it is very much apparent in *John Bull* and other comedies of that period, as well as in melodrama. However, class spirit and class antagonisms permeate Victorian comedy:

Bulwer-Lytton's *Money* (1840),[1] Tom Robertson's *Society* (1865), and Taylor's *New Men and Old Acres* (1869) are examples. This class hostility was not, as in melodrama, the consequence of life-and-death conflict between peasant and landowner, or workman and employer, but rather a product of the social enmity and a struggle for superiority between the established and landed aristocracy and the socially ambitious *nouveaux riches*—usually depicted · as vulgarians—or the new professional and managerial classes, as in Robertson's *Progress* (1869) and *Birth* (1870). Indeed, wealth and social ambition are major themes in Victorian comedy. The idealizing of home, marriage, wife, and mother became much more intense, and the whole ground of comedy shifted from the larger-than-life extravagances of the Colman school to the quieter and more commonplace domestic realism of Robertson and his followers. Right to the end of the century, however, comedy never lost its fundamental component of seriousness, evident in themes, situations, and characters, which coexisted with the more obviously humorous potential of the genre.

The sentimentality, the romantic, rural, and domestic idealism, the exalted virtue, and the righteous morality of so much Victorian comedy did not go unchallenged. Its chief and virtually sole opponent until the 1890s and Shaw and Wilde was W. S. Gilbert, better known for his operatic collaboration with Arthur Sullivan but with an established reputation for comedy, extravaganza, burlesque, and the 'Bab' ballads before he began to write comic operas.[2] In *Engaged* (1877) Gilbert attacked the main premises of Victorian comedy. His characters are entirely motivated by financial considerations even while enraptured by 'love' (not, of course, the traditional love of other comedy); his women twist their men around their little fingers; worthy sentiments are uttered with the utmost hypocrisy; the tender bonds between doting father and loving daughter prove to be a mercenary alliance of calculating selfishness and heartless intrigue; the simple pastoral virtues are a sham. Accepted moralities and social conventions are continually violated by characters who pride themselves ostentatiously upon their sense of decency and honour, and who are blithely unaware of

---

[1] As they also do in his well-known drama, *The Lady of Lyons* (1838).
[2] The first opera with Sullivan was *Thespis* (1871), a classical burlesque.

transgressions on their own part. This point of view and this dramatic material is embodied in a deeply ironic, graceful, and witty comedy which made a considerable stir in its own time and strongly influenced Shaw and Wilde, whose *The Importance of Being Earnest* (1895) is very much in debt to *Engaged*. Gilbert's sophistication and irony carried over to the Mayfair comedies of Jones and Pinero,[1] but were not essential to them; melodramatic material (parodied in *Engaged*) and serious themes continued to be part of the comedies of the 1880s and 1890s, sometimes coexisting with the extremes of eccentric comedy as they had done at the beginning of the century.

Nineteenth-century farce also dealt in the extremes of comedy, but, surprisingly, embraced some of the serious matter of comedy as well. Farce too could be sentimental, moral, and idealistic; although domestic ideals in particular might suffer knocking about on the way to the final curtain, they are always vindicated in the end. The bounds between farce and comedy are difficult to define; indeed, the conventional dramatic genres became in the nineteenth century so blended on the one hand and so fragmented on the other that it is best to forget about definitions altogether. During the eighteenth century farce occupied a regular place on the playbill as the afterpiece. In the nineteenth century it was still relegated to the latter part of the evening's entertainment, although later in the century in the West End theatres it sometimes opened the bill. As in the eighteenth century farce was written in one or two acts; not until the 1870s and the influence of Parisian farce did it develop a three- or four-act structure.[2]

Length and place on the bill is only an external means of characterizing farce; technique and content are much more important determinants. Farcers naturally employed such methods as the sudden reversal of expectation; the telescoping of time so that plots, when they have gained momentum, move with breathtaking speed; the juxtaposition on stage of characters who should on no account meet; and a series of coincidences,

---

[1] Jones's *The Case of Rebellious Susan* (1894) and *The Liars* (1897), together with Pinero's *The Cabinet Minister* (1891) and *The Gay Lord Quex* (1899), are good examples of this kind of comedy.

[2] There had been earlier three-act farces, such as Jerrold's *Mr. Paul Pry* (1826) —a short piece nevertheless—and J. B. Buckstone's *Married Life* (1834) and *Single Life* (1839).

misunderstandings, and calamitous events whose full resolution is delayed until the last moment. Characters in farces before
the 1870s commonly confide in their audiences through direct
and lengthy speeches, and appeal for their indulgence in ritualis-
tic concluding 'tags'; the theatricality of farce is thus frankly
stressed. In content the central predicament of farce is funda-
mentally absurdist. The comic futility of man's existence is
demonstrated by his ridiculous helplessness in the toils of
malignant chance, which governs a universe whose sole purpose
is to drive him to the verge of sanity, to entrap him in incompre-
hensibility, to make him doubt his identity, to turn his perfectly
ordinary domestic life into a maelstrom of preposterous con-
tretemps and desperate entanglements, all entirely beyond his
own control. Such a dramatic viewpoint and such a comic
practice are remarkably similar to contemporary views of man
and contemporary dramatic method.

The pressures of farce are more inexorable in the nineteenth
than in the eighteenth century, when most farce plots centred
upon stock character types such as a father or guardian, a pair of
lovers, a pair of sympathetic friends (who may also be matched),
a stupid or foolish rival, an ingeniously scheming manservant
and chambermaid. The lovers, with the aid of their servants,
commonly outwit parent and rival alike. The love intrigue—
the comic wooing of the servants apart—is invariably aristo-
cratic and upper middle-class; the tone is therefore relatively
elevated and refined, and obvious physical business is uncommon.

In the early nineteenth century farce was still concerned with
plots of this kind, but later they were supplanted by new matter.
A setting of homely domesticity, household affairs, and a lower-
ing of class status is noteworthy in the period 1840–70; the
individual undergoing peculiar and extraordinary pressures
takes the centre of the stage. *Box and Cox* (1847) and *How to
Settle Accounts with Your Laundress* (1847) are fine examples of
these trends. Their comedy is the comedy of domestic material-
ism; comic business involves a wide variety of humble objects,
and much humour is obtained from the preparation, service, and
consumption of food. Box is employed by a printer, Cox by
a hatter; Widgetts is a tailor, Mrs. Bouncer a landlady, Mary
White a laundress. Widgetts finds himself in a quandary so

fearful as to be excessively comic, for this is farce. The grim offstage figure of Penelope Ann darkens the lives of Box and Cox.[1] In farce of this type the very normality and cosy domestic familiarity of setting and characters intensifies by contrast the extreme predicament in which the hapless ordinary man finds himself embroiled.

Such comedy is also the basis of *The Magistrate* (1885) and Pinero's *Dandy Dick* (1887), in which another 'pillar of society' —in this case an Anglican dean of the greatest rectitude— becomes hopelessly involved in shady doings outside the law. In the forty years since *Box and Cox* and *How to Settle Accounts with Your Laundress*, farce had largely abandoned its interest in working- and lower-class material. Socially it became more elevated, but greater social status meant that characters partaking of it, like Posket in *The Magistrate*, had further to fall. It confided less in its audience and on the whole observed the proprieties of the 'fourth wall'. The comedy of physical humiliation remained a part of the severe pressures of hostile chance upon the individual; these pressures intensify in late nineteenth-century farce. The physical battering Posket sustains is directly related to the central philosophical concept of farce and to his position as the chosen victim of the Fates; it is not merely incidental in the way that physical comedy sometimes is in earlier farce. Actually, farce functions quite well without knockabout business—as witness *Box and Cox*—and it was never an indispensable ingredient of the genre. By the 1880s English farce had also been for some years under the influence of Parisian boulevard farce, which dealt much more frankly with bourgeois sin than its English imitators dared or wished to.[2] *The Magistrate* follows a standard technique of such farce in entangling its principal characters in a restaurant of doubtful reputation, but although the idea and the plot mechanisms are French the play remains completely moral and utterly English.

By the end of the nineteenth century the cinema was in its infancy as a new medium of popular entertainment. Slowly the theatre began to contract its appeal to all classes of society, at

---

[1] The reader familiar with melodrama will notice that *Box and Cox* (subtitled 'A Romance of Real Life') is in part a clever parody of melodramatic plot machinery.

[2] The French vogue started in the West End with such adaptations as Gilbert's *The Wedding March* (1873) and James Albery's *Pink Dominos* (1877).

first giving much ground to the cinema and then further retreating to the lonely middle-class fastness from which it can now observe the triumphant legions of television rampaging over what used to be its very own domain. Aside from the cinema, drama and theatre in the nineteenth century were moving steadily towards middle-class respectability in any case, as well as toward social and stage realism. Yet the antecedents of the late-century drama can be clearly seen; an unbroken chain of continuous evolution stretches from 1800 to 1900, from *John Bull* and *The Factory Lad* to *The Magistrate* and *Mrs. Dane's Defence*. No part of that chain can easily be separated, and isolated for critical examination, from any other part. Nineteenth-century drama is unquestionably the father of much in the modern theatre, and that is one reason for reading it; but its inherent interest and significance is a much better reason for serious and respectful consideration.

JOHN BULL

OR THE ENGLISHMAN'S FIRESIDE

A COMEDY IN FIVE ACTS

BY

GEORGE COLMAN THE YOUNGER (1762–1836)

First performed at Covent Garden Theatre
5 March 1803

CAST

PEREGRINE	Mr. Cooke
SIR SIMON ROCHDALE	Mr. Blanchard
FRANK ROCHDALE	Mr. H. Johnston
LORD FITZ-BALAAM	Mr. Waddy
HONOURABLE TOM SHUFFLETON	Mr. Lewis
JOB THORNBERRY	Mr. Fawcett
JOHN BUR	Mr. Atkins
DENNIS BRULGRUDDERY	Mr. Johnstone
DAN	Mr. Emery
MR. PENNYMAN	Mr. Davenport
JOHN	Mr. Abbot
ROBERT	Mr. Truman
SIMON	Mr. Beverly
WILLIAMS	Mr. Klanert
LADY CAROLINE BRAYMORE	Mrs. H. Johnston
MRS. BRULGRUDDERY	Mrs. Davenport
MARY THORNBERRY	Mrs. Gibbs

SCENE
Cornwall

ACT I

SCENE I. *A Public-House on a Heath*, R. *Over the door the sign of the Red Cow, and the name of Dennis Brulgruddery; a finger-post*, R.

Enter DENNIS BRULGRUDDERY *and* DAN, *from the house—* DAN *opening the outward shutters of the house.*

DENNIS. A pretty blustratious night we have had, and the sun peeps through the fog this morning like the copper pot in my kitchen. Devil a traveller do I see coming to the Red Cow.

DAN. Na, measter, nowt do pass by here, I do think, but the carrion crows.

DENNIS. Dan, think you I will be ruined?

DAN. Ees, past all condemption. We be the undonestest family in all Cornwall. Your ale be as dead as my grandmother; mistress do set by the fire and sputter like an apple a-roasting; the pigs ha' gotten the measles; I be grown thinner nor an old sixpence; and thee hast drunk up all the spirity liquors.

DENNIS. By my soul, I believe my setting up the Red Cow a week ago was a bit of a bull—but that's no odds. Haven't I been married these three months—and who did I marry?

DAN. Why, a waddling woman wi' a mulberry feace.

DENNIS. Have done with your blarney, Mr. Dan. Think of the high blood in her veins, you bogtrotter!

DAN. Ees, I always do, when I do look at her nose.

DENNIS. Never you mind Mrs. Brulgruddery's nose. Wasn't she fat widow to Mr. Skinnygauge, the lean exciseman, of Lestwithiel? And didn't her uncle, who is fifteenth cousin to a Cornish baronet, say he'd leave her no money, if he ever happened to have any, becase she had disgraced her parentage by marrying herself to a taxman? Bathershan, man, and don't you think he'll help us out of the mud, now her second husband is an Irish jontleman, bred and born.

DAN. [*Laughing.*] He! he! Thee be'st a rum gentleman.

DENNIS. Troth, and myself, Mr. Dennis Brulgruddery, was brought up to the church.

DAN. Why, zure!

DENNIS. You may say that. I opened the pew doors in Belfast.

DAN. And what made 'em to turn thee out o' the treade?

DENNIS. I snored in sermon time. Dr. Snufflebags, the preacher, said I woke the rest of the congregation. [*Looking off.*] Arrah, Dan, don't I see a tall customer stretching out his arms in the fog?

DAN. Na, that be the road-post.

DENNIS. Faith, and so it is! Och! when I was turned out of my snug birth in Belfast, the tears ran down my eighteen-year old cheeks like buttermilk.

DAN. Pshaw, man, nonsense! Thee'dst never get another livelihood by crying.

DENNIS. Yes, I did; I cried oysters. Then I plucked up——[*Pointing.*] what's that—a customer?

DAN. [*Looking out.*] Na, a donkey.

DENNIS. Well, then I plucked up a parcel of my courage, and carried arms.

DAN. Waunds! What, a musket?

DENNIS. No, a reaping hook. I cut my way half through England, till a German larned me physic at a fair in Devonshire.

DAN. What, poticary's stuff?

DENNIS. I studied it in Doctor Von Quolchigronck's booth at Plympton. He cured the yellow glanders, and restored prolification to families who wanted an heir. I was of mighty use to him as an assistant.

DAN. Were you indeed?

DENNIS. But somehow the doctor and I had a quarrel; so I gave him something and parted.

DAN. And what didst thee give him pray?

DENNIS. I gave him a black eye, and set up for myself at Lestwithiel, where Mr. Skinnygauge, the exciseman, was in his honeymoon. Poor soul! he was my patient, and died one **day**;

but his widow had such a neat notion of my subscriptions that in three weeks she was Mrs. Brulgruddery.

DAN. [*Laughing.*] He! he! So you jumped into the old man's money?

DENNIS. Only a dirty hundred pounds. Then her brother-in-law, bad luck to him, kept the Red Cow upon Muckslush Heath, till his teeth chattered him out of the world, in an ague.

DAN. Why, that be this very house.

DENNIS. Ould Nick fly away with the roof of it! I took the remainder of the lease, per advice of my bride, Mrs. Brulgruddery; laid out her good-looking hundred pound for the furniture and the goodwill, bought three pigs that are going into a consumption, took a sarving-man that——

DAN. That's I. I be going into a consumption too, sin you hired me.

DENNIS. And devil a soul has darkened my doors for a pot of beer since I've been a publican.

DAN. [*Looking off.*] See! See, mun, see! Yon's a traveller, sure as eggs, and a-coming this road!

DENNIS. Och, hubbaboo! A customer at last! St. Patrick send he may be a pure dry one! Be alive, Dan, be alive! Run and tell him there's elegant refreshment at the Red Cow.

DAN. I wull. Oh, dang it, I doesn't mind a bit of a lie.

DENNIS. And hark ye—say there's an accomplished landlord.

DAN. Ees, and a genteel waiter; but he'll see that.

DENNIS. And Dan—sink that little bit of a thunder-storm that has soured all the beer, you know.

DAN. What, dost take me for an oaf? Dang me, if he ha'n't been used to drink vinegar, he'll find it out fast enow of himsel, I'se warrant un.   [*Exit.*

DENNIS. [*Calling.*] Wife! I must tell her the joyful news. Mrs. Brulgruddery! My dear! Devil choak my dear; she's as deaf as a trunkmaker! Mrs. Brulgruddery!

Enter MRS. BRULGRUDDERY, *from the house.*

MRS. BRULGRUDDERY. And what do you want now with Mrs. Brulgruddery? What's to become of us? Tell me that. How are we going on, I should like to know?

DENNIS. Mighty like a mile-stone, standing still at this present writing.

MRS. BRULGRUDDERY. A pretty situation we are in, truly!

DENNIS. Yes, upon Muckslush Heath, and be damned to it.

MRS. BRULGRUDDERY. And where is the fortune I brought you?

DENNIS. All swallowed up by the Red Cow.

MRS. BRULGRUDDERY. Ah, had you followed my advice, we should never have been in such a quandary.

DENNIS. Tunder and turf! Didn't yourself advise me to take this public-house?

MRS. BRULGRUDDERY. No matter for that. I had a relation who always kept it. But who advised you to drink out all the brandy?

DENNIS. No matter for that—I had a relation who always drank it.

MRS. BRULGRUDDERY. [Crying.] Ah! my poor dear Mr. Skinnygauge never brought tears into my eyes as you do.

DENNIS. I know that—I saw you at his funeral.

MRS. BRULGRUDDERY. You're a monster!

DENNIS. Am I? Keep it to yourself, then, my lambkin.

MRS. BRULGRUDDERY. You'll be the death of me—you know you will.

DENNIS. Look up, my sweet Mrs. Brulgruddery, while I give you a small morsel of consolation.

MRS. BRULGRUDDERY. Consolation, indeed!

DENNIS. Yes; there's a customer coming.

MRS. BRULGRUDDERY. [Brightening.] What!

DENNIS. A customer. Turn your neat jolly face over the heath yonder. Look at Dan, towing him along as snug as a cock-salmon into a fish basket.

MRS. BRULGRUDDERY. Jimminy, and so there is! Oh, my dear Dennis! But I knew how it would be if you had but a little patience. Remember, it was all by my advice you took the Red Cow.

DENNIS. Och, ho! it was, was it?

MRS. BRULGRUDDERY. I'll run and spruce myself up a bit. Aye, aye, I haven't prophesied a customer to-day for nothing.

[*Exit into the house.*

DENNIS. Troth, and it's prophesying on the sure side, to foretell a thing when it has happened.

Re-enter DAN, *conducting* PEREGRINE, *who carries a small trunk under his arm.*

PEREGRINE. I am indifferent about accommodations.

DAN. Our'n be a comfortable parlour, zur: you'll find it clean, for I washed un down mysen, wringing wet, five minutes ago.

PEREGRINE. You have told me so, twenty times.

DAN. This be the Red Cow, zur, as ye may see by the pictur; and here be measter—he'll treat ye in an hospital manner, zur, and show you a deal o' contention.

DENNIS. I'll be bound, sir, you'll get good entertainment, whether you are a man or a horse.

PEREGRINE. You may lodge me as either, friend. I can sleep as well in a stable as a bedchamber, for travel has seasoned me. [*Half aside, and pointing to the trunk under his arm.*] Since I have preserved this, I can lay my head upon it with tranquillity, and repose anywhere.

DENNIS. Faith, it seems a mighty decent hard bolster. What is it stuffed with, I wonder?

PEREGRINE. That which keeps the miser awake—money.

DAN. Waunds! All that money!

DENNIS. I'd be proud, sir, to know your upholsterer—he should make me a feather bed gratis of the same pretty materials. If this was all my own, I'd sleep like a pig, though I'm married to Mrs. Brulgruddery.

PEREGRINE. I shall sleep better because it is not my own.

DENNIS. Your own's in a snugger place, then? Safe from the sharks of this dirty world, and be hanged to 'em!

PEREGRINE. Except the purse in my pocket, 'tis now, I fancy, in a place most frequented by the sharks of this world.

DENNIS. London, I suppose?

PEREGRINE. The bottom of the sea.

DENNIS. By my soul, that's a watering place; and you'll find sharks there, sure enough, in all conscience.

Re-enter MRS. BRULGRUDDERY.

MRS. BRULGRUDDERY. [*To* PEREGRINE.] What would you choose to take, sir, after your walk this raw morning? We have any thing you desire.

DENNIS. Yes, sir, we have anything. [*Aside.*] Anything's nothing, they say.

MRS. BRULGRUDDERY. Dan, bustle about, and see the room ready and all tidy; do you hear?

DAN. I wull.

MRS. BRULGRUDDERY. What would you like to drink, sir?

PEREGRINE. Oh, mine is an accommodating palate, hostess. I have swallowed burgundy with the French, hollands with the Dutch, sherbet with the Turk, sloe juice with an Englishman, and water with a simple Gentoo.

DAN. [*Going.*] Dang me, but he's a rum customer! It's my opinion he'll take a fancy to our sour beer.   [*Exit.*

PEREGRINE. Is your house far from the sea-shore?

MRS. BRULGRUDDERY. About three miles, sir.

PEREGRINE. So! And I have wandered upon the heath four hours, before daybreak.

MRS. BRULGRUDDERY. Lack-a-day! Has anything happened to you, sir?

PEREGRINE. Shipwreck—that's all.

MRS. BRULGRUDDERY. Mercy on us! Cast away!

PEREGRINE. On your coast here.

DENNIS. Then, compliment apart, sir, you take a ducking as if you had been used to it.

PEREGRINE. Life's a lottery, friend, and man should make up his mind to the blanks. On what part of Cornwall am I thrown?

MRS. BRULGRUDDERY. We are two miles from Penzance, sir.

PEREGRINE. Ha! from Penzance! That's lucky!

MRS. BRULGRUDDERY. Lucky! [*Aside to* DENNIS.] Then he'll go on, without drinking at our house.

DENNIS. Ahem! Sir, there has been a great big thunder-storm at Penzance, and all the beer in the town's as thick as mustard.

PEREGRINE. I feel chilled—get me a glass of brandy.

DENNIS. [*Aside.*] Oh, the devil! [*Aloud to his wife.*] Bring the brandy bottle for the jontleman, my jewel.

MRS. BRULGRUDDERY. [*Aside to* DENNIS.] Don't you know you've emptied it, you sot you?

DENNIS. [*Aside.*] Draw a mug of beer—I'll palaver him..

MRS. BRULGRUDDERY. [*Aside.*] Ah, if you would but follow my advice!   [*Exit.*

DENNIS. You see that woman that's gone, sir—she's my wife, poor soul! She has got but one misfortune, and that's a wapper.

PEREGRINE. What's that?

DENNIS. We had as neat a big bottle of brandy a week ago, and damn the drop's left. But I say nothing—she's my wife, poor creature, and she can tell who drank it. Wouldn't you like a sup of sour—I mean, of our strong beer?

PEREGRINE. Psha! no matter what. Tell me, is a person of the name of Thornberry still living in Penzance?

DENNIS. Is it one Mr. Thornberry you are asking after?

PEREGRINE. Yes. When I first saw him (indeed, it was the first time and the last), he had just begun to adventure humbly in trade. His stock was very slender, but his neighbours accounted him a kindly man, and I know they spoke the truth. Thirty years ago, after half an hour's intercourse, which proved to me his benevolent nature, I squeezed his hand, and parted.

DENNIS. Thirty years! Faith, after half an hour's dish of talk, that's a reasonable long time to remember.

PEREGRINE. Not at all, for he did me a genuine service; and

gratitude writes her records in the heart that, till it ceases to beat, they may live in the memory.

Re-enter MRS. BRULGRUDDERY, *with a mug of beer.*

MRS. BRULGRUDDERY. [*Aside to* DENNIS.] What have you said about the brandy bottle?

DENNIS. [*Aside.*] I told him you broke it one day.

MRS. BRULGRUDDERY. [*Aside.*] Ah! I am always the shelter for your sins!

DENNIS. Hush! You know sir, I—hem! I mentioned to you poor Mrs. Brulgruddery's misfortune.

PEREGRINE. Ha! ha! You did indeed, friend.

MRS. BRULGRUDDERY. I am very sorry, sir, but——

DENNIS. Be asy, my lambkin, the jontleman excuses it. You are not the first that has cracked a bottle, you know. [*Taking the beer from his wife.*] My jewel, the jontleman was asking after one Mr. Thornberry. [*Delaying to give the beer.*

MRS. BRULGRUDDERY. What, old Job Thornberry of Penzance, sir?

PEREGRINE. The very same. You know him, then?

MRS. BRULGRUDDERY. Very well, by hearsay, sir. He has lived there upwards of thirty years. [*To* DENNIS.] A very thriving man now, and well to do in the world, as others might be too, if they would but follow my advice.

PEREGRINE. I rejoice to hear it. Give me the beer, landlord; I'll drink his health in humble malt, then hasten to visit him.

DENNIS. [*Aside.*] By St. Patrick, then, you'll make wry faces on the road.
        [*Gives the mug to* PEREGRINE, *and, as he is about to drink, a shriek is heard at a small distance.*

PEREGRINE. Ha, the voice of a female in distress! Then 'tis a man's business to fly to her protection!
                [*Dashes the mug on the ground and exit.*

MRS. BRULGRUDDERY. Wheugh! What a whirligig! Why, Dennis, the man's mad!

DENNIS. I think that thing.

MRS. BRULGRUDDERY. He has thrown down all the beer before he tasted a drop.

DENNIS. That's it: if he had chucked it away afterwards, I shouldn't have wondered.

MRS. BRULGRUDDERY. Here he comes again, and, I declare, with a young woman leaning on his shoulder.

DENNIS. A young woman! Let me have a bit of a peep. Och, the crature! Och, the——

MRS. BRULGRUDDERY. Heyday! I shouldn't have thought of your peeping after a young woman, indeed!

DENNIS. Be asy, Mrs. Brulgruddery, it's a way we have in Ireland. There's a face!

MRS. BRULGRUDDERY. Well, and haven't I a face, pray?

DENNIS. That you have, my lambkin! You have had one these fifty years, I'll be bound for you.

MRS. BRULGRUDDERY. Fifty years! You are the greatest brute that ever dug potatoes.

Re-enter PEREGRINE, *supporting* MARY THORNBERRY.

PEREGRINE. This way; cheer your spirits! The ruffian with whom I saw you struggling has fled across the heath, but his speed prevented my saving your property. Was your money, too, in the parcel with your clothes?

MARY. All I possessed in the world, sir, and he has so frightened me! Indeed I thank you, sir; indeed I do!

PEREGRINE. Come, come; compose yourself. Whither are you going, pretty one?

MARY. I must not tell, sir.

PEREGRINE. Then whither do you come from?

MARY. Nobody must know, sir.

PEREGRINE. Umph! Then your proceedings, child, are a secret?

MARY. Yes, sir.

PEREGRINE. Yet you appear to need a friend to direct them. A heath is a rare place to find one. In the absence of a better, confide in me.

MARY. You forget that you are a stranger, sir.

B

PEREGRINE. I always do, when the defenceless want my assistance.

MARY. But perhaps you might betray me, sir.

PEREGRINE. Never, by the honour of a man!

MARY. Pray don't swear by that, sir, for then you'll betray me, I'm certain.

PEREGRINE. Have you ever suffered from treachery, then, poor innocence?

MARY. Yes, sir.

PEREGRINE. And may not one of your own sex have been treacherous to you?

MARY. No, sir; I'm very sure he was a man.

DENNIS. Oh, the blackguard!

MRS. BRULGRUDDERY. Hold your tongue, do!

PEREGRINE. Listen to me, child. I would proffer you friendship for your own sake—for the sake of benevolence. When ages, indeed, are nearly equal, nature is prone to breathe so warmly on the blossoms of a friendship between the sexes, that the fruit is desire; but Time, fair one, is scattering snow on my temples, while Hebe waves her freshest ringlets over yours. Rely, then, on one who has numbered years sufficient to correct his passions; who has encountered difficulties enough to teach him sympathy; and who would stretch forth his hand to a wandering female, and shelter her like a father.

MARY. [*Weeping.*] Oh, sir! I do want protection sadly indeed; I am very miserable!

PEREGRINE. Come, do not droop. The cause of your distress, perhaps, is trifling; but light gales of adversity will make women weep. A woman's tear falls like the dew that zephyrs shake from roses. Nay, confide in me.

MARY. I will, sir, [*Looking round.*] but——

PEREGRINE. [*To* DENNIS.] Leave us a little, honest friends.

DENNIS. Ahem! Come, Mrs. Brulgruddery; let you and I pair off, my lambkin.

MRS. BRULGRUDDERY. [*Going.*] Ah, she's no better than she should be, I'll warrant her.

DENNIS. By the powers, she's well enough, though, for all that!

[*Exeunt.*

PEREGRINE. Now, sweet one, your name?

MARY. Mary, sir.

PEREGRINE. What else?

MARY. Don't ask me that, sir; my poor father might be sorry it was mentioned now.

PEREGRINE. Have you quitted your father, then?

MARY. I left his house at daybreak this morning, sir.

PEREGRINE. What is he?

MARY. A tradesman in the neighbouring town, sir.

PEREGRINE. Is he aware of your departure?

MARY. No, sir.

PEREGRINE. And your mother?

MARY. I was very little when she died, sir.

PEREGRINE. Has your father, since her death, treated you with cruelty?

MARY. He! Oh, bless him, no! He is the kindest father that ever breathed, sir.

PEREGRINE. How must such a father be agonized by the loss of his child!

MARY. Pray, sir, don't talk of that!

PEREGRINE. Why did you fly from him?

MARY. Sir, I—I——but that's my story, sir.

PEREGRINE. Relate it, then.

MARY. Yes, sir. You must know, then, sir, that there was a young gentleman in this neighbourhood that——oh dear, sir, I'm quite ashamed!

PEREGRINE. Come, child, I will relieve you from the embarrassment of narration, and sum up your history in one word—love.

MARY. That's the beginning of it, sir, but a great deal happened afterwards.

PEREGRINE. And who is the hero of your story, my poor girl?

MARY. The hero of——oh, I understand. He is much above me in fortune, sir; to be sure, I should have thought of that before he got such power over my heart to make me so wretched, now he has deserted me.

PEREGRINE. He would have thought of that, had his own heart been generous.

MARY. He is reckoned very generous, sir; he can afford to be so. When the old gentleman dies, he will have all the great family estate. I am going to the house now, sir.

PEREGRINE. For what purpose?

MARY. To try if I can see him for the last time, sir; to tell him I shall always pray for his happiness when I am far away from a place which he has made it misery for me to abide in; and to beg him to give me a little supply of money, now I am penny-less and from home, to help me to London, where I may get into service, and nobody will know me.

PEREGRINE. And what are his reasons, child, for thus deserting you?

MARY. He sent me his reasons by letter yesterday, sir. He is to be married next week to a lady of high fortune; his father, he says, insists upon it. I know I am born below him, but after the oaths we plighted, heaven knows the news was a sad, sad shock to me! I did not close my eyes last night; my poor brain was burning; and as soon as day broke I left the house of my dear father, whom I should tremble to look at when he discovered my story, which I could not long conceal from him.

PEREGRINE. Poor, lovely, heart-bruised wanderer! O wealthy despoilers of humble innocence, splendid murderers of virtue, who make your vice your boast, and fancy female ruin a feather in your caps of vanity—single out a victim you have abandoned, and, in your hours of death, contemplate her: view her, care-worn, friendless, pennyless; hear her tale of sorrows, fraught with her remorse—her want—a hard world's scoffs—her parents' anguish; then, if ye dare, look inward upon your own bosoms, and, if they be not conscience-proof, what must be your compunctions! Who is his father, child?

MARY. Sir Simon Rochdale, sir, of the manor-house hard by.

PEREGRINE. [*Surprised.*] Indeed!

MARY. Perhaps you know him, sir.

PEREGRINE. I have heard of him, and on your account shall visit him.

MARY. Oh pray, sir, take care what you do! If you should bring his son into trouble by mentioning me, I should never, never forgive myself.

PEREGRINE. Trust to my caution. Promise only to remain at this house till I return from a business which calls me immediately two miles hence; I will hurry back to pursue measures for your welfare with more hope of success than your own weak means, poor simplicity, are likely to effect. What say you?

MARY. I hardly know what to say, sir; you seem good, and I am little able to help myself.

PEREGRINE. You consent, then?

MARY. Yes, sir.

PEREGRINE. [*Calling.*] Landlord!

Enter DENNIS, *followed by* MRS. BRULGRUDDERY.

DENNIS. Did you call, sir? Arrah now, Mrs. Brulgruddery, you are peeping after the young woman yourself.

MRS. BRULGRUDDERY. I choose it.

PEREGRINE. Prepare your room, good folks, and get the best accommodation you can for this young person.

DENNIS. That I will, with all my heart and soul, sir.

MRS. BRULGRUDDERY. [*Sulkily.*] I don't know that we have any room at all, for my part.

DENNIS. Whew! She's in her tantrums!

MRS. BRULGRUDDERY. People of repute can't let in young women (found upon a heath, forsooth!) without knowing who's who. I have learned the ways of the world, sir.

PEREGRINE. So it seems, which too often teach you to overrate the little good you can do in it, and to shut the door when the distressed entreat you to throw it open. But I have learnt the ways of the world, too. [*Taking out his purse.*] I shall return in a few hours. Provide all the comforts you can, and here are a couple of guineas to send for any refreshments you have not in the house.

DENNIS. Mighty pretty handsel for the Red Cow, my lambkin!

MRS. BRULGRUDDERY. A couple of guineas! Lord, sir, if I thought you had been such a gentleman! Pray, miss, walk in; your poor dear little feet must be quite wet with our nasty roads. I beg pardon, sir; but character's every thing in our business, and I never lose sight of my own credit.

DENNIS. That you don't, till you see other people's ready money.

PEREGRINE. Go in, child. I shall soon be with you again.

MARY. You will return, then, sir?

PEREGRINE. Speedily; rely on me.

MARY. I shall, sir; I am sure I may. Heaven bless you, sir!

MRS. BRULGRUDDERY. [*Courtesying.*] This way, miss—this way.   [*Exeunt* MRS. BRULGRUDDERY *and* MARY.

DENNIS. Long life to your honour, for protecting the petticoats! Sweet cratures: I'd like to protect them myself, by bushels.

PEREGRINE. Can you get me a guide, friend, to conduct me to Penzance?

DENNIS. Get you a guide? There's Dan, my servant, shall skip before you over the bogs like a grasshopper. Oh, by the powers! my heart's full to see your generosity, and I owe you a favour in return: never you call for any of my beer till I get a fresh tap.   [*Exit.*

PEREGRINE. Now for my friend Thornberry; then hither again to interest myself in the cause of this unfortunate, for which many would call me Quixotic—many would cant out 'Shame!' But I care not for the stoics, nor the puritans. Genuine nature and unsophisticated morality, that turn disgusted from the rooted adepts in vice, have ever a reclaiming tear to shed on the children of error. Then let the sterner virtues, that allow no plea for human frailty, stalk on to Paradise without me. The mild associate of my journey thither shall be charity; and my pilgrimage to the shrine of mercy will not, I trust, be

worse performed for having aided the weak, on my way, who
have stumbled in their progress.

Enter DAN.

DAN. I be ready, zur.

PEREGRINE. For what, friend?

DAN. Measter says you be a going to Penzance; if you be
agreeable, I'll keep you company.

PEREGRINE. Oh, the guide! You belong to the house?

DAN. Ees, zur! I'se enow to do; I be head waiter and hostler,
only we never have no horses, nor customers.

PEREGRINE. The path, I fancy, is difficult to find. Do you never
deviate?

DAN. Na, zur; I always whistles.

PEREGRINE. Come on, friend. It seems a dreary route; but how
cheerily the eye glances over a sterile tract when the habitation of a benefactor, whom we are approaching to requite,
lies in the perspective!   [*Exeunt.*

ACT II

SCENE I. *A Library in the House of* SIR SIMON ROCHDALE—
books scattered on a writing table.

Enter TOM SHUFFLETON.

SHUFFLETON. Nobody up yet? I thought so.

Enter JOHN.

Ah, John, is it you? How d'ye do, John?

JOHN. Thank your honour, I——

SHUFFLETON. Yes, you look so. Sir Simon Rochdale in bed?
Mr. Rochdale not risen? Well, no matter: I have travelled all
night, though, to be with them. How are they?

JOHN. Sir, they are both——

SHUFFLETON. I'm glad to hear it. Pay the postboy for me.

JOHN. Yes, sir. I beg pardon, sir, but when your honour last left
us——

SHUFFLETON. Owed you three pound five. I remember; have
you down in my memorandums. Honourable Tom Shuffleton,
debtor to——what's your name?

JOHN. My christian name, sir, is——

SHUFFLETON. Muggins—I recollect. Pay the postboy, Muggins. And harkye, take particular care of the chaise; I borrowed
it of my friend, Bobby Fungus, who sprang up a peer in the
last bundle of barons: if a single knob is knocked out of his
new coronets, he'll make me a sharper speech than ever he'll
produce in Parliament. And John——

JOHN. Sir.

SHUFFLETON. What was I going to say?

JOHN. Indeed, sir, I can't tell.

SHUFFLETON. No more can I. 'Tis the fashion to be absent—
that's the way I forgot your bill. There, run along. [*Exit*
JOHN.] I've the whirl of Bobby's chaise in my head still.
Cursed fatiguing, posting all night through Cornish roads to

obey the summons of friendship. Convenient in some respects, for all that. If all loungers of slender revenues like mine could command a constant succession of invitations from men of estates in the country, how amazingly it would tend to the thinning of Bond Street! [*Throwing himself into a chair near the writing table.*] Let me see, what has Sir Simon been reading? 'Burn's Justice'—true, the old man's reckoned the ablest magistrate in the county: he hasn't cut open the leaves, I see. 'Chesterfield's Letters'—pooh! his system of education is extinct; Belcher and the Butcher have superseded it. 'Clarendon's History of——'

Enter SIR SIMON ROCHDALE.

SIR SIMON. Ah, my dear Tom Shuffleton!

SHUFFLETON. Baronet, how are you?

SIR SIMON. Such expedition is kind, now. You got my letter at Bath, and——

SHUFFLETON. Saw it was pressing—here I am. Cut all my engagements for you, and came off like a shot.

SIR SIMON. Thank you; thank you, heartily!

SHUFFLETON. Left every thing at sixes and sevens.

SIR SIMON. Gad, I'm sorry if——

SHUFFLETON. Don't apologise—nobody does now. Left all my bills in the place unpaid.

SIR SIMON. Bless me! I've made it monstrous inconvenient!

SHUFFLETON. Not a bit—I give you my honour I didn't find it inconvenient at all. How is Frank Rochdale?

SIR SIMON. Why, my son isn't up yet, and before he's stirring, do let me talk to you, my dear Tom Shuffleton. I have something near my heart, that——

SHUFFLETON. Don't talk about your heart, baronet—feeling's quite out of fashion.

SIR SIMON. Well then, I'm interested in——

SHUFFLETON. Aye, stick to that. We make a joke of the heart nowadays, but when a man mentions his interest, we know he's in earnest.

SIR SIMON. Zounds! I am in earnest. Let me speak, and call my motives what you will.

SHUFFLETON. Speak, but don't be in a passion. We are always cool at the clubs; the constant habit of ruining one another teaches us temper. Explain.

SIR SIMON. Well, I will. You know, my dear Tom, how much I admire your proficiency in the New School of breeding; you are what I call one of the highest finished fellows of the present day.

SHUFFLETON. Psha, baronet! You flatter.

SIR SIMON. No, I don't; only, in extolling the merits of the newest fashioned manners and morals, I am sometimes puzzled by the plain gentlemen who listen to me, here in the country, most consumedly.

SHUFFLETON. I don't doubt it.

SIR SIMON. Why, 'twas but t'other morning I was haranguing old Sir Noah Starchington in my library, and explaining to him the shining qualities of a dasher of the year eighteen hundred and three; and what do you think he did?

SHUFFLETON. Fell fast asleep.

SIR SIMON. No; he pulled down an English dictionary, where (if you'll believe me) he found my definition of stylish living under the word 'insolvency;' a fighting crop turned out a 'docked bull-dog;' and modern gallantry 'adultery and seduction.'

SHUFFLETON. Noah Starchington is a damned old twaddler, but the fact is, baronet, we improve. We have voted many qualities to be virtues now that they never thought of calling virtues formerly. The rising generation wants a new dictionary, damnably.

SIR SIMON. Deplorably, indeed! You can't think, my dear Tom, what a scurvy figure you and the dashing fellows of your kidney make in the old ones. But you have great influence over my son Frank, and I want you to exert it. You are his intimate—you come here and pass two or three months at a time, you know.

SHUFFLETON. Yes, this is a pleasant house.

SIR SIMON. You ride his horses as if they were your own.

SHUFFLETON. Yes, he keeps a good stable.

SIR SIMON. You drink our claret with him till his head aches.

SHUFFLETON. Yours is famous claret, baronet.

SIR SIMON. You worm out his secrets; you win his money; you——in short, you are——

SHUFFLETON. His friend, according to the next new dictionary. That's what you mean, Sir Simon.

SIR SIMON. Exactly. But let me explain. Frank, if he doesn't play the fool and spoil all, is going to be married.

SHUFFLETON. To how much?

SIR SIMON. Damn it now, how like a modern man of the world that is! Formerly, they would have asked to who.

SHUFFLETON. We never do now; fortune's every thing. We say 'a good match' at the west end of the town, as they say 'a good man' in the city; the phrase refers merely to money. Is she rich?

SIR SIMON. Four thousand a year.

SHUFFLETON. What a devilish desirable woman! Frank's a happy dog!

SIR SIMON. He's a miserable puppy. He has no more notion, my dear Tom, of a modern 'good match' than Eve had of pin money.

SHUFFLETON. What are his objections to it?

SIR SIMON. I have smoked him, but he doesn't know that—a silly, sly amour, in another quarter.

SHUFFLETON. An amour! That's a very unfashionable reason for declining matrimony.

SIR SIMON. You know his romantic flights. The blockhead, I believe, is so attached, I shouldn't wonder if he flew off at a tangent and married the girl that has bewitched him.

SHUFFLETON. Who is she?

SIR SIMON. She—hem!—she lives with her father, in Penzance.

SHUFFLETON. And who is he?

SIR SIMON. He—upon my soul, I am ashamed to tell you.

SHUFFLETON. Don't be ashamed; we never blush at anything in the New School.

SIR SIMON. Damn me, my dear Tom, if he isn't a brazier.

SHUFFLETON. The devil!

SIR SIMON. A dealer in kitchen candlesticks, coal-skuttles, coppers, and cauldrons.

SHUFFLETON. And is the girl pretty?

SIR SIMON. So they tell me; a plump little devil, as round as a teakettle.

SHUFFLETON. I'll be after the brazier's daughter tomorrow.

SIR SIMON. But you have weight with him. Talk to him, my dear Tom—reason with him; try your power, Tom, do!

SHUFFLETON. I don't much like plotting with the father against the son—that's reversing the New School, baronet.

SIR SIMON. But it will serve Frank; it will serve me, who wish to serve you. And to prove that I do wish it, I have been keeping something in embryo for you, my dear Tom Shuffleton, against your arrival.

SHUFFLETON. For me?

SIR SIMON. When you were last leaving us, if you recollect, you mentioned, in a kind of a way, a—a sort of an intention of a loan of an odd five hundred pounds.

SHUFFLETON. Did I? I believe I might. When I intend to raise money, I always give my friends the preference.

SIR SIMON. I told you I was out of cash then, I remember.

SHUFFLETON. Yes; that's just what I told you, I remember.

SIR SIMON. I have the sum floating by me now, and much at your service.   [*Presenting it.*

SHUFFLETON. [*Taking it.*] Why, as it's lying idle, baronet, I— I—don't much care if I employ it.

SIR SIMON. Use your interest with Frank, now.

SHUFFLETON. Rely on me. Shall I give you my note.

SIR SIMON. No, my dear Tom; that's an unnecessary trouble.

SHUFFLETON. Why, that's true, with one who knows me so well as you.

SIR SIMON. Your verbal promise to pay is quite as good.

SHUFFLETON. [*Going.*] I'll see if Frank's stirring.

SIR SIMON. [*Going.*] And I must talk to my steward.

SHUFFLETON. Baronet!

SIR SIMON. [*Returning.*] Eh?

SHUFFLETON. Pray, do you employ the phrase, 'verbal promise to pay,' according to the reading of old dictionaries, or as it's the fashion to use it at present?

SIR SIMON. Oh damn it, choose your own reading, and I'm content.   [*Exeunt severally.*

━━━━━

SCENE II. *A Dressing Room—a table and chairs,* C.; *a door,* R.

FRANK ROCHDALE *discovered sitting at the table writing,*
WILLIAMS *attending.*

FRANK. [*Throwing down the pen.*] It don't signify—I cannot write. I blot and tear, and tear and blot, and——come here, Williams—do let me hear you once more. Why the devil don't you come here?

WILLIAMS. I am here, sir.

FRANK. Well, well, my good fellow, tell me. You found means to deliver her the letter yesterday?

WILLIAMS. Yes, sir.

FRANK. And she read it——and——did you say she——she was very much affected when she read it?

WILLIAMS. I told you last night, sir; she looked quite death-struck, as I may say.

FRANK. [*Much affected.*] Did——did she weep, Williams?

WILLIAMS. No, sir, but I did afterwards. I don't know what ailed me, but when I got out of the house into the street I'll be hanged if I didn't cry like a child.

FRANK. You are an honest fellow, Williams. [*A knock at the door.*] See who is at the door.   [WILLIAMS *opens the door.*

Enter JOHN.

WILLIAMS. Well, what's the matter?

JOHN. There's a man in the porter's lodge says he won't go away without speaking to Mr. Francis.

FRANK. See who it is, Williams. Send him to me, if necessary, but don't let me be teazed without occasion.

WILLIAMS. I'll take care, sir.   [*Exeunt* WILLIAMS *and* JOHN.

FRANK. Must I marry this woman whom my father has chosen for me, whom I expect here to-morrow? And must I, then, be told 'tis criminal to love my poor deserted Mary, because our hearts are illicitly attached? Illicit for the heart! Fine phraseology! Nature disowns the restriction. I cannot smother her dictates and fall in or out of love, as the law directs.

Enter DENNIS BRULGRUDDERY.

Well, friend, who do you come from?

DENNIS. I come from the Red Cow, sir.

FRANK. The Red Cow?

DENNIS. Yes, sir, upon Muckslush Heath—hard by your honour's father's house, here. I'd be proud of your custom, sir, and all the good-looking family's.

FRANK. [*Impatiently.*] Well, well, your business?

DENNIS. That's what the porter ax'd me. 'Tell me your business, honest man,' says he. 'I'll see you damn'd first, sir,' says I; 'I'll tell it your betters, and that's Mr. Francis Rochdale, Esquire.'

FRANK. Zounds! then why don't you tell it? I am Mr. Francis Rochdale. Who the devil sent you here?

DENNIS. Troth, sir, it was good-nature whispered me to come to your honour; but I believe I've disremembered her directions, for damn the bit do you seem acquainted with her.

FRANK. Well, my good friend, I don't mean to be violent; only be so good as to explain your business.

DENNIS. Oh, with all the pleasure in life. Give me good words, and I'm as asy as an ould glove; but bite my nose off with mustard, and have at you with pepper; that's my way. There's a little crature at my house—she's crying her eyes out—and she won't get such another pair at the Red Cow, for I've left nobody with her but Mrs. Brulgruddery.

FRANK. With her! With who? Who are you talking of?

DENNIS. I'd like to know her name myself, sir; but I have heard but half of it, and that's Mary.

FRANK. Mary! Can it be she? Wandering on a heath! Seeking refuge in a wretched hovel!

DENNIS. A hovel! Oh, fie for shame of yourself, to misbecall a genteel tavern! I'd have you to know my parlour is clean sanded once a week.

FRANK. Tell me directly—what brought her to your house?

DENNIS. By my soul, it was Adam's own carriage—a ten-toed machine the haymakers keep in Ireland.

FRANK. Damn it, fellow! Don't trifle, but tell your story, and, if you can, intelligibly.

DENNIS. Don't be bothering my brains, then, or you'll get it as clear as mud. Sure the young crature can't fly away from the Red Cow while I'm explaining to you the rights on't. Didn't she promise the gentleman to stay till he came back?

FRANK. Promised a gentleman! Who—who is the gentleman?

DENNIS. Arrah now, where did you larn manners? Would you ax a customer his birth, parentage, and education? 'Heaven bless you, sir, you'll come back again?' says she. 'That's what I will, before you can say parsnips, my darling,' says he.

FRANK. Damnation! what does this mean? Explain your errand clearly, you scoundrel, or——

DENNIS. Scoundrel! Don't be after affronting a housekeeper. Haven't I a sign at my door, three pigs, a wife, and a man-sarvant?

FRANK. Well, go on.

DENNIS. Damn the word more will I tell you.

FRANK. Why, you infernal——

DENNIS. Oh, be asy! See what you get, now, by affronting Mr. Dennis Brulgruddery! [*Searching his pockets.*] I'd have talked for an hour if you had kept a civil tongue in your head, but now you may read the letter.   [*Giving it.*

FRANK. A letter! Stupid booby, why didn't you give it to me at first? Yes, it is her hand!   [*Opens the letter.*

DENNIS. Stupid! If you're so fond of letters, you might larn to behave yourself to the postman.

FRANK. [*Reading, and agitated.*] 'Not going to upbraid you—couldn't rest at my father's—trifling assistance'—oh, heaven! does she then want assistance? 'The gentleman who has befriended me.' Damnation! The gentleman! 'Your unhappy Mary.' Scoundrel that I am! What is she suffering? But who, who is this gentleman? No matter—she is distressed, heart breaking, and I, who have been the cause—I, who——here—— [*Running to the writing table, opening a drawer, and taking out a purse.*] Run! Fly! Despatch!

DENNIS. He's mad!

FRANK. Say I will be at your house myself—remember, positively come or send in the course of the day. In the mean-time take this, and give it to the person who sent you.

DENNIS. A purse! Faith, and I'll take it. Do you know how much is in the inside?

FRANK. Psha, no! No matter.

DENNIS. Troth, now, if I'd trusted a great big purse to a stranger, they'd have called it a bit of a bull. [*Pouring the money on the table.*] But let you and I count it out between us, for damn him, say I, who would cheat a poor girl in distress of the value of a rap! [*Counting.*] One, two, three, &c.

FRANK. Worthy, honest fellow!

DENNIS. Eleven, twelve, thirteen——

FRANK. I'll be the making of your house, my good fellow.

DENNIS. Damn the Red Cow, sir; you put me out. Seventeen, eighteen, nineteen. Nineteen fat yellow boys and a seven shilling piece. Tell 'em yourself, sir; then chalk 'em up over the chimney-piece, or else you'll forget, you know.

FRANK. Oh friend, when honesty so palpably natural as yours keeps the account, I care not for my arithmetic. Fly, now!

Bid the servants give you any refreshment you choose; then hasten to execute your commission.

DENNIS. Thank your honour; good luck to you! I'll taste the beer; but by my soul, if the butler comes the Red Cow over me, I'll tell him I know sweet from sour.   [*Exit.*

FRANK. Let me read her letter once more. 'I am not going to upbraid you, but after I got your letter, I could not rest at my father's, where I once knew happiness and innocence. I wished to have taken a last leave of you, and to beg a trifling assistance, but the gentleman who has befriended me in my wanderings would not suffer me to do so; yet I could not help writing to tell you I am quitting this neighbourhood for ever. That you may never know a moment's sorrow will always be the prayer of your unhappy Mary.' My mind is hell to me! Love, sorrow, remorse, and—yes—and jealousy, all distract me, and no counsellor to advise with—no friend to whom I may——

Enter TOM SHUFFLETON.

FRANK. Tom Shuffleton! You never arrived more apropos in your life!

SHUFFLETON. That's what the women always say to me. I've rumbled on the road all night, Frank. My bones ache, my head's muzzy—and we'll drink two bottles of claret a piece after dinner, to enliven us.

FRANK. You seem in spirits, Tom, I think, now.

SHUFFLETON. Yes; I have had a windfall—five hundred pounds.

FRANK. A legacy?

SHUFFLETON. No. The patient survives who was sick of his money. 'Tis a loan from a friend.

FRANK. 'Twould be a pity, then, Tom, if the patient experienced improper treatment.

SHUFFLETON. Why, that's true; but his case is so rare, that it isn't well understood, I believe. Curse me, my dear Frank, if the disease of lending is epidemic.

FRANK. But the disease of trying to borrow, my dear Tom, I am afraid, is.

SHUFFLETON. Very prevalent indeed, at the west end of the town.

FRANK. And as dangerous, Tom, as the small-pox. They should inoculate for it.

SHUFFLETON. That wouldn't be a bad scheme, but I took it naturally. Psha! damn it, don't shake your head. Mine's but a mere *façon de parler*—just as we talk to one another about our coats. We never say, 'Who's your tailor?' We always ask, 'Who suffers?' Your father tells me you are going to be married; I give you joy.

FRANK. Joy! I have known nothing but torment and misery since this cursed marriage has been in agitation.

SHUFFLETON. Umph! Marriage was a weighty affair formerly; so was a family coach, but domestic duties now are like town chariots; they must be made light to be fashionable.

FRANK. Oh, do not trifle! By acceding to this match, in obedience to my father, I leave to all the pangs of remorse and disappointed love a helpless, humble girl, and rend the fibres of a generous, but too credulous heart, by cancelling, like a villain, the oaths with which I won it.

SHUFFLETON. I understand—a snug thing in the country. Your wife, they tell me, will have four thousand a year.

FRANK. What has that to do with sentiment?

SHUFFLETON. I don't know what you may think, but, if a man said to me, plump, 'Sir, I am very fond of four thousand a year,' I should say, 'Sir, I applaud your sentiment very highly.'

FRANK. But how does he act who offers his hand to one woman at the very moment his heart is engaged to another?

SHUFFLETON. He offers a great sacrifice.

FRANK. And where is the reparation to the unfortunate he has deserted?

SHUFFLETON. An annuity. A great many unfortunates sport a stylish carriage up and down St. James's Street, upon such a provision.

FRANK. An annuity flowing from the fortune, I suppose, of the woman I marry! Is that delicate?

SHUFFLETON. 'Tis convenient. We liquidate debts of play and usury from the same resources.

FRANK. And call a crowd of Jews and gentleman-gamesters together, to be settled with during the debtor's honeymoon.

SHUFFLETON. No, damn it, it wouldn't be fair to jumble the Jews into the same room with our gaming acquaintance.

FRANK. Why so?

SHUFFLETON. Because twenty to one the first half of the creditors would begin dunning the other.

FRANK. Nay, for once in your life be serious. Read this, which has wrung my heart, and repose it as a secret in your own.

[*Giving the letter.*

SHUFFLETON. [*Glancing over it.*] A pretty little crowquill kind of a hand. 'Happiness—innocence—trifling assistance— gentleman befriended me—unhappy Mary.' Yes, I see. [*Returning it.*] She wants money, but has got a new friend. The style's neat, but the subject isn't original.

FRANK. Will you serve me at this crisis?

SHUFFLETON. Certainly.

FRANK. I wish you to see my poor Mary in the course of the day. Will you talk to her?

SHUFFLETON. Oh yes, I'll talk to her. Where is she to be seen?

FRANK. She writes, you see, that she has abruptly left her father; and I learn by the messenger that she is now in a miserable retired house on the neighbouring heath. That musn't deter you from going.

SHUFFLETON. Me? Oh dear, no! I'm used to it. I don't care how retired the house is.

FRANK. Come down to my father, to breakfast. I will tell you afterwards all I wish you to execute. Oh, Tom! this business has unhinged me for society. Rigid morality, after all, is the best coat of mail for the conscience.

SHUFFLETON. Our ancestors, who wore mail, admired it amazingly; but to mix in the gay world with their rigid morality would be as singular as stalking into a drawing-room in their armour; for dissipation is now the fashionable habit with which, like a brown coat, a man goes into company to avoid being stared at.   [*Exeunt.*

SCENE III. *An Apartment in* JOB THORNBERRY's *House.*

Enter JOB THORNBERRY *in a night gown, followed by*
JOHN BUR.

BUR. Don't take on so—don't you, now! Pray, listen to reason.

JOB. I won't!

BUR. Pray do!

JOB. I won't! Reason bid me love my child and help my friend: what's the consequence? My friend has run one way and broke up my trade; my daughter has run another and broke my——no, she shall never have it to say she broke my heart. If I hang myself for grief, she shan't know she made me.

BUR. Well, but master——

JOB. And reason told me to take you into my shop when the fat churchwardens starved you at the workhouse—damn their want of feeling for it!—and you were thumped about, a poor, unoffending, ragged-rumped boy as you were—I wonder you haven't run away from me too!

BUR. That's the first real unkind word you ever said to me. I've sprinkled your shop two and twenty years, and never missed a morning.

JOB. The bailiffs are below, clearing the goods; you won't have the trouble any longer.

BUR. Trouble! Look ye, old Job Thornberry——

JOB. Well! What, are you going to be saucy to me now I'm ruined?

BUR. Don't say one cutting thing after another. You have been as noted, all round our town, for being a kind man, as being a blunt one.

JOB. Blunt or sharp, I've been honest. Let them look at my ledger—they'll find it right. I began upon a little; I made that little great, by industry; I never cringed to a customer to get him into my books, that I might hamper him with an over-charged bill for long credit; I earned my fair profits; I paid my fair way; I break by the treachery of a friend, and my first dividend will be seventeen shillings in the pound. I wish every tradesman in England may clap his hand on his heart and say as much, when he asks a creditor to sign his certificate.

BUR. 'Twas I kept your ledger, all the time.

JOB. I know you did.

BUR. From the time you took me out of the workhouse.

JOB. Psha! Rot the workhouse!

BUR. You never mentioned it to me yourself till to-day.

JOB. I said it in a hurry.

BUR. And I've always remembered it at leisure. I don't want to brag, but I hope I've been faithful. It's rather hard to tell poor John Bur, the workhouse boy, after clothing, feeding, and making him your man of trust for two-and-twenty years, that you wonder he don't run away from you now you're in trouble.

JOB. [*Affected.*] John, I beg your pardon.

[Stretching out his hand.

BUR. [*Taking his hand.*] Don't say a word more about it!

JOB. I——

BUR. Pray now, master, don't say any more! Come, be a man; get on your things, and face the bailiffs that are rummaging the goods.

JOB. I can't, John—I can't. My heart's heavier than all the iron and brass in my shop.

BUR. Nay, consider—what confusion. Pluck up a courage—do, now!

JOB. Well, I'll try.

BUR. Aye, that's right; here's your clothes. [*Taking them from the back of a chair.*] They'll play the devil with all the pots and pans, if you aren't by. Why, I warrant you'll do. Bless you, what should ail you?

JOB. Ail me? Do you go and get a daughter, John Bur; then let her run away from you, and you'll know what ails me.

BUR. Come, here's your coat and waistcoat. [*Going to help him on with his clothes.*] This is the waistcoat young mistress worked with her own hands for your birth-day five years ago. Come, get into it as quick as you can.

JOB. [*Throwing it on the floor violently.*] I'd as lieve get into my coffin! She'll have me there soon. Psha, rot it! I'm going to snivel. Bur, go and get me another.

BUR. Are you sure you won't put it on?

JOB. No, I won't! [BUR *pauses*.] No, I tell you! [*Exit* BUR.] How proud I was of that waistcoat five years ago! I little thought what would happen now, when I sat in it at the top of my table with all my neighbours to celebrate the day. There was Collop on one side of me, and his wife on the other, and my daughter Mary sat at the further end, smiling so sweetly— like an artful, good-for-nothing——I shouldn't like to throw away the waistcoat, neither—I may as well put it on. Yes, it would be poor spite not to put it on. [*Putting his arms into it.*] She's breaking my heart, but I'll wear it, I'll wear it! [*Buttoning it as he speaks, and crying involuntarily.*] It's my child's— she's undutiful, ungrateful, barbarous—but she's my child, and she'll never work me another.

Re-enter JOHN BUR.

BUR. Here's another waistcoat, but it has laid by so long, I think it's damp.

JOB. I was thinking so myself, Bur, and so——

BUR. Eh? what, you've got on the old one? Well now, I declare, I'm glad of that! Here's your coat. [*Putting it on him.*] 'Sbobs! this waistcoat feels a little damp about the top of the bosom.

JOB. [*Confused.*] Never mind, Bur, never mind. A little water has dropped on it, but it won't give me cold, I believe.

[*A noise of voices in altercation, without.*

BUR. Heigh, they are playing up old Harry below! I'll run and see what's the matter. Make haste after me—do, now.

[*Exit.*

JOB. I don't care for the bankruptcy now. I can face my creditors like an honest man, and I can crawl to my grave afterwards as poor as a church mouse. What does it signify? Job Thornberry has no reason now to wish himself worth a groat; the old ironmonger and brazier has nobody to hoard his money for now! I was only saving for my daughter; and she has run away from her doating, foolish father, and struck down my heart—flat—flat!

Enter PEREGRINE.

Well—who are you?

PEREGRINE. A friend.

JOB. Then I'm sorry to see you. I have just been ruined by a friend, and never wish to have another friend again, as long as I live; no, nor any ungrateful, undutiful——poh! I don't recollect your face.

PEREGRINE. Climate and years have been at work on it. But do you remember no trace of me?

JOB. No, I tell you. If you have anything to say, say it. I have something to settle below with my daughter—I mean, with the people in the shop; they are impatient, and the morning has half run away before she knew I should be up—I mean, before I have had time to get on my coat and waistcoat she gave me—I mean—I mean, if you have any business, tell it at once.

PEREGRINE. I will tell it at once. You seem agitated. The harpies whom I passed in your shop informed me of your sudden misfortune, but do not despair yet.

JOB. Aye, I'm going to be a bankrupt—but that don't signify. Go on; it isn't that—they'll find all fair—but go on.

PEREGRINE. I will. 'Tis just thirty years since I left England.

JOB. That's a little after the time I set up in the hardware-business.

PEREGRINE. About that time a lad of fifteen years entered your shop; he had the appearance of a gentleman's son, and told you he had heard by accident, as he was wandering through the streets of Penzance, some of your neighbours speak of Job Thornberry's goodness to persons in distress.

JOB. I believe he told a lie there.

PEREGRINE. Not in that instance, though he did in another.

JOB. I remember him. He was a fine, bluff boy.

PEREGRINE. He had lost his parents, he said; and, destitute of friends, money, and food, was making his way to the next port to offer himself to any vessel that would take him on board, that he might work his way abroad and seek a livelihood.

JOB. Yes, yes, he did. I remember it.

PEREGRINE. You may remember, too, when the boy had finished his tale of distress, you put ten guineas in his hand. They were the first earnings of your trade, you told him, and could not be laid out to better advantage than in relieving a helpless orphan; and, giving him a letter of recommendation to a sea captain at Falmouth, you wished him good spirits and prosperity. He left you with a promise that, if fortune ever smiled upon him, you should one day hear news of Peregrine.

JOB. Ah, poor fellow, poor Peregrine! He was a pretty boy. I should like to hear news of him, I own.

PEREGRINE. I am that Peregrine.

JOB. Eh? What! You are—no! Let me look at you again. Are you the pretty boy that——bless us, how you are altered!

PEREGRINE. I have endured many hardships since I saw you— many turns of fortune, but I deceived you (it was the cunning of a truant lad) when I told you I had lost my parents. From a romantic folly, the growth of boyish brains, I had fixed my fancy on being a sailor, and had run away from my father.

JOB. [*With great emotion.*] Run away from your father! If I had known that, I'd have horse-whipped you within an inch of your life!

PEREGRINE. Had you known it, you had done right, perhaps.

JOB. Right! Ah, you don't know what it is for a child to run away from a father! Rot me if I wouldn't have sent you back to him, tied neck and heels, in the basket of the stage-coach.

PEREGRINE. I have had my compunctions—have expressed them by letter to my father, but I fear my penitence had no effect.

JOB. Served you right.

PEREGRINE. Having no answers from him, he died, I fear, without forgiving me.   [*Sighs.*

JOB. [*Starting.*] What! died without forgiving his child! Come, that's too much. I couldn't have done that, neither. But go on; I hope you've been prosperous. But you shouldn't—you shouldn't have quitted your father.

PEREGRINE. I acknowledge it; yet I have seen prosperity, though I traversed many countries, on my outset, in pain and poverty. Chance at length raised me a friend in India, by whose interest and my own industry I amassed considerable wealth in the factory at Calcutta.

JOB. And have just landed it, I suppose, in England?

PEREGRINE. I landed one hundred pounds last night in my purse, as I swam from the Indiaman, which was splitting on a rock, half a league from the neighbouring shore. As for the rest of my property—bills, bonds, cash, jewels—the whole amount of my toil and application, are, by this time I doubt not, gone to the bottom; and Peregrine is returned after thirty years to pay his debt to you, almost as poor as he left you.

JOB. I won't touch a penny of your hundred pounds—not a penny!

PEREGRINE. I do not desire you; I only desire you to take your own.

JOB. My own?

PEREGRINE. Yes; I plunged with this box, last night, into the waves. You see it has your name on it.

JOB. 'Job Thornberry,' sure enough. And what's in it?

PEREGRINE. The harvest of a kind man's charity, the produce of your bounty to one whom you thought an orphan. I have traded these twenty years on ten guineas (which from the first I had set apart as yours), till they have become ten thousand; take it—it could not, I find, come more opportunely. [*Giving him the box.*] Your honest heart gratified itself in administering to my need, and I experience that burst of pleasure a grateful man enjoys in relieving my reliever.

JOB. [*Squeezing* PEREGRINE's *hand, returning the box, and seeming almost unable to utter.*] Take it again.

PEREGRINE. Why do you reject it?

JOB. I'll tell you as soon as I'm able. T'other day I had a friend—— psha, rot it! I'm an old fool! [*Wiping his eyes.*] I lent a friend t'other day the whole profits of my trade, to save him from sinking. He walked off with them and made me a bankrupt. Don't you think he is a rascal?

PEREGRINE. Decidedly so.

JOB. And what should I be if I took all you have saved in the world and left you to shift for yourself?

PEREGRINE. But the case is different. This money is, in fact, your own. I am inured to hardships; better able to bear them, and am younger than you. Perhaps, too, I still have prospects of——

JOB. I won't take it. I'm as thankful to you as if I left you to starve, but I won't take it.

PEREGRINE. Remember, too, you have claims upon you which I have not. My guide, as I came hither, said you had married in my absence: 'tis true he told me you were now a widower, but it seems you have a daughter to provide for.

JOB. I have no daughter to provide for now.

PEREGRINE. Then he misinformed me.

JOB. No, he didn't. I had one last night, but she's gone.

PEREGRINE. Gone!

JOB. Yes; gone to sea, for what I know, as you did. Run away from a good father, as you did. This is a morning to remember: my daughter has run out, and the bailiffs have run in. I shan't soon forget the day of the month.

PEREGRINE. This morning, did you say?

JOB. Aye, before day-break; a hard-hearted, base——

PEREGRINE. And could she leave you, during the derangement of your affairs?

JOB. She didn't know what was going to happen, poor soul! I wish she had now. I don't think my Mary would have left her old father in the midst of his misfortunes.

PEREGRINE. [*Aside.*] Mary! It must be she! What is the amount of the demands upon you?

JOB. Six thousand. But I don't mind that; the goods can nearly cover it—let 'em take 'em—damn the gridirons and warming-pans! I could begin again, but now my Mary's gone I haven't the heart; but I shall hit upon something.

PEREGRINE. Let me make a proposal to you, my old friend. Permit me to settle with the officers and to clear all demands upon you. Make it a debt, if you please. I will have a hold, if it must be so, on your future profits in trade; but do this, and I promise to restore your daughter to you.

JOB. What? Bring back my child! Do you know where she is? Is she safe? Is she far off? Is——

PEREGRINE. Will you receive the money?

JOB. Yes, yes, on those terms—on those conditions—but where is Mary?

PEREGRINE. Patience—I must not tell you yet, but in four-and-twenty hours I pledge myself to bring her back to you.

JOB. What, here? To her father's house, and safe? Oh, 'sbud! when I see her safe, what a thundering passion I'll be in with her! But you are not deceiving me? You know the first time you came into my shop, what a bouncer you told me when you were a boy.

PEREGRINE. Believe me, I would not trifle with you now. Come, come down to your shop, that we may rid it of its present visitants.

JOB. I believe you dropped from the clouds, all on a sudden, to comfort an old, broken-hearted brazier.   [*Exeunt.*

ACT III

SCENE I. SIR SIMON ROCHDALE'S *Library.*

SIR SIMON ROCHDALE *and* LORD FITZ-BALAAM *discovered sitting at a table,* C.

SIR SIMON. And now, since the marriage is concluded, as I may say, in the families, may I take the liberty to ask, my lord, what sort of a wife my son Frank may expect in Lady Caroline? Frank is rather of a grave, domestic turn; Lady Caroline, it seems, has passed the three last winters in London. Did her ladyship enter into all the spirit of the first circles?

LORD FITZ-BALAAM. She was as gay as a lark, Sir Simon.

SIR SIMON. Was she like the lark in her hours, my lord?

LORD FITZ-BALAAM. A great deal more like the owl, Sir Simon.

SIR SIMON. I thought so. Frank's mornings in London will begin where her ladyship's nights finish. But his case won't be very singular: many couples make the marriage bed a kind of cold matrimonial well, and the two family buckets dip into it alternately.

Enter LADY CAROLINE BRAYMORE.

LADY CAROLINE. Do I interrupt business?

SIR SIMON. Not in the least. Pray, Lady Caroline, come in; his lordship and I have just concluded.

LORD FITZ-BALAAM. And I must go and walk my three miles this morning.

SIR SIMON. Must you, my lord?

LORD FITZ-BALAAM. My physician prescribed it, when I told him I was apt to be dull after dinner.   [*Exit.*

SIR SIMON. I would attend your lordship, but since Lady Caroline favours me with——

LADY CAROLINE. No, no; don't mind me. I assure you, I had much rather you would go.

SIR SIMON. Had you? [*Aside.*] Hum! But the petticoats have their New School of good breeding, too, they tell me. [*Aloud.*] Well, we are gone. We have been glancing over the writings, Lady Caroline, that form the basis of my son's happiness, although his lordship isn't much inclined to read.

LADY CAROLINE. But I am. I came here to study very deeply before dinner.

SIR SIMON. [*Showing the writings.*] What, would your ladyship then wish to——

LADY CAROLINE. To read that? My dear Sir Simon, all that Hebrew, upon parchment as thick as a board! I came to see if you had any of the last novels in your book-room.

SIR SIMON. The last novels! [*Aside.*] Most of the female New School are ghost-bitten, they tell me! [*Aloud, pointing to the table.*] There's Fielding's works, and you'll find Tom Jones, you know.

LADY CAROLINE. Psha, that's such a hack!

SIR SIMON. A hack, Lady Caroline, that the knowing ones have warranted sound.

LADY CAROLINE. But what do you think of those that have had such a run lately?

SIR SIMON. Why, I think most of them have run too much, and want firing.   [*Exit.*

LADY CAROLINE. I shall die of *ennui* in this moping manor-house! Shall I read to-day? No, I'll walk; no, I'll——yes, I'll read first, and walk afterwards. [*Sitting at the table, taking up a book, and ringing the bell.*] Pope. Come, as there are no novels, this may be tolerable. This is the most *triste* house I ever saw.

> 'In these deep solitudes, and awful cells,
> Where heavenly-pensive——'

Enter ROBERT.

ROBERT. Did you ring, my lady?

LADY CAROLINE. 'Contemplation dwells.' Sir? Oh, yes; I should like to walk. Is it damp under foot, sir? 'And ever musing——

ROBERT. There has been a good deal of rain to-day, my lady.

LADY CAROLINE. 'Melancholy reigns.'

ROBERT. My lady?

LADY CAROLINE. Pray, sir, look out and bring me word if it is clean or dirty.

ROBERT. Yes, my lady. [*Exit.*

LADY CAROLINE. This settling a marriage is a strange business. 'What means this tumult in a vestal's veins?'

SHUFFLETON. [*Without.*] Bid the groom lead the horse into the avenue, and I'll come to him.

LADY CAROLINE. Company in the house! Some Cornish squire, I suppose. [*Resumes her reading.*

Enter TOM SHUFFLETON, *followed by* JOHN.

LADY CAROLINE. [*Still reading, and seated with her back to* SHUFFLETON.] 'Soon as thy letters, trembling, I unclose—'

JOHN. What horse will you have saddled, sir?

SHUFFLETON. Slyboots. [*Exit* JOHN.

LADY CAROLINE. 'That well-known name awakens all my woes.'

SHUFFLETON. Lady Caroline Braymore!

LADY CAROLINE. Mr. Shuffleton! Lard! what can bring you into Cornwall?

SHUFFLETON. Sympathy, which has generally brought me near your ladyship, in London at least, for these three winters.

LADY CAROLINE. Psha! But seriously?

SHUFFLETON. I was summoned by friendship. I am consulted on all essential points in this family, and Frank Rochdale is going to be married.

LADY CAROLINE. Then you know to whom?

SHUFFLETON. No; not thinking that an essential point, I forgot to ask. He kneels at the pedestal of a rich shrine, and I didn't inquire about the statue. But dear Lady Caroline, what has brought you into Cornwall?

LADY CAROLINE. Me? I'm the statue.

SHUFFLETON. You?

LADY CAROLINE. Yes; I've walked off my pedestal, to be worshipped at the Land's End.

SHUFFLETON. You to be married to Frank Rochdale! Oh, Lady Caroline! What, then, is to become of me?

LADY CAROLINE. Oh, Mr. Shuffleton! Not thinking that an essential point, I forgot to ask.

SHUFFLETON. Psha, now you're laughing at me! But upon my soul I shall turn traitor, take advantage of the confidence reposed in me by my friend, and endeavour to supplant him.

LADY CAROLINE. What do you think the world would call such duplicity of conduct?

Re-enter ROBERT.

ROBERT. Very dirty, indeed, my lady.   [*Exit.*

SHUFFLETON. That infernal footman has been listening! I'll kick him round his master's park.

LADY CAROLINE. 'Tis lucky, then, you are booted; for you hear he says it is very dirty there.

SHUFFLETON. Was that the meaning of—pooh! But you see, the—the surprise—the—the agitation has made me ridiculous.

LADY CAROLINE. I see something has made you ridiculous, but you never told me what it was before.

SHUFFLETON. Lady Caroline, this is a crisis that—my attentions—that is, the——in short, the world, you know, my dear Lady Caroline, has given me to you.

LADY CAROLINE. Why, what a shabby world it is!

SHUFFLETON. How so?

LADY CAROLINE. To make me a present of something it sets no value on itself.

SHUFFLETON. I flattered myself I might not be altogether invaluable to your ladyship.

LADY CAROLINE. To me! Now I can't conceive any use I could make of you. No, positively, you are neither useful nor ornamental.

SHUFFLETON. Yet you were never at an opera without me at your elbow, never in Kensington Gardens that my horse wasn't constantly in leading at the gate. Haven't you danced with me at every ball? And haven't I, unkind, forgetful Lady Caroline, even cut the Newmarket meetings when you were in London?

LADY CAROLINE. Bless me! these charges are brought in like a bill. 'To attending your ladyship, at such a time; to dancing down twenty couple with your ladyship, at another;' and, pray, to what do they all amount?

SHUFFLETON. The fullest declaration.

LADY CAROLINE. Lard, Mr. Shuffleton! Why, it has, to be sure, looked a—a—a little foolish, but you—you never spoke anything to—that is—to justify such a——

SHUFFLETON. [*Aside.*] That's as much as to say, speak now. [*Aloud.*] To be plain, Lady Caroline, my friend does not know your value. He has an excellent heart—but that heart is— [*Coughing. Aside.*] damn the word, it's so out of fashion, it chokes me!—[*Aloud.*] is irrevocably given to another. But mine—by this sweet hand I swear——

[*Kneeling, and kissing her hand.*

Re-enter JOHN.

Well, sir?   [*Rising hastily.*

JOHN. Slyboots, sir, has been down on his knees, and the groom says he can't get out.

SHUFFLETON. Let him saddle another.

JOHN. What horse, sir, will you——

SHUFFLETON. Psha, any! What do you call Mr. Rochdale's favourite, now?

JOHN. Traitor, sir.

SHUFFLETON. When Traitor's in the avenue, I shall be there.

[*Exit* JOHN.

LADY CAROLINE. Answer me one question candidly, and perhaps I may entrust you with a secret. Is Mr. Rochdale seriously attached?

SHUFFLETON. Very seriously.

LADY CAROLINE. Then I won't marry him.

SHUFFLETON. That's spirited. Now, your secret.

LADY CAROLINE. Why—perhaps you may have heard that my father, Lord Fitz-Balaam, is somehow so much in debt that ——but no matter.

SHUFFLETON. Oh, not at all; the case is fashionable with both lords and commoners.

LADY CAROLINE. But an old maiden aunt, whom, rest her soul, I never saw, for family pride's sake bequeathed me an independence. To obviate his lordship's difficulty, I mean to—to marry into this humdrum Cornish family.

SHUFFLETON. I see—a sacrifice! Filial piety and all that—to disembarrass his lordship. But hadn't your ladyship better——

LADY CAROLINE. Marry to disembarrass you?

SHUFFLETON. By my honour, I'm disinterested.

LADY CAROLINE. By my honour, I am monstrously piqued, and so vexed that I can't read this morning, nor talk, nor— I'll walk.

SHUFFLETON. Shall I attend you?

LADY CAROLINE. No; don't fidget at my elbow as you do at the opera. But you shall tell me more of this by-and-by.

SHUFFLETON. [*Taking her hand.*] When? Where?

LADY CAROLINE. Don't torment me. This evening, or to-morrow, perhaps; in the park, or—psha, we shall meet at dinner! Do let me go now, for I shall be very bad company.

SHUFFLETON. [*Kissing her hand.*] Adieu, Lady Caroline!

LADY CAROLINE. Adieu!   [*Exit.*

SHUFFLETON. My friend Frank, here, I think, is very much obliged to me. I am putting matters pretty well *en train* to disencumber him of a wife; and now I'll canter over the heath, and see what I can do for him with the brazier's daughter.

[*Exit.*
C

SCENE II. *A Mean Parlour at the Red Cow. A window in flat,*
c. *A cupboard in flat,* R. *A clock in flat,* L. *A door,* R.; *a fireplace,*
L. *with plaister parrots on the mantle. Chairs, and table,* c.; *pen, ink,*
and paper on it.

Enter MARY *and* MRS. BRULGRUDDERY.

MRS. BRULGRUDDERY. Aye, he might have been there and
back, over and over again; but my husband's slow enough in
his motions, as I tell him 'till I'm tired on't.

MARY. I hope he'll be here soon.

MRS. BRULGRUDDERY. Ods, my little heart! Miss, why so
impatient? Haven't you as genteel a parlour as any lady in the
land could wish to sit down in? The bed's turned up in a
chest of drawers that's stained to look like mahogany; there's
two poets, and a poll-parrot, the best images the Jew had on
his head, over the mantelpiece; and, was I to leave you all
alone by yourself, isn't there an eight-day clock in the
corner that, when one's waiting lonesome-like for anybody,
keeps going tick tack and is quite company?

MARY. Indeed, I did not mean to complain.

MRS. BRULGRUDDERY. Complain? No, I think not, indeed!
When, besides having a handsome house over your head, the
strange gentleman has left two guineas—though one seems
light, and t'other looks a little brummish—to be laid out for
you, as I see occasion. I don't say it for the lucre of anything
I'm to make out of the money, but I'm sure you can't want to
eat yet.

MARY. Not if it gives any trouble, but I was up before sunrise,
and have tasted nothing to-day.

MRS. BRULGRUDDERY. Eh? Why, bless me, young woman!
Aren't you well?

MARY. I feel very faint.

MRS. BRULGRUDDERY. Aye, this is a faintish time o'year; but
I must give you a little something, I suppose. I'll open the
window and give you a little air.

DENNIS. [*Passing the window and singing without.*]
　　They handed the whiskey about,
　　　　'Till it smoked through the jaws of the piper;

The bride got a fine copper snout,
And the clergyman's pimples grew riper.
                    Whack doodlety bob,
                        Sing pip.

MARY. There's your husband.

MRS. BRULGRUDDERY. There's a hog; for he's as drunk as one, I know, by his beastly bawling.

Enter DENNIS BRULGRUDDERY.

DENNIS. [*Singing.*] Whack doodlety bob,
                        Sing pip.

MRS. BRULGRUDDERY. 'Sing pip,' indeed! Sing sot! And that's to your old tune.

MARY. Haven't you got an answer?

MRS. BRULGRUDDERY. Haven't you got drunk?

DENNIS. Be asy, and you'll see what I've got in a minute.
                        [*Pulls a bottle from his pocket.*

MRS. BRULGRUDDERY. What's that?

DENNIS. Good Madeira it was when the butler at the big house gave it me. It jolted so over the heath, that if I hadn't held it to my mouth, I'd have wasted half. [*Putting it on the table.*] There, miss, I brought it for you; and I'll get a glass from the cupboard, and a plate for this paper of sweet cakes that the gintlefolks eat after dinner in the desert.

MARY. But tell me if——

DENNIS. [*Running to the cupboard.*] Eat and drink, my jewel, and my discourse shall serve for the seasoning. [*Filling a glass.*] Drink now, my pretty one, for you have had nothing, I'll be bound. Och, by the powers! I know the ways of ould mother Brulgruddery.

MRS. BRULGRUDDERY. Old mother Brulgruddery!

DENNIS. Don't mind her; take your prog; she'd starve a saint.

MRS. BRULGRUDDERY. I starve a saint?

DENNIS. Let him stop at the Red Cow as plump as a porker, and you'd send him away in a week like a weasel. [*Offering the plate to* MARY.] Bite a maccaroony, my darling.

MARY. I thank you.

DENNIS. Faith, no merit of mine; 'twas the butler that stole it. Take some. [*Letting the plate fall.*] Slips, by St. Patrick!

MRS. BRULGRUDDERY. [*Screaming.*] Our best China plate broke all to shivers!

DENNIS. Delf, you deceiver, delf! The cat's dining dish, rivetted.

MARY. Pray, now, let me hear your news.

DENNIS. That I will. Mrs. Brulgruddery, I take the small liberty of begging you to get out, my lambkin.

MRS. BRULGRUDDERY. I shan't budge an inch. She needn't be ashamed of anything that's to be told, if she's what she should be.

MARY. I know what I should be if I were in your place.

MRS. BRULGRUDDERY. Marry come up! And what should you be, then?

MARY. More compassionate to one of my own sex, or to any one in misfortune. Had you come to me, almost broken-hearted, and not looking like one quite abandoned to wickedness, I should have thought on your misery and forgot that it might have been brought on by your faults.

DENNIS. At her, my little crature! By my soul, she'll bother the ould one! Faith, the Madeira has done her a deal of service.

MRS. BRULGRUDDERY. What's to be said is said before me, and that's flat.

MARY. [*To* DENNIS.] Do tell it, then; but for others' sakes don't mention names. I wish to hide nothing now on my own account; though the money that was put down for me, before you would afford me shelter, I thought might have given me a little more title to hear a private message.

MRS. BRULGRUDDERY. I've a character for virtue to lose, young woman.

DENNIS. When that's gone, you'll get another—that's of a damned impertinent landlady! Sure, she has a right to her parlour, and haven't I brought her cash enough to swallow the Red Cow's rent for these two years?

MRS. BRULGRUDDERY. Have you? Well, though the young lady misunderstands me, it's always my endeavour to be respectful to gentlefolks.

DENNIS. Och, botheration to the respect that's bought by knocking one shilling against another at an inn! Let the heart keep open house, I say; and if Charity isn't seated inside of it, like a beautiful barmaid, it's all a humbug to stick up the sign of the Christian.

MRS. BRULGRUDDERY. I'm sure miss shall have anything she likes, poor dear thing! There's one chicken——

DENNIS. A chicken! Fie on your double barbarity! Would you murder the tough‧ dunghill cock to choke a customer? [*To* MARY.] A certain person that shall be nameless will come to you in the course of this day, either by himself, or by friend, or by handwriting.

MARY. And not one word—not one, by letter, now?

DENNIS. Be asy—won't he be here soon? In the meantime, here's nineteen guineas and a seven-shilling piece, as a bit of a postscript.

MRS. BRULGRUDDERY. Nineteen guineas and——

DENNIS. Hould your gab, woman! Count them, darling.
             [*He puts the money on the table—*MARY *counts it.*

MRS. BRULGRUDDERY. [*Drawing* DENNIS *aside.*] What have you done with the rest?

DENNIS. The rest?

MRS. BRULGRUDDERY. Why, have you given her all?

DENNIS. I'll tell you what, Mrs. Brulgruddery; it's my notion, in summing up your last accounts, that when you begin to dot Ould Nick will carry one, and that's yourself, my lambkin!

SHUFFLETON. [*Without.*] Hollo! Red Cow!

DENNIS. You are called, Mrs. Brulgruddery.

MRS. BRULGRUDDERY. I, you Irish bear! Go and——[*Looking towards the window.*] Jimminy! A traveller on horseback, and the handsomest gentleman I ever saw in my life! [*Runs out.*

MARY. Oh then it must be he!

DENNIS. No, faith, it isn't the young squire.

MARY. [*Mournfully.*] No!

DENNIS. There—he's got off the outside of his horse: it's that flashy spark I saw crossing the court-yard, at the big house. Here he is.

Enter TOM SHUFFLETON.

SHUFFLETON. [*Aside, looking at* MARY.] Devilish good-looking girl, upon my soul! [*Seeing* DENNIS.] Who's that fellow?

DENNIS. Welcome to Muckslush Heath, sir.

SHUFFLETON. Pray, sir, have you any business here?

DENNIS. Very little this last week, your honour.

SHUFFLETON. Oh, the landlord. Leave the room!

DENNIS. [*Aside.*] Manners! But he's my customer. If he don't behave himself to the young crature, I'll bounce in and thump him blue.   [*Exit.*

SHUFFLETON. [*Looking at* MARY.] Shy, but stylish—much elegance, and no brass: the most extraordinary article that ever belonged to a brazier. [*Addressing her.*] Don't be alarmed, my dear. Perhaps you didn't expect a stranger?

MARY. No, sir.

SHUFFLETON. But you expected somebody, I believe, didn't you?

MARY. Yes, sir.

SHUFFLETON. I come from him; here are my credentials. [*Giving her a letter.*] Read that, my dear little girl, and you shall see how far I am authorised.

MARY. [*Kissing the superscription.*] 'Tis his hand!

SHUFFLETON. [*As she is opening the letter.*] Fine blue eyes, faith, and very like my Fanny's. Yes, I see how it will end—she'll be the fifteenth Mrs. Shuffleton.

MARY. [*Reading.*] 'When the conflicts of my mind have subsided, and opportunity will permit, I will write to you fully. My friend is instructed from me to make every arrangement for your welfare. With heartfelt grief I add, family circumstances have torn me from you for ever.'
                              [*Drops the letter, and is falling.*

SHUFFLETON. [*Supporting her*.] Ha! damn it, this looks like earnest! They do it very differently in London.

MARY. [*Recovering*.] I beg pardon, sir; I expected this, [*Bursting into tears*.] but I—I——

SHUFFLETON. [*Aside*.] Oh, come, we are getting into the old train; after the shower, it will clear. My dear girl, don't flurry yourself; these are things of course, you know. To be sure, you must feel a little resentment at first, but——

MARY. Resentment! When I am never, never to see him again! Morning and night my voice will be raised to heaven, in anguish, for his prosperity! And tell him—pray, sir, tell him,—I think the many, many bitter tears I shall shed will atone for my faults; then you know, as it isn't himself but his station that sunders us, if news should reach him that I have died, it can't bring any trouble to his conscience.

SHUFFLETON. Mr. Rochdale, my love, you'll find will be very handsome.

MARY. I always found him so, sir.

SHUFFLETON. [*Giving her a note*.] He has sent you a hundred pound bank note till matters can be arranged, just to set you a going.

MARY. I was going sir, out of this country, for ever. Sure he couldn't think it necessary to send me this, for fear I should trouble him!

SHUFFLETON. Psha! my love, you mistake; the intention is to give you a settlement.

MARY. I intended to get one for myself, sir.

SHUFFLETON. Did you?

MARY. Yes, sir; in London. I shall take a place in the coach to-morrow morning; and I hope the people of the inn where it puts up at the end of the journey will have the charity to recommend me to an honest service.

SHUFFLETON. Service? Nonsense! You—you must think differently. I'll put you into a situation in town.

MARY. Will you be so humane, sir?

SHUFFLETON. Should you like Marybone parish, my love?

MARY. All the parishes are the same to me, now I must quit my own, sir.

SHUFFLETON. I'll write a line for you to a lady in that quarter, and——oh, here's pen and ink. [*Writing, and talking as he is writing.*] I shall be in London myself in about ten days, and then I'll visit you to see how you go on.

MARY. Oh, sir, you are indeed a friend!

SHUFFLETON. I mean to be your friend, my love. There. [*Giving her the letter.*] Mrs. Brown, Howland Street, an old acquaintance of mine, a very good-natured, discreet, elderly lady, I assure you.

MARY. You are very good, sir, but I shall be ashamed to look such a discreet person in the face if she hears my story.

SHUFFLETON. No, you needn't; she has a large stock of charity for the indiscretions of others, believe me.

MARY. I don't know how to thank you, sir. The unfortunate must look up to such a lady, sure, as a mother.

SHUFFLETON. She has acquired that appellation. You'll be very comfortable, and when I arrive in town I'll——

Enter PEREGRINE.

[*Aside.*] Who have we here? Oh! Ha, ha! This must be the gentleman she mentioned to Frank in her letter. Rather an ancient *ami*.

PEREGRINE. [*Aside.*] So! I suspected this might be the case. [*Aloud.*] You are Mr. Rochdale, I presume, sir?

SHUFFLETON. Yes, sir, you do presume, but I am not Mr. Rochdale.

PEREGRINE. I beg your pardon, sir, for mistaking you for so bad a person.

SHUFFLETON. Mr. Rochdale, sir, is my intimate friend. If you mean to recommend yourself in this quarter, [*Pointing to* MARY.] good breeding will suggest to you that it mustn't be done by abusing him before me.

PEREGRINE. I have not acquired that sort of good breeding, sir, which isn't founded on good sense; and when I call the betrayer of female innocence a bad character, the term, I think, is too true to be abusive.

SHUFFLETON. 'Tis a pity, then, you haven't been taught a little better what is due to polished society.

PEREGRINE. I am always willing to improve.

SHUFFLETON. I hope, sir, you won't urge me to become your instructor.

PEREGRINE. You are unequal to the task. If you quarrel with me in the cause of a seducer, you are unfit to teach me the duties of a citizen.

SHUFFLETON. You may make, sir, a very good citizen, but curse me if you'll do for the west end of the town.

PEREGRINE. I make no distinctions in the ends of towns, sir. The ends of integrity are always uniform; and 'tis only where those ends are most promoted that the inhabitants of a town, let them live east or west, most preponderate in rational estimation.

SHUFFLETON. Pray, sir, are you a Methodist preacher in want of a congregation?

PEREGRINE. Perhaps I'm a quack doctor in want of a Jack Pudding. Will you engage with me?

SHUFFLETON. Damn me if this is to be borne. Sir, the correction I must give you will——

PEREGRINE. [*With coolness.*] Desist, young man, in time, or you may repent your petulance.

MARY. [*Coming between them.*] Oh, gentlemen! Pray, pray don't! I am so frightened! [*To* PEREGRINE.] Indeed, sir, you mistake. [*Pointing to* SHUFFLETON.] This gentleman has been so good to me.

PEREGRINE. Prove it, child, and I shall honour him.

MARY. Indeed, indeed he has. Pray, pray don't quarrel! When two such generous people meet, it would be a sad pity. See, sir, he has recommended me to a place in London, an elderly lady in Marybone parish; and so kind, sir, everybody that knows her calls her mother.

PEREGRINE. [*Looking at the superscription.*] Infamous! Sit down and compose yourself, my love; the gentleman and I shall come to an understanding. [MARY *retires up, and sits.*] One word, sir. I have lived long in India, but the flies who gad thither buzz in our ears till we learn what they have blown upon in England. I have heard of the wretch in whose house you meant to place that unfortunate.

SHUFFLETON. Well? And you meant to place her in snugger lodgings, I suppose?

PEREGRINE. I mean to place her where——

SHUFFLETON. No, my dear fellow, you don't, unless you answer it to me.

PEREGRINE. I understand you. In an hour, then, I shall be at the manor-house, whence I suppose you come. Here we are both unarmed, and there is one at the door who, perhaps, might interrupt us.

SHUFFLETON. Who is he?

PEREGRINE. Her father—her agonised father, to whose entreaties I have yielded and brought him here prematurely. He is a tradesman—beneath your notice, a vulgar brazier; but he has some sort of feeling for his child whom, now your friend has lured her to the precipice of despair, you would hurry down the gulf of infamy. For your own convenience, sir, I would advise you to avoid him.

SHUFFLETON. Your advice now begins to be a little sensible; and if you turn out a gentleman, though I suspect you to be one of the brazier's company, I shall talk to you at Sir Simon's. [*Exit.*

MARY. Is the gentleman gone, sir?

PEREGRINE. Let him go, child, and be thankful that you have escaped from a villain.

MARY. A villain, sir?

PEREGRINE. The basest, for nothing can be baser than manly strength, in the specious form of protection, injuring an unhappy woman. When we should be props to the lily in the storm, 'tis damnable to spring up like vigorous weeds and twine about the drooping flower till we destroy it.

MARY. Then where are friends to be found, sir? He seemed honest—so do you, but perhaps you may be as bad.

PEREGRINE. Do not trust me. I have brought you a friend, child, in whom Nature tells us we ever should confide.

MARY. What, here, sir?

PEREGRINE. Yes. When he hurts you, he must wound himself; and so suspicious is the human heart become, from the treachery of society, that it wants that security. I will send him to you.   [*Exit.*

MARY. Who can he mean? I know nobody but Mr. Rochdale that, I think, would come to me; for my poor dear father, when he knows all my crime, will abandon me as I deserve.

Enter JOB THORNBERRY, *hastily.*

JOB. Mary! [*She shrieks, and falls into her father's arms.*] My dear Mary! Speak to me!

MARY. [*Recovering.*] Don't look kindly on me, my dear father! Leave me! I left you, but I was almost mad.

JOB. I'll never leave you till I drop down dead by your side! How could you run away from me, Mary? [*She shudders.*] Come, come, kiss me, and we'll talk of that another time.

MARY. You haven't heard half the story, or I'm sure you'd never forgive me.

JOB. Never mind the story now, Mary; 'tis a true story that you're my child, and that's enough for the present. I hear you have met with a rascal; I haven't been told who yet. Some folks don't always forgive; braziers do. Kiss me again, and we'll talk on't bye-and-bye. But why would you run away, Mary?

MARY. I couldn't stay and be deceitful, and it has often cut me to the heart to see you show me that affection which I knew I didn't deserve.

JOB. Ah, you jade! I ought to be angry, but I can't. Look here— don't you remember this waistcoat? You worked it for me, you know.

MARY. [*Kissing him.*] I know I did.

JOB. I had a hard struggle to put it on this morning, but I squeezed myself into it, a few hours after you ran away. If I could do that, you might have told me the worst, without much fear of my anger. How have they behaved to you, Mary?

MARY. The landlord is very humane, but the landlady——

JOB. Cruel to you? I'll blow her up like gunpowder in a copper! We must stay here to-night; for there's Peregrine, that king of good fellows—we must stay here till he comes back from a little way off, he says.

MARY. He that brought you here?

JOB. Aye, he. I don't know what he intends, but I trust all to him, and when he returns we'll have such a merry-making! [*Calling.*] Hollo! House! Oh, damn it, I'll be good to the landlord, but I'll play hell with his wife! Come with me, and let us call about us a bit. Hollo, house! Come, Mary. Odsbobs! I'm so happy to have you again! House! Come, Mary.

[*Exeunt.*

ACT IV

SCENE I. *The Outside of the Red Cow.*

Enter DENNIS BRULGRUDDERY, *from the house.*

DENNIS. I've stretched my neck half a yard longer, looking out after that rapscallion, Dan. Och! and is it yourself I see at last? There he comes, in a snail's trot, with a basket behind him, like a stage-coach.

Enter DAN, *with a basket at his back.*

Dan, you divil! Aren't you a beast of a waiter?

DAN. What for?

DENNIS. To stay out so, the first day of company.

DAN. Come, that be a good un! I ha' waited for the company a week, and I defy you to say I ever left the house till they comed.

DENNIS. Well, and that's true. Pacify me with a good reason, and you'll find me a dutiful master. Arrah, Dan, what's that hump grown out at your back, on the road?

DAN. Plenty o' meat and drink. [*Putting the basket on the ground.*] I han't had such a hump o' late at my stomach.

DENNIS. And who harnessed you, Dan, with all that kitchen stuff?

DAN. He as ware racked and took I wi' un to Penzance for a companion. He ordered I, as I said things ware a little famished-like here, to buy this for the young woman and the old man he ha' brought back wi' un.

DENNIS. Then you have been gabbling your ill-looking stories about my larder, you stone-eater!

DAN. Larder! I told un you had three live pigs as ware dying.

DENNIS. Oh, fie! Think you, won't any master discharge a mansarvant that shames him? Thank your luck, I can't blush. But is the old fellow our customer has brought his intimate friend he never saw but once, thirty years ago?

DAN. Ees, that be old Job Thornberry, the brazier; and as sure as you stand there, when we got to his shop they ware a going to make him a banker.

DENNIS. A banker! I never saw one made; how do they do it?

DAN. Why, the bum-baileys do come into his house and claw away all his goods and furniture.

DENNIS. By the powers, but that's one way of setting a man going in business!

DAN. When we got into the shop, there they ware, as grum as thunder. You ha' seen a bum-bailey?

DENNIS. I'm not curious that way. I might have seen one, once or twice; but I was walking mighty fast, and had no time to look behind me.

DAN. My companion—our customer—he went up stairs, and I bided below, and then they began a knocking about the goods and chapels. That ware no business o' mine.

DENNIS. Sure it was not.

DAN. Na, for sartin; so I ax'd 'em what they ware a doing; and they told I, wi' a broad grin, taking an invention of the misfortunate man's defects.

DENNIS. Choke their grinning!

DAN. They comed down stair—our customer and the brazier; and the head bailey he began a bullocking at the old man, in my mind, just as one Christian shouldn't do to another. I had nothing to do wi' that.

DENNIS. Damn the bit!

DAN. Na, nothing at all, and so my blood began to rise. He made the poor old man almost fit to cry.

DENNIS. That wasn't your concern, you know.

DAN. Bless you, mun! 'twould ha' looked busy-like in me to say a word; so I took up a warming-pan, and I banged bumbailey wi' the broad end on't, till he fell o' the floor, as flat as twopence.

DENNIS. Oh, hubbaboo! lodge in my heart, and I'll never ax you for rent. You're a friend in need. Remember, I've a warming-pan—you know where it hangs, and that's enough.

DAN. They had like to ha' warmed I finely, I know. I ware nigh being hauled to prison 'cause, as well as I could make out their cant, it do seem I had rescued myself and broke a statue.

DENNIS. Och, the Philistines!

DAN. But our traveller—I do think he be the devil—he settled all in a jiffy; for he paid the old man's debts, and the bailey's broken head ware chucked into the bargain.

DENNIS. And what did he pay?

DAN. Guess, now.

DENNIS. A hundred pounds.

DAN. Six thousand, by gum!

DENNIS. What! On the nail?

DAN. Na, on the counter.

DENNIS. Whew! six thousand pou——oh, by the powers, this man must be the philosopher's stone! Dan——

DAN. Hush, here he be!

Enter PEREGRINE, *from the house.*

PEREGRINE. So, friend, you have brought provision, I perceive.

DAN. Ees, sir; three boiled fowls, three roast, two chicken pies, and a capon.

PEREGRINE. You have considered abundance more than variety. And the wine?

DAN. A dozen o' capital red port, sir; I axed for the newest they had i' the cellar.

DENNIS. [*Abstractedly.*] Six thousand pounds upon a counter!

PEREGRINE. [*To* DAN.] Carry the hamper in doors; then return to me instantly. You must accompany me in another excursion.

DAN. What, now?

PEREGRINE. Yes; to Sir Simon Rochdale's. You are not tired, my honest fellow?

DAN. Na, not a walking wi' you; but, dang me, when you die, if all the shoemakers shouldn't go into mourning.

[*He takes the hamper into the house.*

DENNIS. [*Ruminating.*] Six thousand pounds! By St. Patrick, it's a sum!

PEREGRINE. How many miles from here to the manor-house?

DENNIS. Six thousand!

PEREGRINE. Six thousand! Yards you mean, I suppose, friend.

DENNIS. Sir! Eh? Yes, sir, I—I mean yards—all upon a counter!

PEREGRINE. Six thousand yards upon a counter! Mine host here seems a little bewildered; but he has been anxious, I find, for poor Mary, and 'tis national in him to blend eccentricity with kindness. John Bull exhibits a plain, undecorated dish of solid benevolence, but Pat has a gay garnish of whim around his good nature; and if now and then 'tis sprinkled in a little confusion, they must have vitiated stomachs who are not pleased with the embellishment.

Re-enter DAN, *booted.*

DAN. Now, sir, you and I'll stump it.

PEREGRINE. Is the way we are to go now so much worse, that you have cased yourself in those boots?

DAN. Quite clean; that's why I put 'em on. I should ha' dirtied 'em in t'other job.

PEREGRINE. Set forward, then.

DAN. Na, sir, axing your pardon; I be but the guide, and 'tisn't for I to go first.

PEREGRINE. Ha, ha! Then we must march abreast, boy, like lusty soldiers, and I shall be side by side with honesty; 'tis the best way of travelling through life's journey, and why not over a heath? Come, my lad.

DAN. Cheek by jowl, by gum! [*Exeunt* PEREGRINE *and* DAN.

DENNIS. That walking philosopher—perhaps he'll give me a big bag of money. Then, to be sure, I won't lay out some of it to make me easy for life; for I'll settle a separate maintenance upon ould mother Brulgruddery.

JOB THORNBERRY *peeps out at the door of the public-house.*

JOB. Landlord!

DENNIS. Coming, your honour!

JOB. [*Coming forward.*] Hush, don't bawl! Mary has fallen asleep. You have behaved like an emperor to her, she says. Give me your hand, landlord.

DENNIS. Behaved! [*Refusing his hand.*] Arrah now, get away with your blarney.

JOB. Well, let it alone. I'm an old fool, perhaps; but as you comforted my poor girl in her trouble, I thought a squeeze from her father's hand—as much as to say, 'thank you for my child'—might not have come amiss to you.

DENNIS. And is it yourself who are that crature's father?

JOB. Her mother said so, and I always believed her. You have heard some'at of what has happened, I suppose? It's all over our town, I take it, by this time. Scandal is an ugly, trumpeting devil. Let 'em talk; a man loses little by parting with a herd of neighbours who are busiest in publishing his family misfortunes, for they are just the sort of cattle who would never stir over the threshhold to prevent 'em.

DENNIS. Troth, and that's true; and some will only sarve you becase you're convenient to 'em for the time present, just as my customers come to the Red Cow.

JOB. I'll come to the Red Cow, hail, rain, or shine, to help the house, as long as you are landlord, though I must say that your wife——

DENNIS. [*Putting his hand before JOB's mouth.*] Decency! Remember your own honour and my feelings. I mustn't hear any thing bad, you know, of Mrs. Brulgruddery, and you'll say nothing good of her without telling damned lies; so be asy!

JOB. Well, I've done, but we mustn't be speaking ill of all the world, neither; there are always some sound hearts to be found among the hollow ones. Now he that has just gone over the heath——

DENNIS. What, the walking philosopher?

JOB. I don't know anything of his philosophy, but if I live these thousand years I shall never forget his goodness. Then there's another: I was thinking, just now, if I had tried him I might have found a friend in my need, this morning.

DENNIS. Who is he?

JOB. A monstrous good young man, and as modest and affable as if he had been bred up a 'prentice instead of a gentleman.

DENNIS. And what's his name?

JOB. Oh, everybody knows him in this neighbourhood; he lives hard by—Mr. Francis Rochdale, the young squire at the manor-house.

DENNIS. Mr. Francis Rochdale!

JOB. Yes; he's condescending, and took quite a friendship for me and mine. He told me t'other day he'd recommend me in trade to all the great families twenty miles round; and said he'd do I don't know what all for my Mary.

DENNIS. He did! Well, faith, you mayn't know what, but by my soul he has kept his word.

JOB. Kept his word! What do you mean?

DENNIS. Harkye: if Scandal is blowing about your little fireside accident, 'twas Mr. Francis Rochdale recommended him to your shop to buy his trumpet.

JOB. Eh! What? No! Yes—I see it at once! Young Rochdale's a rascal! [*Bawling.*] Mary!

DENNIS. Hush! you'll wake her, you know.

JOB. I intend it; I'll——a glossy, oily, smooth rascal! Warming me in his favour like an unwholesome February sun! Shining upon my poor cottage and drawing forth my child—my tender blossom—to suffer blight and mildew! Mary! I'll go directly to the manor-house; his father's in the commission. I mayn't find justice, but I shall find a justice of peace.

DENNIS. Fie now! and can't you listen to reason?

JOB. Reason! Tell me a reason why a father shouldn't be almost mad, when his patron has ruined his child? Damn his protection! Tell me a reason why a man of birth's seducing my daughter doesn't almost double the rascality? Yes, double it—for my fine gentleman, at the very time he is laying his plans to make her infamous, would think himself disgraced in making her the honest reparation she might find from one of her equals!

DENNIS. Arrah, be asy now, Mr. Thornberry.

JOB. And this spark, forsooth, is now canvassing the county, but if I don't give him his own at the hustings! How dare a man set himself up for a guardian of his neighbour's rights, who has robbed his neighbour of his dearest comforts? How dare a seducer come into freeholders' houses and have the impudence to say, send me up to London as your representative? Mary!

Enter MARY, *from the house.*

MARY. Did you call, my dear father?

JOB. [*Passionately.*] Yes, I did call.

DENNIS. Don't you frighten that poor young crature!

MARY. Oh, dear, what has happened? You are angry, very angry. I hope it isn't with me. If it is, I have no reason to complain.

JOB. [*Softened, and folding her in his arms.*] My poor, dear child! I forgive you twenty times more now than I did before.

MARY. Do you, my dear father?

JOB. Yes, for there's twenty times more excuse for you when rank and education have helped a scoundrel to dazzle you. [*Taking her hand.*] Come.

MARY. Come! Where?

JOB. [*Impatiently.*] To the manor-house with me, directly.

MARY. To the manor-house! Oh, my dear father, think of what you are doing—think of me!

JOB. Of you? I think of nothing else. I'll see you righted. Don't be terrified, child—damn it, you know I doat on you; but we are all equals in the eye of the law, and rot me if I won't make a baronet's son shake in his shoes for betraying a brazier's daughter. Come, love, come!   [*Exeunt* JOB *and* MARY.

DENNIS. There'll be a big botheration at the manor-house. My customers are all gone that I was to entertain; nobody's left but my lambkin, who don't entertain me. Sir Simon's butler gives good Madeira; so I'm off after the rest, and the Red Cow and Mother Brulgruddery may take care of one another.
      [*Exit.*

SCENE II. *A Hall at* SIR SIMON ROCHDALE'S.

Enter SIR SIMON ROCHDALE *and* FRANK ROCHDALE,
severally.

SIR SIMON. Why, Frank, I thought you were walking with
Lady Caroline?

FRANK. No, sir.

SIR SIMON. Ha! I wish you would learn some of the gallantries
of the present day from your friend, Tom Shuffleton, but
from being careless of coming up to the fashion, damn it, you
go beyond it; for you neglect a woman three days before
marriage as much as half the Tom Shuffletons three months
after it.

FRANK. As by entering into this marriage, sir, I shall perform
the duties of a son, I hope you will do me the justice to
suppose I shall not be basely negligent as a husband.

SIR SIMON. Frank, you're a fool, and——

Enter a SERVANT.

Well, sir?

SERVANT. A person, Sir Simon, says he wishes to see you on
very urgent business.

SIR SIMON. And I have very urgent business just now with my
steward. Who is the person? How did he come?

SERVANT. On foot, Sir Simon.

SIR SIMON. Oh, let him wait. [*Exit* SERVANT.] At all events,
I can't see this person for these two hours; I wish you would
see him for me.

FRANK. Certainly, sir. [*Aside, going.*] Anything is refuge to me
now from the subject of matrimony.

SIR SIMON. But a word before you go. Damn it, my dear lad,
why can't you perceive I am labouring this marriage for your
good? We shall ennoble the Rochdales; for though my
father, your grandfather, did some service in elections (that
made him a baronet), amassed property, and bought lands
and so on, yet your great-grandfather—come here—[*Half
whispering.*] your great-grandfather was a miller.

FRANK. [*Smiling.*] I shall not respect his memory less, sir, for knowing his occupation.

SIR SIMON. But the world will, you blockhead, and for your sake—for the sake of our posterity, I would cross the cart breed as much as possible by blood; so no more of the miller.

[*Exeunt severally.*

Enter LADY CAROLINE BRAYMORE, *followed by* TOM SHUFFLETON.

SHUFFLETON. 'The time is come for Iphigene to find
            The miracle she wrought upon my mind—'

LADY CAROLINE. Don't talk to me.

SHUFFLETON. 'For now, by love, by force, she shall be mine,
            Or death, if force should fail, shall finish my
                design.'

LADY CAROLINE. I wish you would finish your nonsense.

SHUFFLETON. Nonsense! 'Tis poetry; somebody told me 'twas written by Dryden.

LADY CAROLINE. Perhaps so; but all poetry is nonsense.

SHUFFLETON. Hear me, then, in prose.

LADY CAROLINE. Psha! that's worse.

SHUFFLETON. Then I must express my meaning in pantomime. Shall I ogle you?

LADY CAROLINE. You are a teazing wretch! I have subjected myself, I find, to very ill treatment in this petty family, and begin to perceive I am a very weak woman.

SHUFFLETON. [*Aside.*] Pretty well for that matter!

LADY CAROLINE. To find myself absolutely avoided by the gentleman I meant to honour with my hand, so pointedly neglected!

SHUFFLETON. I must confess it looks a little like a complete cut.

LADY CAROLINE. And what you told me of the low attachment that——

SHUFFLETON. Nay, my dear Lady Caroline, don't say that I told you more than——

LADY CAROLINE. I won't have it denied, and I'm sure 'tis all

true. See here—here's an odious parchment Lord Fitz-
Balaam put into my hand in the park. A marriage license,
I think he calls it, but if I don't scatter it in a thousand
pieces——

SHUFFLETON. [*Preventing her.*] Softly, my dear Lady Caroline!
That's a license of marriage, you know; the names are
inserted of course. Some of them may be rubbed a little in the
carriage, but they may be filled up at pleasure, you know.
Frank's my friend; and if he has been negligent I say nothing,
but the parson of the parish is as blind as a beetle.

LADY CAROLINE. Now don't you think, Mr. Shuffleton, I am a
very ill-used person?

SHUFFLETON. I feel inwardly for you, Lady Caroline, but my
friend makes the subject delicate. Let us change it. Did you
observe the steeple upon the hill, at the end of the park pales?

LADY CAROLINE. Psha! No.

SHUFFLETON. It belongs to one of the prettiest little village
churches you ever saw in your life. Let me show you the
inside of the church, Lady Caroline.

LADY CAROLINE. I am almost afraid; for if I should make a
rash vow there, what is to become of my Lord Fitz-Balaam?

SHUFFLETON. Oh, that's true—I had forgot his lordship; but
as the exigencies of the times demand it, let us hurry the
question through the Commons, and when it has passed, with
such strong independent interest on our side, it will hardly be
thrown out by the peerage.   [*Exeunt.*

ACT V

SCENE I. *A Hall in the Manor-House—voices are heard wrangling without.*

JOB. [*Without.*] I will see Sir Simon!

SIMON. [*Without.*] You can't see Sir Simon!

Enter JOB THORNBERRY, MARY, *and* SIMON.

JOB. Don't tell me! I come upon justice business!

SIMON. Sir Simon be a gentleman justice.

JOB. If the justice allows all his servants to be as saucy as you, I can't say much for the gentleman.

SIMON. But these ben't his hours.

JOB. Hours for justice! I thought one of the blessings of an Englishman was to find justice at any time.

MARY. Pray don't be so——

JOB. Hold your tongue, child! What are his hours?

SIMON. Why, from twelve to two.

JOB. Two hours out of four-and-twenty! I hope all that belong to law are a little quicker than his worship; if not, when a case wants immediate remedy, it's just eleven to one against us. Don't you know me?

SIMON. Na.

JOB. I'm sure I have seen you in Penzance.

SIMON. My wife ha' got a chandler's shop there.

JOB. Haven't you heard we've a fire engine in the church?

SIMON. What o' that?

JOB. Suppose your wife's shop was in flames, and all her bacon and farthing candles frying?

SIMON. And what then?

JOB. Why then, while the house was burning, you'd run to the church for the engine. Shouldn't you think it plaguy hard if the sexton said, 'Call for it to-morrow, between twelve and two?'

SIMON. That be neither here nor there.

JOB. Isn't it? [*Menacing.*] Then do you see this stick?

SIMON. Psha, you be a foolish old fellow!

JOB. Why, that's true. Every now and then a jack-in-office like you provokes a man to forget his years. The cudgel is a stout one, and some'at like your master's justice—'tis a good weapon in weak hands, and that's the way many a rogue escapes a good dressing. What! You are laughing at it?

SIMON. Ees.

JOB. Ees! You Cornish baboon in a laced livery! Here's something to make you grin more. [*Holding up a half-crown between his finger and thumb.*] Here's half-a-crown.

SIMON. [*Laughing.*] He! he!

JOB. He! he! Damn your Land's End chops! 'Tis to get me to your master; but before you have it, though he keeps a gentleman-justice-shop, I shall make free to ring it on his counter. [*Throwing it on the floor.*] There, pick it up! [SIMON *picks up the money.*] I am afraid you are not the first underling that has stooped to pocket a bribe before he'd do his duty. Now, tell the gentleman-justice I want to see him.

SIMON. I'll try what I can do for you.   [*Exit.*

JOB. What makes you tremble so, Mary?

MARY. I can't help it; I wish I could persuade you to go back again.

JOB. I'll stay till the roof falls, but I'll see some of 'em.

MARY. Indeed, you don't know how you terrify me. But if you go to Sir Simon, you'll leave me here in the hall; you won't make me go with you, father?

JOB. Not take you with me? I'll go with my wrongs in my hand, and make him blush for his son.

MARY. I hope you'll think better of it.

JOB. Why?

MARY. Because, when you came to talk, I should sink with shame if he said anything to you that might—that——

JOB. Might what?

MARY. [*Sighing, and hanging down her head.*] Make you blush for your daughter.

JOB. I won't have you waiting like a petitioner in this hall, when you come to be righted—no, no!

MARY. You wouldn't have refused me anything once, but I know I have lost your esteem now.

JOB. Lost! Forgive is forgive, all the world over. You know, Mary, I have forgiven you; and making it up by halves is making myself a brass tea-kettle, warm one minute, cold the next, smooth without and hollow within.

MARY. Then pray don't deny me! I'm sure you wouldn't if you knew half I am suffering.

JOB. Do as you like, Mary, only never tell me again you have lost my esteem; it looks like suspicion o' both sides. Never say that, and I can deny you nothing in reason, or perhaps a little beyond it.

Re-enter SIMON.

Well, will the justice do a man the favour to do his duty? Will he see me?

SIMON. Come into the room next his libery. A stranger who's with young master ha' been waiting for un longer nor you, but I'll get you in first.

JOB. I don't know that that's quite fair to the other.

SIMON. Ees it be, for t'other didn't gi' I half-a-crown.

JOB. Then stay till I come back, Mary. I see, my man, when you take a bribe, you are scrupulous enough to do your work for it; for which, I hope, somebody may duck you with one hand and rub you dry with the other.   [*Exeunt* JOB *and* SIMON.

MARY. I wished to come to this house in the morning, and now I would give the world to be out of it. Hark, here's somebody! Oh, mercy on me, 'tis he himself! What will become of me?
[*Retires up.*

Enter FRANK ROCHDALE.

FRANK. My father, then, shall see this visitor, whatever be the event. I will prepare him for the interview, and—[*Seeing* MARY.] Good heaven! Why—why are you here?

MARY. [*Advancing to him eagerly.*] I don't come willingly to trouble you; I don't, indeed!

FRANK. What motive, Mary, has brought you to this house, and who is the stranger under whose protection you have placed yourself, at the house on the heath? Surely you cannot love him!

MARY. I hope I do.

FRANK. You hope you do!

MARY. Yes; for I think he saved my life this morning, when I was struggling with the robber who threatened to kill me.

FRANK. And had you taken no guide with you, Mary, no protector?

MARY. I was thinking too much of one who promised to be my protector always, to think of any other.

FRANK. Mary, I—I—'twas I then, it seems, who brought your life into such hazard.

MARY. I hope I haven't said anything to make you unhappy.

FRANK. Nothing, my dearest Mary, nothing! I know it is not in your nature even to whisper a reproof. Yet I sent a friend, with full power from me, to give you the amplest protection.

MARY. I know you did, and he gave me a letter that I might be protected when I got to London.

FRANK. Why then commit yourself to the care of a stranger?

MARY. Because the stranger read the direction of the letter— here it is—[*Taking it from her pocket.*] and said your friend was treacherous.

FRANK. [*Looking at the letter.*] Villain!

MARY. Did he intend to lead me into a snare, then?

FRANK. Let me keep this letter. I may have been deceived in the person I sent to you, but—[*Aside.*] damn his rascality! But could you think me base enough to leave you unsheltered? I had torn you from your home—with anguish I confess it— but I would have provided you another home, which want should not have assailed. Would this stranger bring you better comfort?

MARY. Oh, yes, he has; he has brought me my father.

FRANK. Your father! From whom I made you fly!

MARY. Yes; he has brought a father to his child that she might kiss off the tears her disobedience had forced down his aged cheeks, and restored me to the only home which could give me any comfort now. And my father is here.

FRANK. Here!

MARY. Indeed, I couldn't help his coming, and he made me come with him.

FRANK. I—I am almost glad, Mary, that it has happened.

MARY. Are you?

FRANK. Yes: when a weight of concealment is on the mind, remorse is relieved by the very discovery which it has dreaded. But you must not be waiting here, Mary. There is one in the house to whose care I will entrust you.

MARY. I hope it isn't the person you sent to me to-day.

FRANK. He! I would sooner cradle infancy with serpents! Yet this is my friend! I will now confide in a stranger—the stranger, Mary, who saved your life.

MARY. Is he here?

FRANK. He is. Oh, Mary, how painful if, performing the duty of a son, I must abandon at last the expiation of a penitent! But so dependent on each other are the delicate combinations of probity, that one broken link perplexes the whole chain, and an abstracted virtue becomes a relative iniquity. [*Exeunt.*

SCENE II. *The Library in the Manor-House—table and chairs*, C.

SIR SIMON ROCHDALE *and* MR. PENNYMAN, *his steward, discovered at the table.* JOB THORNBERRY *standing at a little distance from them.*

SIR SIMON. Remember, the money must be ready tomorrow, Mr. Pennyman.

MR. PENNYMAN. [*Going.*] It shall, Sir Simon.

SIR SIMON. [*To* JOB.] So, friend, your business, you say, is——

and Mr. Pennyman, give Robin Ruddy notice to quit his cottage directly.

MR. PENNYMAN. I am afraid, Sir Simon, if he's turned out it will be his ruin.

SIR SIMON. He should have recollected that before he ruined his neighbour's daughter.

JOB. [*Starting.*] Eh!

SIR SIMON. What's the matter with the man? [*To* PENNYMAN.] His offence is attended with great aggravation. Why doesn't he marry her?

JOB. [*Emphatically.*] Aye!

SIR SIMON. Pray, friend, be quiet.

MR. PENNYMAN. He says it would make her more unfortunate still; he's too necessitous to provide even for the living consequence of his indiscretion.

SIR SIMON. That doubles his crime to the girl. He must quit. I'm a magistrate, you know, Mr. Pennyman, and 'tis my duty to discourage all such immorality.

MR. PENNYMAN. Your orders must be obeyed, Sir Simon.

[*Exit.*

SIR SIMON. Now, yours is justice-business, you say. You come at an irregular time, and I have somebody else waiting for me; so be quick. What brings you here?

JOB. My daughter's seduction, Sir Simon, and it has done my heart good to hear your worship say 'tis your duty to discourage all such immorality.

SIR SIMON. To be sure it is, but men like you shouldn't be too apt to lay hold of every sentiment justice drops, lest you mis-apply it. 'Tis like an officious footman snatching up his mistress's perriwig and clapping it on again, hind part before. What are you?

JOB. A tradesman, Sir Simon. I have been a freeholder in this district for many a year.

SIR SIMON. A freeholder! [*Aside.*] Zounds! One of Frank's voters, perhaps, and of consequence at his election. [*Aloud.*] Won't you, my good friend take a chair?

JOB. Thank you, Sir Simon; I know my proper place. I didn't come here to sit down with Sir Simon Rochdale because I am a freeholder; I came to demand my right because you are a justice.

SIR SIMON. A man of respectability, a tradesman, and a freeholder, in such a case as yours, had better have recourse to a court of law.

JOB. I am not rich now, Sir Simon, whatever I may have been.

SIR SIMON. A magistrate, honest friend, can't give you damages; you must fee counsel.

JOB. I can't afford an expensive law-suit, Sir Simon; and, begging your pardon, I think the law never intended that an injured man, in middling circumstances, should either go without redress or starve himself to obtain it.

SIR SIMON. Whatever advice I can give you you shall have it for nothing, but I can't jump over justice's hedges and ditches. Courts of law are broad high roads, made for national convenience; if your way lie through them 'tis but fair you should pay the turnpikes. Who is the offender?

JOB. He lives upon your estate, Sir Simon.

SIR SIMON. Oho, a tenant! Then I may carry you through your journey by a short cut. Let him marry your daughter, my honest friend.

JOB. He won't.

SIR SIMON. Why not?

JOB. He's going to marry another.

SIR SIMON. Then he turns out; the rascal shan't disgrace my estate four-and-twenty hours longer! Injure a reputable tradesman, my neighbour—a freeholder! and refuse to—— did you say he was poor?

JOB. No, Sir Simon; and, bye and bye, if you don't stand in his way, he may be very rich.

SIR SIMON. Rich, eh? Why, zounds! is he a gentleman?

JOB. I have answered that question already, Sir Simon.

SIR SIMON. Not that I remember.

JOB. I thought I had been telling you his behaviour.

SIR SIMON. Umph!

JOB. I reckon many of my neighbours honest men, though I can't call them gentlemen, but I reckon no man a gentleman that I can't call honest.

SIR SIMON. Harkye, neighbour: if he's a gentleman (and I have several giddy young tenants with more money than thought), let him give you a good round sum, and there's an end.

JOB. A good round sum! [*Aside.*] Damn me, I shall choke! [*Aloud.*] A ruffian with a crape puts a pistol to my breast and robs me of forty shillings; a scoundrel with a smiling face creeps to my fireside and robs my daughter of her innocence. The judge can't allow restitution to spare the highwayman. Then pray, Sir Simon—I wish to speak humbly—pray don't insult the father by calling money a reparation from the seducer!

SIR SIMON. [*Aside.*] This fellow must be dealt with quietly, I see. [*Aloud.*] Justice, my honest friend, is—is justice. As a magistrate, I make no distinction of persons. Seduction is a heinous offence, and whatever is in my power I——

JOB. The offender is in your power, Sir Simon.

SIR SIMON. Well, well, don't be hasty, and I'll take cognizance of him. We must do things in form, but you mustn't be passionate. [*Going to the table and taking up a pen.*] Come, give me his christian and surname, and I'll see what's to be done for you. Now, what name must I write?

JOB. [*Emphatically.*] Francis Rochdale!

SIR SIMON. [*Dropping the pen, looking at* JOB, *and starting up.*] Damn me, if it isn't the brazier!

JOB. Justice is justice, Sir Simon. I am a respectable tradesman, your neighbour, and a freeholder. Seduction is a heinous offence; a magistrate knows no distinction of persons; and a rascal mustn't disgrace your estate four-and-twenty hours longer.

SIR SIMON. [*Sheepishly.*] I believe your name is Thornberry.

JOB. It is, Sir Simon. I never blushed at my name till your son made me blush for yours.

SIR SIMON. Mr. Thornberry, I—I heard something of my son's—a—little indiscretion some mornings ago.

JOB. Did you, Sir Simon? You never sent to me about it; so I suppose the news reached you at one of the hours you don't set apart for justice.

SIR SIMON. This is a—a very awkward business, Mr. Thornberry, something like a hump back—we can never set it quite straight; so we must bolster it.

JOB. How do you mean, Sir Simon?

SIR SIMON. Why, 'tis a disagreeable affair, and—we—we must hush it up.

JOB. Hush it up! A justice compound with a father to wink at his child's injuries! If you and I hush it up so, Sir Simon, how shall we hush it up here? [*Striking his breast.*] In one word, will your son marry my daughter?

SIR SIMON. What! My son marry the daughter of a brazier?

JOB. He has ruined the daughter of a brazier. If the best lord in the land degrades himself by a crime, you can't call his atonement for it a condescension.

SIR SIMON. Honest friend, I don't know in what quantities you may sell brass at your shop, but when you come abroad, and ask a baronet to marry his son to your daughter, damn me if you aren't a wholesale dealer!

JOB. And I can't tell, Sir Simon, how you may please to retail justice, but when a customer comes to deal largely with you, damn me if you don't shut up the shop-windows!

SIR SIMON. You are growing saucy. Leave the room, or I shall commit you!

JOB. Commit me! You will please to observe, Sir Simon, I remembered my duty till you forgot yours. You asked me at first to sit down in your presence—I knew better than to do so before a baronet and a justice of the peace. But I lose my respect for my superior in rank when he's so much below my equals in fair dealing; and, since the magistrate has left the chair, [*Slamming the chair into the middle of the room.*] I'll sit down on it. [*Sitting down.*] There! 'Tis fit it should be filled by somebody, and damn me if I leave the house till you redress my daughter, or I shame you all over the county!

SIR SIMON. Why, you impudent mechanic! I shouldn't wonder

if the scoundrel called for my clerk and signed my mittimus. [*Ringing the bell.*] Fellow, get out of that chair!

JOB. I shan't stir. If you want to sit down, take another. This is the chair of justice: it's the most uneasy for you of any in the room.

Enter SIMON.

SIR SIMON. Tell Mr. Rochdale to come to me directly.

SIMON. Ees, Sir Simon. [*Seeing* JOB.] He! he!

SIR SIMON. Don't stand grinning, you booby, but go.

SIMON. Ees, Sir Simon. He! he!   [*Exit, laughing.*

JOB. [*Reaching a book from the table.*] 'Burn's Justice!'

SIR SIMON. And how dare you take it up?

JOB. Because you have laid it down. Read it a little better, and then I may respect you more. [*Throwing it on the floor.*] There it is!

Enter FRANK ROCHDALE, *followed by* PEREGRINE.

SIR SIMON. So, sir, prettily I am insulted on your account!

FRANK. Good heaven, sir! What is the matter?

SIR SIMON. The matter! [*Pointing to* JOB.] Lug that old bundle of brass out of my chair directly.
  [FRANK *casts his eyes on* JOB, *then on the ground, and stands abashed.*

JOB. He dare as soon jump into one of your tin mines. Brass! There is no baser metal than hypocrisy. He came with that false coin to my shop, and it passed, but see how conscience nails him to the spot now!

FRANK. [*To* SIR SIMON.] Sir, I came to explain all.

SIR SIMON. Sir, you must be aware that all is explained already. You provoke a brazier almost to knock me down, and bring me news of it when he is fixed as tight in my study as a copper in my kitchen.

FRANK. [*Advancing to* JOB.] Mr. Thornberry, I——

JOB. Keep your distance! I'm an old fellow; but if my daughter's seducer comes near me, I'll beat him as flat as a stew-pan!

FRANK. [*Still advancing.*] Suffer me to speak, and——

JOB. [*Rising from his chair, and holding up his cane.*] Come an inch nearer, and I'll be as good as my word!

PEREGRINE. [*Advancing.*] Hold!

JOB. Eh? you here! Then I have some chance, perhaps, of getting righted at last.

PEREGRINE. Do not permit passion to weaken that chance.

JOB. Oh, plague! You don't know—I wasn't violent till——

PEREGRINE. Nay, nay; cease to grasp that cane. While we are so conspicuously blessed with laws to chastise a culprit, the mace of justice is the only proper weapon for the injured. Let me talk with you.   [PEREGRINE *and* JOB *retire up.*

SIR SIMON. [*To* FRANK.] Well, sir, who may this last person be, whom you have thought proper should visit me?

FRANK. A stranger in this country, sir, and——

SIR SIMON. And a friend, I perceive, of that old ruffian.

FRANK. I have reason to think, sir, he is a friend to Mr. Thornberry.

SIR SIMON. Sir, I am very much obliged to you. You send a brazier to challenge me, and now I suppose you have brought a travelling tinker for his second. Where does he come from?

FRANK. India, sir. He leaped from the vessel that was foundering on the rocks this morning, and swam to shore.

SIR SIMON. Did he? I wish he had taken the jump with the brazier tied to his neck!

[PEREGRINE *and* JOB *come forward.*

PEREGRINE. [*Aside to* JOB.] I can discuss it better in your absence. Be near with Mary: should the issue be favourable, I will call you.

JOB. [*Aside to* PEREGRINE.] Well, well, I will; you have a better head at it than I. Justice! Oh, if I was Lord Chancellor, I'd knock all the family down with the mace in a minute!

[*Exit.*

PEREGRINE. Suffer me to say a few words, Sir Simon Rochdale, in behalf of that unhappy man.   [*Points off.*

SIR SIMON. And pray, sir, what privilege have you to interfere in my domestic concerns?

D

PEREGRINE. None, as it appears abstractedly. Old Thornberry has just deputed me to accommodate his domestic concerns with you; I would willingly not touch upon yours.

SIR SIMON. Pooh, pooh! You can't touch upon one without being impertinent about the other.

PEREGRINE. Have the candour to suppose, Sir Simon, that I mean no disrespect to your house. Although I may stickle lustily with you in the cause of an aggrieved man, believe me, early habits have taught me to be anxious for the prosperity of the Rochdales.

SIR SIMON. Early habits!

PEREGRINE. I happened to be born on your estate, Sir Simon, and have obligations to some part of your family.

SIR SIMON. Then, upon my soul, you have chosen a pretty way to repay them!

PEREGRINE. I know no better way of repaying them than by consulting your family honour. In my boyhood, it seemed as if nature had dropped me a kind of infant subject on your father's Cornish territory and the whole pedigree of your house is familiar to me.

SIR SIMON. Is it? [Aside.] Confound him, he has heard of the miller! [Aloud.] Sir, you may talk this tolerably well, but 'tis my hope—my opinion, I mean—you can't tell who was my grandfather.

PEREGRINE. Whisper the secret to yourself, Sir Simon; and let reason also whisper to you that when honest industry raises a family to opulence and honours, its very original lowness sheds lustre on its elevation; but all its glory fades when it has given a wound and denies a balsam to a man as humble, and as honest, as your own ancestor!

SIR SIMON. But I haven't given the wound! [To FRANK.] And why, good sir, won't you be pleased to speak your sentiments?

FRANK. [Advancing.] The first are obedience to my father, sir; and if I must proceed, I own that nothing in my mind but the amplest atonement can extinguish true remorse for a cruelty.

SIR SIMON. Ha! In other words, you can't clap an extinguisher upon your feelings without a father-in-law who can sell you one. But Lady Caroline Braymore is your wife, or I am no longer your father.

Enter TOM SHUFFLETON *and* LADY CAROLINE
BRAYMORE.

SHUFFLETON. How d'ye do, good folks? How d'ye do?

SIR SIMON. Ha, Lady Caroline! Tom, I have had a little business. The last dinner-bell has rung, Lady Caroline, but I'll attend you directly.

SHUFFLETON. Baronet, I'm afraid we shan't be able to dine with you to-day.

SIR SIMON. Not dine with me!

LADY CAROLINE. No; we are just married.

SIR SIMON. Hell and the devil! Married!

SHUFFLETON. Yes; we are married, and can't stay.

PEREGRINE. [*Aside.*] Then 'tis time to speak to old Thornberry.   [*Exit.*

SIR SIMON. Lady Caroline!

LADY CAROLINE. I lost my appetite in your family this morning, Sir Simon, and have no relish for anything you can have the goodness to offer me.

SHUFFLETON. Don't press us, baronet; that's quite out in the New School.

SIR SIMON. Oh, damn the New School! Who will explain all this mystery?

FRANK. Mr. Shuffleton shall explain it, sir, and other mysteries too.

Enter LORD FITZ-BALAAM.

SIR SIMON. My lord, it is painful to be referred to you, when so much is to be said. What is it all?

LORD FITZ-BALAAM. You are disappointed, Sir Simon, and I am ruined!

SIR SIMON. But my lord——

[SIR SIMON *and* LORD FITZ-BALAAM *retire up.* LADY
CAROLINE *throws herself carelessly into a chair.*

SHUFFLETON. [*Advancing to* FRANK.] My dear Frank, I—I have had a devilish deal of trouble in getting this business off your hands; but you see I have done my best for you.

FRANK. For yourself, you mean.

SHUFFLETON. Come, damn it, my good fellow, don't be ungrateful to a friend.

FRANK. Take back this letter of recommendation you wrote for Mary, as a friend. When you assume that name with me, Mr. Shuffleton, for myself I laugh; for you I blush; but for sacred friendship's profanation I grieve! [*Turns from him.*

SHUFFLETON. That all happens from living so much out of town.

Enter PEREGRINE, JOB THORNBERRY, *and* MARY.

PEREGRINE. Now, Sir Simon, as accident seems to have thwarted a design which probity could never applaud, you may perhaps be inclined to do justice here.

JOB. Justice is all I come for; damn their favours. Cheer up, Mary!

SIR SIMON. [*To* PEREGRINE.] I was in hopes I had got rid of you. You are an orator from the sea-shore, but you must put more pebbles in your mouth before you harangue me into a tea-kettle connexion.

SHUFFLETON. That's my new friend at the Red Cow. He is the new-old *cher ami* to honest tea-kettle's daughter.

FRANK. Your insinuation is false, sir!

SHUFFLETON. [*Advancing towards* FRANK.] False!

LADY CAROLINE. [*Rising, and coming between them.*] Hush, don't quarrel: we are only married to-day.

SHUFFLETON. That's true. I won't do anything to make you unhappy for these three weeks. So, adieu, Sir Simon!
[*Exeunt* SHUFFLETON *and* LADY CAROLINE.

PEREGRINE. Sir Simon Rochdale, if my oratory fail, and which, indeed, is weak, may interest prevail with you?

SIR SIMON. No: rather than consent, I'd give up every acre of my estate.

PEREGRINE. Your conduct proves you unworthy of your estate; and, unluckily for you, you have roused the indignation of an elder brother, who now stands before you and claims it!

SIR SIMON. Eh? Zounds! Peregrine!

PEREGRINE. I can make my title too good in an instant for you to dispute it. My agent in London has long had documents on the secret he has kept, and several old inhabitants here, I know, are prepared to identify me.

SIR SIMON. I had a run-away brother—a boy that everybody thought dead. How came he not to claim till now?

PEREGRINE. Because, knowing he had given deep cause of offence, he never would have asserted his abandoned right had he not found a brother neglecting what no Englishman should neglect—justice and humanity to his inferiors.

Enter DENNIS BRULGRUDDERY.

DENNIS. Stand asy, all of you, for I've big news for my half-drowned customer. [*Seeing* PEREGRINE.] Och, bless your mug! and is it there you are?

SIR SIMON. What's the matter now?

DENNIS. Hould your tongue, you little man! There's a great post just come to your manor-house, and the Indiaman's worked into port.

JOB. [*To* PEREGRINE.] What, the vessel with all your property?

DENNIS. By all that's amazing, they say you have a hundred thousand pounds in that ship!

PEREGRINE. My losses might have been somewhat more without this recovery. [*To* JOB.] I have entered into a sort of partnership with you, my friend, this morning: how can we dissolve it?

JOB. You are an honest man—so am I; so settle that account as you like.

PEREGRINE. [*Handing* MARY *forward.*] Come forth, then, injured simplicity! Of your own cause you shall be now the arbitress.

MARY. Do not make me speak, sir! I am so humbled—so abashed——

JOB. Nonsense! We are sticking up for right!

PEREGRINE. Will you then speak, Mr. Rochdale?

FRANK. My father is bereft of a fortune, sir; but I must hesitate till his fiat is obtained, as much as if he possessed it.

SIR SIMON. Nay, nay; follow your own inclinations now.

FRANK. May I, sir? Oh, then, let the libertine now make reparation, and claim a wife!

> [*Running to* MARY, *and embracing her.*

DENNIS. His wife! Och, what a big dinner we'll have at the Red Cow!

PEREGRINE. [*To* SIR SIMON.] What am I to say, sir?

SIR SIMON. Oh, you are to say what you please.

PEREGRINE. [*To* FRANK *and* MARY.] Then bless you both! And though I have passed so much of my life abroad, English equity, brother, is dear to my heart. Respect the rights of honest John Bull, and our family concerns may be easily arranged.

JOB. That's upright. [*To* FRANK.] I forgive you, young man, for what has passed; but no one deserves forgiveness who refuses to make amends when he has disturbed the happiness of an Englishman's fireside!

THE MILLER AND HIS MEN

A MELODRAMA IN TWO ACTS

BY

ISAAC POCOCK (1782–1835)

———

*First performed at Covent Garden Theatre
21 October 1813*

———

CAST

GRINDOFF, the miller	Mr. Farley
COUNT FREDERICK FRIBERG	Mr. Vining
KARL, his servant	Mr. Liston
LOTHAIR, a young peasant	Mr. Abbott
KELMAR, an old cottager	Mr. Chapman
KRUITZ, his son	Master Gladstanes
RIBER ⎫	Mr. Jefferies
GOLOTZ ⎬ Banditti	Mr. King
ZINGRA ⎭	Mr. Sladen
CLAUDINE ⎫ Kelmar's daughters	Miss Booth
LAURETTE ⎬	Miss Carew
RAVINA	Mrs. Egerton

The Miller's Men, Banditti, Officers of Count Friberg

———

SCENE

*The Banks of a River on the Borders of a Forest
in Bohemia*

ACT I

SCENE I. *The Banks of a River in Bohemia. On the right, in the distance, a rocky eminence, on which is a windmill at work—a cottage in front,* R. *Sunset.*

Music. The MILLER'S MEN *are seen in perspective, descending the eminence—they cross the river in boats, and land near the cottage, with their sacks, singing the following round:*

> When the wind blows,
>   When the mill goes,
> Our hearts are all light and merry;
>   When the wind drops,
>   When the mill stops,
> We drink and sing, hey down derry.

[*Exeunt.*

Enter KELMAR *from the cottage.*

KELMAR. What! more sacks, more grist to the mill! Early and late the miller thrives: he that was my tenant is now my landlord; this hovel, that once sheltered him, is now the only dwelling of bankrupt broken-hearted Kelmar—well, I strove my best against misfortune, and thanks be to heaven have fallen respected, even by my enemies.

Enter CLAUDINE *with a basket.*

So, Claudine, you are returned. Where stayed you so long?

CLAUDINE. I was obliged to wait ere I could cross the ferry— there were other passengers.

KELMAR. Amongst whom I suppose was one in whose company time flew so fast—the sun had set before you had observed it.

CLAUDINE. No, indeed, father: since you desired me not to meet Lothair—and I told him what you had desired—I have never seen him but in the cottage here, when you were present.

KELMAR. You are a good girl—a dutiful child, and I believe you—you never yet deceived me.

CLAUDINE. Nor ever will, dear father—but—

KELMAR. But what?

CLAUDINE. I—I find it very lonely passing the borders of the forest without—without—

KELMAR. Without Lothair.

CLAUDINE. You know 'tis dangerous, father.

KELMAR. Not half so dangerous as love—subdue it, child, in time.

CLAUDINE. But the robbers?

KELMAR. Robbers! what then? They cannot injure thee or thy father—alas! we have no more to lose—yet thou hast one treasure left, innocence! Guard well thy heart, for should the fatal passion there take root, 'twill rob thee of thy peace.

CLAUDINE. You told me once, love's impulse could not be resisted.

KELMAR. When the object is worthless, it should not be indulged.

CLAUDINE. Is Lothair worthless?

KELMAR. No; but he is poor, almost as you are.

CLAUDINE. Do riches without love give happiness?

KELMAR. Never.

CLAUDINE. Then I must be unhappy if I wed the miller Grindoff.

KELMAR. Not so—not so; independence gives comfort, but love without competence is endless misery. You can never wed Lothair.

CLAUDINE [*sighing*]. I can never love the miller.

KELMAR. Then you shall never marry him—though to see you Grindoff's wife be the last wish of your old father's heart. Go in, child; go in, Claudine. [CLAUDINE *kisses his hand, and exit into cottage.*] 'Tis plain her heart is riveted to Lothair, and honest Grindoff yet must sue in vain.

Enter LOTHAIR, *hastily.*

LOTHAIR. Ah! Kelmar, and alone! Where is Claudine?

KELMAR. At home, in her father's house—where should she be?

LOTHAIR. Then she has escaped—she is safe, and I am happy—
I did not accompany her in vain.

KELMAR. Accompany! Accompany! Has she then told me a
falsehood? Were you with her, Lothair?

LOTHAIR. No—ye—yes. [*Aside.*] I must not alarm him.

KELMAR. What mean these contradictions?

LOTHAIR. She knew not I was near her—you have denied our
meeting, but you cannot prevent my loving her—I have
watched her daily through the village and along the borders
of the forest.

KELMAR. I thank you, but she needs no guard; her poverty will
protect her from a thief.

LOTHAIR. Will her beauty protect her from a libertine?

KELMAR. Her virtue will.

LOTHAIR. I doubt it: what can her resistance avail against the
powerful arm of villainy?

KELMAR. Is there such a wretch?

LOTHAIR. There is.

KELMAR. Lothair, Lothair! I fear you glance at the miller Grindoff. This is not well; this is not just.

LOTHAIR. Kelmar, you wrong me; 'tis true, he is my enemy, for
he bars my road to happiness. Yet I respect his character;
the riches that industry has gained him he employs in assisting the unfortunate—he has protected you and your child,
and I honour him.

KELMAR. If not to Grindoff, to whom did you allude?

LOTHAIR. Listen: as I crossed the hollow way in the forest, I
heard a rustling in the copse. Claudine had reached the bank
above. As I was following, voices, subdued and whispering,
struck my ear. Her name was distinctly pronounced: 'She
comes,' said one: 'Now! now we may secure her,' cried the
second; and instantly two men advanced. A sudden exclamation burst from my lips, and arrested their intent; they
turned to seek me, and with dreadful imprecations vowed
death to the intruder. Stretched beneath a bush of holly, I lay
concealed; they passed within my reach. I scarcely breathed,

while I observed them to be ruffians, uncouth and savage—they were banditti.

KELMAR. Banditti! Are they not yet content? All that I had—all that the hand of Providence had spared, they have deprived me of; and would they take my child?

LOTHAIR. 'Tis plain they would. Now, Kelmar, hear the last proposal of him you have rejected. Without Claudine my life is but a blank—useless to others and wretched to myself; it shall be risked to avenge the wrongs you have suffered. I'll seek these robbers! If I should fall, your daughter will more readily obey your wish, and become the wife of Grindoff. If I should succeed, promise her to me. The reward I shall receive will secure our future comfort, and thus your fears and your objections both are satisfied.

KELMAR [affected]. Lothair, thou art a good lad, a noble lad, and worthy my daughter's love; she had been freely thine, but that by sad experience I know how keen the pangs of penury are to a parent's heart. My sorrows may descend to her when I am gone, but I have nothing to bequeath her else.

LOTHAIR. Then you consent?

KELMAR. I do, I do; but pray be careful. I fear 'tis a rash attempt; you must have help.

LOTHAIR. Then, indeed, I fail as others have before me. No, Kelmar, I must go alone, pennyless, unarmed, and secretly. None but yourself must know my purpose, or my person.

KELMAR. Be it as you will; but pray be careful. Come, thou shalt see her. [*The mill stops.*]

LOTHAIR. I'll follow; it may be my last farewell.

KELMAR. Come in—I see the mill has stopped. Grindoff will be here anon; he always visits me at nightfall, when labour ceases. Come.

[*Exit* KELMAR *into the cottage.*

LOTHAIR. Yes, at the peril of my life, I'll seek them. With the juice of herbs my face shall be discoloured, and in the garb of misery I'll throw myself within their power—the rest I leave to Providence. [*Music.*] But the miller comes.

[*Exit to the cottage. The* MILLER *appears in perspective coming from the crag in the rock—the boat disappears on the opposite side.*

Enter the two ROBBERS, RIBER *and* GOLOTZ, *hastily—they rush up to the cottage and peep in at the window.*

RIBER [*retiring from the window*]. We are too late—she has reached the cottage.

GOLOTZ. Curse on the interruption that detained us; we shall be rated for this failure.

RIBER. Hush! not so loud. [*Goes again cautiously to the window of the cottage.*] Ha! Lothair.

GOLOTZ. Lothair! 'twas he, then, that marred our purpose; he shall smart for't.

RIBER. Back! back! he comes. On his return he dies; he cannot pass us both.

[*Music. They retire behind a tree—a boat passes in the distance from the mouth of the cavern in the rock beneath the mill; then draws up to the bank.*

Enter GRINDOFF, *the* MILLER, *in the boat, who jumps ashore. Re-enter* LOTHAIR, *at the same moment, from the cottage.*

GRINDOFF [*disconcerted*]. Lothair!

LOTHAIR. Ay, my visit here displeases you, no doubt.

GRINDOFF. Nay, we are rivals, but not enemies, I trust. We love the same girl; we strive the best we can to gain her. If you are fortunate, I'll wish you joy with all my heart; if I should have the luck on't, you'll do the same by me, I hope.

LOTHAIR. You have little fear; I am poor, you are rich. He needn't look far that would see the end on't.

GRINDOFF. But you are young and likely. I am honest and rough; the chances are as much yours as mine.

LOTHAIR. Well, time will show. I bear you no enmity. Farewell!

GRINDOFF [*aside*]. He must not pass the forest. [*To* LOTHAIR.] Whither go you?

LOTHAIR. To the village; I must haste, or 'twill be late ere I reach the ferry. [*It begins to grow dark.*]

RIBER [*who with* GOLOTZ *is watching them*]. He will escape us yet.

GRINDOFF. Stay, my boat shall put you across the river. Besides, the evening looks stormy—come, it will save your journey half a league.

RIBER [*aside*]. It will save his life.

LOTHAIR. Well, I accept your offer, and I thank you.

GRINDOFF. Your hand.

LOTHAIR. Farewell! [*He goes into the boat, and pushes off.*]

GRINDOFF. So, I am rid of him. If he had met Claudine! But she is safe—now then for Kelmar.

[*Exit into the cottage.*

Re-enter RIBER *and* GOLOTZ.

RIBER. Curse on this chance! We have lost him!

GOLOTZ. But a time may come.

RIBER. A time shall come, and shortly, too.

[*Exeunt.*

SCENE II. *The Forest—distant thunder—stage dark.*

Enter KARL, *dragging after him a portmanteau.*

KARL. Here's a pretty mess! here's a precious spot of work! Pleasant upon my soul—lost in a labyrinth, without love or liquor—the sun gone down, a storm got up, and no getting out of this vile forest, turn which way you will.

COUNT [*calling without*]. Halloo! Karl! Karl!

KARL. Ah, you may call and bawl, master of mine; you'll not disturb anything here but a wild boar or two, and a wolf, perhaps.

Enter COUNT FREDERICK FRIBERG.

COUNT. Karl, where are you?

KARL. Where am I! that's what I want to know—this cursed wood has a thousand turnings, and not one that turns right.

COUNT. Careless coxcomb! said you not you could remember the track?

KARL. So I should, sir, if I could find the path—but trees will grow, and since I was here last, the place has got so bushy and briery that—that I have lost my way.

COUNT. You have lost your senses.

KARL. No, sir, I wish I had; unfortunately my senses are all in the highest state of perfection.

COUNT. Why not use them to more effect?

KARL. I wish I'd the opportunity; my poor stomach can testify that I taste—

COUNT. What?

KARL. Nothing; it's as empty as my head; but I see danger, smell a tempest, hear the cry of wild beasts, and feel—

COUNT. How?

KARL. Particularly unpleasant. [*Thunder and rain.*] Oh, we are in for it; do you hear, sir?

COUNT. We must be near the river; could we but reach the ferry 'tis but a short league to the Château Friberg.

KARL. Ah, sir, I wish we were there, and I seated in the old arm-chair in the servant's hall, taking of—holloa!

COUNT. What now?

KARL. I felt a spot of rain on my nose as big as a bullet. [*Thunder and rain.*] There, there, it's coming on again—seek some shelter, sir; some hollow tree, whilst I, for my sins, endeavour once more to find the way, and endure another curry-combing among these cursed brambles. Come sir. [*The storm increases.*] Lor', how it rumbles—this way, sir—this way.

[*Exeunt.*

———

SCENE III. *A Room in the Cottage—a door*, R. *flat—a window*, L. *flat—a fire*, R.—*tables*, R. *and* L.—*chairs, etc.*

GRINDOFF *and* KELMAR *discovered sitting at the table—thunder and rain.*

KELMAR. 'Tis a rough night, miller: the thunder roars, and, by the murmuring of the flood, the mountain torrents have descended. Poor Lothair! he'll scarcely have crossed the ferry.

GRINDOFF. Lothair by this is safe at home, old friend; before the storm commenced I passed him in my boat across the river. [*Aside.*] He seems less anxious for his daughter than for this bold stripling.

KELMAR. Worthy man! you'll be rewarded for all such deeds hereafter. Thank heaven, Claudine is safe! Hark!

[*Thunder heard.*

GRINDOFF [*aside*]. She is safe by this time, or I am much mistaken.

KELMAR. She will be here anon.

GRINDOFF [*aside*]. I doubt that. [*To* KELMAR.] Come, here's to her health, old Kelmar—would I could call you father!

KELMAR. You may do soon; but even your protection would now, I fear, be insufficient to—

GRINDOFF. What mean you? Insufficient!

KELMAR. The robbers—this evening in the forest—

GRINDOFF [*rising*]. Ha!

KELMAR [*rising*]. Did not Lothair, then, tell you?

GRINDOFF. Lothair?

KELMAR. Yes; but all's well; be not alarmed—see, she is here.

GRINDOFF. Here!

Enter CLAUDINE. GRINDOFF *endeavours to suppress his surprise.*

GRINDOFF. Claudine! Curse on them both!

KELMAR. Both! how knew you there were two?

GRINDOFF. 'Sdeath! you—you said robbers, did you not? They never have appeared singly; therefore, I thought you meant two.

KELMAR. You are right. But for Lothair they had deprived me of my child.

GRINDOFF. How! Did Lothair—humph! he's a courageous youth.

CLAUDINE, That he is; but he's gentle, too. What has happened?

KELMAR. Nothing, child, nothing. [*Aside to* GRINDOFF.] Do not speak on't, 'twill terrify her. Come, Claudine, now for supper. What have you brought us?

CLAUDINE. Thanks to the miller's bounty, plenty.

KELMAR. The storm increases!

KARL [*calling without*]. Holloa! holloa!

KELMAR. And hark! I hear a voice—listen!

KARL [*calling again without*]. Holloa!

CLAUDINE. The cry of some bewildered traveller.

> [*The cry repeated, and a violent knock at the door.*

KELMAR. Open the door.

GRINDOFF. Not so; it may be dangerous.

KELMAR. Danger comes in silence and in secret; my door was never shut against the wretched while I knew prosperity, nor shall it be closed now to my fellows in misfortune. [*To* CLAUDINE.] Open the door, I say.

> [*The knock is repeated, and* CLAUDINE *opens the door.*
>
> *Enter* KARL *with a portmanteau.*

KARL. Why, in the name of dark nights and tempests, didn't you open the door at first? Have you no charity?

KELMAR. In our hearts plenty, in our gift but little; yet all we have is yours.

KARL. Then I'll share all you have with my master. Thank you, old gentleman; you won't fare the worse for sheltering honest Karl and Count Frederick Friberg.

GRINDOFF. Friberg!

KARL. Ay, I'll soon fetch him; he's waiting now, looking as melancholy as a mourning coach in a snow-storm, at the foot of a tree, wet as a drowned rat; so stir up the fire, bless you! clap on the kettle, give us the best eatables and drinkables you have, a clean table-cloth, a couple of warm beds, and don't stand upon ceremony. We'll accept every civility and comfort you can bestow upon us without scruple.

> [*Throws down the portmanteau and exit.*

GRINDOFF. Friberg, did he say?

CLAUDINE. 'Tis the young count, so long expected.

KELMAR. Can it be possible? Without attendants, and at such a time, too?

GRINDOFF [*looking at the portmanteau, on which is the name in brass nails*]. It must be the same! Kelmar, good night.

KELMAR. Nay, not yet—the storm rages.

GRINDOFF. I fear it may increase; besides, your visitors may not like my company; good night.

Enter COUNT FREDERICK FRIBERG, *followed by* KARL—*he stops suddenly, and eyes the* MILLER, *as if recollecting him.* GRINDOFF *appears to avoid his scrutiny.*

COUNT. Your kindness is well timed; we might have perished. Accept my thanks. [*Aside.*] I should know that face.

GRINDOFF. To me your thanks are not due.

COUNT. That voice, too!

GRINDOFF. This house is Kelmar's.

[KARL *places the portmanteau on the table.*

COUNT. Kelmar's!

KELMAR. Ay, my dear master; my fortunes have deserted me, but my attachment to your family still remains.

COUNT. Worthy old man. How happens this: the richest tenant of my late father's land—the honest, the faithful Kelmar, in a hovel?

KELMAR. It will chill your hearts to hear.

KARL [*at the fire, drying and warming himself*]. Then don't tell us, pray, for our bodies are cramped with cold already.

KELMAR. 'Tis a terrible tale.

KARL [*advancing*]. Then, for the love of a good appetite and a dry skin, don't tell it, for I've been terrified enough in the forest tonight to last me my life.

COUNT. Be silent, Karl. [*Retires to fire with* KELMAR.]

GRINDOFF. In—in the forest?

KARL. Ay.

GRINDOFF. What should alarm you there?

KARL. What should alarm me there? come, that's a good one. Why, first I lost my way; trying to find that, I lost the horses; then I tumbled into a quagmire, and nearly lost my life.

GRINDOFF. Psha! this is of no consequence.

KARL. Isn't it? I have endured more hardships since morning than a knight-errant. My head's broken; my body's bruised, and my joints are dislocated. I haven't three square inches about me but what are scarified with briers and brambles; and, above all, I have not tasted a morsel of food since sunrise. Egad! instead of my making a meal of anything, I've been in constant expectation of the wolves making a meal of me.

GRINDOFF. Is this all?

KARL. All! No, it's not all; pretty well, too, I think. When I recovered the path, I met two polite gentlemen with long knives in their hands.

GRINDOFF. Hey!

KARL. And because I refused a kind invitation of theirs, they were affronted, and were just on the point of ending all my troubles when up came my master.

GRINDOFF. Well!

KARL. Well! yes, it was well indeed, for after a struggle they made off. One of them left his sting behind, though; look, here's a poker to stir up a man's courage with! [*Showing a poniard.*]

GRINDOFF. A poniard!

KARL. Ay.

GRINDOFF [*snatching at it*]. Give it me.

KARL [*refusing the dagger*]. For what? It's lawful spoil—didn't I win it in battle? No! I'll keep it as a trophy of my victory.

[*During this time*, KELMAR *and* CLAUDINE *have taken and hung up the* COUNT'S *cloak, handed him a chair, and are conversing.*]

GRINDOFF. It will be safer in my possession: it may lead to a discovery of him who wore it—and—

KARL. It may—you are right—therefore I'll deliver it into the hands of Count Frederick: he'll soon ferret the rascals out; set a reward on their heads—five thousand crowns, dead or alive! that's the way to manoeuvre 'em. [*Poking* GRINDOFF *in the ribs.*]

GRINDOFF. Indeed! humph!

KARL. Humph! don't half like that chap—never saw such a ferocious black muzzle in my life—that miller's a rogue in grain.

COUNT [*advancing*]. Nay, nay, speak of it no more. I will not take an old man's bed to ease my youthful limbs; I have slept soundly on a ruder couch—and that chair shall be my resting-place.

CLAUDINE. The miller's man, Riber, perhaps can entertain his excellency better—he keeps the Flask here, on the hill, sir.

GRINDOFF. His house contains but one bed.

KARL. Only one?

GRINDOFF. And that is occupied.

KARL. The devil it is!

COUNT. It matters not; I am contented here.

KARL. That's more than I am.

GRINDOFF. But stay; perchance his guest has left it; if so, 'tis at Count Frederick's service. I'll go directly and bring you word. [*Aside.*] I may now prevent surprise—the storm has ceased; I will return immediately.

> [*Unseen he drops the sheath of a dagger and exit.*

COUNT [*eagerly*]. Kelmar, tell me, who is that man?

KELMAR. The richest tenant, sir, you have; what Kelmar was when you departed from Bohemia, Grindoff now is.

COUNT. Grindoff! I remember in my youth a favoured servant of my father's, who resembled him in countenance and voice —the recollection is strong upon my memory but I hope deceives me, for he was a villain who betrayed his trust.

KELMAR. I have heard the circumstance; it happened just before I entered your good father's service—his name was Wolf.

COUNT. The same.

KARL. And if this is not the same, I suspect he is a very near relation.

KELMAR [*angrily*]. Nay, sir, you mistake—Grindoff is my friend. Come, Claudine, is all ready?

KARL. Oh, it's a sore subject is it?

                              [*Exeunt* KELMAR *and* CLAUDINE.

Your friend, is he, old gentleman? Sir—sir—

COUNT [*who has become thoughtful*]. Well! what say you?

KARL. I don't like our quarters, sir; we are in a bad neighbourhood.

COUNT. I fear we are; Kelmar's extreme poverty may have
tempted him to league with—yet his daughter?

KARL. His daughter—a decoy! nothing but a trap; don't
believe her, sir; we are betrayed, murdered, if we stay here.
I'll endure anything, everything, if you will but depart, sir.
Dark nights, bad roads, hail, rain, assassins, and—hey! what's
this? [*Sees and picks up the scabbard dropped by* GRINDOFF.]
Oh, Lord, what's the matter with me? My mind misgives me;
and here—[*He sheaths the dagger in it and finds it fits.*] fits to
a hair—we are in the lion's den!

COUNT. 'Tis evident we are snared, caught.

KARL. Oh, lord! don't say so.

Re-enter KELMAR *and* CLAUDINE, *followed by* LAURETTE *and*
KRUITZ *with supper things, etc.*

KELMAR. Come, come, youngsters, bestir—spread the cloth,
and—

COUNT. Kelmar, I have bethought me; at every peril, I must on
tonight.

KELMAR. Tonight!

CLAUDINE. Not tonight, I beseech you; you know not half your
danger. [*Goes to the table and places her hand carelessly on the
portmanteau.*]

KARL. Danger! [*Aside.*] Cockatrice! [*To* CLAUDINE.] I'll thank
you for that portmanteau.

COUNT. Let it remain—it may be an object to them, 'tis none to
me—it will be safer here with honest Kelmar.

KELMAR. But why so sudden?

KARL. My master has recollected something that must be done
tonight—or tomorrow it may be out of his power.

CLAUDINE. Stay till the miller returns.

KARL. Till he returns! [*Aside.*] Ah, the fellow's gone to get assistance, and if he comes before we escape, we shall be cut and hashed to mincemeat.

COUNT. Away! [*Advancing to the door.*]

Enter GRINDOFF, *suddenly.*

KARL. It's all over with us.

KELMAR. Well, friend, what success?

GRINDOFF. Bad enough—the count must remain here.

COUNT. Must remain!

GRINDOFF. There is no resource.

KARL. I thought so.

GRINDOFF. Tomorrow Riber can dispose of you both.

KARL. Dispose of us! [*Aside.*] Ay, put us to bed with a spade— that fellow's a gravedigger.

COUNT. Then I must cross the ford tonight.

GRINDOFF. Impossible; the torrent has swept the ferry barge from the shore, and driven it down the stream.

COUNT. Perhaps your boat—

GRINDOFF. Mine! 'twould be madness to resist the current now —and in the dark, too.

COUNT. What reward may tempt you?

GRINDOFF. Not all you are worth, sir, until tomorrow.

KARL. Tomorrow! [*Aside.*] Ah! we are crow's meat to a certainty.

GRINDOFF [*aside, looking askance around the room*]. All is right: they have got the scabbard, and their suspicions now must fall on Kelmar.

[*Exit* GRINDOFF, *bidding them all good night.*

COUNT. Well, we must submit to circumstances. [*Aside to* KARL.] Do not appear alarmed; when all is still, we may escape.

KARL. Why not now? There are only two of 'em.

COUNT. There may be others near.

Sestette.

CLAUDINE. Stay, prithee, stay—the night is dark,
            The cold wind whistles—hark! hark! hark!

COUNT. ⎫ [*Together.*] ⎧ We must away.
KARL. ⎭   ⎩ Pray, come away.

CLAUDINE.   The night is dark,
            The cold wind whistles.

ALL.   Hark! hark! hark!

CLAUDINE. Stay, prithee, stay—the way is lone,
            The ford is deep—the boat is gone.

KELMAR.   And mountain torrents swell the flood,
            And robbers lurk within the wood.

ALL.   Here ⎧ you ⎫ must stay till morning bright
               ⎩ we ⎭
            Breaks through the dark and dismal night,
            And merry sings the rising lark,
            And hush'd the night bird—hark! hark! hark!

[CLAUDINE *tenderly detains the* COUNT—KELMAR *detains*
KARL, *and the scene closes.*]

SCENE IV. *The Depth of the Forest—stage dark.*

Enter LOTHAIR, *with his dress and complexion entirely changed;
his appearance is extremely wretched.*

LOTHAIR. This way, this—in the moaning of the blast, at inter-
vals, I heard the tread of feet—and as the moon's light burst
from the stormy clouds, I saw two figures glide like departed
spirits to this deep glen. Now heaven prosper me, for my
attempt is desperate! [*Looking off.*] Ah, they come! [*Retires.*]

[*Music.* Enter RIBER, GOLOTZ *follows; they look around
cautiously, then advance to a particular rock,* L. C., *which is
nearly concealed by underwood and roots of trees.*

LOTHAIR [*advancing*]. Hold! [*The* ROBBERS *start, and eye him with ferocious surprise.*] So, my purpose is accomplished—at last I have discovered you.

RIBER. Indeed! it will cost you dear.

LOTHAIR. It has already—I have been hunted through the country, but now my life is safe.

RIBER. Safe!

LOTHAIR. Ay, is it not? Would you destroy a comrade? Look at me, search me—I am unarmed, defenceless!

GOLOTZ. Why come you hither?

LOTHAIR. To join your brave band—the terror of Bohemia.

RIBER. How knew you our retreat?

LOTHAIR. No matter. In the service of Count Friberg I have been disgraced—and fly from punishment to seek revenge.

GOLOTZ [*to* RIBER]. How say you?

LOTHAIR [*aside*]. They hesitate—the young Count is far from home, and his name I may use without danger. [*To the* ROBBERS.] Lead me to your chief.

RIBER. We will—not so fast; your sight must be concealed. [*Offering to bind his forehead.*]

LOTHAIR. Ah! [*Hesitates.*] May I trust you?

GOLOTZ. Do you doubt?

RIBER. Might we not despatch you as you are?

LOTHAIR. Enough; bind me, and lead on.

[*Music. They conceal his sight.* GOLOTZ *leads* LOTHAIR *to the rock, pushes the brushwood aside, and both exeunt, followed by* RIBER, *watching that they are not observed.*]

SCENE V. *A Cavern.*

BANDITTI *discovered variously employed, chiefly sitting carousing around tables on which are flasks of wine, etc.—steps rudely cut in the rock, in the background, leading to an elevated recess, C., on which is inscribed* 'Powder Magazine'—*other steps leading to an opening in the cave—a grated door, R.—stage light.*

Chorus. BANDITTI.

Fill, boys, and drink about—
   Wine will banish sorrow;
Come, drain the goblet out,
   We'll have more tomorrow.

[*The* ROBBERS *all rise and come forward.*

Slow Movement.

We live free from fear,
In harmony here,
Combin'd just like brother and brother;
   And this be our toast,
   The free-booter's boast,
Success and good-will to each other!

Chorus   Fill, boys, &c.

Enter RAVINA *through the grated door, as they conclude.*

RAVINA. What, carousing yet—sotting yet!

ZINGRA. How now, Ravina, why so churlish?

RAVINA. To sleep, I say—or wait upon yourselves. I'll stay no longer from my couch to please you. Is it not enough that I toil from daybreak, but you must disturb me ever with your midnight revelry?

ZINGRA. You were not wont to be so savage, woman.

RAVINA. Nor you so insolent. Look you repent it not!

FIRST ROBBER. Psha! heed her no more. Jealousy hath soured her.

ZINGRA. I forgive her railing.

RAVINA. Forgive!

ZINGRA. Ay, our leader seeks another mistress; and 'tis rather hard upon thee, I confess, after five years captivity, hard service too, and now that you are accustomed to our way of life—we pity thee.

RAVINA. Pity me! I am indeed an object of compassion: five long years a captive, hopeless still of liberty. Habit has almost made my heart cold as these rude rocks that screen me from the light of heaven. Miserable lost Ravina! by dire necessity become an agent in their wickedness: yet I pine for virtue and for freedom.

ZINGRA. Leave us to our wine. Come, boys, fill all, fill full, to our captain's bride.

ROBBERS. To our captain's bride!

> [*A single note on the bugle is heard from below.*

ZINGRA. Hark! 'tis from the lower cave. [*Bugle note repeated.*] She comes! Ravina, look you receive her as becomes the companion of our chief—remember!

RAVINA. I shall remember. So, another victim to hypocrisy and guilt. Poor wretch! she loves perhaps, as I did, the miller Grindoff; but, as I do, may live to execrate the outlaw and the robber!

> [*Music—the trap in the floor is thrown open.*

Enter RIBER *through the floor, followed by* GOLOTZ *and*
LOTHAIR.

ROBBERS. Hail to our new companion!

RAVINA. A man!

> [LOTHAIR *tears the bandage from his eyes as he arrives in the cave—the* ROBBERS *start back on perceiving a man.*

LOTHAIR. Thanks for your welcome!

ZINGRA. Who have we here? Speak!

RIBER. A recruit. Where is the captain?

ZINGRA. Where is the captain's bride?

RIBER. Of her hereafter. [*A bugle is heard above.*]

ROBBERS. Wolf! Wolf!

Enter GRINDOFF *in robber's apparel—he descends the opening, and advances.*

ZINGRA. ⎫
ROBBERS. ⎭ Welcome, noble captain!

GRINDOFF [*starts at seeing* LOTHAIR]. A stranger!

LOTHAIR [*aside*]. Grindoff!

　　　　　　　[*The* ROBBERS *lay hands on their swords, etc.*

GRINDOFF. Ha, betrayed! Who has done this?

RIBER. I brought him hither to—

GRINDOFF. Riber! humph! You have executed my orders well, have you not? Where is Claudine?

LOTHAIR. Claudine! [*Aside.*] Villain! hypocrite!

GRINDOFF. Know you Claudine likewise?

RIBER. She escaped us in the forest. Some meddling fool thwarted our intent, and—

GRINDOFF. Silence; I know it all. A word with you presently. Now, stranger—but I mistake; we should be old acquaintance—my name is so familiar to you. What is your purpose here?

LOTHAIR. Revenge!

GRINDOFF. On whom?

LOTHAIR. On one whose cruelty and oppression well deserve it.

GRINDOFF. His name?

LOTHAIR [*aside*]. Would I dare mention it!

GRINDOFF. His name, I say?

RIBER. He complains of Count Friberg.

GRINDOFF. Indeed! then your purpose will soon be accomplished: he arrived this night, and shelters at old Kelmar's cottage. He shall never pass the river; should he once reach the Château Friberg, it would be fatal to our band.

LOTHAIR. Arrived! [*Aside.*] What have I done! My fatal indiscretion has destroyed him. [*To* GRINDOFF.] Let him fall by my hand.

GRINDOFF. It may tremble—it trembles now. The firmest of our band have failed. [*Looking at* RIBER.] Henceforth the enterprise shall be my own.

LOTHAIR. Let me accompany you.

GRINDOFF. Not tonight.

LOTHAIR. Tonight.

GRINDOFF. Ay, before the dawn appears, he dies! Riber!

> [LOTHAIR *clasps his hands in agony.*

RAVINA. What, more blood! must Friberg's life be added to the list?

GRINDOFF. It must; our safety claims it.

RAVINA. Short-sighted man! Will not his death doubly arouse the sluggish arm of justice? The whole country, hitherto kept in awe by dissension and selfish fear, will join; reflect in time; beware their retribution!

GRINDOFF. When I need a woman's help and counsel, I'll seek it of the compassionate Ravina. Begone! [*Exit* RAVINA.] Riber, I say!

RIBER. I wait your orders.

GRINDOFF. Look you execute them better than the last—look to't! The Count and his companion rest at Kelmar's; it must be done within an hour: arm, and attend me—at the same time I will secure Claudine—and should Kelmar's vigilance interpose to mar us, he henceforth shall be an inmate here.

LOTHAIR. Oh, villain!

GRINDOFF [*rushing towards* LOTHAIR]. How mean you?

LOTHAIR. Friberg—let me go with you.

GRINDOFF. You are too eager; I will not trust thy inexperience. Trust you! What surety have we of your faith?

LOTHAIR. My oath.

GRINDOFF. Swear, then, never to desert the object, never to betray the cause for which you sought our band—revenge on—

LOTHAIR. On him who has deeply, basely injured me, I swear it.

GRINDOFF. 'Tis well—your name?

LOTHAIR. Spiller.

GRINDOFF [*to* RIBER]. Quick! arm and attend me. [RIBER *retires.*] Are those sacks in the mill disposed of as I ordered?

ZINGRA. They are, captain.

GRINDOFF. Return with the flour tomorrow, and be careful that
all assume the calmness of industry and content. With such
appearance, suspicion itself is blind; 'tis the safeguard of our
band. Fill me a horn, and then to business. [*A* ROBBER *hands
him a horn of wine; he drinks.*] The Miller and his Men!

ROBBERS [*drinking*]. The Miller and his Men!

[GRINDOFF *and* ROBBERS *laugh heartily.* GRINDOFF *puts on
his miller's frock, hat, etc.* RIBER, *armed with pistols in his
belt, advances with a dark lantern, and exeunt with* GRINDOFF
through the rocks.

Chorus. BANDITTI.

Now to the forest we repair,
Awhile like spirits wander there;
In darkness we secure our prey,
And vanish at the dawn of day.

ACT II

SCENE I. *The Interior of* KELMAR'S *Cottage, as before.*

COUNT FREDERICK FRIBERG *discovered asleep in a chair, reclining on a table, and at the opposite side, near the fire,* KARL *is likewise seen asleep,* R. *The* COUNT'S *sword lies on the table,* L.—*the fire is nearly extinguished—stage dark—music as the curtain rises. Enter* CLAUDINE, *with a lamp, down the stairs.*

CLAUDINE. All still, all silent! The Count and his companions are undisturbed! What can it mean? My father wanders from his bed, restless as myself. Alas! the infirmities of age and sorrow afflict him sorely. Night after night I throw myself upon a sleepless couch, ready to fly to his assistance, and —hush—hush!

Enter KELMAR. CLAUDINE *extinguishes the light, and conceals herself.*

KELMAR. They sleep—sleep soundly—ere they wake I may return from my inquiry. If Grindoff's story was correct, I still may trust him—still may the Count confide in him; but his behaviour last night, unusual and mysterious, hangs like a fearful dream upon my mind—his anxiety to leave the cottage, his agitation at the appearance of Count Friberg— but above all, his assertion that the ferry-barge was lost, disturbs me. My doubts shall soon be ended. At this lone hour I may pass the borders unperceived, and the grey dawn that now glimmers in the east will direct my path.

[*Looks about him fearful of disturbing the sleepers, and exit.*

CLAUDINE [*advancing*]. My father appears unusually agitated. Ah, it may be! Sometimes he wanders on the river's brink, watching the bright orb of day bursting from the dark trees, and breathes a prayer, a blessing for his child; yet 'tis early, very early—yet it may be. Oh, father, my dear—dear father!

[*Exit.*

KARL. Yaw! [*Snoring.*] Damn the rats! Yaw, what a noise they keep up! Hey, where am I? Oh, in this infernal hovel; the night-mare has rode me into a jelly; then such horrible dreams, yaw! [*A light from the dark lantern borne by* RIBER *is seen passing the window.*] And such a swarm of rats—damn the rats! [*Lays his hand on his poniard.*] They'd better keep off, for I'm hungry enough to eat one. Bew—eu. [*Shivering.*] I wish it were morning. [*Music.*]

Enter RIBER; *he suddenly retires, observing a light occasioned by* KARL's *stirring the fire with his dagger.*

KARL. What's that? [*Listens.*] Nothing but odd noises all night; wonder how my master can sleep for such a—yaw—aw! Damn the rats! [*Lies down.*]

[*Music. Enter* RIBER *cautiously, holding forward the lantern.* GRINDOFF *follows.* RIBER, *on seeing the* COUNT, *draws a poniard—he raises his arm,* GRINDOFF *catches it, and prevents the blow. Appropriate music.*

GRINDOFF. Not yet; first secure my prize, Claudine; these are safe.

KARL. How the varmint swarm!

GRINDOFF. Hush! he dreams.

RIBER. It shall be his last.

KARL. Rats, rats!

RIBER. What says he?

KARL. Rats! they all come from the mill.

RIBER. Do they so?

KARL. Ay, set traps for 'em, poison 'em.

[RIBER, *again attempting to advance, is detained by* GRINDOFF.

GRINDOFF. Again so rash—remember!

KARL. I shall never forget that fellow in the forest.

RIBER. Ha! do you mark?

GRINDOFF. Fear them not; be still till I return. He is sound; none sleep so hard as those that babble in their dreams. Stir not, I charge you; yet should Kelmar—ay—should you hear a noise without, instantly despatch.

[*Exit* GRINDOFF *up the stairs.*

RIBER. Enough! [KARL *wakes again—he observes* RIBER, *grasps his dagger, and, watching the motion of the* ROBBER, *acts accordingly*.] This delay is madness, but I must obey. [*Looking at the priming of his pistol, then towards the table—*KARL *drops to his position*.] Hey, a sword! [*Advancing to the table and removing the sword*.] Now all is safe. Hark! [*A noise without, as of something falling*.] 'Tis time! If this should fail, my poniard will secure him.

> [*Music.* RIBER *advances hastily, and, in the act of bringing his pistol to the level against the* COUNT, *is stabbed by* KARL, *who has arisen and closely followed his every movement; at the same moment enter* GRINDOFF. *The* COUNT, *rushing from the chair at the noise of the pistol, seizes him by the collar—the group stand amazed. Tableau.*

COUNT. Speak! What means this?

KARL. They've caught a tartar, sir, that's all. Hey, the miller!

GRINDOFF. Ay!

COUNT. How came you here?

GRINDOFF. To—to do you service.

COUNT. At such an hour!

GRINDOFF. 'Tis never too late to do good.

COUNT. Good!

GRINDOFF. Yes; you have been in danger.

KARL. Have we? Thank you for your news.

GRINDOFF. You have been watched by the banditti.

COUNT. So it appears.

KARL. But how did you know it?

GRINDOFF [*confused*]. There is my proof. [*Pointing to the body of* RIBER.]

KARL. But how the plague got you into the house? Through a rat-hole?

COUNT. Explain.

GRINDOFF. Few words will do that: on my return to the mill, I found you might repose there better than in this house; at all events, I knew you would be safer in my care.

COUNT. Safer! Proceed, what mean you?

KARL [*aside*]. Safer!

GRINDOFF. Kelmar—

COUNT. Hah!

GRINDOFF. Had you no suspicion of him—no mistrust of his wish to—to detain you?

COUNT. I confess, I—

GRINDOFF [*to* KARL]. The poniard you obtained in the forest, that you refused to give me—

KARL. This?

GRINDOFF. Is Kelmar's.

COUNT. Wretch!

KARL. I thought so; I found the sheath here.

GRINDOFF. I knew it instantly; my suspicions were aroused— now they are confirmed; Kelmar is in league with these marauders. I found the door open—you still slept. I searched the house for him; he is no where to be found—he and his daughter have absconded. Now sir, are you satisfied?

COUNT. I am.

KARL. I am not. I wish we were safe at home. I'm no coward by daylight, but I hate adventures of this kind in the dark. Lord, how a man may be deceived! I took you for a great rogue; but I now find you are a good Christian enough, though you are a very ill-looking man.

GRINDOFF. Indeed; we can't all be as handsome as you are, you know.

KARL [*pertly*]. No; nor as witty as you are, you know.

GRINDOFF. Come, sir, follow me. You can't mistake; see, 'tis day-break; at the cottage close to the narrow bridge that passes the ravine you will find repose.

COUNT. We'll follow you.

[*Exit* GRINDOFF.

KARL. I don't half like that fellow yet. [*Gets the portmanteau from table.*] Now, the sooner we are off the better, sir. As for this fellow, the rats may take care of him. [CLAUDINE's *shrieks heard without.*]

E

COUNT [*drawing his sword*]. Ha, a woman's voice! Karl, follow me!

KARL. What, more adventures! [*Drawing his sword.*] I'm ready. I say, [*To the body of* RIBER.] take care of the portmanteau, will you?

[*Exit.*

SCENE II.—*The Forest. Stage partly dark.*

Music. Enter GRINDOFF, *with* CLAUDINE *in his arms.*

COUNT [*without*]. Karl! Karl! Follow, this way!

GRINDOFF [*resting*]. Ha, so closely pursued! Nay, then—

[*Going hastily, he pushes aside the leaves of the secret pass, and they disappear.*

Enter COUNT FREDERICK FRIBERG, *hastily.*

COUNT. Gone! Vanished! Can it be possible? Sure 'tis witchcraft. I was close upon him—Karl! The cries of her he dragged with him, too, have ceased, and not the faintest echo of his retiring footsteps can be heard—Karl!

Enter KARL.

KARL. Oh, Lord! Pho, that hill's a breather! Why, where is he? Didn't you overtake him?

COUNT. No! in this spot he disappeared, and sunk, as it should seem, ghost-like into the very earth. Follow!

KARL. Follow! Follow a will-o'-the-wisp!

COUNT. Quick—aid me to search!

KARL. Search out a ghost! Mercy on us! I'll follow you through the world, fight for you the best cock-giant robber of 'em all, but if you're for hunting goblins I'm off. Hey! where the devil's the woman, though? If she was a spirit, she made more noise than any lady alive.

COUNT. Perchance the villain, so closely pursued, has destroyed his victim.

KARL. No doubt on't; he's killed her to a certainty; nothing but death can stop a woman's tongue.

COUNT [*having searched in vain*]. From the miller we may gain assistance: Grindoff, no doubt, is acquainted with every turn and outlet of the forest; quick, attend me to the mill.

[*Exeunt.*

SCENE III. *The Cavern.*

Music. ROBBERS *discovered asleep in different parts,* R. *and* L. LOTHAIR *on guard, with a carbine, stands beneath the magazine—stage partly light.*

LOTHAIR. Ere this it must be daylight—yet Grindoff returns not. Perchance their foul intent has failed—the fatal blow designed for Friberg may have fallen upon himself. How tedious drags the time, when fear, suspense, and doubt thus weigh upon the heart. Oh Kelmar, beloved Claudine, you little know my peril. [*Looks at the various groups of* BANDITTI, *and carefully rests his carbine at the foot of the rugged steps leading to the magazine.*] While yet this drunken stupor makes their sleep most death-like, let me secure a terrible but just revenge. If their infernal purpose be accomplished, this is their reward. [*Draws a coil of fuse from his bosom.*] These caverns, that spread beneath the mill, have various outlets, and in the fissures of the rock the train will lie unnoticed. Could I but reach the magazine.

[*Music.* LOTHAIR *retires cautiously up—he places his foot over the body of a* ROBBER, *who is seen asleep on the steps leading to the magazine—by accident he touches the carbine, which slips down—the* ROBBER, *being disturbed, alters his position while* LOTHAIR *stands over him, and again reposes.* LOTHAIR *advances up the steps—as he arrives at the magazine,* WOLF'S *signal, the bugle, is heard from above. The* ROBBERS *instantly start up, and* LOTHAIR *at the same moment springs from the steps, and seizing his carbine stands in his previous attitude.*

F   WOLF [GRINDOFF] *descending the steps of the opening, with* CLAUDINE *senseless in his arms.*

ROBBERS. The signal!

GOLOTZ. Wolf, we rejoice with you.

LOTHAIR. Have you been successful?

WOLF [*setting down* CLAUDINE]. So far, at least, I have.

LOTHAIR [*aside*]. Claudine—merciful powers! [*To* WOLF.] But Kelmar—

WOLF. Shall not long escape me—Kelmar once secure, his favourite, my redoubted rival, young Lothair, may next require attention—bear her in, Golotz. [GOLOTZ *bears* CLAUDINE *off*.] Where is Ravina?

Enter RAVINA.

Oh, you are come!

RAVINA. I am; what is your will?

WOLF. That you attend Claudine; treat her as you would treat me.

RAVINA. I will, be sure on't.

WOLF. Look you, fail not. I cannot wait her recovery—danger surrounds us.

ROBBERS. Danger!

WOLF. Ay, everyone must be vigilant, every heart resolved. Riber has been stabbed.

LOTHAIR. Then Friberg—

WOLF. Has escaped.

LOTHAIR. Thank heaven!

WOLF. How?

LOTHAIR. Friberg is still reserved for me.

WOLF. Be it so—your firmness shall be proved.

RAVINA. So—one act of villainy is spared you; pursue your fate no farther—desist, be warned in time.

WOLF. Fool! could woman's weakness urge me to retreat, my duty to our band would now make such repentance treachery.

ROBBERS. Noble captain!

WOLF. Mark you, my comrades: Kelmar has fled; left his house —no doubt for the Château Friberg. The suspicions of the

Count are upon *him*. All mistrust of me is banished from his mind, and I have lured him and his companion to the cottage of our lost comrade, Riber.

LOTHAIR. How came Claudine to fall into your power?

WOLF. I encountered her alone, as I left Kelmar's cottage. She had been to seek her father; I seized the opportunity, and conveyed her to the secret pass in the forest. Her cries caused me to be pursued, and one instant later I had fallen into their hands—by this time they have recovered the pathway to the mill. Spiller shall supply Riber's place—be prepared to meet them at the Flask, and prove yourself—

LOTHAIR. The man I am; I swear it.

WOLF. Enough—I am content!

RAVINA. Content! such guilt as thine can never feel content. Never will thy corroded heart have rest—years of security have made you rash, incautious—wanton in thy cruelty—and you will never rest until your mistaken policy destroys your band.

WOLF. No more of this—her discontent is dangerous. Spiller! when you are prepared to leave the cavern, make fast the door; Ravina shall remain here confined until our work above is finished.

LOTHAIR. I understand—

WOLF. Golotz and the rest—who are wont to cheer our revels with your music—be in waiting at the Flask, as travellers, wandering Savoyards, till the Count and his followers are safe within our toils; the delusion may spare us trouble. I know them resolute and fierce; and should they once suspect, though our numbers overpower them, the purchase may cost us dear. Away—time presses—Spiller—remember—

LOTHAIR. Fear me not—you soon shall know me.

[*Exit* WOLF *and* ROBBERS *up the steps.* LOTHAIR *immediately runs up the steps to the magazine, and places the fuse within, closes the door and directs it towards the trap by which he first entered the cave.*

RAVINA. Now then, hold firm, my heart and hand; one act of

vengeance, one dreadful triumph, and I meet henceforth the
hatred, the contempt of Wolf, without a sigh.

[*In great agitation she advances to the table, and taking a vial
from her bosom pours the contents into a cup, and goes cautiously
across to where* CLAUDINE *has been conducted.*

RAVINA. As she revives—ere yet her bewildered senses pro-
claim her situation, she will drink—and—

[LOTHAIR, *who has watched the conduct of* RAVINA, *seizes
her arm, takes away the cup, and throws it off.*

LOTHAIR. Hold, mistaken woman! Is this your pity for the
unfortunate—of your own sex, too? Are you the advocate
of justice and of mercy—who dare condemn the cruelty of
Wolf, yet with your own hand would destroy an innocent
fellow-creature, broken-hearted, helpless, and forlorn? Oh,
shame, shame!

RAVINA. And who is he that dares to school me thus?

LOTHAIR. Who am I?

RAVINA. Ay! that talk of justice and of mercy, yet pant to shed
the blood of Friberg!

LOTHAIR [*aside*]. Now, dared I trust her—I must, there is no
resource, for they'll be left together. [*To* RAVINA.] Ravina
—say what motive urged you to attempt an act that I must
believe is hateful to 'your nature?

RAVINA. Have I not cause—ample cause?

LOTHAIR. I may remove it.

RAVINA. Can you remove the pangs of jealousy?

LOTHAIR. I can—Claudine will never be the bride of Wolf.

RAVINA. Who can prevent it?

LOTHAIR. Her husband.

RAVINA. Is it possible?

LOTHAIR. Be convinced. Claudine, Claudine! [*Music.*]

CLAUDINE [*without*]. Ha! that voice!

LOTHAIR. Claudine!

Enter CLAUDINE.

CLAUDINE. 'Tis he, 'tis he! then I am safe! Ah! who are these,
and in what dreadful place am I?

LOTHAIR. Beloved Claudine, can this disguise conceal me?

CLAUDINE. Lothair! I was not deceived.

[*Falls into his arms.*

RAVINA. Lothair!

LOTHAIR. Ay, her affianced husband. Ravina, our lives are in your power; preserve them and save yourself. One act of glorious repentance, and the blessings of the surrounding country are yours. Observe!

[*Music.* LOTHAIR *points to the magazine—shows the train to* RAVINA, *and explains his intention—then gives a phosphorous bottle, which he shows the purpose of—she comprehends him.* CLAUDINE'S *action expresses astonishment and terror.* LOTHAIR *opens the trap up the stage.*

RAVINA. Enough, I understand.

LOTHAIR. Be careful, be cautious, I implore you—convey the train where I may distinctly see you from without the mill; and above all let no anxiety of mind, no fear of failure, urge you to fire the train till I give the signal. Remember, Claudine might be the victim of such fatal indiscretion.

RAVINA. But Wolf.

Re-enter WOLF, *who, hearing his name, halts at the back of the cavern.*

LOTHAIR. Wolf, with his guilty companions, shall fall despised and execrated. [*Seeing* WOLF.] Ah! [*Aside to* CLAUDINE.] Remove the train.

WOLF. Villain! [*Levels a pistol at* LOTHAIR. RAVINA *utters an exclamation of horror.* CLAUDINE *retreats, and removes the train to the foot of the steps.*]

LOTHAIR. Hold! you are deceived.

WOLF. Do you acknowledge it? But 'tis the last time. [*Seizing* LOTHAIR *by the collar.*]

LOTHAIR. One moment.

WOLF. What further deception?

LOTHAIR. I have used none—hear the facts.

WOLF. What are they?

LOTHAIR. Hatred to thee—jealousy of the fair Claudine urged this woman to attempt her life. [*Points to* CLAUDINE.]

WOLF. Indeed! for what purpose was that pass disclosed? [*Pointing to the trap.*]

LOTHAIR. I dared not leave them together.

WOLF. Vain subterfuge—your threat of destruction on me and my companions—

LOTHAIR. Was a mere trick, a forgery, a fabrication to appease her disappointed spirit—induce her to quit the cave, and leave Claudine in safety.

WOLF [*going up to, and closely observing* RAVINA]. Plausible hypocrite, Ravina has no weapon of destruction—how then? [*Crossing back to* LOTHAIR.]

LOTHAIR [*looking toward* RAVINA, *who holds up the vial, unseen by* WOLF]. Ah! [*Aside.*] We are saved. [*Crossing and snatching the vial, which she had retained in her hand.*] Behold, let conviction satisfy your utmost doubts.

WOLF [*looking on the label*]. Poison! you then are honest, Wolf unjust—I can doubt no longer. [*Seizes* RAVINA *by the arm.*] Fiend! descend instantly; in darkness and despair anticipate a dreadful punishment.

[*Music.* RAVINA *clasps her hands in entreaty, and descends the trap, which is closed violently by* WOLF.

WOLF. Now, Spiller, follow me to the Flask. [*Music.*] Be sure, make fast yon upper door.

[*He takes his broad miller's hat, for which he had returned—exit up steps,* LOTHAIR *following and looking back significantly at* CLAUDINE, *who then advances cautiously, opens the trap, and gives the train to* RAVINA—*appropriate music.* RAVINA *and* CLAUDINE *remain in attitude, the latter watching* LOTHAIR, *with uplifted hands.*

SCENE IV. *The cottage of Riber—The sign of the Flask at the door, L. in flat.*

Enter COUNT FREDERICK FRIBERG *and* KARL.

COUNT. This must be the house.

KARL. Clear as daylight; look, sir, 'The Flask!' Oh, and there stands the mill! I suppose old rough-and-tough, master Grindoff, will be here presently. Well, I'm glad we are in the right road at last; for such ins and outs, and ups and downs, and circumbendibuses in that forest, I never—

COUNT. True; we may now obtain guides and assistance to pursue that ruffian!

KARL [*aside*]. Pursue again! not to save all the she sex! Flesh and blood can't stand this.

COUNT [*abstracted*]. Yet, after so long an absence, delay is doubly irksome—could I but see her my heart doats on!

KARL. Ah! could *I* but see what my heart doats on.

COUNT. My sweet Lauretta!

KARL. A dish of saur-kraut!

COUNT. Fool!

KARL. Fool! so I mustn't enjoy a good dinner even in imagination.

COUNT. Still complaining!

KARL. How can I help it, sir? I can't live upon air, as you do.

COUNT. You had plenty last night.

KARL. So I had last Christmas, sir; and what sort of a supper was it, after all? One apple, two pears, three bunches of sour grapes, and a bowl of milk; one of your forest meals— I can't abide such a cruel cold diet—oh, for a bumper of brandy! But unfortunately my digestion keeps pace with my appetite—I'm always hungry. Oh, for a bumper of brandy!

[*Music heard within the Flask.*

COUNT. Hush!

KARL. What's that? Somebody tickling a guitar into fits; soft music always makes me doleful.

COUNT. Go into the house—stay; remember, I would be private.

KARL. Private—in a public-house. Oh, I understand, incog. But the miller knows you, sir.

COUNT. That's no reason all his people should.

KARL. I smoke—they'd be awed by our dignity and importance —poor things, I pity 'em—they are not used to polished society. Holloa! house! landlord! Mr. Flask!

Enter LOTHAIR *as landlord.*

KARL. Good entertainment here for man and beast, I'm told.

LOTHAIR. You are right.

KARL. Well, here am I, and there's my master!

LOTHAIR. You are welcome. [*Aside.*] I dare not say otherwise; Wolf is on the watch.

[WOLF *appears, watching at a window.*

KARL. Have you got anything ready? [*Smacking his lips.*]

LOTHAIR. Too much, I fear.

KARL. Not a bit, I'll warrant. I'm devilish sharp set.

LOTHAIR. Well, you are just in time.

KARL. Pudding-time, I hope! Have you got any meat?

LOTHAIR. I must ask him. [*Aside and looking round anxiously.*] Won't your master—

KARL. No, he lives upon love; but don't be alarmed, I'll make it worth your while. I'm six meals in arrear, and can swallow enough for both of us.

[*Exit* KARL, *with* LOTHAIR, *to the Flask.* WOLF *closes the window.*

COUNT. Yes, I'm resolved—the necessity for passing the river must by this time have urged the peasantry to re-establish the ferry—delay is needless. I'll away instantly to the Château Friberg, and with my own people return to redress the wrongs of my oppressed and suffering tenantry.

Enter KARL.

COUNT. Well, your news?

KARL. Glorious! The landlord, Mr. Flask, is a man after my own heart, a fellow of five meals a day.

COUNT. Psha! Who are the musicians?

KARL. Ill-looking dogs, truly; Savoyards, I take it; one plays on a thing like a frying-pan, the other turns something that sounds like a young grindstone.

COUNT. What else?

KARL. As fine an imitation of a shoulder of mutton as ever I clapp'd my eyes on.

Enter KELMAR, *exhausted by haste and fatigue.*

COUNT. Kelmar!

KELMAR. Ah, the Count and his companion! Thank heaven, I am arrived in time! my master will be saved, though Claudine, my poor unhappy child, is lost. Fly, I beseech you, fly from this spot! Do not question me; this is no time for explanations; one moment longer, and you are betrayed— your lives irrecoverably sacrificed.

COUNT. Would you again deceive us?

KELMAR. I have been myself deceived—fatally deceived! Let an old man's prayers prevail with you! Leave, oh leave this accursed place, and—

Enter WOLF, *in his miller's dress.*

KELMAR. Ah, the miller! then has hope forsaken me. Yet one ray, one effort more, and—

WOLF. Thy treachery is known. [*He seizes* KELMAR *by the collar.*]

KELMAR. One successful effort more, and death is welcome.

WOLF. Villain!

KELMAR. Thou art the villain—see—behold!

[*With a violent effort of strength, the old man suddenly turns upon* WOLF *and tears open his vest, beneath which he appears armed.* WOLF, *at the same instant, dashes* KELMAR *from him, who impelled forward is caught by the* COUNT. *The* COUNT *draws his sword—*WOLF *draws pistols in each hand from his side-pockets, and his hat falls off at the same instant— appropriate music.*]

COUNT. 'Tis he, the same! 'tis Wolf.

WOLF. Spiller! Golotz! [*Rushes out.*]

KARL. Is it Wolf? Damn his pistols! This shall reach him. [*Draws his sword, and hastens after* WOLF—*the report of a pistol is immediately heard.*

[*Exit* COUNT FRIBERG *and* KELMAR. *At the same moment,* GOLOTZ *and another* ROBBER, *disguised as minstrels, followed by* LOTHAIR, *burst from the house.*

GOLOTZ. We are called; Wolf called us! Ah, they have discovered him!

LOTHAIR. 'Tis too late to follow him; he has reached the bridge.

GOLOTZ. Then he is safe; but see, at the foot of the hill armed men in the Friberg uniform press forward to the mill.

LOTHAIR. This way we must meet them, then; in to the subterranean pass! [*Exeunt* GOLOTZ *and* ROBBER *to house.*] Now, Claudine, thy sufferings shall cease, and thy father's wrongs shall be revenged. [*Exit to house.*]

━━━━━━

SCENE V. *A near View of the Mill,* C., *standing on an elevated projection—from the foreground a narrow bridge passes to the rocky promontory across the ravine.*

Music. Enter RAVINA, *ascending the ravine with the fuse, which she places carefully in the crannies of the rock.*

RAVINA. My toil is over; the train is safe. From this spot I may receive the signal from Lothair, and at one blow the hapless victims of captivity and insult are amply, dreadfully avenged. [*A pistol is fired without.*] Ah, Wolf! [*She retires.*]

Enter WOLF *pursued, and turning, fires his remaining pistol off; then hurries across the bridge, which he instantly draws up.* KARL *rushes on.*

WOLF [*with a shout of great exultation*]. Ha, ha! you strive in vain!

KARL. Cowardly rascal! you'll be caught at last. [*Shaking his sword at* WOLF.]

WOLF. By whom?

KARL. Your only friend, Beelzebub: run as fast as you will, he'll trip up your heels at last.

WOLF. Fool-hardy slave, I have sworn never to descend from this spot alive, unless with liberty.

KARL. Oh, we'll accommodate you; you shall have *liberty* to *ascend* from it; the wings of your own mill shall be the gallows, and fly with every rascal of you into the other world.

WOLF. Golotz! Golotz, I say! [*Calling toward the mill.*]

Enter COUNT FRIBERG, *with* KELMAR *and the* ATTENDANTS *from the Château Friberg, in uniform, and armed with sabres.*

COUNT. Wretch! your escape is now impossible. Surrender to the injured laws of your country.

WOLF. Never! The brave band that now await my commands within the mill double your number. Golotz!

Enter GOLOTZ *from a small door in the mill.*

WOLF. Quick! let my bride appear.

[*Exit* GOLOTZ.

Enter RAVINA—WOLF *starts.*

RAVINA. She is here! What would you?

WOLF. Ravina! Traitress!

RAVINA. Traitress! What then art thou? But I come not here to parley; ere it be too late, make one atonement for thy injuries—restore this old man's child.

KELMAR. Does she still live?

WOLF. She does; but not for thee, or for the youth Lothair.

RAVINA. Obdurate man! Then do I know my course.

Re-enter LOTHAIR, *conducting* CLAUDINE *from the mill, a cloak concealing him.*

CLAUDINE. Oh, my dear father!

KELMAR. My child—Claudine! Oh, spare, in pity spare her!

WOLF. Now mark me, Count: unless you instantly withdraw your followers and let my troop pass free, by my hand she dies!

KELMAR. Oh, mercy!

COUNT. Hold yet a moment!

WOLF. Withdraw your followers.

COUNT. Till thou art yielded up to justice, they never shall depart.

WOLF. For that threat, be this your recompense!

LOTHAIR [*throwing aside his cloak*]. And this my triumph!

> [*Music.* LOTHAIR *places himself before* CLAUDINE *and receives* WOLF's *attack—the* ROBBER *is wounded, staggers back, sounds his bugle, and the mill is crowded with* BANDITTI. LOTHAIR *throws back the bridge, and crosses it with* CLAUDINE *in his arms.*

Ravina, fire the train.

> [RAVINA *instantly sets fire to the fuse, the flash of which is seen to run down the side of the rock into the gully under the bridge, and the explosion immediately takes place.* KELMAR, *rushing forward, catches* CLAUDINE *in his arms.*

CURTAIN

THE FACTORY LAD

A DOMESTIC DRAMA IN TWO ACTS

BY

JOHN WALKER

════

First performed at the Surrey Theatre,
15 October 1832

════

CAST

GEORGE ALLEN		Mr. Waldron
WILSON		Mr. Lee
SIMS	Lately discharged from	Mr. Brunton
SMITH	the factory of ******	Mr. Gardner
HATFIELD		Mr. C. Hill
WILL RUSHTON, an outcast		Mr. Stuart
SQUIRE WESTWOOD, master of the factory		Mr. Dibdin Pitt
TAPWELL, landlord of the 'Harriers'		Mr. Young
GRIMLEY		Mr. Bannister
JUSTICE BIAS		Mr. Clarkson
CRINGE, his clerk		Mr. Smith
JANE ALLEN		Mrs. W. West
MARY, her eldest girl, about eleven		Miss. H. Pitt
MILLY, her second, about six		Miss Clarke
A CHILD IN CRADLE		

Constables, Soldiers

ACT I

SCENE I. *Exterior of a Factory, lighted.*

As the curtain rises the clock strikes eight, and the men, including ALLEN, WILSON, SMITH, SIMS, *and* HATFIELD, *enter from Factory.*

ALLEN. Now my lads, the glad sound—eight o'clock, Saturday night. Now for our pay, and for the first time from our new master, the son of our late worthy employer.

WILSON. The poor man's friend!

HATFIELD. And the poor man's father, too!

ALLEN. Aye; who, as he became rich by the industry of his men, would not desert them in a time of need, nor prefer steam machinery and other inventions to honest labour.

WILSON. May his son be like him!

ALLEN. Aye; he was a kind man, truly. Good as good could be, an enemy to no man but the slothful! Ah, a tear almost starts when I think of him! May he be happy, may—. He must be as happy above as he made those on this earth. But come, come, we won't be melancholy. Saturday night! We won't put a dark side upon things, but let us hope his son, our present master, may be like his father, eh?

HATFIELD. Ah, half like, and I shall be content!

WILSON. And I—and all of us.

ALLEN. Hush! He comes.

Enter WESTWOOD, *from Factory.*

WESTWOOD. Gentlemen!

HATFIELD [*aside to* ALLEN *and rest*]. Gentlemen! There's a pleasing way.

ALLEN. Gentlemen, sir! We're no gentlemen, but only poor, hard-working men, at your honour's service.

HATFIELD. Hard-working and honest, we hope.

WESTWOOD. Well, well, gentlemen or hard-working men, it's not what I've come about.

ALLEN. No complaint, I hope? Work all clean and right?

WESTWOOD. It may be.

HATFIELD. It may be! It is, or I'll forfeit my wages. Your father, sir, never spoke in doubt, but always looked, spoke his mind, and—

WESTWOOD. And that's what *I've* come to do. I've come to speak my mind. Times are now altered!

ALLEN. They are indeed, sir. A poor man has now less wages for more work.

WESTWOOD. The master having less money, resulting from there being less demand for the commodity manufactured.

ALLEN. Less demand!

WESTWOOD. Hear me! If not less demand, a greater quantity is thrown into the markets at a cheaper rate. Therefore, to the business I've come about. As things go with the times, so must men. To compete with my neighbours—that is, if I wish to prosper as they do—in plain words, in future I have come to the resolution of having my looms propelled by steam.

ALLEN.
HATFIELD. } By steam!
WILSON.

WESTWOOD. Which will dispense with the necessity of manual labour, and save me some three thousand a year.

ALLEN. And not want us, who have been all our lives working here?

WESTWOOD. I can't help it. I am sorry for it; but I must do as others do.

ALLEN. What, and turn us out, to beg, starve, steal, or—

HATFIELD. Aye; or rot for what he cares.

WESTWOOD. Turn you out are words I don't understand. I don't want you, that's all. Surely I can say that? What is here is mine, left me by my father to do the best with, and that is now my intention. Steam supersedes manual labour. A ton of coals will do as much work as fifty men, and for less wages than ten will come to, is it not so?

ALLEN. It may be as you say, sir; but your poor father made the old plan do, and died, they say, rich. He was always well satisfied with the profits our industry brought him, he lived cheerful himself and made others so; and often I have heard him say his greatest pleasure was the knowledge that so many hard-working men could sit down to a Sunday's dinner in peace, and rear up their children decently through his means.

WILSON. Ah, heaven bless him!

HATFIELD. Heaven has blessed him, I trust, for he was a man— an Englishman who had feeling for his fellow creatures, and who would not, for the sake of extra gain, that he might keep his hounds and his hunters, turn the poor man from his door who had served him faithfully for years.

WESTWOOD. I hear you, and understand you, sir. Sentiments in theory sound well, but not in practice; and as you seem spokes-man in this affair, I will—though I consider myself in no way compelled—reply to you in your own way. Don't you buy where you please, at the cheapest place? Would you have bought that jerkin of one man more than another, if he had charged you twice the sum for it, or even a sixpence more? Don't you, too, sow your garden as you please, and dig it as you please?

HATFIELD. Why, it's my own!

WESTWOOD. There it is! Then have *I* not the same right to do as I please with *my own*?

ALLEN. Then you discharge us?

HATFIELD. Oh, come along! What's the use of asking or talking either? You cannot expect iron to have feelings!

WESTWOOD. I stand not here to be insulted; so request you'll to the counting-house, receive your wages, and depart.

ALLEN. And for ever?

WESTWOOD. For ever! I want you not.

ALLEN. Will you not think of it again once more?

WESTWOOD. I'm resolved.

ALLEN [*aside*]. My poor wife and children! [*To* WESTWOOD.] No, no; not quite—not quite resolved! Things, mayhap ha' run cross, so you be hasty! Think, think again! [*Kneels*.] On my knees hear a poor man's prayer.

WESTWOOD. It is useless! I *have* thought and decided!

ALLEN [*rises*]. My wife! My children!   [*Rushes off*.

WILSON. Poor fellow!

HATFIELD. Then, if ye will not hear a poor man's prayer, hear his curses! May thy endeavours be as sterile land, which the lightning has scath'd, bearing nor fruit, nor flower, nor blade, but never-dying thorns to pierce thee on thy pillow! Hard-hearted, vain, pampered thing as thou art, remember, the day will come thou'lt be sorry for this night's work! Come, comrades—come!

[HATFIELD, WILSON, SIMS, *and* SMITH *exeunt.* WESTWOOD *into Factory, sneeringly.*

━━━━━━

SCENE II. *A Country Lane. Dark.*

Enter RUSHTON, *cautiously, with snare, bag, and gun. Sets a snare.*

RUSHTON. That be sure for a good 'un! Ha, ha! The Game Laws, eh? As if a poor man hadn't as much right to the bird that flies and the hare that runs as the rich tyrants who want all, and gripe and grapple all too? I care not for their laws. While I have my liberty, or power, or strength, I will live as well as the best of 'em. [*Noise without*.] But who comes here? Ah, what do I see? Some of the factory lads, and this way too! What can this mean? I'll listen!   [*Stands aside*.

Enter HATFIELD, WILSON, SIMS, *and* SMITH.

WILSON. Well, here's a pretty ending to all our labours, after nine years, as I've been—

SIMS. And I ten.

SMITH. And I, since I was a lad.

HATFIELD. And I, all my life. But so it is. What are working men like us but the tools that make others rich, who, when we become old—

OMNES. Ah!

HATFIELD. We're kicked from our places, like dogs, to starve, die, and rot, for what they care!

SIMS. Or beg!

HATFIELD. Ah, that I'll never do!

WILSON. Nor I!

SMITH. Nor I, either!

SIMS. Then rob, mayhap?

WILSON. That may be!

HATFIELD. Aye; be like poor Will Rushton—an outcast, a poacher, or anything!

RUSHTON [*starting forward. The others stand amazed*]. Aye, or a pauper, to go with your hat in your hand, and after begging and telling them what they know to be the truth—that you have a wife and five, six, or eight children, one perhaps just born, another mayhap just dying—they'll give you eighteen pence to support them all for the week; and if you dare to complain, not a farthing; but place you in the stocks, or scourge you through the town as a vagabond! This is parish charity! I have known what it is. My back is still scored with the marks of their power. The slave abroad, the poor black whom they affect to pity, is not so trampled on, hunted, and ill-used as the peasant or hard-working fellows like your-selves, if once you have no home nor bread to give your children!

WILSON. But this I'll never submit to!

SIMS. Nor I!

SMITH. Nor I!

HATFIELD. Nor I! I'll hang first!

WILSON. Thank heaven, I have no children!

SMITH. Nor more have I, nor Sims; but some have both, wives and children.

WILSON. 'Tis true. I have a wife, but she's as yet young, healthy, and can work and does work; but think of poor

Allen, with a wife and three small children and an aged mother to support.

RUSHTON. What! And is he discharged too? What, Allen— George Allen?

HATFIELD. Aye, along with the rest. Not wanted now!

RUSHTON. My brother George, as I do call him still—for though my poor wife be dead and gone, she were his wife's sister. Ah, but let me not think of that. Where—where be poor George? He be not here!

WILSON. He rushed off home, I do believe, like to one broken-hearted.

RUSHTON. Ah, to his poor wife and children! There will I go to him, and say though all the world do forsake him, Will Rushton never will! No; while there be a hare or bird he shall have one; and woe to the man who dare prevent or hold my hand!

HATFIELD. You're a brave and staunch fellow.

RUSHTON. Aye, and desperate and daring, too.

WILSON. Give me your hand.

HATFIELD And here's mine. What say you? Suppose we go to the 'Harriers', and, in the back room by ourselves, just ha' a drop of something and talk o' things a bit.

WILSON. We will go.

SMITH. Aye, we will.

HATFIELD [*to* RUSHTON]. And you to George, and say where we are.

RUSHTON. I will—and bring him with me! But he'll not want asking. These times cannot last long. When man be so worried that he be denied that food that heaven sends for all, then heaven itself calls for vengeance! No, the time has come when the sky shall be like blood, proclaiming this shall be the reward of the avaricious, the greedy, the flinty-hearted, who, deaf to the poor man's wants, make him what he now is, a ruffian—an incendiary!

WILSON. Remember Allen. Yet stay! Now I think again, will it not alarm his wife to see *you*?

RUSHTON. Ah!

HATFIELD. And bring things to mind that had not best be thought of just now.

RUSHTON. Ah, my wife—

HATFIELD. Was her sister. So, suppose Smith here goes instead. She do not know him, does she, Smith?

SMITH. But bare—perhaps not. I ha' passed her once or twice.

HATFIELD. 'Twill do then. You go then and whisper in his ear where we are.

SMITH. Aye, the 'Harriers'.

HATFIELD [to RUSHTON]. What say you, isn't it better so?

RUSHTON. Aye, aye!

WILSON. 'Tis much better.

HATFIELD. Remember then! To the 'Harriers'.

RUSHTON. And shall I be there?

SMITH. To be sure.

WILSON. But won't our all meeting in a room by ourselves, and Will with us too, excite suspicion?

HATFIELD. That's well thought again. Then we'll drop in one by one, or two together so—and Will, you can look in too, as 'twere by accident, for a drink o' summat—that way.

RUSHTON. I care not how, lads. In Will Rushton you see one who has been so buffetted he thinks not of forms. But be it as you will. To the last drop I have, I'll be your friend—aye, the friend of poor George Allen!

HATFIELD. George! Away—away!

[*Music. They shake hands earnestly and exeunt.*

———

SCENE III. *Interior of* ALLEN's *House. Fireplace, saucepan on. A Clock—time twenty minutes past eight. A Cradle with Child.*
JANE ALLEN, *and* MARY *and* MILLY *assisting her in pearling lace, and drawing ditto.*

MARY. I've done another length, mother, and that makes five, and sister hasn't done four yet.

JANE. Never mind! She does very well. You're both very good children! Only now you may lay the cloth, and get out the supper. It's past eight, and your father will be coming home, and he'll be very tired, I dare say, and hungry too, and at the end of the week a bit of supper and a draught of ale is a thing he looks for! And, his family around him, who so happy as George Allen?

MARY. And you too, mother, and me too, and sister too, and little brother in the cradle.

JANE. All—all, bless you, and thank heaven!

MARY. Then I'll not begin another, mother?

JANE. No; but make haste and lay the cloth.

MILLY. And shan't I finish mine neither, mother?

JANE. No, never mind, that's a good girl. Get out the bread, and be quick. [*Clock chimes half-past.*] Hear? It's half-past! A fork—the potatoes must be done.

MARY. Yes, mother.

[*Hands fork.* JANE *goes to fire, and* MILLY *gets bread out.*

JANE. Oh, I think I hear him!

MARY. And so do I, mother—I can hear him! But oh dear, how he's banging to the gate!

Enter GEORGE ALLEN, *who throws himself in a chair fretfully.*

JANE. Why, George, what's the matter? Dear me, how pale you are! Are you not well, George? You seem feverish.

ALLEN. I am—I am!

JANE. You'll be better after supper. Children, quick!

MARY. Oh, father, we've been so busy, and done such a deal! See, father!

[*Shows him lace.* ALLEN *takes it, throws it down, rises, and stamps on it.*

ALLEN. Curses on it!

MARY. Oh, mother—mother, father's thrown down all my work and has stamped on it, and I'm sure it's done very well! [*Cries.*]

MILLY. Oh, mother, see what father's done!

JANE. George, oh, tell me what means this!

ALLEN. It means that—

MARY. What, father? What makes you angry?

JANE. Say, George!

ALLEN [*looks at his children, and then clasps them*]. God—God bless you! [*Picks up the lace and gives it them.*] There, there! You're good children!   [*Sits down.*

MARY. I'm sure, father, I never do anything to make you angry.

MILLY. No more do I, father—do I?

MARY. Nor does mother, either?

ALLEN. No—no, I know she does not!

JANE. Then what is it, George? I never saw you thus before? You're so pale, and you tremble so. Why did you throw down the lace, that which is a living to us?

ALLEN. Because it will never be so again!

JANE. Not a living to us?

ALLEN. No! George Allen must beg now! Ah, beg or as bad—work and starve. And that I'll never do!

JANE. Oh, speak! Work and starve? Impossible!

ALLEN. Naught be impossible these days! What has ruined others will now ruin us. It's been others' turn first, now it be ours.

JANE. What, George?

ALLEN. That steam—that curse on mankind, that for the gain of a few, one or two, to ruin hundreds, is going to be at the factory! Instead of five-and-thirty good hands, there won't be ten wanted now, and them half boys and strangers. Yes, steam be now going to do all the work, and poor, hard-working, honest men, who ha' been for years toiling to do all for the good of a master, be now turned out o' doors to do what they can or what they like. And you know what that means, and what it must come to.

JANE. Oh, dreadful—dreadful! But don't fret, husband—don't fret! We will all strive to do something!

ALLEN [*again rising*]. But what be that something? Think I can hear my children cry for food and run barefoot? Think I don't know what 'twill come to?

JANE. But some other place will perhaps give us employ.

ALLEN. Aye, some foreign outlandish place; to be shipped off like convicts to die and starve. Look at Will Rushton, who was enticed, or rather say ensnared there with his wife and four children. Were not the children slaughtered by the natives, who hate white men and live on human flesh? And was not his wife seized too, your own sister, and borne away and never returned; shared perhaps the same fate as her children, or perhaps worse? And has not poor Will, since he returned, been crazed, heart-broken, a pauper, a poacher, or anything?

JANE. Oh, no, no! We shall meet with friends here, George.

ALLEN. Aye, Jane, such friends that if thou wert dying, starving, our children stretched lifeless, and I but took a crust of bread to save thee, would thrust me in a prison, there to rot. I have read, Jane—I have seen, Jane, the fate of a poor man. And you know we have nothing now, no savings after the long sickness of father and burying, and the little one we lost, too.

JANE. They are in heaven now, I hope!

Door opens and SMITH *appears.*

ALLEN. Who's there?

SMITH. It's only me, George.

ALLEN. Ah! [SMITH *approaches and whispers in* ALLEN'S *ear.*] I will!

JANE [*apart*]. What can this mean?

SMITH. Be secret.

ALLEN. As the grave!

SMITH [*whispers again*]. There, too!

ALLEN. He will?

SMITH. As by chance, you know.

JANE [*apart*]. Heaven, what can it mean?

ALLEN. I'll be there.

> [*Shakes* SMITH *by the hand, who leaves at door.*

JANE. Oh, George—George, what is this, that your eyes roll so? Now think!

ALLEN. I do think, Jane.

JANE. Sit—come, come, sit—sit down and have some supper, then you'll be better! Remember it is Saturday night. I know it is enough to make you vexed; but think, George—think, and remember there is One who never forsakes the good man, if he will but pray to him.

ALLEN. I will—I will; but I must now to see the lads that be like myself, poor fellows—just to talk, you know—to think, as like—to plan—e'es to plan—merely to plan.

JANE. But not yet. Sit awhile. Take some ale.

ALLEN. Why, I can get ale there, and I can't eat, my tongue and throat be so dry. God bless you!   [*Going.*

MARY. Not going, father?

MILLY. Not going, father?

JANE. See, George! Don't go yet!

ALLEN [*kisses children*]. I must—I must! Only for a short time, and it be growing late.

> [*Approaches door.*

JANE. Don't! Stay, George—stay!

> [*Kneels and catches hold of him.*

ALLEN. I must—I must!

> [*Rushes out. Music.* JANE *falls.*

MARY [*cries*]. Mother—mother! Oh, father!

> [*They fall on their mother, and scene closes.*

━━━━━

SCENE IV. *An Apartment in* WESTWOOD'S *House.*

Enter WESTWOOD.

WESTWOOD. I must be on the alert, and keep my doors well fastened, and have, too, an armed force to welcome these desperadoes if they should dare to violate the laws, well framed to subject them to obedience. I did not half like the menace of that fellow. However, I'll be secure, and if they dare, let them take the consequences. [*Muses, and repeats* HATFIELD's *words.*] 'The day will come, I shall be sorry for what I have done!' Ha, ha! Sorry! Fool, and fools! What have I to fear or dread? Is England's proud aristocracy to tremble when brawling fools mouth and question? No; the hangman shall be their answer.

Enter SERVANT.

SERVANT. The dinner's ready, sir.

WESTWOOD. Is it eight, then?

SERVANT. Yes, sir.

WESTWOOD. Is that old grumbler, my father's late housekeeper, gone, who dared to talk and advise, as she called it?

SERVANT. She went at six, sir. We trundled her out, sir.

WESTWOOD. And the French cook, is he arrived yet?

SERVANT. He has sent his valet to say he'll be here in three days, after his excursion to Brighton.   [*Exit.*

WESTWOOD. What, because our fathers acted foolishly, shall we also plod on in the same dreary route? No; science has opened to us her stores, and we shall be fools indeed not to take advantage of the good it brings. The time must come, and shortly, when even the labourer himself will freely acknowledge that our improvements in machinery and the aid afforded us by the use of steam will place England on a still nobler eminence than the proud height she has already attained.   [*Exit.*

=====

SCENE V. *A Room in the 'Harriers'.*

WILSON, SIMS, SMITH, *and* HATFIELD *discovered at a table, drinking.* TAPWELL, *the Landlord, just entering.*

TAPWELL. *Another* mug, did you say?

HATFIELD. Aye, and another to that. What stare you at?

TAPWELL. Eh? Oh, very well!   [*Exit.*

SIMS. Master Tapwell seems surprised at our having an extra pot.

HATFIELD. Let him be. We care not, no more will he, if we have twenty, so he gets the money.

WILSON [*to* SMITH]. He said he'd come, did he—Allen?

SMITH. For certain.

HATFIELD. His wife, no doubt, was there? Did you manage all well? Whisper secretly?

SMITH. Not a word out.

HATFIELD. That's well, for women are bad to trust in these things. I've read in books where the best plots have failed through women being told what their husbands or their fathers were going to do, though it was to free a nation from the yoke of tyranny.

WILSON. Aye, right; and so have I.

Re-enter TAPWELL, *with beer.*

TAPWELL. The beer.

[*Holds out his hand without delivering it.*

WILSON. What's that for?

TAPWELL. Another mug, and you didn't pay for the last, which makes one-and-fourpence.

HATFIELD. What, you know, do you, already, that we're discharged?

TAPWELL. Why, yes, if truth must be told, young Squire—

HATFIELD. Young who?

TAPWELL. Young Squire—Master Westwood.

HATFIELD. Young damnation! Squire such a rascal as that again while we're here, and this pot with its contents shall make you call for a plaster quicker than you may like. Squire Westwood! Squire Hard-heart! No man, no feeling! Call a man like that a squire! An English gentleman—a true English gentleman is he who feels for another, who relieves the distressed, and not turns out the honest hard-working man to beg or starve because he, forsooth, may keep his hunters and drink his foreign wines.

SIMS. Aye; and go to foreign parts. Englishmen were happy when they knew naught but Englishmen; when they were plain, blunt, honest, upright, and downright—the master an example to his servant, and both happy with the profits of their daily toil.

ALLEN *enters at door.*

SMITH. Allen!

HATFIELD [*to* TAPWELL]. Off, thou lickshoe! There, take that. That will do, I suppose, for another pot, or a gallon?

          [*Throws him down a crown piece on the floor.*

TAPWELL. Oh, certainly, Master Hatfield—certainly gentlemen! Another pot now, did you say?

SMITH. Off!   [*Thrusts him out and shuts the door.*

HATFIELD [*to* ALLEN]. Come, come, don't look so down—come, drink!

WILSON. Aye, drink!

ALLEN. Nay, I—

HATFIELD. Not drink? Not 'Destruction to steam machinery'?

ALLEN. Destruction to steam machinery! Aye, with all my heart! [*Drinks.*] Destruction to steam machinery!

HATFIELD. Aye, our curse—our ruin!

WILSON. Aye, aye; we've been talking about that, and one thing and t'other like, and about what we shall do, you know—

ALLEN. Ah!

SIMS. I say poaching.

ALLEN. And for a hare, to get sent away, perhaps, for seven long years.

SMITH. So I said.

SIMS. But we mayn't be caught, you know, not if we are true to each other. Four or five tightish lads like us can't be easily taken, unless we like, you know!

ALLEN. And if we carry but a stick in our defence, and use it a bit, do you know the law? Hanging!

HATFIELD. Right! Hanging for a hare!

SIMS. Not so—not hanging. Don't Will Rushton carry on the sport pretty tidishly, and has only been—

ALLEN. In the stocks twice, whipped publicly thrice, and in gaol seven times. And what has he for his pains? Not a coat to his back worth a groat, no home but the hedge's shelter or an outhouse, and himself but to keep. What would he then do had he, as I have, a wife and three young children to support? Besides, isn't he at times wild with thinking of the past—of his lost wife and murdered children? He, poor unhappy wretch, cannot feel more or sink lower—the gaol to him is but a resting-place!

HATFIELD. 'Tis true, indeed. I remember him once a jovial fellow, the pride of all that knew him; but now—

ALLEN [*to* SMITH]. But said you not he would be here?

WILSON. Aye, as by accident.

RUSHTON *partly opens door, when* TAPWELL *stops him.*

ALLEN. Ah, 'tis he!

WILSON [*to* ALLEN]. Be not over anxious.

TAPWELL. No, you can't. You remember the bag you left here the last time, and the scrape it got me into?

RUSHTON. But only a minute or so.

TAPWELL. Not for half a minute.

HATFIELD [*to* ALLEN]. Shall I cleave the dastard down?

ALLEN. Leave it to me. [*Approaches* TAPWELL.] Come, sir landlord, mercy a bit, though you may not like his rags and for bread he snares a hare now and then, he may wear as honest a heart as many who wear a better garment; therefore, let him in. The outcast should sojourn with the outcast. Come, another gallon, and take that.   [*Gives* TAPWELL *money.*

TAPWELL. Oh well, certainly, if you have no objection, gentlemen, and he has no game or snares about him.

HATFIELD. Off!

[*Exit* TAPWELL.

ALLEN. Rushton!

RUSHTON. Allen!

ALLEN. Thy hand.

RUSHTON. 'Tis here, with my heart.

ALLEN. Drink.   [*Gives beer*.

RUSHTON. Thanks. Many's the day since I was welcomed thus.

SIMS. Not since, I dare say, you lost your poor wife.

                              [RUSHTON *stands transfixed*.

ALLEN. That was foolish to mention his wife.

SIMS. I forgot.

RUSHTON. Who spoke of my wife? Ah, did she call? Ah, she
   did—I hear her screams! They are—are tearing her from me!
   My children, too! I see their mangled forms, bleeding, torn
   piecemeal! My wife—my children! [*Subsides.*] My wife—
   my—[*Looks about.*] Where, where am I? [*Sees* ALLEN.] Allen,
   Allen!

ALLEN. To be sure—George Allen! Don't you know me? Your
   brother, your friend George, who—

RUSHTON. I know. Sent me food while I was in prison! [*Clasps*
   ALLEN's *hand and sobs.*] Heaven, heaven bless you!

ALLEN. Come, come, an end to this! I am now like thyself, an
   outcast—one driven, after years of hard toil, upon the world.
   These the same! [*Pointing to his comrades.*] Come now, say
   honestly, as a man who has seen much and whose hairs are
   gray, what would you advise us to do?

RUSHTON. I know all. You are discharged.

WILSON. Aye, from where we've worked since lads, nearly, if
   not all, and our fathers before us.

HATFIELD. And we are turned beggars on the world, for no
   reason but to make room for that which has ruined hundreds,
   to suit the whims and finery of a thing unworthy the name of
   man!

RUSHTON [*stands absorbed awhile*]. I would, but I dare not
   advise, for my blood now boils, and my flesh is gored with the
   lash of power! Hush! Hither! [*Beckons them round him.*] A
   word. Are you all good here? [*Touching his heart.*] Sound?
   Prime?

HATFIELD. Who dare to doubt?

RUSHTON. Enough. Hush! [*Whispers in their ears, and ends with:*] Dare you?

HATFIELD. I dare!

SMITH. And I!

WILSON. And I!

SIMS. And I!

ALLEN. And I!

RUSHTON. 'Tis well! [*Shakes them by the hand.*] Now then, come lads, the time answers. Hush!

[*Music. Exeunt.*

SCENE VI. *A Country Lane. Dark.*

Enter RUSHTON, ALLEN, WILSON, SIMS, SMITH, *and* HATFIELD, *armed variously.*

RUSHTON. Steady—steady, lads, and resolute!

WILSON. 'Tis well no one crosses our path.

HATFIELD. What if they did?

ALLEN. My heart almost begins to sicken; a fear, ever unknown to me, seems to shake me from head to foot.

RUSHTON. Pshaw, fear! Fear is the coward's partner, and the companion of the guilty; not of men who are about to act in their own right, and crush oppression.

WILSON. 'Tis true we are oppressed!

SMITH. We are!

SIMS. Aye, we are!

HATFIELD. And we'll be revenged!

SIMS. Aye, revenged!

ALLEN. But if we meet with resistance—I mean if they attack us?

RUSHTON. Return their attack—blow for blow, if they will have it; aye, and blood for blood. Give in, and you're lost for ever! You'll have no mercy. Look at me, Will Rushton, honest Will

F

Rushton that was once—hard-working Will Rushton. You know my fate—torture upon torture, the insult of the proud and the pity of the poor have been my lot for years. Trampled on, crushed, and gored to frenzy! My blood boils now I think on't! The pale spectre of my wife, with my slaughtered children now beckons me on! Revenge, revenge! Come, revenge!

[Takes ALLEN'S *hand and exeunt.*

HATFIELD. Aye, revenge—revenge!

OMNES. Aye, revenge!

[They follow RUSHTON *and* ALLEN.

SCENE VII. *Exterior of the Factory. Dark.*

Enter RUSHTON *with a torch, followed by* ALLEN, WILSON, SIMS, SMITH, *and* HATFIELD.

RUSHTON. Now, to the work—to the work! Break, crack, and split into ten thousand pieces these engines of your disgrace, your poverty, and your ruin! Now!

HATFIELD. Aye, now destruction!

WILSON. Aye, spare not a stick! Come, come, Allen!

*[*RUSHTON, WILSON, SIMS, *and* SMITH *rush into the Factory. The Factory is seen blazing.*

WESTWOOD *rushes in, followed by* CONSTABLES.

WESTWOOD. Ah, villain, stay! It is as I was told; but little did I think they dared. Seize them!

HATFIELD. Ah, surprised!

RUSHTON *comes from the Factory, with firebrand, followed by his comrades.*

WESTWOOD. Submit, I say!

RUSHTON. Ah!

[Seizes him by the throat, hurls him to the earth, and waves the lighted ember above him in wild triumph.

ACT II

SCENE I. *Moonlight. Open Country, with View of Factory burning in the distance.*

Enter RUSHTON, *with firebrand.*

RUSHTON. Ha, ha! This has been a glorious night, to see the palace of the tyrant levelled to the ground—to hear his engines of gain cracking—to hear him call for help, and see the red flame laugh in triumph! Ah, many a day have I lain upon the cold damp ground, muttering curses—many a night have I called upon the moon, when she has frenzied my brain, to revenge my wrongs; for days and nights I have never slept—misery and want, and the smart of the lash, with visions of bygone days, have been like scorpions, rousing me to revenge, and the time has come. I have had partners, too, in the deed—men who, like myself, glory in the act. But where can Allen be, and the rest? They must away now. I'll to his cottage, and if the minions of power dare but touch a hair of his head, this brand shall lay them low.

[*Exit.*

SCENE II. *Interior, as before, of* ALLEN'S *House. The casement open, and the blaze of the Factory seen in the distance.*

JANE *watching at the window.* MARY *and* MILLY *near her.*

JANE. Oh, horror—horror!

MARY. It's not out yet, mother; it seems as if some other house was on fire.

MILLY. See, mother!

JANE. 'Tis too true, child! Oh, mercy—mercy! The flames have caught the farm next to it. I can no longer look. The worst of thoughts crowd upon my brain. My husband's absence—his wild and distracted look—the factory in flames!

Enter ALLEN, *hurriedly.*

Ah, my husband! Oh say, George, where—where is it you have been?

ALLEN. Jane—my children! [*Embraces them in silent anguish.*] Some ale, water, or something! My throat is parched!

MARY. Some ale, father?

JANE. You've seen the fire?

ALLEN. Yes, yes. Some ale, I said.

MARY. Here it is, father! [*Gives jug.* ALLEN *drinks.*

ALLEN. Ha, that be sweet! [*To his wife in an undertone.*] Hush! Here—here, take this—[*Gives money.*]—it be all I have, and this, too. [*Gives watch.*] There be, too, a little up-stairs. Take care of thyself, Jane, and of children.

JANE. Oh, George, say not that! You would not leave your Jane, who has ever loved you, and ever will?

MARY. Oh, mother, don't cry!

ALLEN. Mother's not crying. [*Standing before her.*] See to the child; it wakes! [*Fire blazes vividly. To* JANE.] See you that? All be broken and burnt down. Say, if they come, you ha' not seen me, you know. They cannot harm thee.

JANE. Oh, George, say, for mercy's sake, you've had no hand in this!

ALLEN. What be done, Jane, cannot now be altered.

JANE. Oh, George, bad advice has led you to this! I know you would not have done so of yourself.

ALLEN. It matters not now, Jane; it be done, and I must away; but you shall hear from me, Jane, where'er I be. I will send thee all I get.

[*A noise without.*

JANE. Ah, that noise—

ALLEN. It be they come—come to take me.

ALLEN *rushes towards the door, when* WESTWOOD *and* CONSTABLES *appear at the window.*

Ah, 'tis useless!

WESTWOOD. He's here.

Enter WESTWOOD, *followed by* GRIMLEY *and* CONSTABLES.

Seize him! [*They seize* ALLEN.

JANE [*kneels*]. Oh, mercy, mercy! Spare him—spare my husband!

MARY. Oh, spare my father!

MILLY. Don't hurt father!

JANE. He is not guilty, indeed he's not!

WESTWOOD. Not guilty, when I saw him with the rest?

JANE. But he did not set fire the place. I know he did not—he would not.

WESTWOOD. What matters what hand did the deed? Is not all a heap of ashes—all burnt and destroyed?

JANE. Yet mercy!

WESTWOOD. Mercy! What mercy had he to me? Cast thy eye yonder, and petition to the flames.

JANE. Oh, George, George!

WESTWOOD. Away with him! Now for the outcast!

Enter RUSHTON, *frantically, with a piece of burnt machinery in his hand.*

RUSHTON. Who calls for the outcast? Stay! What are you about? Seizing an innocent man? Here stands the incendiary! I, Will Rushton, the outcast, the degraded! Ha, ha! Yes, and the revenged! 'Twas I led them on, and this hand lit the fire brand, and I am satisfied.

WESTWOOD. Seize him! 'Tis the instigator—the ringleader!

[*They attempt to seize him.*

RUSHTON [*in a menacing attitude*]. Approach not, or your grave is at my feet!

[*They retreat, intimidated.*

WESTWOOD. Cowards, do you fear a madman? Surrender, idiot, fiend, wretch, outcast, or this shall tame thee!

[*Presents a pistol.*

ALLEN. Rushton, you escape, I care not.

WESTWOOD. Ah! then stir but one foot, and—

RUSHTON. And what? [*Seizes him by the collar and hurls him to the ground,* WESTWOOD *firing the pistol.*] Away, I say!

JANE. Oh, fly—fly, George!

> [WESTWOOD *attempts to rise.* RUSHTON *stands over him and, waving the ember, secures the retreat of* ALLEN. *As he is rushing out, the scene closes.*

——————

SCENE III. *Exterior of an Out-house or Hovel, in Lane. Moonlight.*

Enter ALLEN, *frantic, as if pursued.*

ALLEN. Where shall I fly? My brain is giddy, my legs feeble. I can no further. Oh, my wife—Jane, Jane—my children, too!

> [*Falls exhausted.*

WILSON *and* HATFIELD *look out from hovel.*

HATFIELD. It was Allen's voice, I'm sure, yet I see no one.

WILSON. See, who lies there?   [*They come out.*

HATFIELD. Ah, it is he!

WILSON. What is this? Not dead—killed himself! Allen—Allen!

HATFIELD. Allen, lad!

ALLEN [*staring*]. Ah, who calls on Allen? Was't my wife— my children! I'm here! Don't you see me? What—what's—

> [*Looks about wildly.*

WILSON. Allen, it's but us, your old friends, Wilson and Hatfield. Don't you know us?

ALLEN. Ah, is it? [*They assist him to rise. He clasps their hands earnestly.*] Have you seen my wife—my children?

HATFIELD. I thought you'd been to see them.

ALLEN. Ah, I remember! Like a wild dream it comes across my brain; but where—where's the rest—Smith and—

> [*Voices without cry* 'This way—this way!'

ALLEN. Ah, they come!

HATFIELD. In—in there! Would you be taken?

ALLEN. I care not. Ah, 'tis he—'tis Rushton! Never will I fly. He who would desert his comrade in the hour of peril is worse than coward.

Enter RUSHTON *in haste, followed by* WESTWOOD *and* SOLDIERS.

WESTWOOD. Ah, here are the rest. Seize them all and spare none.

RUSHTON. Hell-hounds, would you murder the poor wretches you have deprived of bread!

WESTWOOD. Villain, have you not deprived me of bread, and set fire to my dwelling, reckless who might perish in the flame?

RUSHTON. That *you had*, then justice had been done and my revenge satisfied!

WESTWOOD. Officer, your duty! Let them not escape.

OFFICER. In the King's name, I desire you to yield!

HATFIELD. Never!

RUSHTON. That's right, my lads—never yield!

[*They stand on the defensive.*

OFFICER. Then at your peril!

[*Presents pistol.* SOLDIERS *advance and a confused combat ensues, ending in the disarming of* HATFIELD *and* WILSON, *and capture of* ALLEN *with a wound across his forehead.*

At that moment JANE ALLEN *enters, distracted.*

JANE [*she screams on seeing her husband wounded and taken*]. Oh, mercy—mercy, my husband! Do not—do not murder him! Oh, George!   [*Kneels and clasps him round the knee.*

ALLEN. Who calls on George Allen?

JANE. It is thy wife! Don't you know me? Thy wife, you know, George. Jane, Jane, thy wife!

ALLEN. Ah, Jane, my doom is fixed! Leave me, and clasp those who are helpless—my little ones!

RUSHTON. There, monster, dost thou see that? Thy doing.

WESTWOOD. 'Tis false! Liar, fiend, reprobate!

RUSHTON. 'Tis true! Liar, fiend, and reprobate again! Didst thou not turn these poor men from their honest employ to beg, steal, starve, or do as they have done—be revenged?

ALLEN. Peace, peace, it is over now! Jane, I feel my life fast ebbing! Home, home!

WESTWOOD. Away with them!

JANE. Oh, pity, mercy! Tear him not away from me.

OFFICER. The law's imperative!

> [*The* SOLDIERS *march them off.* JANE *falls fainting.*
> JANE *is lying senseless.* MARY *enters.*

MARY. Mother, mother, where are you? Oh, what do I see on the cold ground? It can't be mother? Mother! [*Approaches nearer.*] Mother! Oh, it can't be my mother—she would hear me—yet it looks my mother! Oh, dear, it is, I know it can be no other! Mother, mother! [*Cries and falls on her mother.*] Mother, why don't you speak? Mother!

> [*Kneels and kisses her.* JANE, *recovering, looks about her in wild disorder.*

JANE. Where am I?

MARY. Here, mother, on the cold ground!

JANE [*seeing her child*]. Ah, my child, bless you—bless you! But what are we doing here in the open air?

MARY. You came out after father, mother.

JANE. Your father! [*Screams.*] Ah, I now remember all! They are tearing him from me, to take him to a loathsome dungeon! All now crosses me like a wild dream. The factory—the red sky—flames whirling in the air! My eye-balls seem cracked—my brain grows dizzy—I hear chains and screams of death! My husband—they shall not tear him from me!

MARY. Mother, mother, where are you going?

JANE. To thy father—to the gaol—they will not refuse his poor, weak, and broken-hearted wife!

MARY. Nor me either, will they, mother?

JANE [*takes her up*]. Bless you—bless you! Never, never shall they part us!

> [*Exeunt.*

SCENE IV. *Interior of a Justice Room.*

The JUSTICE *and* CLERK *discovered seated at table.* GEORGE
ALLEN, SIMS, WILSON, *and* HATFIELD *discovered handcuffed.*
WESTWOOD, CONSTABLES, OFFICER, *and* SOLDIERS, *dragging
in* RUSHTON, *struggling.*

RUSHTON. Why do you drag me thus? Do you think I'm afraid?
Do you think I fear to own that I was the man who led them
on? No! I glory in the act—'tis the sweet triumph I've oft
longed for!

BIAS. Silence, sirrah!

RUSHTON. I speak or am silent as I please! Talking is not
hanging, is it? What are you more than I am? I remember
when you were overseer—the man appointed to protect the
poor.

BIAS. And what has that to do with the present business?

RUSHTON. It has this—to show that an honest man at least
should sit in that seat, and not one who has crept into it by
robbery and oppression.

BIAS. Maniac!

RUSHTON. Aye, but I was not so when the cart, laden with
provisions for the workhouse, by your order stopped at your
own door to pretend to deliver some articles ordered for
yourself, but which belonged to the poor famished creatures
who had no redress but the lash if they dared to complain.

BIAS. It is false!

RUSHTON. Is it false, too, that through your means alone, when
but seven years of age, I was condemned to six weeks' hard
labour in a prison for stealing, as you called it, but a handful
of apples from your orchard?

BIAS. 'Tis false, or why not have made your charge before? Is
it to be supposed one so vindictive, a common thief, an incendiary, would have concealed this so long? The law is open
to you, is it not?

RUSHTON. No; I am poor!

BIAS. And what of that? The law is made alike for rich and poor.

RUSHTON. Is it? Why, then, does it so often lock the poor man in a gaol, while the rich one goes free?

BIAS. No more of this. Clerk, draw out the commitment!

RUSHTON. Commitment? Who would you commit? Not these poor men. 'Twas I broke into and destroyed the engines of power. 'Twas I set fire to the mass, and reduced to ashes what has reduced others to beggary. Think you I regret— think you I fear? No, I glory in the act. There! I have confessed, and as in me you see the avenger of the poor man's wrongs, on me, and me alone, heap your vengeance.

BIAS. Clerk, record the prisoner's confession; and Charles George Westwood, proprietor of the factory and buildings adjoining thereunto, lately burnt, stand forth and make your further allegations, and name the prisoners charged in this atrocious act.

WESTWOOD. I charge all the prisoners now standing here as being concerned in the destruction of the factory, dwelling-house, and out-houses. First, their leader there, William, or Will Rushton, as I believe he is called; second, John Hatfield; third, Walter Sims; fourth, Francis Wilson; fifth, Joseph Smith, not here through being wounded; sixth, and last, George Allen.

BIAS. And this you are willing to swear?

WESTWOOD. I am.

BIAS. Prisoners, you have heard the charge, have you aught to say?

HATFIELD. No! If it is to be, let it be; we may as well die on a scaffold as be starved!

WILSON. Don't look down, George; let's bear it up like men.

ALLEN. Yet my wife and children!

BIAS. 'Tis well. This silence shows a proper sense of shame. 'Tis written, they who defy the law must suffer by the law. Prisoners, though it is not my duty to pronounce judgment, still I deem it so to apprize you of the fate likely to await you. To-morrow will commence the assizes at the neighbouring town, where you will be removed and arraigned before a tribunal, which will hear your defence, and give the verdict according to the evidence produced. Further I have naught to say. Officer, remove the prisoners.

JANE [*without*]. Unhand me, I will enter!

She enters. ALLEN *conceals himself.*

He is here—must be here! Is it that agony has dimmed my sight, or that reason has left her seat and madness mocks me? [*Sees him.*] Ah, he's there! Oh, George, is this the end of all our former bliss? Torn from me, and for ever? My husband, he whom I have pressed to my breast—my heart's blood—the father of my children—oh horror, horror, exposed like a common felon to the gaze of thousands on a gibbet! Hung? Oh, my heart sickens! No, no, it cannot be—must not be! Never shall it be said that my husband, George Allen, died like a felon, a common robber, a murderer!

BIAS. Seize this frantic woman, and let her be removed.

[*They approach to take her.*

JANE. Oh, touch me not! Off—off, I say! Yet have pity on me, I know not what I say. A whirlwind rushes through my brain! [*Falls at* WESTWOOD's *feet clasping his knees.*] Mercy—mercy, to you I kneel! Pity my poor husband, and I will pray for thee, work for thee; my children, all—all, shall be your slaves for ever—ever, but spare him!

WESTWOOD. Cling not to me, justice shall have its due!

[*Spurns her from him.*

RUSHTON. Spurn a helpless and imploring woman, whose heart is broken—whose mind is crazed? If her *voice* is weak, my *arm* is not. Justice shall have its due. Die, tyrant! Quick, to where water quencheth not!

[*Fires.* WESTWOOD *falls, and the curtain drops on picture of* RUSHTON *standing in centre, laughing hysterically, pointing at* WESTWOOD. JANE *in the arms of* ALLEN. HATFIELD, SIMS, *and* WILSON, *in an attitude of surprise, the* SOLDIERS *with their muskets levelled at* RUSHTON.

HOW TO SETTLE ACCOUNTS
WITH YOUR LAUNDRESS

AN ORIGINAL FARCE IN ONE ACT

BY

JOSEPH STIRLING COYNE (1803–1868)

═══

First performed at the Adelphi Theatre
26 July 1847

═══

CAST

WHITTINGTON WIDGETTS, a West-end tailor	Mr. Wright
BARNEY TWILL, Widgetts's page and light porter	
	Mr. Ryan
JACOB BROWN, a hairdresser at the opera	Mr. Munyard
POSTMAN	Mr. Lindon
WAITER	Mr. Mitchenson
MLLE. CHERI BOUNCE, an opera dancer	Miss E. Harding
MARY WHITE, a young laundress	Miss Woolgar

SCENE. *A Tailor's Show-room, Jermyn-street, handsomely fitted up with cheval-glass, large round table in centre, fashionable chairs, &c. A dummy figure, dressed in the extreme mode, near window. Articles of gentlemen's attire exhibited in window,* L. *Door of entrance to street,* L. *Fire-place and chimney glass,* R. *Door to* WIDGETTS's *chamber,* R. *Large pair of folding-doors,* C., *opening towards the stage; beyond these doors a passage to the kitchen, in which stands a stillion, with a water-butt standing on it. At the end of this passage, the door of the kitchen. A round table,* C., *with writing materials and lighted candle upon it. A print of the fashions and tailor's patterns cut in brown paper on the wall. Table at back,* L., *on which is a table lamp. Another table at back,* R., *on which is a bottle of brandy and glasses.* TWILL *discovered brushing the coat on the dummy figure, and singing a verse of an Irish song. A postman's knock at door,* L.

TWILL. Whist! I'll bet a pinny that's the post. [*Runs to door and opens it;* POSTMAN *appears.*]

POSTMAN. Mr. Widgetts. [*Gives letter to* TWILL.]

TWILL. Thank you, sir. Maybe you've got a bit of a letter for me, from my poor mother in Ireland? I'm not particular—the first that comes to hand in the bundle will do.

POSTMAN. No, I haven't one for you.

TWILL. Thank you, sir. Maybe you'd have one the next time. Good-bye, sir. [POSTMAN *goes away.* TWILL *reads the address on the letter.*] 'Whittington Widgetts, Esquire.' Ow wow! Esquire! The devil a ha'porth less. 'Whittington Widgetts, Esquire, Hierokosma, Jarmyn Street.' Hierokosma! That's French for a tailor's shop. By the Attorney-General, 'twould give a man a headache in his elbow to write such a cramp word. [*Smells the letter.*] Why then, it smells elegant intirely. [*Goes to door* R. *and enters while speaking.*] Mr. Widgetts, here's a letter for you, sir.
     [*Returns immediately from the room, re-commences his song, and begins to brush the figure again. A church clock in the neighbourhood strikes eight.*

WIDGETTS. Twill!   [*Speaking from the door of chamber.*

TWILL. There, listen to that row. That master of mine will persist in calling me Twill, though he knows my name is Barney Toole, because Twill, he says, is genteeler.

WIDGETTS. What o'clock is that, Twill?

TWILL. Eight o'clock, sir.

WIDGETTS. Put up the shutters.

TWILL. What the devil can he mean? We never shut until nine o'clock.

Enter WIDGETTS *from chamber, kissing a note which he holds.*

WIDGETTS. Well, don't you hear me? Put up the shutters and close the establishment, directly.

TWILL. Of coorse, sir; never say it twice.
[TWILL *runs out and is seen putting up the window shutters outside.*

WIDGETTS. This night I devote to the tender union of love and lobsters. The adorable Ma'amselle Cheri Bounce, the ballet dancer, at last consents to partake a little quiet supper with me here this evening. I must read her charming note once more. 'Ma'amselle Cheri Bounce presents compliments to Mr. Whittington Widgetts, will feel happy to sup with Mr. W. W. this evening. Ma'amselle C. B. fears that female notions don't correspond with supping with a single gent, but lobsters is stronger than prudence, therefore trusts to indulgence; at nine o'clock precise. P.S. I'll come in my blue *visite* and my native innocence, and hopes you'll treat them with proper delicacy.' Glorious! Angelic creature! [*Kisses the letter and puts it in his waistcoat pocket.*] Oh, Widgetts, you lucky rascal, to have the happiness of a private and confidential supper with that magnificent girl, whose image has never left my mind since the evening I danced with her at the Casino! Twill!

Enter TWILL.

TWILL. Sir?

WIDGETTS. You must run directly to the tavern over the way, and order them to send a roast fowl and lobster in the shell, here at nine o'clock.

TWILL. Roast fowl, sir?

WIDGETTS. And lobster. He—hem! I expect a particular **party** to sup with me.

TWILL. Coorse you'll want cigars, sir?

WIDGETTS. No. The party, Twill, is a lady and don't **smoke**.

TWILL. A lady! Tare my agers, sir. Does the lady bring **the** lady's maid with her?

WIDGETTS. Don't be impertinent, Twill, but listen to me. **The** party I expect is Ma'amselle Cheri Bounce, a splendid creature, who dances on a limited income, with the strictest regard to propriety, at the Opera House, and gives lessons to private pupils in the *pokar* and the waltz *ah do tongs*.

TWILL. Whoo! She must be a switcher. [*Going.*] I'll run directly, sir!

WIDGETTS. Stay; I must make myself attractive for the inter-esting occasion. Give me the coat that has just been finished for Sir Chippin Porrage, and the waistcoat that's to be sent home to-morrow morning for the Honourable Cecil Harrowgate's wedding. [TWILL *hands a dress coat and waist-coat from the table*, L.] I'll give them an air of gentility by wearing them this evening. That will do. There, be off now.

TWILL. Ha, ha! By the powers o' war, when you get them on your back, sir, you'll be like Mulligan's dog; your own father wouldn't know you.

WIDGETTS *carries the coat and waistcoat into his bed-room.* TWILL *is going towards door, when* MARY WHITE *enters, carrying a basket of clothes under her arm.*

MARY. Here, Twill, take my basket, good chap. Is master at home?

TWILL. [*Takes basket.*] Yes, he *is* at home. [*Aside.*] Take my basket—good chap—well, there's no bearing the impidence of the lower orders. [*Sets down basket, and calls at door*, R.] Please, sir, here's the laundress come for your clothes. [*Aside.*] Good chap! [*Exit.*

Enter WIDGETTS.

WIDGETTS. [*Aside.*] She always comes at an awkward crisis. Mary, my dear, you're rather late this evening.

MARY. Oh dear, yes. I've been half over the town for my

customers' washing and I'm almost tired to death, but I left yours for last, that we might have a comfortable chat together. Stop a minute though, till I take off my clogs.

[She goes into the kitchen passage through the folding-doors.

WIDGETTS. The poor creature loves me to distraction, but she's painfully familiar; she forgets that our positions are materially altered since I was a journeyman tailor in a two pair back, struggling to make love and trowsers for the small remuneration of fifteen shillings a week. Mary White is an uncommon nice girl—as a laundress, but my sentiments is changed respecting her as a wife.

Re-enter MARY.

MARY. Now, Widgy dear—oh, good gracious, what a love of a waistcoat you've on! Let me look at it, do! Well, it's a real beauty.

WIDGETTS. Stylish, eh? The last Paris touch.

MARY. You used not to wear such waistcoats as that when you lived in Fuller's Rents.

WIDGETTS. Oh no, no! Ha, ha! *[Aside.]* I wish she'd cut Fuller's Rents.

MARY. Do you know, Widgy, I don't think you're at all improved since you fell in for that fortune by a legacy you never expected. When you lived in Fuller's Rents you used to walk out with me on a Sunday; you never walk with me at all now.

WIDGETTS. Walking's vulgar, my dear.

MARY. And you sometimes used to take me at half-price to the theatres.

WIDGETTS. Theatres is low, my dear.

MARY. And you remember how we used to go together to Greenwich, with a paper of ham sandwiches in my basket, and sit under the trees in the park, and talk, and laugh—law, how we used to laugh to be sure—and then you used to talk of love and constancy and connubial felicity in a little back parlour, and a heap of beautiful things.

WIDGETTS. *[Aside.]* A heap of rubbish.

MARY. And you know, Widgy dear, when we enter that happy state—

WIDGETTS. What state do you allude to, Miss White?

MARY. The marriage state, of course.

WIDGETTS. Oh, indeed. Ah!

MARY. You don't forget, I hope, that I have your promissory note on the back of twenty-nine unpaid washing bills to make me your lawful wife. [*Produces several papers.*] There they are —and there's the last of them. 'Six months after date I promise to marry Miss Mary White.' There, sir, you're due next Monday.

WIDGETTS. Am I! Then I'm afraid I shan't be prepared to take myself up. I'll let myself be protested.

MARY. No, you shan't; you've been protested often enough. I can't be put off any longer, and understand me, Mr. Widgetts, I *won't* neither.

WIDGETTS. [*Aside.*] There's a savage hymeneal look in her eye that makes me shiver in my Alberts. I must soothe her a little or I shall have a scene. Why, Mary my dear, now don't be angry; you know it's one of my jokes.

MARY. Well, you'd better not try any more of them, for I don't like them. No woman does.

WIDGETTS. No, of course, no woman does. Ha, ha, ha! Quite proper too, my dear.

MARY. Well, now that matter's settled, I'll go and collect your soiled things, for it's getting late.

WIDGETTS. Do so, Mary; you'll find them in my room as usual. I'll make out the list as you call them out. [MARY *enters room*, R., *and* WIDGETTS *prepares to write.*] She's resolved to make me her victim and I don't know how to get rid of her. I'd give—

MARY. [*Inside.*] Four shirts.

WIDGETTS. [*Writes.*] Four shirts. She's a perfect treasure at shirt buttons, but what is shirt buttons to a bosom that beats for another?

MARY. [*Inside.*] One false front.

WIDGETTS. [*Writes.*] One false front. She'd make a comfortable little wife if she only had—

MARY. [*Inside.*] A pair of white trowsers.

WIDGETTS. [*Writes.*] A pair of white trowsers. Ah! I wore those ducks at the Casino last Wednesday, and Ma'amselle Cheri Bounce observed, while I was handing her a glass of champagne—ecod, 'tis well I recollected it—I've forgotten to order champagne for my supper. I must run over to the tavern myself and tell them to send some.

[*Snatches up his hat and exit.*

Enter MARY, *with the white waistcoat worn at first by* WIDGETTS, *and a note in her hand.*

MARY. Well, you're a pretty careless fellow, to leave your letters in your waistcoat pocket. Where is he gone to? [*Examines the note curiously.*] 'Whittington Widgetts, Esq.' It's a woman's hand. I've a good mind to read it. I've no secrets from him and he has none from me—or at least he oughtn't to; so it can be no harm. [*Opens note and reads hastily.*] 'Ma'amselle Cheri Bounce'—ah!—'compliments— happy to sup with Mr. W. W. this evening—female notions —single gent—lobsters is stronger than prudence—therefore trusts to indulgence, at nine o'clock precise.' Oh, the minx! 'P.S. I'll come in my blue *visite* and my native innocence.' Oh, Widgetts, the false deceitful wretch! To deceive me and wash out all his promises; to wring my heart and mangle my affections like that. [*Sobbing.*] But I—I—don't care not a pin's point, no—I despise him and hate him worse than poison, and I'll—I'll—I'll—tell him so. [*Sobbing.*] I'll—I'll—

Enter JACOB BROWN.

BROWN. [*Angrily.*] Where's Widgetts! I want to see Widgetts.

MARY. Then you want to see a good-for-nothing fellow.

BROWN. Exactly, and I shouldn't mind adding that I consider him an humbug.

MARY. A wretch!

BROWN. Most decidedly.

MARY. A puppy!

BROWN. Not a doubt of it. You see we're unanimous in our verdict. That man, ma'am, has been a *reptile* in my path, a *wiper* to all my hopes, and an *adder* to all my woes; he has lacerated my heart and singed the tender buds of young affection here. [*Lays his hands on his bosom.*

MARY. Ah! What has he done?

BROWN. He has *done me*, ma'am, *me*, Brown; that's what he's done. Cut me out with Ma'amselle Cheri Bounce.

MARY. Cheri Bounce! Ah! [*Aside.*] She that's to sup tonight with Widgetts.

BROWN. I'm an 'airdresser, ma'am; my name's Brown, and I've a professional engagement at the Opera House, where I cultivate romance and ringlets amongst the ladies of the ballet. There I first beheld the lovely Cheri Bounce, the very image of the wax Wenus in my shop window. I loved her, not for her foreign grace, but for her native hair. Oh, she had such a head of real hair, and, oh, the showers of tears and the bottles of Macassar oil that I've poured upon it nobody would believe! Well, I toasted her for two years regularly, and at length she consented to become *Brown*. Well, we were to have been married; I had bought my wedding suit, when this fellow Widgetts came to take the curl out of my happiness. We quarrelled about him last Saturday, and grew so warm that we've been cool ever since. But that's not all. This very day I heard that she had accepted an invitation to sup with him to-night, but I'll prevent *that*; he shall fight me—one of us must fall—let him choose his own weapons—curling irons if he likes.

MARY. Don't be rash, Brown. Widgetts has deceived *me* and wronged *you*; we must take a better way of being revenged on him.

BROWN. How? What way? Tell me! I'll do anything to be down on Widgetts.

MARY. Then you must assist me in a scheme I've just thought of. Here, carry this stuffed gentleman into the kitchen there.
[*Pointing to dummy figure.*

BROWN. This chap! Come along, old fellow. [*Takes him up.*] Why, he's a regular railway speculator—nothing but a man of straw.

MARY. [*Taking a gown and other articles of female attire out of her basket.*] Aye, here's a gown, petticoat, and stockings, [*Takes a pair of green boots out of her pocket.*] and a pair of green boots. Now, Brown, you must dress the figure in these clothes.

[*Gives him clothes.*

BROWN. Dress him in these! Why, bless you, I don't know how. I'm not a lady's maid.

MARY. Oh, never mind; you'll manage very well. There, make haste, and do as I tell you.

BROWN. Well, I'm only made to order, so I'll try and do my best.

[*Exit through the folding-doors into the passage and then through the door beyond into kitchen.*

MARY. Now to write to Widgetts and tell him of my melancholy end. [*Writes and reads.*] 'Base man—I have discovered the truth of your falsity, and know all about the lobsters and the creetur that's to sup with you to-night. Oh, Widgetts! Once, you swore to love none but Mary *White*—but now your vows is *blew* to the winds. I shan't trouble you no more with my *mangled* feelings, for I'm going to drown myself in the water-butt in your kitchen, where you'll find me. Adieu, Widgetts—I forgive you, but I know that my ghost and them lobsters will sit heavy on your stomach to-night; so no more at present from your departed—MARY WHITE.'

Enter BROWN.

BROWN [*Showing the figure dressed in the clothes given him by* MARY.] Here she is; will she do?

MARY. Oh, beautifully! Ha, ha, ha, ha! I can't help laughing at the droll figure I cut. [*Folds and directs the letter.*] There lies the train that's to blow up Widgetts. Now, Brown, we must pop her head-downwards into the water-butt.

BROWN. Well, that's easily done.

MARY. [WIDGETTS *heard singing in the street.*] Hark! I hear Widgetts coming—quick, we must get out by the back door quietly.

[*Exeunt into the passage, closing the folding-doors after them.*

Enter WIDGETTS *by street door.*

WIDGETTS. I've ordered the champagne—these opera girls all drink champagne, when they can get it. I wonder is *she* here still. [*Looks into chamber.*] Ah, bravo! She's gone. [*Sees the letter on table.*] Ah, a letter—for me! [*Opens it carelessly, starts and reads to himself.*] Oh, oh, oh! What? 'Mary White—I'm going to drown myself in the water-butt, where you'll find me.' Gracious powers! 'Adieu, Widgetts, I forgive you.' Poor dear soul. 'But my ghost and them lobsters will sit heavy on your stomach to-night.' Horrible idea! It can't be true—she'd never go to commit such a catastrophe in my establishment. Make a coroner's inquest of herself in my private water-butt, when the Thames is open to all! No, she's only said so to frighten me. [*Throws letter on the floor and goes to folding doors.*] Why, Mary, Mary, my dear, don't be foolish, ha, ha, ha, ha! I know it's one of your jokes, ha, ha! Little rogue— ha, ha, ha, ha! [*Throws open folding doors and discovers the dummy figure, which has been dressed in female garments, with the legs and part of the dress sticking out of the water-butt, a pair of women's green boots on the feet of the figure.* WIDGETTS *totters back, horrified at the sight.*] Oh, oh, oh! She's done it; she's there, with her legs sticking out of the water-butt, and her green Sunday boots on her feet—and the vital spark extinct! Oh! It's too dreadful a sight for human feelings: them legs, and them green boots. [*Returns and closes the folding doors.*] What an awful sensation 'twill make when its found out; they'll have my *head* in all the print-shops and my *tale* in all the newspapers—I shall be brought out at half the theatres too. They'll make *three* shocking acts of one fatal act at the Victoria, and they'll have the real water and water-butt at the Surrey. What's to be done? I'm in a desperate state of mind, and feel as if I could take my own measure for an unmade coffin.

Enter TWILL, *at the last words.*

TWILL. I've ordered it, sir, for nine precisely.

WIDGETTS. [*Starts.*] Ordered it? What?

TWILL. The fowl and the lobster in the shell.

WIDGETTS. Oh! Ha! I was thinking of another *shell*. Ha, ha, ha, ha! Light the lamp, Twill. [*With forced gaiety.*] We'll have a jolly night, ha, ha, ha, ha!

Old King Cole was a jolly old soul, and a jolly old soul was he;
He called for his pipe, and he called for his bowl,
    And he called for his fiddlers three.

TWILL. Aye, master, that's the way to drown old care.

WIDGETTS. Drown who, sir? Do you mean sir, that any one is drowned in this establishment?

TWILL. Me sir, not I, sir—I only—

WIDGETTS. Go and lay the table for supper.

> [TWILL *picks up* MARY's *letter from the floor, twists it into an allumette, and, lighting it at the candle, lights with it the lamp on table at back.* WIDGETTS *walks about in a state of agitation and endeavours to sing.*

WIDGETTS. It's an awful business—but at all events they can't charge me with the deed. I have her letter to prove she made away with herself; *that* will clear me. [*Searches his pockets hastily.*] Where is it? What have I done with it? [*Looking about the floor.*] Eh! No, no! Twill, Twill, have you seen a letter lying about here?

TWILL. Letter! I found a piece of crumpled paper on the floor that I've lighted the lamp with; there's a bit of it left though.
> [*Gives him a fragment of the burnt letter.*

WIDGETTS. [*Glances hastily at it.*] Oh, heivings! You've lighted the lamp, and snuffed out the candle of my precious existence!

TWILL. Why, what's the matter, Mr. Widgetts? You are going to faint; stop till I'll fetch you a glass of water from the water-butt.

WIDGETTS. [*Interposing to prevent* TWILL *going to the kitchen.*] Water! Forbear!

TWILL. Bless me, how dreadful you look!

WIDGETTS. Do I? Ah, very likely! I've been seized with a sudden swimming in the water-butt—the head—the head, I mean.

TWILL. By my sowl—I see how it is: the murder's out.

WIDGETTS. [*Collaring him.*] Murder—what murder do you allude to? Who's done it, sir? Speak!

TWILL. Asy, Mr. Widgetts—asy, sir—sure I know you've been taking a drop too much.

WIDGETTS. A drop! [*Aside.*] The word puts me in a cold perspiration. Oh, aye—ha, ha, ha! You may go, Twill; I shan't want you any longer. Stop! You haven't had any enjoyment lately; there's an order for the Adelphi; go there my boy, and be happy. [*Gives him a card.*]

TWILL. Oh, thank you, sir, may be I'm not a lucky boy.
[*Exit hastily.*

WIDGETTS. Now he's gone, I can reflect upon my terrible situation. *She* must be removed—but how? That's the point.
[*He stands, buried in thought.*

Enter MARY, *disguised as a boy, wearing an old blouse.*

MARY. Aei—aei—yoo—

WIDGETTS. Eh! Who are you? What do you want?

MARY. E-eh? You must speak up; I'm rather hard of hearing.

WIDGETTS. [*Bawling.*] I say, what do you want?

MARY. I'm Mary White the laundress's young man, and I'm come to carry home her basket of clothes.

WIDGETTS. The devil! [*Speaking very loud.*] She's gone, my good fellow; she's been gone these two hours.

MARY. Two hours! Well, I'm in no hurry; I can stop, but I may as well eat my supper while I'm waiting. I've got a plummy slice of ham in my pocket, [*Pulls a crust of bread and a slice of ham, wrapped in a play-bill, from her pocket.*] and a play-bill too, for a table-cloth. [*Spreading bill on table.*] I think that's coming it rather genteel. [*Takes a clasp knife out of her pocket.*] Fond of ham, old fellow?

WIDGETTS. Why, you impudent young vagabond, you don't mean to say you're going to sup here? Be off, and be damn'd to you.

MARY. Well, you *are* a regular brick, and I don't mind if I do take some of your pickles.

WIDGETTS. [*Bawls.*] Zounds! I say, you mustn't sup here.

MARY. Mustn't sup here? Why didn't you say so at once? Never mind, I'll go into the kitchen and take it there. [*Going.*

WIDGETTS. [*Alarmed.*] To the kitchen! [*Holds her.*] Not for the world; you quite misunderstood me—don't disturb yourself; sit down, do. [*Pushes her again into the chair—aside.*] What's to become of me? I'd pitch him into the street, only I'm afraid of making a disturbance. There's no making him hear. Ecod! I know what I'll do; I'll run and borrow the speaking-trumpet that I saw this morning hanging at Smith, the broker's, door, and speak to him through that. [*Going, returns.*] Stay, the devil might tempt him to peep into the kitchen; I'll lock the door.

[*Locks the folding-door, goes through pantomime, expressive of sorrow for his victim in the water-butt, and exit.*]

MARY. [*Jumping up and laughing.*] Ha, ha, ha, ha, ha! Ho, ho, ho, ho! Oh, dear, never was anything managed so cleverly. Ha, ha, ha, ha! [*Throwing off cap and neckerchief.*] To think that he didn't know me, and what a rage he was in. Well, now I'm ready for him in another character. [*Takes off her leggings and blouse, and appears dressed as a young man of fashion. Surveys herself in the cheval-glass.*] Yes, it will do—it will do—a very smart little fellow, not extensive, but uncommonly well got up. These were the clothes that poor Brown got to be married in; they fit me to a nicety. [*Knock at door.*] Come in.

Enter two WAITERS, *carrying tray with supper, covered dishes, plates, bottles, glasses, &c.*

WAITER. Supper, sir, ordered by Mr. Widgetts.

MARY. Supper! Oh, yes. All right. Mr. Widgetts is out, but he'll be back presently; leave it on this table if you please. [WAITER *places tray on table at back,* R.] There, that will do; plates, knives, and forks. All right—you need not wait, young man.

WAITER. Thank you, sir. Anything else, sir?

MARY. No; everything is beautiful, thank you.

WAITER. Thank you, sir. Good night, sir.

MARY. Good night. [*Exit* WAITERS. MARY *looks under the covers.*] Lobsters, roast fowl, kidneys. Ah! the ungrateful wretch never asked me to such a supper, but never mind. Hark, I hear him returning.

[*She throws the blouse, hat, and gaiters, into the clothes-basket and carries all into the chamber.*

Enter WIDGETTS.

WIDGETTS. [*Shouting through speaking-trumpet.*] Now young fell—low I sa—a—ay! Hey! he's gone and the coast's clear. [*Sees supper-tray.*] Oh! What! They've sent the supper from the tavern. I quite forgot it. Dear me, this dreadful affair has so upset me and given me such a turn that I doubt I'll never come straight again. What will Ma'amselle Cheri Bounce think of me? I dare say she's been here and gone? Everybody's gone but my interesting victim. Ah! She's still there, standing with all her imperfections on her head in the water-butt. Well, I suppose every one has his lot, but mine's a lot I don't know how to dispose of. I must remove the body from the establishment at all events, and I'll do it now while the house is still. [*Goes to folding-doors and puts key in the lock.*] Oh! I haven't strength to open the door with them green boots kicking at my conscience. Courage, Widgetts, courage! Be a man— though you are but a tailor. Stay, I'll take a thimbleful of brandy first. [*Takes bottle from table and pours out a glass which he drinks.*] Ah, that's a reviver. [*Drinks and comes down.*] Betts has raised the standard of British spirit in my heart. [*Drinks.*] Well, we all want comfort in this miserable world. [*Drinks.*] There's poor Mary White gone on a weeping and *wailing* voyage to that bourne from whence no traveller gets a return ticket. [MARY *laughs in room.*] Ah, what's that? A laugh—it had a hollow and inhuman sound—could it be *she*? [*Points to folding-doors.*] Mary—a—a—a—how do I know—she may have been turned into something horrible. The fiend of the water-butt, perhaps. She may come to me at night; she said she would. Oh, Lord! The idea of the ghost of a damp laundress at your back. [*Shudders.*] W—h—h—h—hew! [MARY *laughs.*] There, there it is again, that demoniac laugh. I wish I could peep into the kitchen, but I daren't lest I should see her glaring at me with one eye through the bung-hole of the water-butt. Bless me, how my knees keep giving double knocks upon each other! [MARY *sings in room.*] Ah! Surely that's singing. [*Listens.*] Ghosts haven't got a singing license. Hark! 'Tis somebody committing vocal violence in my bedroom. [*Goes to door of bed-chamber and looks in.*] Hey! there's a young fellow making himself quite at home in my establishment. I am not aware I ever saw him before. What had I better do? Go in and ask him what he wants—no—that might be dangerous; 'twill be safer in my present peculiar position to appear as a stranger. Let me see—I have it—capital idea—the waiter from the tavern with the supper—I think I could do a waiter; it's only, 'Coming, sir, in *one* minute, coming; two brandies and water, coming, sir.' [*He ties one of the supper napkins round his neck for a white cravat, changes his coat for an old black one that hangs on the back of a chair; while doing so he looks into the room now and again.*] There goes my Macassar oil and my Circassian cream. There, my *eau de cologne* too, that cost me half-a-guinea a bottle. An impudent rascal! D——n me if he's not rummaging my drawers! That's free and easy at all events. Come, I think I'm pretty well disguised now. [*Looks at himself in the cheval-glass.*] No, confound it! This face of mine will never do—it might be known—I want a pair of whiskers to hide it. Ecod, I've hit it again; this chair —[*Takes knife from table and cuts open the stuffed seat of the chair.*] there's enough hair in it to whisker a regiment of Turks.

[*Pulls a handful of the hair out of the chair-seat, goes to the chimney-glass and arranges it round his chin so as to look like a pair of large whiskers.*

Enter MARY, *still dressed as a young man, and drying her hands with a towel.*

MARY. [*Aside and laughing.*] Heavens, what a figure!

WIDGETTS. Hem! A—I beg your pardon—but you seem—a—eh?

MARY. Exactly. And who are you?

WIDGETTS. Me—I—a—ah—I'm—a—the waiter—from the tavern.

MARY. Perhaps, then, you can tell me where I can find Mr. Widgetts?

WIDGETTS. Not exactly. You've particular business with him?

MARY. Rather. In fact—I don't mind telling you—I'm one of the detective police.

WIDGETTS. [*Alarmed.*] You! A gentleman?

MARY. Oh yes, we go about in all manner of disguises when we want to pick up a shy bird. Now, I'm looking for Widgetts, and I shouldn't mind giving five pounds if you could tell me where to lay my hand upon him.

[*Lays her hand on* WIDGETTS's *shoulder, who starts.*

WIDGETTS. Ah! Ha, ha, ha! Five pounds! Is it a—very serious business, eh?

MARY. Merely a hanging matter.

WIDGETTS. Nothing more? [*Aside.*] The dreadful deed's discovered. I'll be off. Hem! Well, I'll go and look after Mr. Widgetts.

MARY. No, no, you must stop here; I've no doubt I shall want you presently.

Enter MADEMOISELLE CHERI BOUNCE.

CHERI. I beg pardon.

WIDGETTS. [*Aside.*] Zounds, Ma'amselle Cheri Bounce!

CHERI. I expected to meet a gent—Mr. Widgetts.

MARY. Who invited you to supper.

WIDGETTS. [*Aside.*] How did the fellow know that?

MARY. My friend Widgetts has been obliged to leave home rather suddenly, but he has left me here to perform the agreeable for him. Supper, you see, is waiting, ma'amselle.

WIDGETTS. [*Coming forward.*] Allow me to observe—

MARY. Lay the table.

WIDGETTS. [*Aside.*] The rascal's not going to·eat my supper!

[*Lays the table.*

CHERI. [*Aside.*] Really a very nice young man.

MARY. My name is Spraggs—Spraggs, ma'amselle—like my friend Widgetts I'm dotingly fond of the girls—aw—pawsitive fact—can't help it, never could, and don't think I ever shall. Let me take your shawl. [*Takes off* CHERI BOUNCE's *shawl.*] A divine figure—demme!

WIDGETTS. [*Coming between them.*] Allow me to observe—

MARY. Lay the table, *waiter*.

WIDGETTS. [*Aside.*] D—n the table.
   [*Lays the plates and dishes and places the chairs.* MARY *gallants* CHERI BOUNCE *apart.*

WIDGETTS. [*Polishing a plate; furiously.*] Here's a pleasant situation: waiter at my own supper, and afraid to open my mouth. The rascal's making love to her, and she likes it— hang 'em, I wish I could strangle them.
   [MARY *and* CHERI BOUNCE *laugh.*

CHERI. Oh, you droll wretch, you're ten times funnier than that stupid Widgetts.

MARY. Hang Widgetts.

WIDGETTS. [*Coming between them.*] I beg your pardon.

MARY. What d'ye want? Is the table laid?

WIDGETTS. [*Aside.*] D—n the table. [*Returns to table, and bawls out.*] Supper's ready!

MARY. Ah! [*To* CHERI BOUNCE.] Come, my dear.
   [WIDGETTS *seats himself at table.*
What!

WIDGETTS. [*Jumps up.*] Beg pardon—I vacate.
   [MARY *and* CHERI BOUNCE *seat themselves.*

MARY. Now, my dear ma'amselle, here are fowl, and lobster, and kidneys.

WIDGETTS. [*Aside.*] I wish they were sticking in his gizzard.

MARY. Now then, waiter, be alive, and take your tin.
   [*Claps one of the dish covers on* WIDGETTS'S *head, who snatches it off and flings it away in a rage.*

WIDGETTS. Allow me to observe—

MARY. There's no bread, my good fellow.

WIDGETTS. Coming. [*Aside.*] D—n the bread.
   [*Goes to a table at back, on which is a loaf of bread and rolls.*

MARY. What part of the fowl shall I send you, ma'amselle?

CHERI. The funny idea, Mr. Spraggs, if you please.

MARY. The funny idea; well, I never!

CHERI. The merry thought, you know.

MARY. Oh, to be sure, yes, the funny idea.   [*Cutting the fowl.*

WIDGETTS. Bread.
   [*Claps the loaf of bread on the dish before* MARY, *who throws it at him.*

MARY. Roll, stupid. Plates, waiter. [WIDGETTS *puts the roll under his arm, and hands plates to* MARY.] Allow me to add a kidney; they look beautiful.

CHERI. Thank you.
   [MARY *puts some fowl and a sausage on the plate, which she gives to* WIDGETTS *for* CHERI BOUNCE, *and then helps herself.*

WIDGETTS. [*Comes down with the plate in his hand.*] How uncommon savoury it smells! He's not looking.
   [*Takes the kidney off the plate, and puts it in his pocket.*

MARY. Waiter.
   [WIDGETTS *lays the plate before* CHERI BOUNCE.
   Open that champagne, waiter.

WIDGETTS. [*Aside.*] My champagne, too!
   [*Opening a bottle of champagne.*

MARY. [*Helps* CHERI BOUNCE.] I hope you liked your kidney.

CHERI. What kidney, Mr. Spraggs?

WIDGETTS. [*Snatching the kidney out of his pocket, and putting it, unperceived, on* CHERI BOUNCE's *plate.*] Why, *that* kidney.

CHERI. Dear me, I didn't perceive it before.
   [WIDGETTS *places champagne on the table.*

MARY. Celery, waiter.
   [WIDGETTS *goes to table at back for celery.* MARY *fills two glasses of champagne, and drinks with* CHERI BOUNCE. WIDGETTS *returns with stalks of celery in his coat pocket, and without being perceived takes the champagne bottle, fills a glass for himself, comes down and drinks.*
   I say, ma'amselle, this is rare fun.

CHERI. Glorious!

MARY. I'll give you, the absent Widgetts.

CHERI. I've no objection to drink poor Widgetts' health, but I don't at all wish for his company; he's such a particularly conceited fool.

WIDGETTS. [*Aside, and scarcely able to restrain himself.*] Do I look like a fool?   [*They drink.* WIDGETTS *comes to the table.*

As the sole surviving friend of Mr. Widgetts, will you allow me to say—
                              [*Presses the plate to his breast. Knock at door.*

MARY. Hold your tongue, and open the door.

CHERI. Perhaps 'tis Widgetts.

WIDGETTS. No it isn't; Widgetts is—elsewhere.
                              [*Knocking at door.*

BROWN. [*Outside.*] Open the door! I must come in.

CHERI. [*Alarmed.*] Heavens! That's Brown's voice. If he finds me here I shall be ruined.

WIDGETTS. Don't let him in.   [*Runs to door.*

CHERI. Where on earth can I conceal myself? Ah, here!
[*Throws open folding doors.* WIDGETTS *stands transfixed with terror;* CHERI BOUNCE *screams in a state of dreadful alarm.*] Oh, oh, oh! There's a woman drowned in the water-butt!

MARY. 'Tis Mary White, the laundress—Widgetts murdered her.

WIDGETTS. I'll be d——d if he did!

MARY. Never mind, he'll be hanged for it all the same.
            [*Exit through folding doors which she closes after her.*

WIDGETTS. Widgetts hanged! You might as well hang me.

CHERI. Good heavens! What a horrid place I've got into.
[*Knocking at door.* BROWN *outside calling,* 'Let me in! Open the door.'] Oh! That Brown will make another victim of *me*.
                              [*Runs into chamber.*

            Enter BROWN.

BROWN. Where is she? Where's Mademoiselle Cheri Bounce? I know she's here.

WIDGETTS. I beg your pardon—she left here half an hour ago. I called the cab for her myself, a patent hansom, No. 749.

BROWN. Where's Widgetts then? Where's the villain Widgetts, the destroyer of my happiness?

WIDGETTS. My good fellow, don't be outrageous! Mr. Widgetts is unfortunately absent—he's gone to close the eyes of a dying uncle, and won't be back to-night.

Enter TWILL.

TWILL. Oh, please, sir, they wouldn't admit the order at the Adelphi. [*Sees* WIDGETTS *and bursts into a fit of laughter.*] Ha, ha, ha, ha! Why, surely this ain't Guy Faux day, Mr. Widgetts?

BROWN. Widgetts!

CHERI. [*At door.*] Widgetts? [*Retires.*

TWILL. Of course! That's Mr. Widgetts, my master—I'll never deny him.

WIDGETTS. [*Aside.*] Then I've nothing for it but a bolt—out of my bed-room window.
[*Rushes into chamber.* CHERI BOUNCE *screams inside.* WIDGETTS *rushes out again followed by* CHERI BOUNCE *beating him with her umbrella.*

CHERI. Stop him! Don't let him escape—he has murdered a woman!

TWILL. Murdered a woman? Oh, the dirty blackguard! What a taste he had!
[BROWN *attempts to seize him, but* WIDGETTS *strikes his hat over his eyes, runs round the table, and runs to door,* L., *against which* TWILL *has placed his back.*

[*In a boxing attitude.*] No, you don't!
[BROWN *now collars him, and* CHERI BOUNCE *beats him with her umbrella.*

BROWN. Ha, have I got you at last—[*Shaking him.*] villain!

WIDGETTS. Help! Murder—police—help!

TWILL. [*Dancing at door.*] Police! Here's an illigant row—go it, little one—fire away, umbrella! She don't lay it into him at all.

WIDGETTS. Stop—stop—stop! Spare the remnant of an injured tailor's life. You think I cut off Mary White's thread, but I

G

didn't; the horrid act was her own deed. She got jealous of me and mixed her proud spirit with too much water; she'd tell you so herself, poor soul, if she could.

MARY. [*Speaking inside folding doors, in a solemn voice.*] No, she wouldn't.

WIDGETTS. Angels and bannisters support me. [*Drops on his knees.* CHERI BOUNCE *throws herself into the arms of* BROWN. *General consternation.*] 'Tis her voice—her ghost is come back to walk the earth in them green boots. Injured shade—speak for me, if ghosts have parts of speech, and tell them I'm innocent.

MARY. You caused my death by your falsity.

WIDGETTS. O-oh! I know it; but sooner than you should have made an object of yourself, I'd have married you ten times over.

MARY. And would you marry me now, if I was living?

WIDGETTS. I would—to-morrow morning.   [MARY *runs out.*

MARY. Then, Whittington, I'm your loving Mary again!

WIDGETTS. [*Jumps up and tries to avoid her; she follows him.*] Hollo! No—keep off. [*She embraces him.*] Hey! Bless me; you're neither damp or dead! On the contrary, you're remarkably warm and lively. But are you sure you're not a water nymph, and that you have not got private apartments in the Thames or the New River?

MARY. No, Widgy, don't be afraid; 'twas only a trick of mine to plague you for your inconstancy. [*Pointing to water-butt.*] She's not *me*, but the dummy figure dressed up in some of my clothes.

WIDGETTS. Ah! I've been finely hoaxed. And where's the detective policeman that eat my lobster and drank my wine?

MARY. Why, of course, he's here.   [*Points to herself.*

WIDGETTS. Oh, you villain! But what's to be done with Brown? [BROWN *and* CHERI BOUNCE, *who have been conversing at the back during the latter part of the dialogue, come down.*

BROWN. Ask ma'amselle here, for she's consented to be Mrs. Brown next Monday, and as for this little affair of the supper, I was in the plot with Mary.

WIDGETTS. I hope you were not in the water-butt with her; but, never mind, I don't want any further explanation. I've had my lesson—[*To audience.*] and I hope you have all profited by it. Now, if there's any single, good-looking young fellow here wants a bit of advice—eh, there's my friend, Smith. Smith, my dear boy, when you invite a female friend to a quiet bit of supper, mind there's no water-butt on the premises; and—I mention this confidentially to all you bachelors—if your laundress is young and pretty, you had better pay your washing bills regularly; and don't, like me, get yourself into a scrape by not knowing HOW TO SETTLE ACCOUNTS WITH YOUR LAUNDRESS.

BOX AND COX

A ROMANCE OF REAL LIFE IN ONE ACT

BY

JOHN MADDISON MORTON (1811–1891)

———

First performed at the Lyceum Theatre
1 November 1847

———

CAST

JOHN BOX, a journeyman printer	Mr. Buckstone
JAMES COX, a journeyman hatter	Mr. Harley
MRS. BOUNCER, a lodging-house keeper	Mrs. Macnamara

SCENE. *A room decently furnished; at* c. *a bed with curtains closed; at* L. C. *a door; at* L. *a door; at* L. *a chest of drawers; at back,* R., *a window; at* R. *a door; at* R. *fire-place, with mantel-piece; table and chairs; a few common ornaments on chimney-piece.* COX, *dressed with the exception of his coat, is looking at himself in a small looking-glass, which he holds in his hand.*

COX. I've half a mind to register an oath that I'll never have my hair cut again! [*His hair is very short.*] I look as if I had been just cropped for the Militia, and I was particularly emphatic in my instructions to the hairdresser only to cut the ends off. He must have thought I meant the other ends. Never mind; I shan't meet anybody to care about so early. Eight o'clock! I declare I haven't a moment to lose. Fate has placed me with the most punctual, particular and peremptory of hatters, and I must fulfil my destiny. [*Knock at door.*] Open locks, whoever knocks!

Enter MRS. BOUNCER.

MRS. BOUNCER. Good-morning, Mr. Cox. I hope you slept comfortably, Mr. Cox.

COX. I can't say I did, Mrs. Bouncer. I should feel obliged to you if you could accommodate me with a more protuberant bolster, Mrs. B. The one I've got now seems to me to have about a handful and a half of feathers at each end, and nothing whatever in the middle.

MRS. BOUNCER. Anything to accommodate you, Mr. Cox.

COX. Thank you. Then perhaps you'll be good enough to hold this glass while I finish my toilet.

MRS. BOUNCER. Certainly. [*Holding glass before* COX, *who ties on his cravat.*] Why, I do declare, you've had your hair cut!

COX. Cut! It strikes me I've had it mowed! It's very kind of you to mention it, but I'm sufficiently conscious of the absurdity of my personal appearance already. [*Puts on his coat.*] Now for my hat. [*Puts on his hat, which comes over his eyes.*] That's the effect of having one's hair cut. This hat fitted me quite tight before. Luckily I've got two or three more. [*Goes in and returns with three hats of different shapes, and puts them on, one after the other, all of which are too big for him.*] This is pleasant! Never mind. This one appears to me to wabble about rather less than the others—[*Puts on hat.*] and now I'm off! By the bye, Mrs. Bouncer, I wish to call your attention to a fact that has been evident to me for some time past—and that is, that my coals go remarkably fast——

MRS. BOUNCER. Lor, Mr. Cox!

COX. It is not only the case with the coals, Mrs. Bouncer, but I've lately observed a gradual and steady increase of evaporation among my candles, wood, sugar, and lucifer matches.

MRS. BOUNCER. Lor, Mr. Cox! You surely don't suspect me?

COX. I don't say I do, Mrs. B.; only I wish you distinctly to understand that I don't believe it's the cat.

MRS. BOUNCER. Is there anything else you've got to grumble about, sir?

COX. Grumble! Mrs. Bouncer, do you possess such a thing as a dictionary?

MRS. BOUNCER. No, sir.

COX. Then I'll lend you one—and if you turn to the letter G, you'll find 'Grumble, verb neuter—to complain without a cause.' Now that's not my case, Mrs. B. And now that we are upon the subject, I wish to know how it is that I frequently find my apartment full of smoke?

MRS. BOUNCER. Why, I suppose the chimney——

COX. The chimney doesn't smoke tobacco. I'm speaking of tobacco smoke, Mrs. B. I hope, Mrs. Bouncer, *you're* not guilty of cheroots or Cubas?

MRS. BOUNCER. Not I, indeed, Mr. Cox!

COX. Nor partial to a pipe?

MRS. BOUNCER. No, sir.

COX. Then how is it that——

MRS. BOUNCER. [*Confused.*] Why, I suppose—yes—that must be it——

COX. At present I am entirely of your opinion—because I haven't the most distant particle of an idea what you mean.

MRS. BOUNCER. Why, the gentleman who has got the attic is

hardly ever without a pipe in his mouth; and there he sits with his feet on the mantelpiece——

cox. The mantelpiece! That strikes me as being a considerable stretch, either of your imagination, Mrs. B., or the gentleman's legs. I presume you mean the fender, or the hob.

mrs. bouncer. Sometimes one, sometimes t'other. Well, there he sits for hours, and puffs away into the fireplace.

cox. Ah, then you mean to say that this gentleman's smoke, instead of emulating the example of all other sorts of smoke, and going *up* the chimney, thinks proper to affect a singularity by taking the contrary direction.

mrs. bouncer. Why——

cox. Then I suppose the gentleman you are speaking of is the same individual that I invariably meet coming up stairs when I'm going down, and going down when I'm coming up?

mrs. bouncer. Why—yes—I——

cox. From the appearance of his outward man, I should unhesitatingly set him down as a gentleman connected with the printing interest.

mrs. bouncer. Yes, sir, and a very respectable young gentleman he is.

cox. Well, good morning, Mrs. Bouncer.

mrs. bouncer. You'll be back at your usual time, I suppose, sir?

cox. Yes—nine o'clock. You needn't light my fire in future, Mrs. B.; I'll do it myself. Don't forget the bolster! [*Going— stops.*] A halfpenny worth of milk, Mrs. Bouncer, and be good enough to let it stand—I wish the cream to accumulate.

[*Exit.*

mrs. bouncer. He's gone at last! I declare I was all in a tremble for fear Mr. Box should come in before Mr. Cox went out. Luckily they've never met yet, and what's more, they're not very likely to do so; for Mr. Box is hard at work at a newspaper office all night, and doesn't come home till the morning, and Mr. Cox is busy making hats all day long, and doesn't come home till night; so that I'm getting double rent for my room, and neither of my lodgers are any wiser for it.

It was a capital idea of mine, that it was! But I haven't an instant to lose. First of all, let me put Mr. Cox's things out of Mr. Box's way. [*She takes the three hats,* cox's *dressing gown and slippers, opens door at* L *and puts them in; then shuts door and locks it.*] Now then, to put the key where Mr. Cox always finds it. [*Puts the key on the ledge of the door.*] I really must beg Mr. Box not to smoke so much. I was dreadfully puzzled to know what to say when Mr. Cox spoke about it. Now then, to make the bed, and don't let me forget that what's the head of the bed for Mr. Cox becomes the foot of the bed for Mr. Box; people's tastes do differ so. [*Goes behind the curtains of the bed, and seems to be making it; then appears with a very thin bolster in her hand.*] The idea of Mr. Cox presuming to complain of such a bolster as this!

[*She disappears again behind curtains.*

BOX. [*Without.*] Pooh, pooh! Why don't you keep your own side of the staircase, sir?

Enter BOX, *dressed as a printer.*

[*Puts his head out of door again, shouting.*] It was as much your fault as mine, sir. I say, sir, it was as much your fault as mine, sir!

MRS. BOUNCER. [*Emerging from behind the curtains of bed.*] Lor, Mr. Box, what is the matter?

BOX. Mind your own business, Bouncer.

MRS. BOUNCER. Dear, dear, Mr. Box, what a temper you are in, to be sure! I declare you are quite pale in the face.

BOX. What colour would you have a man be who has been setting up long leaders for a daily paper all night?

MRS. BOUNCER. But then, you've all the day to yourself.

BOX. [*Looking significantly at* MRS. BOUNCER.] So it seems. Far be it from me, Bouncer, to hurry your movements, but I think it right to acquaint you with my immediate intention of divesting myself of my garments and going to bed.

MRS. BOUNCER. Oh, Mr. Box! [*Going.*

BOX. Stop! Can you inform me who the individual is that I invariably encounter going down stairs when I'm coming up, and coming up stairs when I'm going down?

MRS. BOUNCER. [*Confused.*] Oh—yes—the gentleman in the attic, sir.

BOX. Oh! There's nothing particularly remarkable about him, except his hats. I meet him in all sorts of hats—white hats and black hats—hats with broad brims, and hats with narrow brims, hats with naps, and hats without naps—in short, I have come to the conclusion that he must be individually and professionally associated with the hatting interest.

MRS. BOUNCER. Yes, sir. And by the bye, Mr. Box, he begged me to request of you, as a particular favour, that you would not smoke quite so much.

BOX. Did he? Then you may tell the gentle hatter, with my compliments, that if he objects to the effluvia of tobacco he had better domesticate himself in some adjoining parish.

MRS. BOUNCER. [*Pathetically.*] Oh! Mr. Box, you surely wouldn't deprive me of a lodger.

BOX. It would come to precisely the same thing, Bouncer, because if I detect the slightest attempt to put my pipe out, I at once give you warning that I shall give you warning at once.

MRS. BOUNCER. Well, Mr. Box, do you want anything more of me?

BOX. On the contrary—I've had quite enough of you.

MRS. BOUNCER. Well, if ever! What next, I wonder?
[*Exit, slamming door after her.*

BOX. It's quite extraordinary, the trouble I always have to get rid of that venerable female. She knows I'm up all night, and yet she seems to set her face against my indulging in a horizontal position by day. Now, let me see—shall I take my nap before I swallow my breakfast, or shall I take my breakfast before I swallow my nap—I mean, shall I swallow my nap before—no—never mind! I've got a rasher of bacon somewhere. [*Feeling in his pockets.*] I've the most distinct and vivid recollection of having purchased a rasher of bacon. Oh, here it is—[*Produces it, wrapped in paper, and places it on table.*] and a penny roll. The next thing is to light the fire. Where are my lucifers? [*Looking on mantelpiece, and taking box, opens it.*] Now, 'pon my life, this is too bad of Bouncer—this is by several degrees too bad! I had a whole box full three days ago, and now there's only one! I'm perfectly aware that she purloins my coals and my candles and my sugar, but I did think—oh, yes, I did think that my lucifers would be sacred! [*Takes candlestick off the mantelpiece, in which there is a very small end of candle—looks at it.*] Now I should like to ask any unprejudiced person or persons their opinion touching this candle. In the first place, a candle is an article that I don't require, because I'm only at home in the daytime—and I bought this candle on the first of May—Chimney-sweepers' Day—calculating that it would last me three months, and here's one week not half over, and the candle three parts gone! [*Lights the fire—then takes down a gridiron, which is hanging over fire-place.*] Mrs. Bouncer has been using my gridiron! The last article of consumption that I cooked upon it was a pork chop, and now it is powerfully impregnated with the odour of red herrings! [*Places gridiron on fire, and then with a fork lays rasher of bacon on the gridiron.*] How sleepy I am, to be sure! I'd indulge myself with a nap if there was anybody here to superintend the turning of my bacon. [*Yawning again.*] Perhaps it will turn itself. I must lie down—so here goes.

[*He lies down on the bed, closing the curtains around him.*

After a short pause, enter COX, *hurriedly.*

COX. Well, wonders will never cease! Conscious of being eleven minutes and a half behind time, I was sneaking into the shop in a state of considerable excitement, when my venerable employer, with a smile of extreme benevolence on his aged countenance, said to me—'Cox, I shan't want you to-day—you can have a holiday.' Thoughts of 'Gravesend and back—fare One Shilling,' instantly suggested themselves, inter-mingled with visions of 'Greenwich for Fourpence.' Then came the Twopenny Omnibuses, and the Halfpenny Boats—in short, I'm quite bewildered! However, I must have my breakfast first—that'll give me time to reflect. I've bought a mutton chop, so I shan't want any dinner. [*Puts chop on table.*] Good gracious! I've forgot the bread. Holloa, what's this? A roll, I declare. Come that's lucky! Now, then, to light

the fire. Holloa—[*Seeing the lucifer box on table.*] who presumes
to touch my box of lucifers? Why, it's empty! I left one in it—
I'll take my oath I did. Heyday! Why the fire *is* lighted!
Where's the gridiron? *On* the fire, I declare. And what's that
on it? Bacon? Bacon it is! Well, now, 'pon my life, there's a
quiet coolness about Mrs. Bouncer's proceedings that's
almost amusing. She takes my last lucifer—my coals, and my
gridiron, to cook her breakfast by. No, no—I can't stand this!
Come out of that! [*Pokes fork into bacon, and puts it on a plate on
the table; then places his chop on the gridiron, which he puts on the
fire.*] Now, then, for my breakfast things.

[*Taking key, opens door, L., and goes out, slamming the door
after him with a loud noise.*

BOX. [*Suddenly showing his head from behind curtains.*] Come in!
If it's you, Mrs. Bouncer, you needn't be afraid. I wonder how
long I've been asleep? [*Suddenly recollecting.*] Goodness
gracious—my bacon! [*Leaps off bed and runs to fire-place.*]
Holloa, what's this? A chop? Whose chop? Mrs. Bouncer's,
I'll be bound! She thought to cook her breakfast while I was
asleep—with my coals, too, and my gridiron! Ha, ha! But
where's my bacon? [*Seeing it on the table.*] Here it is. Well,
'pon my life, Bouncer's going it! And shall I curb my
indignation? Shall I falter in my vengeance? No! [*Digs the
fork into the chop—opens window and throws chop out—shuts
window again.*] So much for Bouncer's breakfast, and now for
my own! [*With fork he puts the bacon on the gridiron again.*] I
may as well lay my breakfast things.

[*Goes to mantelpiece, takes key out of one of the ornaments,
opens door, R. and exit, slamming door after him.*

COX. [*Putting his head in quickly at door, L.*] Come in, come in!
[*Opens door and enters with a small tray, on which are tea-
things, etc., which he places on drawers, and suddenly recollects.*]
Oh, goodness, my chop! [*Running to fireplace.*] Holloa—
what's this! The bacon again! Oh, pooh! Zounds—confound
it—dash it—damn it—I can't stand this! [*Pokes fork into
bacon, opens window and flings it out—shuts window again and
returns to drawers for tea-things; encounters BOX coming from
his cupboard with his tea-things—they walk down stage together.*]
Who are you, sir?

BOX. If you come to that—who are *you*?

COX. What do you want here, sir?

BOX. If you come to that—what do *you* want?

COX. [*Aside.*] It's the printer!   [*Puts tea-things on the drawers.*

BOX. [*Aside.*] It's the hatter!   [*Puts tea-things on table.*

COX. Go to your attic, sir.

BOX. *My* attic, sir? *Your* attic, sir!

COX. Printer, I shall do you a frightful injury if you don't instantly leave my apartment.

BOX. *Your* apartment? You mean *my* apartment, you contemptible hatter, you!

COX. *Your* apartment? Ha, ha! Come, I like that! Look here, sir—[*Produces a paper out of his pocket.*] Mrs. Bouncer's receipt for the last week's rent, sir!

BOX. [*Produces a paper and holds it close to* COX's *face.*] Ditto, sir!

COX. [*Suddenly shouting.*] Thieves!

BOX. Murder!

BOX *and* COX. Mrs. Bouncer! Mrs. Bouncer!
                              [*Each running to door, calling.*

MRS. BOUNCER *runs in.*

MRS. BOUNCER. What is the matter?
     [COX *and* BOX *seize* MRS. BOUNCER *by the arm, and drag her forward.*

BOX. Instantly remove that hatter!

COX. Immediately turn out that printer!

MRS. BOUNCER. Well, but gentlemen——

COX. Explain!   [*Pulling her round to him.*

BOX. Explain! [*Pulling her round to him.*] Whose room is this?

COX. Yes, woman, whose room is this?

BOX. Doesn't it belong to me?

MRS. BOUNCER. No!

COX. There! You hear, sir—it belongs to me.

MRS. BOUNCER. No—it belongs to both of you!   [*Sobbing.*

BOX *and* COX. Both of us?

MRS. BOUNCER. Oh, dear gentlemen, don't be angry; but you see, this gentleman—[*Pointing to* BOX.] only being at home in the daytime, and that gentleman—[*Pointing to* COX.] at night, I thought I might venture—until my little back second-floor room was ready——

BOX *and* COX [*Eagerly.*] When will your little back second-floor room be ready?

MRS. BOUNCER. Why, to-morrow——

COX. I'll take it!

BOX. So will I!

MRS. BOUNCER. Excuse me, but if you both take it, you may just as well stop where you are.

BOX *and* COX. True.

COX. I spoke first, sir!

BOX. With all my heart, sir! The little back second-floor room is yours, sir—now go!

COX. Go? Pooh, pooh!

MRS. BOUNCER. Now, don't quarrel, gentlemen. You see, there used to be a partition here——

BOX *and* COX. Then put it up!

MRS. BOUNCER. Nay, I'll see if I can't get the other room ready this very day. Now, do keep your tempers.   [*Exit.*

COX. What a disgusting position!

                              [*Walking rapidly round the stage.*

BOX. [*Sitting down on chair at one side of table, and following* COX's *movements.*] Will you allow me to observe, if you have not had any exercise to-day, you'd better go out and take it?

COX. I shall not do anything of the sort, sir.

                    [*Seating himself at the table opposite* BOX.

BOX. Very well, sir!

COX. Very well, sir! However, don't let me prevent *you* from going out.

BOX. Don't flatter yourself, sir. [COX *is about to break a piece of the roll off.*] Holloa! That's my roll, sir.

     [*Snatches it away, puts a pipe in his mouth, and lights it with a piece of tinder. Puffs smoke across the table towards* COX.

cox. Holloa! What are you about, sir?

box. What am I about? I'm about to smoke.

cox. Wheugh!   [*Goes to the window and flings it open.*

box. Holloa! [*Turning round.*] Put down that window, sir!

cox. Then put your pipe out, sir!

box. There!   [*Puts pipe on the table.*

cox. There!   [*Slams down window and re-seats himself.*

box. I shall retire to my pillow.
 [*Gets up, takes off his jacket, then goes towards bed and sits upon it.*

cox. [*Jumps up, goes to bed and sits down.*] I beg your pardon, sir—I cannot allow anyone to rumple my bed.

box. *Your* bed? Hark ye, sir—can you fight?

cox. No, sir.

box. No? Then come on.   [*Sparring at* cox.

cox. Sit down, sir, or I'll instantly vociferate 'Police!'

box. [*Seats himself;* cox *does the same.*] I say, sir——

cox. Well, sir?

box. Although we are doomed to occupy the same room for a few hours longer, I don't see any necessity for our cutting each other's throat, sir.

cox. Not at all. It's an operation that I should decidedly object to.

box. And after all, I've no violent animosity against you, sir.

cox. Nor have I any rooted antipathy to you, sir.

box. Besides, it was all Mrs. Bouncer's fault, sir.

cox. Entirely, sir.   [*Gradually approaching chairs.*

box. Very well, sir!

cox. Very well, sir!   [*Pause.*

box. Take a bit of roll, sir?

cox. Thank ye, sir.   [*Breaking a bit off. Pause.*

box. Do you sing, sir?

cox. I sometimes join in a chorus.

BOX. Then give us a chorus. [*Pause.*] Have you seen the Bosjesmans, sir?

COX. No, sir; my wife wouldn't let me.

BOX. Your *wife*?

COX. That is—my *intended* wife.

BOX. Well, that's the same thing. I congratulate you.

[*Shaking hands.*

COX. [*With a deep sigh.*] Thank ye. [*Seeing* BOX *about to get up.*] You needn't disturb yourself, sir; she won't come here.

BOX. Oh! I understand. You've got a snug little establishment of your own here—on the sly—cunning dog. [*Nudging* COX.

COX. [*Drawing himself up.*] No such thing, sir—I repeat, sir, no such thing, sir; but my wife—I mean my *intended* wife— happens to be the proprietress of a considerable number of bathing machines——

BOX. [*Suddenly.*] Ha! Where?   [*Grasping* COX's *arm.*

COX. At a favourite watering place. How curious you are!

BOX. Not at all. Well?

COX. Consequently, in the bathing season—which luckily is rather a long one—we see but little of each other; but as that is now over I am daily indulging in the expectation of being blessed with the sight of my beloved. [*Very seriously.*] Are *you* married?

BOX. Me? Why—not exactly.

COX. Ah, a happy bachelor?

BOX. Why—not precisely.

COX. Oh, a—widower?

BOX. No—not absolutely.

COX. You'll excuse me, sir—but at present I don't exactly understand how you can help being one of the three.

BOX. Not help it?

COX. No, sir—not you, nor any other man alive!

BOX. Ah, that may be—but I'm not alive!

COX. [*Pushing back his chair.*]—You'll excuse me, sir—but I don't like joking upon such subjects.

BOX. But I am perfectly serious, sir; I've been defunct for the last three years.

COX. [*Shouting*.] Will you be quiet, sir?

BOX. If you won't believe me, I'll refer you to a very large, numerous, and respectable circle of disconsolate friends.

COX. My very dear sir—my *very* dear sir—if there does exist any ingenious contrivance whereby a man on the eve of committing matrimony can leave this world, and yet stop in it, I shouldn't be sorry to know it.

BOX. Oh, then I presume I'm not to set you down as being frantically attached to your intended?

COX. Why, not exactly; and yet at present I'm only aware of one obstacle to my doting upon her—and that is, that I can't abide her.

BOX. Then there's nothing more easy. Do as I did.

COX. [*Eagerly*.] I will! What was it?

BOX. Drown yourself.

COX. [*Shouting again*.] Will you be quiet, sir?

BOX. Listen to me. Three years ago it was my misfortune to captivate the affections of a still blooming, though somewhat middle-aged widow, at Ramsgate.

COX. [*Aside*.] Singular enough—just my case three months ago at Margate!

BOX. Well, sir, to escape her importunities, I came to the determination of enlisting into the Blues or Life Guards.

COX. [*Aside*.] So did I. How very odd!

BOX. But they wouldn't have me; they actually had the effrontery to say I was too short——

COX. [*Aside*.] And I wasn't tall enough!

BOX. So I was obliged to content myself with a marching regiment. I enlisted!

COX. [*Aside*.] So did I. Singular coincidence!

BOX. I'd no sooner done so than I was sorry for it.

COX. [*Aside*.] So was I.

BOX. My infatuated widow offered to purchase my discharge on condition that I'd lead her to the altar.

cox. [*Aside.*] Just my case!

box. I hesitated; at last I consented.

cox. [*Aside.*] I consented at once!

box. Well, sir, the day fixed for the happy ceremony at length drew near—in fact, too near to be pleasant—so I suddenly discovered that I wasn't worthy to possess her, and I told her so; when, instead of being flattered by the compliment, she flew upon me like a tiger of the female gender. I rejoined, when suddenly something whizzed past me within an inch of my ear, and shivered into a thousand fragments against the mantelpiece. It was the slop-basin. I retaliated with a tea cup. We parted, and the next morning I was served with a notice of action for breach of promise.

cox. Well, sir?

box. Well, sir, ruin stared me in the face; the action proceeded against me with gigantic strides. I took a desperate resolution. I left my home early one morning, with one suit of clothes on my back and another tied up in a bundle under my arm. I arrived on the cliffs, opened my bundle, deposited the suit of clothes on the very verge of the precipice, took one look down in the yawning gulf beneath me—and walked off in the opposite direction.

cox. Dear me! I think I begin to have some slight perception of your meaning. Ingenious creature! You disappeared—the suit of clothes was found——

box. Exactly; and in one of the pockets of the coat, or waistcoat, or the pantaloons—I forget which—there was also found a piece of paper with these affecting farewell words: 'This is thy work, oh Penelope Ann!'

cox. Penelope Ann! [*Starts up, takes* box *by the arm, and leads him slowly to front of stage.*] Penelope Ann?

box. Penelope Ann.

cox. Originally widow of William Wiggins?

box. Widow of William Wiggins.

cox. Proprietor of bathing machines?

box. Proprietor of bathing machines.

cox. At Margate?

box. And Ramsgate.

cox. It must be she! And you, sir—you are Box—the lamented, long-lost Box?

box. I am!

cox. And I was about to marry the interesting creature you so cruelly deceived.

box. Ah, then you are Cox!

cox. I am!

box. I heard of it. I congratulate you—I give you joy! And now I think I'll go and take a stroll.   [*Going*.

cox. No you don't! [*Stopping him*.] I'll not lose sight of you till I've restored you to the arms of your intended.

box. *My* intended? You mean *your* intended.

cox. No, sir—yours!

box. How can she be *my* intended now that I am drowned?

cox. You're no such thing, sir, and I prefer presenting you to Penelope Ann.

box. I've no wish to be introduced to your intended.

cox. *My* intended? How can that be, sir? You proposed to her first!

box. What of that, sir? I came to an untimely end, and you popped the question afterwards.

cox. Very well, sir!

box. Very well, sir!

cox. You are much more worthy of her than I am, sir. Permit me, then, to follow the generous impulse of my nature—I give her up to you.

box. Benevolent being! I wouldn't rob you for the world! [*Going*.] Good-morning, sir.

cox. [*Seizing him*.] Stop!

box. Unhand me, hatter, or I shall cast off the lamb and assume the lion!

cox. Pooh!   [*Snapping his fingers in* box's *face*.

BOX. An insult to my very face—under my very nose! [*Rubbing it.*] You know the consequences, sir—instant satisfaction, sir!

COX. With all my heart, sir!
[*They begin ringing bells violently, and pull down bell pulls.*

BOX *and* COX. Mrs. Bouncer! Mrs. Bouncer!

MRS. BOUNCER *runs in.*

MRS. BOUNCER. What is it, gentlemen?

BOX. Pistols for two!

MRS. BOUNCER. Yes, sir.   [*Going.*

COX. Stop! You don't mean to say, thoughtless and imprudent woman, that you keep loaded firearms in the house?

MRS. BOUNCER. Oh, no—they're not loaded.

COX. Then produce the murderous weapons instantly!
[*Exit* MRS. BOUNCER.

BOX. I say, sir.

COX. Well, sir?

BOX. What's your opinion of duelling, sir?

COX. I think it's a barbarous practice, sir.

BOX. So do I, sir. To be sure, I don't so much object to it when the pistols are not loaded.

COX. No, I dare say that *does* make some difference.

BOX. And yet, sir—on the other hand—doesn't it strike you as rather a waste of time for two people to keep firing pistols at one another, with nothing in 'em.

COX. No, sir—not more than any other harmless recreation.

BOX. Hark ye! Why do you object to marry Penelope Ann?

COX. Because, as I have observed already, I can't abide her. You'll be very happy with her.

BOX. Happy? Me? With the consciousness that I have deprived *you* of such a treasure? No, no, Cox!

COX. Don't think of me, Box—I shall be sufficiently rewarded by the knowledge of my Box's happiness.

BOX. Don't be absurd, sir!

COX. Then don't you be ridiculous, sir!

BOX. I won't have her!

COX. No more will I!

BOX. I have it! Suppose we draw lots for the lady—eh, Mr. Cox?

COX. That's fair enough, Mr. Box.

BOX. Or what say you to dice?

COX. [*Eagerly*.] With all my heart! Dice by all means.

BOX. [*Aside*.] That's lucky! Mrs. Bouncer's nephew left a pair here yesterday. He sometimes persuades me to have a throw for a trifle, and as he always throws sixes, I suspect they are good ones.   [*Goes to cupboard and brings out dice-box*.

COX. [*Aside*.] I've no objection at all to dice. I lost one pound seventeen and sixpence at last Barnet Races to a very gentlemanly looking man who had a most peculiar knack of throwing sixes. I suspected they were loaded, so I gave him another half-crown, and he gave me the dice.   [*Takes dice out of his pocket*.

BOX. Now then, sir.

COX. I'm ready, sir. [*They seat themselves at opposite sides of the table*.] Will you lead off, sir?

BOX. As you please, sir. The lowest throw, of course, wins Penelope Ann?

COX. Of course, sir.

BOX. Very well, sir!

COX. Very well, sir!

BOX. [*Rattling dice and throwing*.] Sixes!

COX. That's not a bad throw of yours, sir. [*Rattling dice— throws*.] Sixes!

BOX. That's a pretty good one of yours, sir. [*Throws*.] Sixes!

COX. [*Throws*.] Sixes!

BOX. Sixes!

COX. Sixes!

BOX. Sixes!

COX. Sixes!

BOX. Those are not bad dice of yours, sir.

COX. Yours seem pretty good ones, sir.

BOX. Suppose we change?

COX. Very well, sir.   [*They change dice.*

BOX. [*Throwing.*] Sixes!

COX. Sixes!

BOX. Sixes!

COX. Sixes!

BOX. [*Flinging down the dice.*] Pooh! It's perfectly absurd your going on throwing sixes in this sort of way, sir!

COX. I shall go on till my luck changes, sir!

BOX. Let's try something else. I have it! Suppose we toss for Penelope Ann?

COX. The very thing I was going to propose!
            [*They each turn aside and take out a handful of money.*

BOX. [*Aside, examining money.*] Where's my tossing shilling? Here it is.

COX. [*Aside, examining money.*] Where's my lucky sixpence? I've got it.

BOX. Now then, sir, heads wins?

COX. Or tails lose, whichever you prefer.

BOX. It's the same to me, sir.

COX. Very well, sir—heads I win; tails you lose.

BOX. Yes. [*Suddenly.*] No—heads wins, sir.

COX. Very well—go on.

BOX. [*Tossing.*] Heads!

COX. [*Tossing.*] Heads!

BOX. [*Tossing.*] Heads!

COX. [*Tossing.*] Heads!

BOX. Ain't you rather tired of turning up heads, sir?

COX. Couldn't you vary the monotony of our proceedings by an occasional tail, sir?

BOX. [*Tossing.*] Heads!

COX. [*Tossing.*] Heads!

BOX. Heads? Stop, sir! Will you permit me? [*Taking* COX's *sixpence.*] Holloa, your sixpence has got no tail, sir!

COX. [*Seizing* BOX's *shilling*.] And your shilling has got **two** heads!

BOX. Cheat!

COX. Swindler!
  [*They are about to rush upon each other, then retreat to some distance and commence sparring and striking fiercely at one another.*

Enter MRS. BOUNCER.

BOX *and* COX. Is the little back second-floor room ready?

MRS. BOUNCER. Not quite, gentlemen. I can't find the pistols, but I have brought you a letter—it came by the General Post yesterday. I am sure I don't know how I came to forget it, for I put it carefully in my pocket.

COX. And you've kept it carefully in your pocket ever since?

MRS. BOUNCER. Yes, sir. I hope you'll forgive me, sir. [*Going.*] By the bye, I paid twopence for it.

COX. Did you? Then I *do* forgive you. [*Exit* MRS. BOUNCER.] 'Margate.' The postmark decidedly says 'Margate.'

BOX. Oh, doubtless a tender epistle from Penelope Ann.

COX. Then read it, sir.   [*Handing letter to* BOX.

BOX. Me, sir?

COX. Of course. You don't suppose I'm going to read a letter from your intended.

BOX. *My* intended? Pooh! It's addressed to you—C.O.X.

COX. Do you think that's a Ç? It looks to me like a B.

BOX. Nonsense! Fracture the seal.

COX. [*Opens letter—starts.*] Goodness gracious!

BOX. [*Snatching letter—starts.*] Gracious goodness!

COX. [*Taking letter again.*] 'Margate, May the 4th. Sir—I hasten to convey to you the intelligence of a melancholy accident, which has bereft you of your intended wife.' He means *your* intended.

BOX. No, *yours*! However, it's perfectly immaterial—but she unquestionably was yours.

COX. How can that be? You proposed to her first.

BOX. Yes, but then you—now don't let us begin again. Go on.

COX. [*Resuming letter.*] 'Poor Mrs. Wiggins went out for a short excursion in a sailing boat. A sudden and violent squall soon after took place, which it is supposed upset her, as she was found two days afterwards, keel upwards.'

BOX. Poor woman!

COX. The boat, sir! [*Reading.*] 'As her man of business, I immediately proceeded to examine her papers, amongst which I soon discovered her will, the following extract from which will, I have no doubt, be satisfactory to you: "I hereby bequeath my entire property to my intended husband." ' Excellent, but unhappy creature!   [*Affected.*

BOX. Generous ill-fated being!   [*Affected.*

COX. And to think that I tossed up for such a woman!

BOX. When I remember that I staked such a treasure on the hazard of a die!

COX. I'm sure, Mr. Box, I can't sufficiently thank you for your sympathy.

BOX. And I'm sure, Mr. Cox, you couldn't feel more if she had been your own intended.

COX. *If* she'd been *my own* intended! She *was* my own intended.

BOX. *Your* intended? Come, I like that! Didn't you very properly observe just now, sir, that I proposed to her first?

COX. To which you very sensibly replied that you'd come to an untimely end.

BOX. I deny it!

COX. I say you have!

BOX. The fortune's mine!

COX. Mine!

BOX. I'll have it!

COX. So will I!

BOX. I'll go to law!

COX. So will I!

BOX. Stop; a thought strikes me. Instead of going to law about the property, suppose we divide it.

COX. Equally?

BOX. Equally, I'll take two-thirds.

COX. That's fair enough, and I'll take three-fourths.

BOX. That won't do. Half and half.

COX. Agreed! There's my hand upon it.

BOX. And mine.

　　　[*About to shake hands. A postman's knock heard at street door.*

COX. Holloa! Postman again?

BOX. Postman yesterday—postman to-day.

Enter MRS. BOUNCER.

MRS. BOUNCER. Another letter, Mr. Cox—twopence more.

COX. I forgive you again. [*Taking letter. Exit* MRS. BOUNCER.]
Another trifle from Margate. [*Opens letter—starts.*] Goodness
gracious!

BOX. [*Snatching letter—starts.*] Gracious goodness!

COX. [*Snatching letter again—reads.*] 'Happy to inform you,
false alarm.'

BOX. [*Overlooking.*] 'Sudden squall—boat upset—Mrs. Wiggins,
your intended——'

COX. 'Picked up by a steamboat——'

BOX. 'Carried into Boulogne——'

COX. 'Returned here this morning——'

BOX. 'Will start by early train to-morrow——'

COX. 'And be with you at ten o'clock exact.'

　　　　　　　[*Both simultaneously pull out their watches.*

BOX. Cox, I congratulate you!

COX. Box, I give you joy!

BOX. I'm sorry that most important business at the Colonial
Office will prevent my witnessing the truly happy meeting
between you and your intended. Good morning!　　[*Going.*

COX. [*Stopping him.*] It's obviously for me to retire. Not for
worlds would I disturb the rapturous meeting between you
and your intended. Good morning!

BOX. You'll excuse me, sir, but our last arrangement was that
she was *your* intended.

COX. No, yours!

BOX. Yours!

BOX *and* COX. Yours! [*Ten o'clock strikes—noise of an omnibus.*

BOX. Ha, what's that? A cab's drawn up at the door! [*Running to window.*] No, it's a twopenny omnibus!

COX. [*Leaning over* BOX's *shoulder.*] A lady's got out——

BOX. There's no mistaking that majestic person—it's Penelope Ann!

COX. Your intended!

BOX. Yours!

COX. Yours!   [*Both run to door, and eagerly listen.*

BOX. Hark! She's coming upstairs!

COX. Shut the door!
   [*They slam the door, and both lean against it with their backs.*

MRS. BOUNCER. [*Without, and knocking.*] Mr. Cox! Mr. Cox!

COX. [*Shouting.*] I've just stepped out!

BOX. So have I!

MRS. BOUNCER. [*Without.*] Mr. Cox! [*Pushing at the door;* COX *and* BOX *redouble their efforts to keep the door shut.*] Open the door! It's only me, Mrs. Bouncer!

COX. Only you? Then where's the lady?

MRS. BOUNCER. Gone!

COX. Upon your honour?

BOX. As a gentleman?

MRS. BOUNCER. Yes, and she's left a note for Mr. Cox.

COX. Give it to me.

MRS. BOUNCER. Then open the door!

COX. Put it under. [*A letter is put under the door;* COX *picks up the letter and opens it.*] Goodness gracious!

BOX. [*Snatching letter.*] Gracious goodness!
                              [COX *snatches the letter.*

COX. [*Reading.*] 'Dear Mr. Cox, pardon my candour——'

BOX. [*Looking over and reading.*] 'But being convinced that our feelings, like our ages, do not reciprocate——'

COX. 'I hasten to apprise you of my immediate union——'

BOX. 'With Mr. Knox.'

cox. Huzza!

box. Three cheers for Knox. Ha, ha, ha!
  [*Tosses the letter in the air and begins dancing;* cox *does the same.*

mrs. bouncer. [*Putting her head in at door.*] The little second-floor back room is quite ready.

cox. I don't want it!

box. No more do I!

cox. What shall part us?

box. What shall tear us asunder?

cox. Box!

box. Cox! [*About to embrace;* box *stops, seizes* cox's *hand, and looks eagerly in his face.*] You'll excuse the apparent insanity of the remark, but the more I gaze on your features, the more I'm convinced that you're my long-lost brother.

cox. The very observation I was going to make to you!

box. Ah, tell me—in mercy tell me—have you such a thing as a strawberry mark on your left arm?

cox. No!

box. Then it is he!   [*They rush into each other's arms.*

cox. Of course we stop where we are?

box. Of course!

cox. For, between you and me, I'm rather partial to this house.

box. So am I—I begin to feel quite at home in it.

cox. Everything so clean and comfortable——

box. And I'm sure the mistress of it, from what I have seen of her, is very anxious to please.

cox. So she is—and I vote, Box, that we stick by her.

box. Agreed! There's my hand upon it—join but yours—agree that the house is big enough to hold us both, then Box——

cox. And Cox——

box *and* cox. Are satisfied!   [*Curtain.*

THE CORSICAN BROTHERS

A DRAMATIC ROMANCE IN THREE ACTS

BY

DION BOUCICAULT (1820–1890)

———

*First performed at the Princess's Theatre
24 February 1852*

———

CAST

FABIEN DEI FRANCHI ⎫ Twin brothers	Mr. Charles Kean
LOUIS DEI FRANCHI ⎭	
CHÂTEAU-RENAUD	Mr. Alfred Wigan
BARON DE MONTGIRON	Mr. James Vining
BARON GIORDANO MARTELLI	Mr. C. Wheatleigh
ALFRED MEYNARD	Mr. G. Everett
ORLANDO ⎫ The heads of two Corsican	Mr. Ryder
COLONNA ⎭ families	Mr. Meadows
BEAUCHAMP	Mr. Stacey
VERNER	Mr. Rolleston
GRIFFO, a domestic	Mr. Paulo
ANTONIO SANOLA, judge of the district	Mr. F. Cooke
BOISSEC, a woodcutter	Mr. Addison
TOMASO, a guide	Mr. Stoakes
SURGEON	Mr. Daly
SERVANTS	⎧ Mr. Haines
	⎩ Mr. Wilson
SAVILIA DEI FRANCHI	Miss Phillips
ÉMILIE DE LESPARRE	Miss Murray
MARIE, a domestic	Miss Robertson
CORALIE	Miss Carlotta Leclercq
CÉLESTINE ⎱ Ladies of the ballet	Miss Daly
ESTELLE ⎰	Miss Vivash

Ladies, Gentlemen, Masks, Dominoes, Male and Female
Corsican Peasants, Débardeurs, Grotesques, Servants, etc.

———

*The incidents of the First Act in Corsica
and of the Second Act in Paris
are supposed to occur at the same time*

ACT I

SCENE I. *The Principal Saloon, or Hall in the Château of* MADAME LA CONTESSA SAVILIA DEI FRANCHI *at Sullacao in Corsica. Folding door at back, door* L., *door* R., *door* R. *flat. Sideboard* L. *flat. Table, 2 chairs,* L.C. *4 other chairs. Portfolio, paper, inkstand, pens, sealing wax, seal on sideboard. Spinning wheel* C.

MARIE *discovered singing while she sits at her spinning wheel.*

Song

Oh! that I were a crowned King
    Upon a throne of gold,
And mine was all, and everything
    That I could there behold.
I'd give my throne and crown away,
    And all that I could see,
If I could woo Marie to say
    She'd give her heart to me.
If I could woo Marie to say
    She'd give her heart to me. La! la! *etc.*

[*Knocking heard without.*

MARIE. Someone knocks. [*Knocking repeated.*] Yes; I am not deceived. Griffo! Griffo!

Enter GRIFFO.

GRIFFO. What's the matter? Is the house on fire?

MARIE. No, but there's somebody knocking at the gate.

GRIFFO. Well, go and open it.

MARIE. At this late hour? By myself? No thank you.

GRIFFO. Timid individual.   [*Exit.*

MARIE [*pulling her spinning wheel off* R.]. Go and open it! Yes, to be agreeably saluted by a pistol or a stiletto. Well, who is it?

Re-enter GRIFFO.

GRIFFO. A French Gentleman—a traveller, who requests our hospitality.

MARIE. A French gentleman! I hope you haven't refused him.

GRIFFO. Refused! Refuse hospitality in Corsica! Go, and announce his arrival to the Countess.

MARIE. I should like to have a peep at him first.

GRIFFO [*stopping her*]. Go, I tell you.

MARIE. Just one glimpse. Is he young and handsome?

GRIFFO. That's nothing to you; he stays all night.

MARIE. Oh! Then I can wait a little. I fly to tell Madame.
        [*Music. Exit.* GRIFFO *shows in* ALFRED MEYNARD *and* TOMASO.

GRIFFO. This way your excellency. I have sent to inform the Signora Savilia of your arrival.

ALFRED. My good friend, I fear this unseasonable intrusion—

GRIFFO. Intrusion! We have no such word in Corsica: here a stranger honours the house he stops at. Ah! honest Tomaso, is that you? [*Shaking hands.*]

ALFRED. I can dismiss you now; here are two piastres.

TOMASO. Thank you, sir. [*Placing valise on table, takes up the money and exit.*]

GRIFFO. Is your excellency acquainted with the Countess?

ALFRED. I have not yet that honour; but I bring a letter from her son.

GRIFFO. From Monsieur Louis?

ALFRED. Yes; he is my intimate friend.

Enter MADAME DEI FRANCHI, *followed by* MARIE *with candles, which she places on table.*

MADAME. From my son Louis, did you say?

ALFRED. Madame, I ought to apologize for this intrusion; but the well known hospitality of your country, and this letter, will, I trust, plead my excuse.

MADAME [*opens letter*]. I thank you, sir. You can understand a mother's joy, when she sees the handwriting of an absent son. [*Reads.*] Ah! my dear Louis; he recommends you to us as one of his most valued friends; there needed not this to insure your welcome. In Corsica, every traveller may throw his bridle on his horse's neck and stop where he conducts him: his stay is limited by his own pleasure; and the only regret he occasions is when he announces his departure. Marie.

MARIE. Yes, Madame.

MADAME. Tell them to prepare the chamber Louis occupied before he left us. [*Exit* MARIE.] Griffo, carry there the luggage of our guest. While he stays with us, you will devote yourself entirely to him.

[*Exit* GRIFFO *with valise and cloake.*

ALFRED. I know not how to thank you, Madame.

MADAME. On my son's part, as well as my own, I repeat your hearty welcome.

ALFRED. Ah! I recollect—your second son, Monsieur Fabien.

MADAME. I have two sons, twins.

ALFRED. I have heard of the extraordinary resemblance which exists between them.

MADAME. You shall judge for yourself, when you have seen Fabien. He went this morning early to the mountains: I expect his return every instant.

Enter GRIFFO.

ALFRED. I long to take him by the hand.

GRIFFO. Madame, Monsieur Fabien has returned.

MADAME. Fabien! Where is he?

GRIFFO. Just entering the gate, he stopped to speak to the judge. [*To* ALFRED.] Your excellency's apartment is ready.

ALFRED. I thank you. I am not tired. My welcome here has driven away fatigue.

Music. Enter FABIEN DEI FRANCHI *with rifle.*

MADAME. My son, you have been expected home.

FABIEN. By you, dearest mother?

H

MADAME. Yes, and by some one else. How late you are this evening.

FABIEN. Yes, that devil Orlando is a true Corsican. I could hardly persuade him; at last, however, I succeeded, and all is settled. This unhappy feud will now be terminated; he and Colonna have promised to meet here this evening with their kinsmen and friends; and having once promised, they are sure to come.

MADAME. And now let me introduce to you Monsieur Alfred Meynard, a friend of your brother.

FABIEN. A friend of Louis! Sir, you are most welcome.

ALFRED. Good heavens! It is identity! I could swear that I held by the hand my old friend.

FABIEN. Believe it, sir; for Louis and myself are one.

ALFRED. The voice, too, is tone for tone the same.

MADAME. Monsieur is the bearer of a letter.

FABIEN. A letter—from Louis? Dear mother, allow me to look at it. [*Runs his eye eagerly over the letter, then, with an altered tone, turning to* ALFRED.] By the date, you have not seen Louis for three weeks; then you know nothing.

MADAME. What say you, Fabien?

FABIEN. Nothing, mother, nothing. How did you leave my brother when you saw him last?

ALFRED. His health was excellent.

FABIEN. So much for his body: but his mind; did he appear thoughtful, harassed, in low spirits?

ALFRED. Far from it; he seemed entirely occupied in preparing for his degree, which he felt confident of obtaining.

FABIEN. At that time, then, you observed in him no trace of secret vexation.

ALFRED. None whatever. Have you any reason to think otherwise? Have you received more recently any evil tidings?

FABIEN. Received! No—that is, not in the sense in which you use the word.

MADAME. My son!

ALFRED. I scarcely comprehend you.

MADAME. Fabien, I trust nothing of consequence has happened to your brother?

FABIEN. I hope not; yet—

MADAME. The fears you entertained yesterday on account of Louis—

FABIEN. I have them still; they never leave me.

MADAME. But you have had no further warning?

FABIEN [*after a pause*]. No, none.

MADAME. But if your brother's life were threatened?

FABIEN. Mother!

MADAME. If he were dead, you would have known it?

FABIEN. Yes, for I should have seen him.

ALFRED [*aside*]. He would have seen him!

MADAME. And you would have told me?

FABIEN. Assuredly, dearest mother.

MADAME. Fabien, I thank you. The absent are in the hands of Providence—you know that Louis lives. Let us endeavour to dismiss anxiety for the moment, and think of nothing but to do honour to our guest.

> [*Music. She bows to* ALFRED MEYNARD, *who crosses to her and kisses her hand.* FABIEN *opens the door;* MADAME DEI FRANCHI *exits.*

ALFRED. All this is very strange, but I am in the land of adventures and this old chateau appears the head quarters of romance.

FABIEN [*sitting at table*]. You will excuse us, sir, for speaking before you of family affairs, but we cannot treat you with reserve, having come from our dear Louis. The last few words exchanged between me and my mother appear to you a little unintelligible.

ALFRED. I confess it: you have received no recent tidings of your brother. Why, then, do you suppose him restless, melancholy, or in pain?

FABIEN. Because for the last three days, I am restless, melancholy, and in pain myself.

ALFRED. Excuse me, but I cannot follow the coincidence.

FABIEN. You know, probably, that Louis and I are twins?

ALFRED. He has often told me so, and the Countess also mentioned it when I arrived. [*Sits.*]

FABIEN. There is a strange, mysterious sympathy between us; no matter what space divides us, we are still one in body, in feeling, in soul. Any powerful impression which the one experiences is instantly conveyed by some invisible agency to the senses of the other.

ALFRED. This is most singular.

FABIEN. For the last few days, in spite of myself, my temperament has changed. I have become sad, uneasy, gloomy, with a depression of the heart I cannot conquer. I am convinced my brother is unhappy.

ALFRED. And you attribute this mysterious feeling of apprehension to some danger impending over your brother?

FABIEN. I am sure of it.

ALFRED. And the nature of this unhappiness—cannot you divine it?

FABIEN. No; I feel the effect, but the cause is hid from me.

ALFRED. Perhaps some trifling professional annoyance.

FABIEN. Not so: it implicates the heart.

ALFRED. I should have thought him too much occupied with his studies to care for the attractions of the sex.

FABIEN. For the sex generally, yes; but he is deeply in love with one.

ALFRED. And that one is—but I am indiscreet; pray pardon me. [*Rising.*]

FABIEN. You shall know all. [*Rising and taking his hand.*] From my brother's friend I will have no secrets. About a year since, the daughter of the general commanding in Corsica came on a visit of two months, with her father, to Ajaccio. She was young, amiable, beautiful. Louis and I had frequent opportunities of seeing her, and as all our feelings are in unison, need I tell you that we both saw and loved her. Each perceived the passion of the other, and tried to extinguish his own. I know not whether I succeeded, but Louis thought I had, and his increased affection proved his gratitude. The general was recalled to France, his daughter accompanied him, and the lovely vision was dissolved. Some time after, Louis asked me whether I intended to go to Paris, to study law or medicine. We had always promised never to leave our mother solitary. I told him I had no desire to travel. His countenance beamed with joy. He left us, and I remained. Most probably I shall never quit my native village.

ALFRED. What! at your age—in the springtime of life—bury yourself from the active world?

FABIEN. You wonder, naturally, that any one should choose to live in such a wild and ignorant land; but I am native to the soil, like the green oak, or laurel rose. I love to explore the forest, and to rove over chasm and torrent with my rifle for a companion—to sit upon the mountain ledge, with the theatre of nature at my feet, and revel in the sense of liberty and boundless space. In the city I should be stifled as in a prison. No, let Louis obey his destiny; he will become great and noble—

ALFRED. While you—

FABIEN. Am free, and Corsican.

ALFRED. A characteristic reply. And this lady, you think, is the cause of your brother's uneasiness?

FABIEN. Yes, although he never names her in his letters. His love increases—the wound is a deep one.

ALFRED. Such wounds are seldom mortal, and if you have no other subject of inquietude—

FABIEN. Something else has happened to my brother.

ALFRED. Do you imagine he is in any danger?

FABIEN. I do most certainly.

ALFRED. Or dead?

FABIEN. No, not dead; had it been so, as I told my mother, I should have seen him since.

ALFRED. You would have seen him. [*Smiling.*]

FABIEN. Ah! I see by your incredulous smile—

ALFRED. Oh, believe me—

FABIEN. No, do not apologize. You dwellers in cities, what you gain in art you lose in nature; you are more prone to believe the miracles of a science which you have unveiled than to believe the wonders of that creation which a divinity has formed.

ALFRED. Nay, do not mistake surprise for disbelief. I accuse nothing of being impossible.

FABIEN. As a man of the world you scoff at idle tales of superstition; yet I could relate a legend existing in our family three hundred years ago which might shake your scepticism. Do you believe in apparitions?

ALFRED. Why, no; I can't say I believe, but at the same time, nothing proves their non-existence.

FABIEN. Give me, then, your attention, while I recount a story well attested in the annals of the Dei Franchi. Three hundred years ago our immediate ancestor, Count Bartolomeo dei Franchi, died, leaving two orphan sons. The extraordinary attachment of these children to each other was the theme of Corsica. Arrived at the age of manhood, they bound themselves by a solemn oath that not even death itself should separate them. This vow each registered in his own blood on a parchment they exchanged. The conditions prescribed were that he who died first should appear to the other, not only at the moment of his death, but as a warning to foretell it.

ALFRED. An oath more easily made than kept.

FABIEN. About two months after, one of the two brothers was waylaid and murdered. At that very moment the other, residing in this very house, being seized with a vague sense of danger, was engaged in writing to him, and as he impressed his seal upon the burning wax he heard a sigh behind him. He turned and saw his brother standing by his side, his hand upon his shoulder, although he felt no touch or weight. The figure shook its head mournfully, and waving its arm towards the wall the masonry seemed to obey the gesture— it opened, and the living man beheld the murder in all its harrowing identity.

ALFRED. This was a dream.

FABIEN. No, no. The archives of justice at Bastia attest its truth; for on the deposition of the surviving brother, the murderers were detected and arrested. Terrified by what they thought the intervention of heaven, they confessed that the crime had been perpetrated exactly as seen in the vision, and at the very same hour.

ALFRED. This is very strange indeed, and terrible. Do you fear, then, that Louis is dead?

FABIEN. No, he lives; but I fear he is wounded.

ALFRED. Wounded! How? By whom?

FABIEN. This morning, on my way to the mountains—[*Music.*] My mother returns. Do not speak of this before her, I entreat you.

ALFRED. Rely on my discretion.

Enter MADAME DEI FRANCHI, GRIFFO, *and* MARIE *with supper which they place on table.*

MADAME. Now, gentlemen, when you are disposed, supper is ready. Well, Fabien!

FABIEN. Well, mother, my passing gloom has vanished; I am gay and joyous. Monsieur Meynard, take your seat. [*They sit.*] And so you have come to visit Corsica? You do well not to postpone your visit. In a few years our laws, our manners, will exist no longer; all will be swept away before the modern mania of improvement. We are degenerating hourly from our ancient habits.

ALFRED. But in this house, at least, I find a noble picture of the earlier times.

FABIEN. In my mother always. But for me, I am at this moment engaged in an action my ancestors would have deemed disgraceful to them.

ALFRED. You! Impossible.

FABIEN. You'll wonder more when I explain it. Our peasantry in this district have been long divided into two factions, who hate each other mortally—the Orlandos and Colonnas; but for the first time in Corsica a quarrel has been compromised.

Surrounded by muskets, rapiers, and stilettos, I am selected as the arbiter of peace. This evening is fixed for the formality of pacification.

ALFRED. And how originated this famous quarrel, which your good offices have put an end to?

FABIEN. Like many others, from a very trifling cause; so insignificant I cannot name it without smiling. A hen!

ALFRED. A hen!

FABIEN. Yes, a wretched barn door hen. Ten years ago this hen escaped from the farm yard of the Orlandos to that of the Colonnas. The former demanded the hen, the others said it was theirs. During the dispute, the aged grandmother of the Colonnas, who held the fowl, wrung its neck and flung it in the face of the mother of the Orlandos. One of the Orlandos seized the hen, and was about to throw it back when a Colonna, who had a loaded carbine, fired and shot him on the spot.

ALFRED. And how many lives have been sacrificed in this silly altercation?

FABIEN. The killed are nine, the wounded five.

ALFRED. And all for a poor hen! No doubt both parties are worn out, and entreated you to interfere.

FABIEN. Far from it: they would have exterminated each other rather than have made the slightest overture. Our prefect wrote to Louis, who is gentleness itself, to say that if I interfered all might be well. He pledged his word for me, and I was bound in honour to redeem it. This evening, in this hall, the ceremony will take place.

Music. Enter GRIFFO, *who removes the supper things, and* MARIE, *who places pens, ink, portfolio, and paper on the table and exit. Bell strikes.*

Hark! The village bell announces the hour when all are summoned to attend.

GRIFFO. Monsieur Fabien, here's one without desires to speak with you.

FABIEN. Who is he?

GRIFFO. Orlando.

FABIEN. In right good time. Come in, honest Orlando.

> [*Goes to door and drags in* ORLANDO.

ORLANDO. I beg pardon, but—

FABIEN. But what?

ORLANDO. Why this—that is—I don't exactly know, but—
[*Bolting off again*—FABIEN *stops him.*]

FABIEN. Come in, man, come in.

ORLANDO. Oh—yes—come in—that's easily said, and easily
done too—but when I am in—

FABIEN. Well, what then?

ORLANDO. Monsieur Fabien dei Franchi, it chokes a man to be
reconciled to an enemy.

FABIEN. Remember, Orlando, you have given your word.

ORLANDO. Yes, yes I have. Oh! if I hadn't!

FABIEN. Recollect, too, your side has had the advantage. Five
Colonnas killed against four Orlandos.

MARIE enters.

ORLANDO. That's some consolation, but nevertheless—

MARIE. Monsieur Fabien, someone without enquires for you.

FABIEN. Where?

MARIE. There. [*Pointing* L.]

FABIEN. Who is it?

MARIE. Colonna.

FABIEN. Good; desire him to walk in. Griffo, go round by that
door, and lock it on the outside. [*Exit* GRIFFO, *locks door on
the outside and re-enters.*] I repeat, Orlando, you have the
advantage.

ORLANDO. But mind, he must bring a hen with him.

FABIEN. Decidedly.

ORLANDO. A white hen.

FABIEN. Oh, white or black, that makes no difference.

ORLANDO [*furious*]. White, white, nothing but white.

FABIEN. Well, it shall be white.

ORLANDO. And alive?

FABIEN. And alive.

ORLANDO. If it should be dead, remember, the contract fails.

FABIEN. Be satisfied, it *shall* be alive.

ORLANDO. And he must offer his hand first.

FABIEN. No, you both offer at the same time; you agreed to this.

ORLANDO. I don't remember that part of the agreement.

FABIEN. How! can an Orlando's memory fail when he has pledged his word?

ORLANDO. Ah, if I hadn't! It's very hard, nevertheless. But five dead Colonnas against four Orlandos, that's something.

MARIE [*without*]. Go in, I tell you.

COLONNA [*without*]. Well, if I must, I must.

Enter COLONNA *and* MARIE.

[ORLANDO, *on seeing* COLONNA, *tries to escape by the door* R., *but finding it locked, savagely takes a chair and sits.* GRIFFO *remonstrates with him for sitting in the presence of the Countess.* ORLANDO *rises.*

FABIEN [*to* COLONNA]. Remember, you have given your word.

COLONNA. You see, Monsieur Fabien, here's the point: there has been one more killed on one side than on the other; the terms are not equal.

FABIEN. Granted so far; but there are four Orlandos wounded against one Colonna.

COLONNA. Wounded don't count.

FABIEN. It's too late now to argue. Have you brought the hen?

COLONNA. The hen! What hen?

FABIEN. You remember your promise; come, you must have brought it.

COLONNA. Yes, yes.

FABIEN. Well, where is it?

COLONNA. Here.

FABIEN. Here! Where?

COLONNA. In my wallet.

FABIEN. Of course a white one?

COLONNA. Yes, white, certainly; there's one small black spot.

FABIEN. No matter, I'll take that on myself. Is it alive?

COLONNA. It was when I started, but on the way I sat down once or twice, and perhaps—

FABIEN. Produce it. Griffo, lock that door on the outside as you did the other. [*Exit* GRIFFO; *locks the door* L. *on the outside and re-enters.*] Hold your fowl in your hand and be ready.

COLONNA. As I bring the fowl, he must be the first to offer his hand.

FABIEN. No, no, both together, that's the agreement.

COLONNA. Is it positively so written down?

FABIEN. Positively.

COLONNA. Oh, if I hadn't promised—but a Colonna must keep his word.

FABIEN [*to* ORLANDO.] Who is your surety?

ORLANDO. Andrea Mari.

FABIEN [*to* COLONNA]. And yours?

COLONNA. My surety? I forgot that entirely.

ORLANDO. A failure on his side: I declare the treaty void. [*Trying to escape.* FABIEN *stops him.*]

FABIEN. No, no, he has one here. Monsieur Alfred Meynard, will you stand surety to Colonna?

ALFRED. With all my heart.

FABIEN. Good, the preliminaries are complete; throw open the gate, and admit the company.

Music. GRIFFO *opens the door at back. Enter the* JUDGE *with* COLONNA *and* ORLANDO: PEASANTS, *male and female.*

JUDGE [*at head of table*]. My worthy friends, we are assembled here by Monsieur Fabien dei Franchi, in his ancestral mansion, to witness one of those delightful scenes which are acceptable above, and do honour to the human heart.

[ORLANDO *and* COLONNA *groan.*

Receive each of you this peaceful olive branch, and vow oblivion for the past with friendship for the future.

COLONNA. Oblivion, *perhaps*; friendship, *never*.

ORLANDO. You hear him?

COLONNA. Diavolo! 'Tis I, not thou, that must restore the hen.

FABIEN [*presenting olive branch to* ORLANDO]. Now then, Orlando, friendship for the future.

ORLANDO. I'll make an effort. [*Takes the branch.*]

FABIEN [*presenting another branch to* COLONNA]. Now, Colonna, friendship for the future.

COLONNA. Well, I'll try. [*Takes the branch.*]

FABIEN. Good; that point's disposed of; now shake hands. [*Music.*] Your hands, I say. [FABIEN *takes a hand of each, and forces them to shake hands, both evincing disgust and unwillingness.*]

JUDGE [*reading paper*]. 'Before us, Antonio Sanola, justice of the peace for the district of Sullacaro, it has been solemnly and formally agreed between Carbano Orlando, and Marco Colonna, that from this day forth, the 22nd of March, 1841, the vendetta declared between them since the 11th of February, 1830, shall cease for ever. [*Groan from the two adversaries.*] In token of which they have severally signed these presents, before the principal inhabitants of the village, their respective sureties, friends, and relatives; and which are further ratified by Monsieur Fabien dei Franchi, elected as arbitrator, and by me, Antonio Sanola, judge of the district as aforesaid.' Now, gentlemen, your signatures.

ORLANDO. I can't sign; I don't know how to write.

JUDGE. Then you must affix your mark; a cross will do.

[*Music.* ORLANDO, *after some difficulties, makes a large cross.* COLONNA, *with a great deal of ceremony, contrives to write his name. The sureties also sign.*]

FABIEN. Now then, Colonna, restore the hen.

[COLONNA *takes the hen from one of the* PEASANTS *to whom he had previously given it before signing, and is about to dash it in the face of* ORLANDO, *but being checked by* FABIEN *delivers it very politely.* ORLANDO *receives it after the same fashion.*]

ORLANDO. Excellenza! The hen is miserably thin.

COLONNA [*aside to* FABIEN]. It isn't a hen, it's a little cock.

[*Music. Exeunt* JUDGE, ORLANDO, COLONNA, *and* PEASANTS.

FABIEN [*to* ALFRED]. Well sir, you have seen our social manners in Corsica; judge whether we are entitled to rank with civilized nations.

ALFRED. At least I have a new incident to add to my adventures.

MADAME. You will relate to our dear Louis how his brother has redeemed his pledge.

ALFRED. I shall not fail to do so.

MADAME. It grows late; you are doubtless fatigued. Griffo, conduct our guest to his apartment.

FABIEN. Select another servant; I have some particular orders for Griffo.

MADAME. In that case I will attend on him myself. [*Takes candle from* GRIFFO, *and goes to door.*]

ALFRED. Impossible, Madame, I cannot suffer it.

MADAME. In the olden times, the lady of the castle always acted as chamberlain, and in Corsica we are still in the sixteenth century.

ALFRED. If you are peremptory, I must obey. [*To* FABIEN.] Goodnight. Remember, we were interrupted; you owe me the remainder of a story.

FABIEN. Yes, tomorrow. Good night.

[*Music. Exeunt* MADAME DEI FRANCHI *and* ALFRED MEYNARD.

Griffo!

GRIFFO. Sir.

FABIEN. You must instantly set out for Ajaccio; there wait the arrival of a letter from Paris: the moment you receive it, gallop back as if life and death were on your speed.

GRIFFO. You fear something has happened to your brother?

FABIEN. Griffo, he is wounded. I must know whether his wound is slight or dangerous.

GRIFFO. Have you received a warning?

FABIEN. Yes; this morning on my way to the mountains, I felt a sudden pang, as if a sword had pierced my chest. I looked round and saw no one. I laid my hand upon the place, there was no wound. My heart felt crushed, and the name of my brother leapt unbidden to my lips. I looked at my watch; it was ten minutes after nine. [*Music.*] Look! Look! The clock—it points to the same hour, although it must be close on midnight—the clock has stopped.

MADAME *re-enters.*

MADAME. Yes, I noticed it before. The clock stopped this morning and without apparent cause.

FABIEN. This morning! They must have forgot to wind it up.

MADAME. On the contrary, it was wound up the day before yesterday.

FABIEN. There's no mistaking this; 'tis a second warning.

MADAME. What say you, Fabien?

FABIEN. Nothing—nothing. Good night.

MADAME. Bless you my son; good night. If evil hovers over us, may Providence avert it. [*Exit.*

FABIEN. To horse! To horse! Griffo, lose not a moment. At all hazards I will write to Louis. Put the letter in the post the moment you arrive; 'twill catch the steamer which starts for France to-morrow. Haste, haste; I'll bring the letter before your foot is in the stirrup.

[*Music. Exit* GRIFFO. FABIEN *takes off his jacket.*

The sudden pang in my side, the strange coincidence between my watch and the clock—but perhaps 'tis nothing after all. [*Sits at table and writes.*] 'My brother, my dearest Louis, if this finds you still alive, write instantly, though but two words, to reassure me—I have received a terrible admonition; write, write.'

[*He folds the letter, seals it, during which* LOUIS DEI FRANCHI *has gradually appeared rising through the floor, in his shirt sleeves, with blood upon his breast; and as* FABIEN *is about to place his seal on the wax* LOUIS *touches him on the shoulder.*

FABIEN [*looking up*]. My brother! Dead! [*Music changes.*]

MADAME *enters.*

MADAME. Who uttered that word?

[LOUIS DEI FRANCHI *waves his arm towards the wall, and disappears; at the same time the back of the scene opens and discloses a glade in the Forest of Fontainebleau. On one side is a young man wiping the blood from his sword with a pocket handkerchief. Two seconds are near him. On the other side,* LOUIS DEI FRANCHI *extended on the ground, supported by his two seconds and a surgeon. Act drop slowly descends. Tableau.*

ACT II

SCENE I. *Masked Ball at the Opera. Various crowds dancing; end of which enter* CORALIE, *followed by* MONTGIRON.

MONTGIRON. Stay, my angel! One word.

CORALIE. Let it be a short one.

MONTGIRON. Love! Is that short enough?

CORALIE. Short and sweet; but it has too long a meaning.

MONTGIRON. Not so fast, my pretty Coralie.

CORALIE. Ah, you know me. [*Unmasks.*] Well, Baron, what now?

MONTGIRON. I give a supper to-night after the ball; will you join us?

Enter ESTELLE *and* VERNER.

CORALIE. I say, Estelle, here's the Baron has a supper to-night, and is in want of guests.

ESTELLE [*unmasking*]. Let him address his invitations to us ladies of the ballet.

CORALIE. And we'll undertake to provide a full company.

Enter BEAUCHAMP.

ESTELLE. So you may ice your champagne with full confidence, my dear Baron.

MONTGIRON. Then I may depend upon you?

CORALIE [*taking the arm of* BEAUCHAMP]. Here is my security. Monsieur Beauchamp, you are to retain me in custody until— oh, by the bye, what hour?

MONTGIRON. Three o'clock precisely.

CORALIE. Until three o'clock, at which disgracefully late hour you are to surrender me at the table of the Baron de Montgiron.

BEAUCHAMP. Accepted.   [*Exit with* CORALIE.

ESTELLE. Monsieur Verner, till then I confide myself to your sense of propriety.

VERNER. Agreed.

[*Music. All remask and join the crowd: short dance; end of which enter* LOUIS DEI FRANCHI.

LOUIS. It is close on half past one; that was the time named, and this the place. The anonymous letter I have received assured me she would be here. I have examined every domino that passed me, but I cannot find her. Perhaps I have been deceived; oh, would it were so! Émilie, dear Émilie! For you I have suffered much, and will endure still more.

[*Music. Three* DÉBARDEURS *advance, dancing; and a basket figure, with bladders, comes down dancing and hitting every one that comes in his way.* MONTGIRON *returns with* GIORDANO *and two* GENTLEMEN.

MONTGIRON. Yes, every one his own master at present; but remember you sup with me at three o'clock.

GENTLEMEN. At three! We understand. [*They go and mix with crowd.*]

LOUIS. I seek in vain; I cannot find her.

MONTGIRON. Louis!

GIORDANO. Louis dei Franchi!

LOUIS. Giordano! My friend! My countryman!

GIORDANO. My dear Louis, I rejoice to meet you.

LOUIS. I thought you were in Algiers with your regiment.

GIORDANO. I arrived in Paris this morning, on leave of absence.

MONTGIRON. And now, like a true Anacreon, he seeks the Opera, to blend the myrtle with his laurels.

GIORDANO. And you—how chances it I meet you in Paris?

MONTGIRON. He is studying the law; that accounts for his melancholy and abstracted air. Come, cheer up, man; to-night you must be one of us, and sup with me; you'll meet all our own set: Beauchamp, Verner, Château-Renaud.

LOUIS. Château-Renaud!

MONTGIRON. You know him?

LOUIS. I have met him once or twice.

MONTGIRON. Oh, he's in great request: a most accomplished fellow, acknowledged as the best swordsman in France; and by his own account resistless with the fair.

LOUIS [*aside*]. Should it be so? Can I have wronged her?

MONTGIRON. Well, we may reckon on you.

LOUIS. You must excuse me. I have an appointment here; besides I am not in spirits for such a party.

MONTGIRON. An appointment! Oh, bring the fair lady with you.

LOUIS. You mistake me. I am not here to seek proofs of love, but to save one who seeks her own destruction.

MONTGIRON. Louis, are you serious?

LOUIS. I am indeed. Thank you once again, but I must decline.

[*Music. Retires up.* MONTGIRON *and* GIORDANO *retire off. Short dance. Three men run across, carrying another, with their arms extended.* MONTGIRON *and* GIORDANO *re-enter.*

GIORDANO. Poor fellow, I hope he hasn't got into a scrape.

MONTGIRON. Oh no, a love affair; six days will settle it.

GIORDANO. Who is the lady to whom he refers?

MONTGIRON. I cannot tell. Louis is reserved, and not a talker like Château-Renaud.

Enter CHÂTEAU-RENAUD.

RENAUD. I beg pardon, but I heard my name; I fear I interrupt you.

MONTGIRON. Not in the least; 'tis of you we were speaking.

RENAUD. Then I am one too many here.

MONTGIRON. No, no, pray stay. Monsieur de Château-Renaud, the Baron Giordano Martelli, Captain in the First Chasseurs of Africa—both distinguished heroes—the one in the field of Mars, the other in that of Venus.

RENAUD. Now Montgiron, positively you give me a reputation I do not deserve. How I have ever earned the character you honour me with I cannot imagine.

MONTGIRON. Indeed! That's strange; for they do say you gave it to yourself.

RENAUD. Who says so?

MONTGIRON. It was mentioned here not five minutes ago.

RENAUD. By whom?

MONTGIRON. First, I believe, by me.

RENAUD. You said that I boasted of success?

MONTGIRON. Yes, and I added, which you did not always achieve.

RENAUD. The devil you did: name a single instance.

MONTGIRON. Fifty if you please.

Enter ÉMILIE DE L'ESPARRE.

RENAUD. For example, name one.

MONTGIRON. Well, without going very far

RENAUD. Name—name!

MONTGIRON. Madame de L'Esparre.

RENAUD. Émilie de L'Esparre!

ÉMILIE [*advancing*]. M. de Château-Renaud?

RENAUD. Ha! Émilie, you are here; you seem alarmed. [*Aloud to* MONTGIRON.] Excuse me a moment.

[MONTGIRON *and* GIORDANO *retire up.*

ÉMILIE. As I entered, I met Louis dei Franchi. Spite of my mask he seemed to recognize me; he followed me as if to determine his suspicions.

RENAUD. Seek refuge in the adjoining saloon. I will follow you.

ÉMILIE. Oh, sir, why did you compel me to seek, in such a place as this, that justice your honour should have prompted you to do me unsolicited? You wished to humiliate me, and you have succeeded. I will await you.   [*Exit.*

RENAUD. Aha! fair Émilie, you despise my devotion and recall your plighted love; you shall repent it, my lovely traitoress.

MONTGIRON. Come, Château-Renaud, I accord you that creature, whoever she may be, as a conquest.

RENAUD. But you deny me Émilie de L'Esparre.

LOUIS *re-enters.*

MONTGIRON. They say you have compromised her name, although she never gave you the least encouragement.

RENAUD. That is the general opinion, is it?

MONTGIRON. It is.

RENAUD. Then you take me for a coxcomb, a braggart, a would-be Don Juan? Do you feel inclined to back your opinion? Will you bet?

MONTGIRON. On what?

RENAUD. That I prove to you this very night my influence with the lady you have just named.

MONTGIRON. How will you prove it?

RENAUD. You shall see her in a few minutes, leaning on my arm, here at this very ball.

MONTGIRON. Madame de L'Esparre here! But no, were it even so that proves nothing.

[LOUIS *has been watching every female and on hearing the name stops suddenly.*

RENAUD. What, not if I brought her to your house to supper?

MONTGIRON. Château-Renaud, this is too bad. As I know it is impossible, I defy you!

RENAUD. Do you? Name your wager.

MONTGIRON. Well, a thousand francs, and I will give you till four o'clock.

RENAUD. By which hour I engage to bring Madame de L'Esparre to your bachelor party. If I am one moment late I lose.

MONTGIRON. Agreed.

RENAUD. Adieu till then. [*Sees* LOUIS, *aside.*] What a pity that he is not to be of the party.   [*Exit.*

LOUIS. My dear Baron, you were kind enough to ask me to your supper, which I declined; will you permit me now to accept your invitation?

MONTGIRON. Bravo! Our party will then be complete, if Château-Renaud keeps his word. I shall expect you.

LOUIS *and* GIORDANO. We shall be there.

[*Exeunt. Music. Gallopade and polka, during which the scene closes.*

SCENE II. *The lobby of the Opera. Enter* ÉMILIE *and* CHATEAU-RENAUD.

ÉMILIE. You requested my presence here; I am come, although at the risk of my motives being misinterpreted by you and by the world.

RENAUD. What have you to fear? Behind that mask no one can recognize you.

ÉMILIE. I have obeyed the conditions you demanded; now keep your promise and restore to me those letters.

RENAUD. Certainly, since you insist on it.

ÉMILIE. Give them to me at once, and let me go.

RENAUD. You must first hear me: you must tell me at least the cause of this sudden change. Why did you ever encourage my addresses? Why write those letters, pledges of assured affection, and now so coldly ask their restitution?

EMILIE. My first affections, as you know, were yours; my father saw and crushed our hopes at once. The fate of my poor sister, the miserable marriage of Louise, was ever present to his mind. A marriage which lost him a daughter— me a sister. Unhappy girl, where is she now? Perhaps deserted, struggling with misery and want. Some cause, of which I am ignorant, taught his distempered mind to see in you a copy of my sister's husband. To snatch me from the fate he so much dreaded, he obliged me to accept the hand of the Admiral de L'Esparre. The disparity of our years, our total want of sympathy, rendered it impossible for me to love, although I respect and honour him. It is now a sacred duty I owe to my husband, as well as myself, to claim from you the evidences of our plighted troth.

RENAUD. You demand of me no trifling sacrifice.

ÉMILIE. Be not deluded by a thought so vain, so false, as to suppose I can again receive you with the feelings that inspired those letters: cease to claim possession of a heart which, with all its sufferings, all its anguish, belongs now to another; such sentiments are unworthy of you, and their avowal tends to degrade us both.

RENAUD. Who has dared to impugn my actions thus?

ÉMILIE. Those letters have been seen by others, and thus through the thoughtlessness of vanity, you assist to wound the honour you are bound to guard.

RENAUD. You act not from your own impulse: you have been urged on to this.

ÉMILIE. I cannot disregard the warning of a friend.

RENAUD. And this *friend*, this devoted, meddling friend, doubtless is Louis dei Franchi.

ÉMILIE. It matters not. The letters—I implore you—the letters—

RENAUD. I have them not about me.

ÉMILIE. Sir, in reliance on your promise to restore them here, I have consented most reluctantly to meet you.

RENAUD. Émilie, you bid me restore to you the only relics of our unhappy attachment.

ÉMILIE. Aye, now that its very mention is a crime.

RENAUD. Ungrateful! Ah! would I could be thus unfeeling; but no. Listen! That sister, whose name, whose memory you still so fondly cherish, I have traced out to her obscure retreat; I have rescued her from despair, perhaps from death, to restore her to your arms.

ÉMILIE. Oh, heavens!

RENAUD [*aside*]. Quarter to four. [*Aloud.*] Ungrateful Émilie! While you were seeking to complete my misery, I was labouring in silence to effect your happiness.

ÉMILIE. Oh! forgive me. When—when can I see her?

RENAUD. This very night she awaits your coming.

ÉMILIE. You do not deceive me?

RENAUD. This is too much. I have a carriage at the door, and will escort you to her lodgings instantly. There I will leave you, while I hasten to procure those letters you insist on my restoring; and thus, at the same moment, give you a double proof of my respect—my devotion.

ÉMILIE. Haste, haste! Forgive me if I doubted you.

RENAUD. I do—I do. Ah, Émilie! [*Looking at his watch.*] Ten minutes to four; I shall win my wager.

[*Exeunt.*

SCENE III. *An elegant Saloon in the house of* MONTGIRON. *Door* L., *door* R., *fire place* L. *Tables, chairs, sofa. Candelabras lighted.*

Two SERVANTS *discovered arranging the furniture: Bell heard.* SERVANTS *go off. First* SERVANT *re-enters, showing in* LOUIS DEI FRANCHI *and* GIORDANO.

SERVANT. This way, gentlemen.

GIORDANO. The Baron de Montgiron is not yet returned from the Opera, I presume?

SERVANT. No sir; my master ordered supper at four precisely. Do you wish for anything, gentlemen?

GIORDANO. No thank you; you can leave us. [*Advancing to* LOUIS, *who has seated himself and appears absorbed in thought.*] Louis, pardon me, but I see you are unhappy. Before others I said nothing; now that we are alone, tell me your secret: the grief that is confided to another loses half its bitterness. I am your friend—your countryman—you do not doubt me.

LOUIS. No, Giordano; I will treat you with the frankness of a brother. I love and I am wretched.

GIORDANO. Ah! I guessed as much.

LOUIS. This love first dawned in Corsica. A breeze, as soft and balmy as the odour of our orange groves, wafted it towards my heart; a rude tempest has torn it from me. When the object of my affection left Ajaccio for Paris, I resolved to follow her. I left my home, my country, my parent, and my noble generous brother, who sacrificed his own feelings from regard to mine. I came here full of hope, rejoicing to be near her. I came too late; she was already married to another.

GIORDANO [*sitting*]. Married!

LOUIS. Yes, married without affection; married at the very moment when I thought to offer her my hand.

GIORDANO. And have you seen her since?

LOUIS. Chance threw me into the society of her husband, and he invited me to his house.

GIORDANO. A dangerous guest.

LOUIS. Oh, no, you know me not. The sainted shrine is not more safe from desecration by the kneeling pilgrim than is the wife of him whose proffered friendship I accepted. I resolved to stifle my unhappy passion and become worthy of his confidence; but I mistook my strength, and ceased my visits.

GIORDANO. What cause did you assign for your absence?

LOUIS. There needed none; he was ordered on a foreign service. During her husband's absence, she lived almost in seclusion, when there suddenly appeared a man who assumed a fatal influence over her—that man was Château-Renaud.

GIORDANO. Château-Renaud! The lady of your love, then, is Madame de L'Esparre?

LOUIS. You have guessed truly. 'Tis she—'tis Émilie! [*They rise.*] This Château-Renaud, unrestrained by heart or conscience, has boasted publicly that having once been an accepted lover he still retains that character, although she is now married to another. The idle gossip of the world reached me in my lone retreat; claiming the freedom of a friend, I wrote to Émilie, and pointed out the selfish vanity by which she was thus compromised. I received no answer, but from some unknown quarter was informed that I should meet her at this ball. Impelled by the fatality that governs me I came, and was a witness of that shameful wager in which her name and honour are involved.

GIORDANO. Louis, be advised; let us leave this place before the party meets.

LOUIS. I feel, Giordano, that you are right. It were better that I should quit this place; but do we always act as reason dictates? I cannot go. I must remain.

[Music. Goes up with GIORDANO. *Bell.* SERVANT *enters and exits. Pause. Then a laugh is heard outside, and enter* MONT-GIRON, BEAUCHAMP *and* CORALIE, VERNER *and* ESTELLE, CÉLESTINE, *two* GENTLEMEN, *and two* LADIES.

MONTGIRON. This way, ladies; you are welcome to my poor habitation. Off with your masks, ladies, disguise is useless here.

CORALIE. Why, Baron, you are lodged like an eastern sultan.

ESTELLE. What a delicious chair.

CÉLESTINE. What beautiful furniture! I hope it's all paid for.

BEAUCHAMP. Montgiron has an old aunt with heavy dividends.

VERNER. What a lucky fellow! I have an old aunt with nothing but ill temper.

CORALIE. Where is the supper?

ALL. Aye, where is the supper?

MONTGIRON. You must excuse me ladies; we are not quite ready.

LADIES. Oh!

MONTGIRON. We cannot sup until the clock strikes four.

LADIES. Oh!

MONTGIRON. A circumstance—

CORALIE. Nothing happened to the champagne, I hope?

Two SERVANTS *enter with wine and biscuits etc., which they hand round.*

ESTELLE. I should expire.

CORALIE. Oh! Thank heaven, here it is. *[Taking a glass and biscuit.]*

MONTGIRON. Our number is not complete. I have promised to wait for Château-Renaud.

LADIES. Château-Renaud!

CORALIE. Here's to his speedy arrival.

MONTGIRON. Until four o'clock; a wager depends on it.

LADIES. A wager! Oh lor'!

MONTGIRON. He has laid me a thousand francs that he will bring here, to join our party, a certain lady of our acquaintance.

LOUIS [*aside*]. This is torture.

MONTGIRON. If he is one minute late, he loses.

ESTELLE. How ferociously proper she must be.

CORALIE. I wish somebody would ask me to supper, and bet me a thousand francs I would come.

CÉLESTINE. Who is the heroine?

BEAUCHAMP. A vestal of the lamp.

VERNER. Or Joan of Arc at least.

MONTGIRON. Oh, there is no breach of confidence in telling you. 'Tis Madame—

LOUIS [*advancing*]. Montgiron, will you accord me one favour?

MONTGIRON. A favour, my dear Louis?

LOUIS. Do not name the lady you expect.

CORALIE. Why not?

LOUIS. Because, Mademoiselle, that lady is married to a friend of mine.

CORALIE. Oh!

BEAUCHAMP. A married woman! The wager improves.

MONTGIRON. The husband is at this moment cruising off the coast of Mexico.

LOUIS. In a few weeks he will return, and I would have him spared all knowledge of his wife's imprudence.

ESTELLE. Poor fellow! How I pity him.

CORALIE. Serve him right.

CÉLESTINE. Certainly.

CORALIE. 'Twill teach him not to go cruising on the coast of Jericho again.

ESTELLE. Mexico, you dunce—Mexico.

CORALIE. Well then, Mexico, but I suppose it makes no difference to his wife. A husband six thousand miles off must be the same thing as none at all.

MONTGIRON. I respect your scruples, Louis. Since you desire it, we will treat the lady in question with the most profound discretion.

LOUIS. Thank you.

MONTGIRON. Ladies—gentlemen—whether Château-Renaud come alone or not—whether he win or lose his wager—I pledge you all to silence on this adventure.

GENTLEMEN. Certainly—we promise.

MONTGIRON [to LADIES]. And you all promise?

LADIES. We swear. [Raising their glasses.]

BEAUCHAMP. I would advise Château-Renaud to make haste; it wants but three minutes of his time.

VERNER. Is your clock right?

MONTGIRON. To a minute. I sent word to set it by his watch; the rest is his affair.

GIORDANO. Courage, Louis, she will not come.

LOUIS. It wants one minute yet. How slowly move those fatal hands; and yet my life hangs upon their speed. Will they never achieve the goal? Will the hour never strike to release me from this agony?

[Clock strikes four. At the fourth stroke of the clock, the bell of the house rings violently. SERVANT crosses and exits.

LOUIS. 'Tis he!

GIORDANO. Perhaps she is not with him.

MONTGIRON. Is he alone?   [Exit.

LOUIS. She's there, Giordano, she's there; her footfall strikes upon my heart.

GIORDANO. Courage, courage.

Re-enter MONTGIRON.

Enter, Madame, enter, I entreat you.

Music. CHÂTEAU-RENAUD *enters with* ÉMILIE.

RENAUD. Come in, dear Émilie, you needn't unmask unless you like. Bear witness, all of you, it was striking four when we arrived.

MONTGIRON. You have fairly won. Gentlemen, I have lost my wager.

ÉMILIE. Won! He has won. What? I am betrayed; my fears were well founded. My presence here, then, was the subject of a wager.

RENAUD. Émilie, I—

ÉMILIE [*to* MONTGIRON]. Speak, sir; you seem to be the master here: I turn to you for a reply.

MONTGIRON. I confess, Madame, that Monsieur de Château-Renaud induced me to hope that you would join our party.

ÉMILIE. To win this infamous wager, he has stooped to falsehood and to treachery. It was to visit a suffering relative he feigned to conduct me. I came on an errand of charity and affection. [*All express disbelief.*] Oh! I fear not to face you now. If there be any here whose brows should wear a blush, I know 'tis not the wife of the Admiral de L'Esparre. [*Unmasks.*]

RENAUD. Madame, you treat the jest too seriously; since you are here, you will surely stay.

ÉMILIE. I recognize at least *one friend*, and in his hands I place myself. Monsieur Louis dei Franchi, will you afford me your protection to conduct me home.

LOUIS [*advancing*]. My life is yours.

RENAUD. One moment; allow me to observe, sir, that I brought this lady here, and I alone will escort her hence.

ÉMILIE. Gentlemen, I place myself beneath the shelter of your honour; you will shield me from further insult.

LOUIS. Fear nothing, Madame, I am by your side.

RENAUD. I know now to whom to look for explanation.

LOUIS. If you allude to me, sir, I shall be at home in half an hour.

RENAUD. In less than that you will find a friend to represent me.

ÉMILIE. A duel!

ALL. Gentlemen! Gentlemen!

LOUIS. A challenge in the presence of a lady! Oh, sir, it lacked but this to give a finish to your character. Come, Madame, my blood to the last drop is yours; my life is nothing to the honour, the happiness you now confer upon me.

> [*Music. Exit with* ÉMILIE; GIORDANO *follows.*

RENAUD. Well, gentlemen, I suppose I have lost after all; but I shall sup with none the worse appetite.

> *Enter* SERVANT.

SERVANT. Supper is ready.

ALL. Come.

> [*Music till end of act.* MONTGIRON *and* CORALIE, CHÂTEAU-RENAUD *and* CÉLESTINE, LADIES *and* GENTLEMEN *exeunt. Curtains descend and close on the scene, ascending again for the next scene.*

———

SCENE IV. *The Forest of Fontainebleau.* LOUIS DEI FRANCHI *discovered lying wounded, supported by* GIORDANO *and* SECOND; SURGEON *feeling his pulse;* CHÂTEAU-RENAUD *wiping his sword.* MONTGIRON *and* VERNER *as seconds.*

GIORDANO. Well, sir, what hope?

SURGEON. None; the lungs are pierced. Ten minutes past nine! He has not five minutes more to live.

GIORDANO. My poor friend!

LOUIS. Giordano, where are you?

GIORDANO. Here, Louis, by your side; speak, what would you? Is there no wish you would have conveyed to your mother— to your brother, Fabien?

LOUIS. No, none; they will know all.

GIORDANO. When?

LOUIS. Tonight.

GIORDANO. Tonight! And by what means?

LOUIS. By me. Your hand, Giordano; yours, sir—Émilie, farewell. [*Dies.*]

> [*The back of the scene opens, and discovers the exact scene of the first act. The clock pointing to ten minutes after nine.* MADAME DEI FRANCHI *and* FABIEN *in the same position as before. Act drop slowly.*]

ACT III

SCENE I. *The Glade in the Forest of Fontainebleau where* LOUIS *was killed.*

BOISSEC *discovered at work and singing.*

Song

Oho! oho! my heart is low,
I've asked Jeannette, and she has said no no.
Oho! Oho! Oho! Oho!
The jade has said me no.
Oho! Oho! I don't much care.
I know a lass as tall, and quite as fair.
Tol, lol, tol, lol,
And thus I show how deep is my despair.

[*The noise of a carriage is heard at a distance, with the bells of the horses and the cracking of the postillion's whip.*

BOISSEC. Click, clack! click, clack! How they do scamper along yonder—a post chaise tearing away at full gallop. It's a fine thing to be rich. But what is the postillion about? He's taking them right against a heap of stones. If that man isn't drunk, I'm not sober. He'll upset them, ten to one. [*Loud crash heard without.*] A hollow bet, won already. There's an end of your journey, whoever you are. Ah! Two gentlemen get up and shake themselves. They don't seem much hurt after all. They are looking about for assistance. These gentry often give a great deal of trouble, and pay nothing for it. I'll pretend not to see them; but they see me and are making signs. [CHÂTEAU-RENAUD *and* MONTGIRON *call without.*] Now they call. I'm blind and deaf.

[*Sits down and commences tying up faggots.*

Enter CHÂTEAU-RENAUD *and* MONTGIRON.

RENAUD. I say, my good fellow. [BOISSEC *continues singing, pretending not to hear him.* CHÂTEAU-RENAUD *touches him with his foot.*] My good friend, are you deaf?

BOISSEC. Did you speak to me, sir?

RENAUD. Yes, I did.

BOISSEC. Beg pardon, but I was so busy with my work.

MONTGIRON. Listen to me. If we take you from your work, we will gladly repay you for your lost time.

BOISSEC. The case is entirely altered; gentlemen, I am at your service.

MONTGIRON. The axle tree of our carriage is broke. Do you know any wheelwright in Fontainebleau who could mend it?

BOISSEC. A first rate one—my cousin. He should have been a coachmaker in Paris, but there's no such thing as justice in this world.

MONTGIRON. Fly, then, and bring him here, with his tools, instantly.

BOISSEC. 'Tis a good mile to his shop.

MONTGIRON. Ten francs are yours if you despatch.

BOISSEC. Ten francs! I'm off like a flash of lightning. [*Running off—returns.*] I beg pardon, have you broke any bones in your tumble?

MONTGIRON. No, no.

BOISSEC. Because, you see, my cousin is a famous veterinary surgeon also, and can set an arm or leg with any man in Paris.

MONTGIRON. We have no need of his skill in that line.

BOISSEC. Ah! I am sorry for that. [*Running off again—returns.*] I beg pardon, again, but an upset in the dust makes people thirsty; my cousin sells capital wine, almost as good as [*Aside.*] vinegar.

MONTGIRON. Begone, I tell you, or the ten francs will dwindle to five.

BOISSEC. Au revoir.

[*Runs off.* CHÂTEAU-RENAUD, *during this dialogue, has seated himself on a trunk of a tree in a desponding attitude.*]

MONTGIRON. Château-Renaud, what ails you, man?

RENAUD. Montgiron, if I were superstitious, I should give up this journey.

MONTGIRON. It has commenced badly enough, that must be admitted.

RENAUD. We should have done far better to have remained in Paris.

MONTGIRON. I think differently, and have determined to be missing for the present. Your duel with Louis, in spite of our precautions, has taken wind. The Attorney General and the Minister of Police are making tender enquiries after us.

RENAUD. I care little for their enquiries.

MONTGIRON. But I tell you they are serious this time, and resolved to make an example. Unfortunately, this is not your first affair—

RENAUD. And for a trifling mishap or two, like this—

MONTGIRON. You wish to figure in a court of justice; I have no such ambition. We should be acquitted perhaps; but in the mean time three months in prison, on spare diet, is anything but amusing. Besides, you have forgot another trifling inconvenience.

RENAUD. Indeed! Of what nature?

MONTGIRON. Louis dei Franchi is dead, but he has left a brother.

RENAUD. Well, what of him?

MONTGIRON. Only this—he is a true Corsican. As soon as he hears of what has happened, he will traverse the whole world to obtain revenge.

RENAUD. I see no reason, because I have fought with one brother, why I should run the gauntlet through the whole family.

MONTGIRON. In France no, in Corsica yes. Take my advice, and keep out of the way for a few weeks, until this unhappy affair has blown over.

RENAUD. Well, as you wish it, and our plans are formed, let us proceed. I cannot conceal the sensations which oppress me. For the first time I feel as if urged on by some controlling influence to something fatal.

I

MONTGIRON. You, Château-Renaud, grown superstitious?

RENAUD. 'Tis weak, I own; but the strongest minds are sometimes moved by trifles—the breaking of a mirror, or the
howling of a dog. I have laughed at all these things a hundred
times, and now my nerves are shaken by the overturn of our
post chaise—and in what locality? In the forest of Fontainebleau, in the very glade where, five days since—stay, do you
not recognize the spot—this path—that tree—

MONTGIRON. Yes, 'tis the very place. The accident is strange.

RENAUD. Montgiron, there's more than *accident* in this; 'tis
destiny—perhaps the hand of Providence.

MONTGIRON. Our man returns.

Enter BOISSEC.

Well friend, you have lost no time. Is the blacksmith at work?

BOISSEC. Look yonder, and you can see him at work; in a few
moments all will be right again.

MONTGIRON. Here is the money I promised you.

BOISSEC. Thank you sir. With ten francs in my pocket I am a
gentleman for the rest of the day. [*Whip heard.*] Ah! another
carriage! If it would only break down like the first, I might
double the ten francs. [*Taking up axe and faggots.*] Good day,
Messieurs, and a pleasant journey.   [*Exit singing.*

RENAUD. Let us leave this spot; let us get beyond this forest, it
feels like a grave. In the whisper of the wind I hear the
dying sigh of Louis dei Franchi; and at every turn I dread to
meet his ghost.

MONTGIRON. What folly!

RENAUD. It may be folly, but I cannot conquer it; let us be gone.

As they are going up, FABIEN *enters.*

FABIEN. Stay!

MONTGIRON. What do I see?

RENAUD [*in great terror*]. What would you?

FABIEN. Can you not guess?

RENAUD. Louis dei Franchi!

FABIEN. You take me for the spectre of your victim—no; I am one more terrible, more implacable. I am Fabien dei Franchi, come from the wilds of Corsica to demand of you where is my brother.

RENAUD. Of me? Of me? What have I to do with him?

FABIEN. You answer as the first murderer. Five days since, at the remotest end of Corsica, I learnt how I had lost a loved and only brother; how you drew your serpent slime across his path, blighted the bright vision of his days, tried to bring dishonour on a woman it was the devoted object of his life to guard. By a base lie you decoyed that woman into a snare from which he rescued her: then, taking advantage of a mere bravo's skill, you murdered him.

[CHÂTEAU-RENAUD *and* MONTGIRON *evince indignation.*

Yes—you are the assassin of my brother.

RENAUD. Assassin!

FABIEN. Ay, assassin. For when a man is deadly with his weapon and goads another less practised than himself to quarrel, he fights him not, he murders him.

[CHÂTEAU-RENAUD *makes an action as if about to rush on* FABIEN.

MONTGIRON [*interposing*]. Hold, hold! Gentlemen, I entreat you. Monsieur Fabien dei Franchi, I cannot comprehend you. Five days ago, you say you were in Corsica. How is it possible these sad details could have reached you in so short a space of time?

FABIEN. The dead travel quickly.

MONTGIRON. We are not children, sir, to be terrified with nursery tales.

FABIEN. On the same evening of my brother's death I was informed of all, [MONTGIRON *and* CHÂTEAU-RENAUD *appear incredulous.*] nay more. I saw it all. [*A look of surprise and fear from* CHÂTEAU-RENAUD.] In five days I have traversed two hundred and eighty leagues. When I reached your house, they told me you had just left Paris. I ascertained the route you had taken. I saw your carriage overturned and I exclaimed 'The hand of the avenger is upon him'.

RENAUD [*recovering himself*]. Well, sir, I am found. What would you with me?

FABIEN. A mortal combat. Know you not that the Corsican race is like the fabled Hydra—kill one, another supplies his place? You have shed my brother's blood—I am here to demand yours.

RENAUD. You wish to take my life! And how?

FABIEN. Not after the practice of my country, but in the manner sanctioned here, according to rule—according to fashion: you see I am in proper costume.

RENAUD. I would have avoided this most earnestly. I was flying from it. But if I accept the challenge, it is on one condition.

FABIEN. Name it.

RENAUD. That this quarrel ends here, and that I am not again to be called upon—let this be the *last* encounter.

FABIEN. The last it *shall* be. I am the only living relative of Louis, and after me, Monsieur de Château-Renaud, be assured none will trouble you.

RENAUD. Name your hour, place, and weapons.

FABIEN. The hour! I have sworn it should be at the moment when I met you. The weapons! With a sword you killed my brother, with a sword you shall encounter me. The place! The spot where we now stand.

RENAUD [*recoiling*]. This spot?

FABIEN. Yes, this spot; you chose it five days since. At the foot of that tree my brother fell; the traces of his blood remain there still.

RENAUD. Since you are determined, be it so.

[*Takes off coat, vest, handkerchief, etc.*

MONTGIRON. Gentlemen, this cannot be. The duel is impossible; at least at present. Here is but one witness, and you are both unarmed.

FABIEN. You are mistaken, sir; I come prepared. Meynard, approach!

Enter ALFRED MEYNARD *with two swords.*

Here is my second—here are arms for both.

MONTGIRON. Meynard, perhaps we may yet find means—

FABIEN [*taking off coat, etc*]. Monsieur Meynard, sir, knows his duty.

RENAUD. I am ready.

FABIEN. Meynard, request Monsieur de Château-Renaud to take his choice.

> [ALFRED *presents the swords to* CHÂTEAU-RENAUD, *who selects one, after trying the length, etc.*

RENAUD. Now sir.   [*A distant clock strikes nine.*

FABIEN [*very coolly*]. If you have any last instructions for your friend, you have still an opportunity.

RENAUD. Why should I use it?

FABIEN. Because, as surely as yon sky is now above us, in ten minutes you take your place there, where my brother fell.

RENAUD. This is no time for empty boasting, sir.

FABIEN. Come, sir—on guard!

> [*They fight for some moments.* CHÂTEAU-RENAUD *exhausts himself in useless efforts.*

Pause for a moment, you are out of breath.

RENAUD [*to* MONTGIRON, *sitting on trunk*]. His wrist is made of iron. [*To* FABIEN.] When you are ready. [*In rising from the trunk of tree his sword catches against the ground and breaks.*]

MONTGIRON. Gentlemen—the sword of Monsieur de Château-Renaud is broken: the duel is over, the chances are no longer equal.

FABIEN. You are mistaken, sir. [*Breaks his sword.*] I have made them equal. Take up that fragment, and let us try once more.

MONTGIRON. Are you still implacable?

FABIEN. As destiny.

RENAUD. I shall fall, Montgiron; I feel sure of it. You will continue your journey alone. In eight days write to my mother, and say I had a fall from my horse. In a fortnight tell her I am dead. If she learned the fatal news abruptly, it would kill her.

MONTGIRON. Château-Renaud, you are mad.

RENAUD. No, but in ten minutes I am a dead man.

[*Shakes hands with* MONTGIRON.

ALFRED. Gentlemen, are you ready?

[CHÂTEAU-RENAUD *and* FABIEN DEI FRANCHI *close in mortal conflict.* CHÂTEAU-RENAUD *overthrows him; but just as he is going to strike,* FABIEN *plunges his weapon into his breast.* CHÂTEAU-RENAUD *falls into* MONTGIRON'S *arms, who places him under the tree where* LOUIS DEI FRANCHI *fell.*

FABIEN. Louis! Louis! I can weep for you now.

[*Music. Throws himself into* MEYNARD'S *arms—comes down and sits on stump of tree.* LOUIS DEI FRANCHI *appears rising gradually through the earth, and placing his hand on his shoulder.*

LOUIS. Mourn not, my brother; we shall meet again.

Curtain slowly descends.

ENGAGED

AN ENTIRELY ORIGINAL FARCICAL COMEDY
IN THREE ACTS

BY

WILLIAM SCHWENCK GILBERT
(1836–1911)

═══

First performed at the Haymarket Theatre
3 October 1877

═══

CAST

CHEVIOT HILL, a young man of property	Mr. George Honey
BELVAWNEY, his friend	Mr. Harold Kyrle
MR. SYMPERSON	Mr. Howe
ANGUS MACALISTER, a Lowland peasant lad	Mr. Dewar
MAJOR McGILLICUDDY	Mr. Weathersby
BELINDA TREHERNE	Miss Marion Terry
MINNIE, Symperson's daughter	Miss Lucy Buckstone
MRS. MACFARLANE, a Lowland widow	Miss Emily Thorne
MAGGIE, her daughter, a Lowland lassie	Miss Julia Stewart
PARKER, Minnie's maid	Miss Julia Roselle

═══

Three months' interval is supposed to elapse between the First and Second Act. Three days' interval is supposed to elapse between the Second and Third Acts.

ACT I

SCENE. *Garden of a humble but picturesque cottage, near Gretna, on the border between England and Scotland. The cottage,* R., *is covered with creepers, and the garden is prettily filled with flowers. The door faces audience. A wooden bridge leads off* L. *The whole scene is suggestive of rustic prosperity and content.* MAGGIE MACFARLANE, *a pretty country girl, is discovered spinning at a wheel,* L., *and singing as she spins. A rustic stool,* R. ANGUS MACALISTER, *a good-looking peasant lad, appears at back and creeps softly down to* MAGGIE *as she sings and spins, and places his hands over her eyes.*

ANGUS. Wha is it?

MAGGIE. Oh, Angus, ye frightened me sae! [*He releases her.*] And see there—the flax is a' knotted and scrubbled—and I'll do naething wi' it!

ANGUS. Meg! My Meg! My ain bonnie Meg!

MAGGIE. Angus, why, lad, what's wrang wi' 'ee? Thou hast tear-drops in thy bonnie blue een.

ANGUS. Dinna heed them, Meg. It comes fra glowerin' at thy bright beauty. Glowerin' at thee is like glowerin' at the noon-day sun!

MAGGIE. Angus, thou'rt talking fulishly. I'm but a puir brown hill-side lassie. I dinna like to hear sic things from a straight honest lad like thee. It's the way the dandy toun-folk speak to me, and it does na come rightly from the lips of a simple man.

ANGUS. Forgive me, Meg, for I speak honestly to ye. Angus Macalister is not the man to deal in squeaming compliments. Meg, I love thee dearly, as thou well knowest. I'm but a puir lad, and I've little but twa braw arms and a straight hairt to live by, but I've saved a wee bit siller—I've a braw housie and a scrappie of gude garden-land—and it's a' for thee, lassie, if thou'll gie me thy true and tender little hairt!

MAGGIE. Angus, I'll be fair and straight wi' ee. Thou askest me for my hairt. Why, Angus, thou'rt tall and fair and brave. Thou'st a gude, honest face, and a gude, honest hairt, which is mair precious than a' the gold on earth! No man has a word to say against Angus Macalister—no, nor any woman neither. Thou hast strong arms to work wi', and a strong hairt to help thee work. And wha am I that I should say that a' these blessings are not enough for me? If thou, gude, brave, honest man, will be troubled wi' sic a puir little humble mousie as Maggie Macfarlane, why, she'll just be the proudest and happiest lassie in a' Dumfries!

ANGUS. My ain darling!   [*They embrace.*

Enter MRS. MACFARLANE, *from cottage.*

MRS. MACFARLANE. Why, Angus—Maggie, what's a' this?

ANGUS. Mistress Macfarlane, dinna be fasht wi' me; dinna think worse o' me than I deserve. I've loved your lass honestly these fifteen years, but I never plucked up the hairt to tell her so until noo; and when she answered fairly, it wasna in human nature to do aught else but hold her to my hairt and place one kiss on her bonnie cheek.

MRS. MACFARLANE. Angus, say nae mair. My hairt is sair at losing my only bairn, but I'm nae fasht wi' ee. Thou'rt a gude lad, and it's been the hope of my widowed auld heart to see you twain one. Thou'lt treat her kindly—I ken that weel. Thou'rt a prosperous, kirk-going man, and my Mag should be a happy lass indeed. Bless thee, Angus; bless thee!

[*Kisses him.*

ANGUS. [*Wiping his eyes.*] Dinna heed the water in my ee—it will come when I'm ower glad. Yes, I'm a fairly prosperous man. What wi' farmin' a bit land, and gillieing odd times, and a bit o' poachin' now and again; and what wi' my illicit whusky still—and throwin' trains off the line, that the poor distracted passengers may come to my cot, I've mair ways than one of making an honest living—and I'll work them a' nicht and day for my bonnie Meg!

MRS. MACFARLANE. D'ye ken, Angus, I sometimes think that thou'rt losing some o' thine auld skill at upsetting railway trains. Thou hast not done sic a thing these sax weeks, and the cottage stands sairly in need of sic chance custom as the poor delayed passengers may bring.

MAGGIE. Nay, mither, thou wrangest him. Even noo, this very day, has he not placed twa bonnie braw sleepers across the up-line, ready for the express from Glaisgie, which is due in twa minutes or so?

MRS. MACFARLANE. Gude lad! Gude thoughtfu' lad! But I hope the unfortunate passengers will na' be much hurt, puir unconscious bodies!

ANGUS. Fear nought, mither. Lang experience has taught me to do my work deftly. The train will run off the line, and the traffic will just be blocked for half a day, but I'll warrant ye that, wi' a' this, nae mon, woman, or child amang them will get sae much as a bruised head or a broken nose.

MAGGIE. My ain tender-hearted Angus! He wadna hurt sae much as a blatherin', buzzin' bluebottle flee!

[*Railway whistle heard.*

ANGUS. Nae, Meg, not if takin' care and thought could help the poor dumb thing. [*Wiping his eyes.*] There, see lass, [*Looking off.*] the train's at a standstill, and there's nae harm done. I'll just go and tell the puir distraught passengers that they may rest them here in thy cot, gin they will, till the line is cleared again. Mither, get thy rooms ready, and put brose i' the pot, for mebbe they'll be hungry, puir souls. Farewell, Meg; I'll be back ere lang, and if I don't bring 'ee a full half-dozen o' well-paying passengers, thou may'st just wed the red-headed exciseman! [*Exit.*

MAGGIE. Oh, mither, mither, I'm ower happy! I've nae deserved sic a good fortune as to be the wife o' yon brave and honest lad!

MRS. MACFARLANE. Meg, thine auld mither's hairt is sair at the thought o' losin' ye, for hitherto she's just been a' the world to 'ee; but now thou'lt cleave to thine Angus, and thou'lt learn to love him better than thy puir auld mither! But it mun be—it mun be!

MAGGIE. Nay, mither, say not that. A gude girl loves her husband wi' one love and her mither wi' anither. They are not alike, but neither is greater nor less than the ither, and they dwell together in peace and unity. That is how a gude girl loves.

MRS. MACFARLANE. And thou art a gude girl, Meg?

MAGGIE. I am a varra gude girl indeed, mither—a varra, varra gude girl!

MRS. MACFARLANE. I'm richt sure o' that. Well, the puir belated passengers will be here directly, and it is our duty to provide for them sic puir hospitality as our humble roof will afford. It shall never be said o' Janie Macfarlane that she ever turned the weary traveller fainting from her door.

MAGGIE. My ain gentle-hearted mither!

[*Exeunt together into cottage.*

Enter ANGUS *with* BELVAWNEY *and* MISS TREHERNE, *over bridge. She is in travelling costume, and both are much agitated and alarmed.*

ANGUS. Step in, sir—step in, and sit ye doun for a wee. I'll just send Mistress Macfarlane to ye. She's a gude auld bodie, and will see to your comforts as if she was your ain mither.

BELVAWNEY. Thank you, my worthy lad, for your kindness at this trying moment. I assure you we shall not forget it.

ANGUS. Ah, sir, wadna any mon do as muckle? A dry shelter, a bannock and a pan o' parritch is a' we can offer ye, but sic as it is ye're hairtily welcome.

BELVAWNEY. It is well—we thank you.

ANGUS. For wha wadna help the unfortunate?

BELVAWNEY. [*Occupied with* MISS TREHERNE.] Exactly— every one would.

ANGUS. Or feed the hungry?

BELVAWNEY. No doubt.

ANGUS. It just brings the tear-drop to my ee' to think——

BELVAWNEY. [*Leading him off.*] My friend, we would be alone, this maiden and I. Farewell. [*Exit* ANGUS *into cottage.*] Belinda—my own—my life! Compose yourself. It was in truth a weird and gruesome accident. The line is blocked— your parasol is broken, and your butterscotch trampled in the dust, but no serious harm is done. Come, be cheerful. We are safe—quite safe.

MISS TREHERNE. Safe! Ah, Belvawney, my own own Belvawney—there is, I fear, no safety for us so long as we are liable to be overtaken by that fearful Major to whom I was to have been married this morning!

BELVAWNEY. Major McGillicuddy? I confess I do not feel comfortable when I think of Major McGillicuddy.

MISS TREHERNE. You know his barbaric nature, and how madly jealous he is. If he should find that I have eloped with you, he will most surely shoot us both!

BELVAWNEY. It is an uneasy prospect. [*Suddenly.*] Belinda, do you love me?

MISS TREHERNE. With an impetuous passion that I shall carry with me to the tomb!

BELVAWNEY. Then be mine to-morrow! We are not far from Gretna, and the thing can be done without delay. Once married, the arm of the law will protect us from this fearful man, and we can defy him to do his worst.

MISS TREHERNE. Belvawney, all this is quite true. I love you madly, passionately; I care to live but in your heart; I breathe but for your love; yet, before I actually consent to take the irrevocable step that will place me on the pinnacle of my fondest hopes, you must give me some definite idea of your pecuniary position. I am not mercenary, heaven knows, but business is business, and I confess I should like a little definite information about the settlements.

BELVAWNEY. I often think that it is deeply to be deplored that these grovelling questions of money should alloy the tenderest and most hallowed sentiments that inspire our imperfect natures.

MISS TREHERNE. It is unfortunate, no doubt, but at the same time it is absolutely necessary.

BELVAWNEY. Belinda, I will be frank with you. My income is £1000 a year, which I hold on certain conditions. You know my friend Cheviot Hill, who is travelling to London in the same train with us, but in the third class?

MISS TREHERNE. I believe I know the man you mean.

BELVAWNEY. Cheviot, who is a young man of large property, but extremely close-fisted, is cursed with a strangely amatory disposition, as you will admit when I tell you that he has contracted a habit of proposing marriage, as a matter of course, to every woman he meets. His haughty father (who comes of a very old family—the Cheviot Hills had settled in this part of the world centuries before the Conquest) is compelled by his health to reside in Madeira. Knowing that I exercise an all but supernatural influence over his son, and fearing that his affectionate disposition would lead him to contract an undesirable marriage, the old gentleman allows me £1000 a year so long as Cheviot shall live single; but at his death or marriage the money goes over to Cheviot's uncle Symperson, who is now travelling to town with him.

MISS TREHERNE. Then so long as your influence over him lasts, so long only will you retain your income?

BELVAWNEY. That is, I am sorry to say, the state of the case.

MISS TREHERNE. [*After a pause.*] Belvawney, I love you with an imperishable ardour which mocks the power of words. If I were to begin to tell you now of the force of my indomitable passion for you, the tomb would close over me before I could exhaust the entrancing subject. But, as I said before, business is business, and unless I can see some distinct probability that your income will be permanent, I shall have no alternative but to weep my heart out in all the anguish of maiden solitude— uncared for, unloved, and alone!

[*Exit* MISS TREHERNE *into cottage.*

BELVAWNEY. There goes a noble-hearted girl indeed! Oh for the gift of Cheviot's airy badinage—oh for his skill in weaving a net about the hearts of women! If I could but induce her to marry me at once before the dreadful Major learns our flight! Why not? We are in Scotland. Methinks I've heard two loving hearts can wed, in this strange country, by merely making declaration to that effect. I will think out some cunning scheme to lure her into marriage unawares.

Enter MAGGIE, *from cottage.*

MAGGIE. Will ye walk in and rest a wee, Maister Belvawney?

There's a room ready for ye, kind sir, and ye're heartily
welcome to it.

BELVAWNEY. It is well. [MAGGIE *going*.] Stop! Come hither,
maiden.

MAGGIE. Oh, sir! You do not mean any harm towards a puir,
innocent, unprotected cottage lassie?

BELVAWNEY. Harm! No, of course I don't. What do you mean?

MAGGIE. I'm but a puir, humble mountain girl; but let me tell
you, sir, that my character's just as dear to me as the richest
and proudest lady's in the land. Before I consent to approach
ye, swear to me that you mean me no harm.

BELVAWNEY. Harm? Of course, I don't. Don't be a little fool!
Come here.

MAGGIE. [*Aside.*] There is something in his manner that
reassures me. It is not that of the airy trifler with innocent
hairts. [*Aloud.*] What wad ye wi' puir, harmless Maggie
Macfarlane, gude sir?

BELVAWNEY. Can you tell me what constitutes a Scotch
marriage?

MAGGIE. Oh, sir, it's nae use asking me that, for my hairt is not
my ain to give. I'm betrothed to the best and noblest lad in a'
the bonnie Borderland. Oh, sir, I canna be your bride!

BELVAWNEY. My girl, you mistake. I do not want you for my
bride. Can't you answer a simple question? What constitutes
a Scotch marriage?

MAGGIE. Ye've just to say before two witnesses, 'Maggie
Macfarlane is my wife;' and I've just to say, 'Maister
Belvawney is my husband,' and nae mon can set us asunder.
But, sir, I canna be your bride, for I am betrothed to the best
and noblest——

BELVAWNEY. I congratulate you. You can go.

MAGGIE. Yes, sir. [*Exit* MAGGIE.

BELVAWNEY. It is a simple process; simple, but yet how
beautiful! One thing is certain—Cheviot may marry any day,
despite my precautions, and then I shall be penniless. He may
die, and equally I shall be penniless. Belinda has £500 a year;
it is not much, but it would at least save me from starvation.
[*Exit.*

Enter SYMPERSON *and* CHEVIOT HILL, *over bridge. They both show signs of damage—their hats are beaten in and their clothes disordered through the accident.*

SYMPERSON. Well, here we are at last——

CHEVIOT. Yes; here we are at last, and a pretty state I'm in, to be sure.

SYMPERSON. My dear nephew, you would travel third class, and this is the consequence. After all, there's not much harm done.

CHEVIOT. Not much harm? What d'ye call that? [*Showing his hat.*] Ten and ninepence at one operation! My gloves split—one and four! My coat ruined—eighteen and six! It's a coarse and brutal nature that recognizes no harm that don't involve loss of blood. I'm reduced by this accident from a thinking, feeling, reflecting human being, to a moral pulp—a mash—a poultice. Damme, sir, that's what I am! I'm a poultice!

SYMPERSON. Cheviot, my dear boy, at the moment of the accident you were speaking to me on a very interesting subject.

CHEVIOT. Was I? I forget what it was. The accident has knocked it clean out of my head.

SYMPERSON. You were saying that you were a man of good position and fortune, that you derived £2000 a year from your bank, that you thought it was time you settled. You then reminded me that I should come into Belvawney's £1000 a year on your marriage, and I'm not sure, but I rather think you mentioned, casually, that my daughter Minnie is an Angel of Light.

CHEVIOT. True, and just then we went off the line. To resume—Uncle Symperson, your daughter Minnie is an Angel of Light, a perfect being, as innocent as a new-laid egg.

SYMPERSON. Minnie is indeed all that you have described her.

CHEVIOT. Uncle, I'm a man of few words. I feel and I speak. I love that girl, madly, passionately, irresistibly. She is my whole life, my whole soul and body, my Past, my Present, and my To Come. I have thought for none but her; she fills my mind, sleeping and waking; she is the essence of every

hope—the tree upon which the fruit of my heart is growing—
my own To Come!

SYMPERSON. [*Who has sunk overpowered on to stool during this
speech.*] Cheviot, my dear boy, excuse a father's tears. I won't
beat about the bush. You have anticipated my devoutest wish.
Cheviot, my dear boy, take her; she is yours!

CHEVIOT. I have often heard of rapture, but I never knew what
it was till now. Uncle Symperson, bearing in mind the fact
that your income will date from the day of the wedding, when
may this be?

SYMPERSON. My boy, the sooner the better! Delicacy would
prompt me to give Belvawney a reasonable notice of the
impending loss of his income, but should I, for such a mere
selfish reason as that, rob my child of one hour of the happiness that you are about to confer upon her? No! Duty to my
child is paramount!

CHEVIOT. On one condition, however, I must insist. This must
be kept from Belvawney's knowledge. You know the strange,
mysterious influence that his dreadful eyes exercise over me.

SYMPERSON. I have remarked it with astonishment.

CHEVIOT. They are much inflamed just now, and he has to wear
green spectacles. While this lasts I am a free agent, but under
treatment they may recover. In that case, if he knew that I
contemplated matrimony, he would use them to prevent my
doing so—and I cannot resist them—I cannot resist them!
Therefore, I say, until I am safely and securely tied up,
Belvawney must know nothing about it.

SYMPERSON. Trust me, Cheviot, he shall know nothing about
it from *me*. [*Aside.*] A thousand a year! I have endeavoured,
but in vain, to woo Fortune for fifty-six years, but she smiles
upon me at last; she smiles upon me at last!   [*Exit.*

CHEVIOT. At length my hopes are to be crowned! Oh, my own
—my own—the hope of my heart—my love—my life!

Enter BELVAWNEY, *who has overheard these words.*

BELVAWNEY. Cheviot! Whom are you apostrophizing in those
terms? You've been at it again, I see.

CHEVIOT. Belvawney, that apostrophe was private; I decline to admit you to my confidence.

BELVAWNEY. Cheviot, what is the reason of this strange tone of defiance? A week ago I had but to express a wish to have it obeyed as a matter of course.

CHEVIOT. Belvawney, it may not be denied that there was a time when, owing to the remarkable influence exercised over me by your extraordinary eyes, you could do with me as you would. It would be affectation to deny it; your eyes withered my will; they paralyzed my volition. They were strange and lurid eyes, and I bowed to them. Those eyes were my Fate— my Destiny—my unerring Must—my inevitable Shall. That time has gone—for ever!

BELVAWNEY. Alas for the days that are past and the good that came and went with them!

CHEVIOT. Weep for them if you will. I cannot weep with you, for I loved them not. But, as you say, they are past. The light that lit up those eyes is extinct—their fire has died out— their soul has fled. They are no longer eyes; they are poached eggs. I have not yet sunk so low as to be the slave of two poached eggs.

BELVAWNEY. Have mercy. If any girl has succeeded in en- slaving you—and I know how easily you are enslaved— dismiss her from your thoughts; have no more to say to her, and I will—yes, I will bless you with my latest breath.

CHEVIOT. Whether a blessing conferred with one's latest breath is a superior article to one conferred in robust health we need not stop to inquire. I decline, as I said before, to admit you to my confidence on any terms whatever. Begone! [*Exit* BELVAWNEY.] Dismiss from my thoughts the only woman I ever loved! Have no more to say to the tree upon which the fruit of my heart is growing! No, Belvawney, I cannot cut off my tree as if it were gas or water. I do not treat women like that. Some men do, but I don't. I am not that sort of man. I respect women; I love women. They are good; they are pure; they are beautiful; at least many of them are.

Enter MAGGIE; *he is much fascinated.*

This one, for example, is very beautiful indeed!

MAGGIE. If ye'll just walk in, sir, ye'll find a bannock and a pan o' parritch waitin' for ye on the table.

CHEVIOT. This is one of the loveliest women I ever met in the whole course of my life!

MAGGIE. [*Aside.*] What's he glowerin' at? [*Aloud.*] Oh, sir, ye mean no harm to a poor Lowland lassie?

CHEVIOT. Pardon me; it's very foolish. I can't account for it— but I am arrested, fascinated.

MAGGIE. Oh, gude sir, what's fascinated ye?

CHEVIOT. I don't know; there is something about you that exercises a most remarkable influence over me; it seems to weave a kind of enchantment around me. I can't think what it is. You are a good girl, I am sure. None but a good girl could so powerfully affect me. You *are* a good girl, are you not?

MAGGIE. I am a varra gude girl indeed, sir.

CHEVIOT. I was quite sure of it.

[*Gets his arm round her waist.*

MAGGIE. I am a much better girl than nineteen out of twenty in these pairts. And they are all gude girls too.

CHEVIOT. My darling!　　　　　　　　　　　　[*Kisses her.*

MAGGIE. Oh, kind sir, what's that for?

CHEVIOT. It is your reward for being a good girl.

MAGGIE. Oh, sir, I did na look for sic a recompense; you are varra varra kind to puir little Maggie Macfarlane.

CHEVIOT. I cannot think what it is about you that fascinates me so remarkably.

MAGGIE. Maybe it's my beauty.

CHEVIOT. Maybe it is. It is quite possible that it may be, as you say, your beauty.

MAGGIE. I am remarkably pretty, and I've a varra neat figure.

CHEVIOT. There is a natural modesty in this guileless appreciation of your own perfection that is, to me, infinitely more charming than the affected ignorance of an artificial town-bred beauty.

MAGGIE. Oh, sir, can I close my een to the picture that my

looking-glass holds up to me twenty times a day? We see the rose on the tree, and we say that it is fair; we see the silver moon sailing in the braw blue heavens, and we say that she is bright; we see the brawling stream purling over the smooth stanes i' the burn, and we say that it is beautiful; and shall we close our een to the fairest of nature's works—a pure and beautiful woman? Why, sir, it wad just be base ingratitude! No, it's best to tell the truth about a' things: I am a varra, varra, beautiful girl!

CHEVIOT. Maggie Macfarlane, I'm a plain, blunt, straight-forward man, and I come quickly to the point. I see more to love in you than I ever saw in any woman in all my life before. I have a large income, which I do not spend recklessly. I love you passionately; you are the essence of every hope; you are the tree upon which the fruit of my heart is growing— my Past, my Present, my Future—you are my own To Come. Tell me, will you be mine—will you join your life with mine?

Enter ANGUS, *who listens.*

MAGGIE. Ah, kind sir, I'm sairly grieved to wound sae true and tender a love as yours, but ye're ower late. My love is nae my ain to give ye; it's given ower to the best and bravest lad in a' the bonnie Borderland!

CHEVIOT. Give me his address that I may go and curse him!

MAGGIE. Ah, ye must not curse him. Oh, spare him, spare him, for he is good and brave, and he loves me, oh, sae dearly, and I love him, oh, sae dearly too. Oh, sir, kind sir, have mercy on him, and do not—do not curse him, or I shall die!

[*Throwing herself at his feet.*

CHEVIOT. Will you, or will you not, oblige me by telling me where he is, that I may at once go and curse him?

ANGUS. [*Coming forward.*] He is here, sir, but dinna waste your curses on me. Maggie, my bairn, [*Raising her.*] I heard the answer ye gave to this man, my true and gentle lassie. Ye spake well and bravely, Meg—well and bravely! Dinna heed the water in my ee—it's a tear of joy and gratitude, Meg— a tear of joy and gratitude!

CHEVIOT. [*Touched.*] Poor fellow! I will *not* curse him! [*Aloud.*] Young man, I respect your honest emotion. I don't want to distress you, but I cannot help loving this most charming girl. Come, is it reasonable to quarrel with a man because he's of the same way of thinking as yourself?

ANGUS. Nay, sir, I'm nae fasht, but it just seems to drive a' the bluid back into my hairt when I think that my Meg is loved by anither! Oh, sir, she's a fair and winsome lassie, and I micht as justly be angry wi' ye for loving the blue heavens. She's just as far above us as they are!

[*Wiping his eyes and kissing her.*

CHEVIOT. [*With decision.*] Pardon me, I cannot allow that.

ANGUS. Eh?

CHEVIOT. I love that girl madly—passionately—and I cannot possibly allow you to do that—not before my eyes, I beg. You simply torture me.

MAGGIE. [*To* ANGUS.] Leave off, dear, till the puir gentleman's gone, and then ye can begin again.

CHEVIOT. Angus, listen to me, You love this girl?

ANGUS. I love her, sir, a'most as weel as I love mysel'.

CHEVIOT. Then reflect how you are standing in the way of her prosperity. I am a rich man. I have money, position, and education. I am a much more intellectual and generally agreeable companion for her than you can ever hope to be. I am full of anecdote, and all my anecdotes are in the best possible taste. I will tell you some of them some of these days, and you can judge for yourself. Maggie, if she married me, would live in a nice house in a good square. She would have wine—occasionally. She would be kept beautifully clean. Now, if you really love this girl almost as well as you love yourself, are you doing wisely or kindly in standing in the way of her getting all these good things? As to compensation—why, I've had heavy expenses of late—but if—yes, if thirty shillings——

ANGUS. [*Hotly.*] Sir, I'm puir in pocket, but I've a rich hairt. It is rich in a pure and overflowing love, and he that hath love hath all. You canna ken what true love is, or you wadna dare to insult a puir but honest lad by offering to buy his treasure for money.

MAGGIE. My ain true darling!   [*They embrace.*

CHEVIOT. Now, I'll not have it! Understand me, I'll not have it. It's simple agony to me. Angus, I respect your indignation, but you are too hasty. I do not offer to buy your treasure for money. You love her; it will naturally cause you pain to part with her, and I prescribe thirty shillings, not as a cure, but as a temporary solace. If thirty shillings is not enough, why, I don't mind making it two pounds.

ANGUS. Nae, sir, it's useless, and we ken it weel, do we not, my brave lassie? Our hearts are one as our bodies will be some day; and the man is na born and the gold is na coined that can set us twain asunder!

MAGGIE. Angus, dear, I'm varra proud o' sae staunch and true a love; it's like your ain true self, an' I can say nae more for it than that. But dinna act wi'out prudence and forethought, dear. In these hard times twa pound is twa pound, and I'm nae sure that ye're acting richtly in refusing sae large a sum. I love you varra dearly—ye ken that right weel—an' if ye'll be troubled wi' sic a poor little mousie I'll mak' ye a true an' loving wife, but I doubt whether, wi' a' my love, I'll ever be worth as much to ye as twa pound. Dinna act in haste, dear; tak' time to think before ye refuse this kind gentleman's offer.

ANGUS. Oh, sir, is not this rare modesty? Could ye match it amang your toun-bred fine ladies? I think not! Meg, it shall be as you say. I'll tak' the siller, but it'll be wi' a sair and broken hairt! [CHEVIOT *gives* ANGUS *money*.] Fare thee weel, my love—my childhood's—boyhood's—manhood's love! Ye're ganging fra my hairt to anither, who'll gie thee mair o' the gude things o' this world than I could ever gie 'ee, except love, an' o' that my hairt is full indeed! But it's a' for the best; ye'll be happier wi' him—and twa pound is twa pound. Meg, mak' him a gude wife, be true to him, and love him as ye loved me. Oh, Meg, my poor bruised hairt is well nigh like to break!   [*Rushes out in great agony.*

MAGGIE. [*Looking wistfully after him.*] Puir laddie, puir laddie! Oh, I did na ken till noo how weel he loved me!

CHEVIOT. Maggie, I'm almost sorry I—poor lad, poor fellow! He has a generous heart. I am glad I did not curse him. [*Aside.*] This is weakness! [*Aloud.*] Maggie my own—ever and for always my own, we will be very happy, will we not?

MAGGIE. Oh, sir, I dinna ken, but in truth I hope so. Oh, sir, my happiness is in your hands noo; be kind to the puir cottage lassie who loves ye sae weel. My hairt is a' your ain, and if ye forsake me my lot will be a sair one indeed! [*Exit, weeping*.

CHEVIOT. Poor little Lowland lassie! That's my idea of a wife. No ridiculous extravagance; no expensive tastes. Knows how to dress like a lady on £5 a year; ah, and does it too! No pretence there of being blind to her own beauties; she knows that she is beautiful, and scorns to lie about it. In that respect she resembles Symperson's dear daughter, Minnie. My darling Minnie. [*Looks at miniature*.] My own darling Minnie. Minnie is fair, Maggie is dark. Maggie loves me! That excellent and perfect country creature loves me! She is to be the light of my life, my own To Come! In some respects she is even prettier than Minnie—my darling Minnie, Symperson's dear daughter, the tree upon which the fruit of my heart is growing; my Past, my Present, and my Future, my own To Come! But this tendency to reverie is growing on me; I must shake it off.

Enter MISS TREHERNE.

Heaven and earth, what a singularly lovely girl!

MISS TREHERNE. A stranger! Pardon me, I will withdraw.
[*Going*.

CHEVIOT. A stranger indeed, in one sense, inasmuch as he never had the happiness of meeting you before—but, in that he has a heart that can sympathize with another's misfortune, he trusts he may claim to be regarded almost as a friend.

MISS TREHERNE. May I ask, sir, to what misfortunes you allude?

CHEVIOT. I—a—do not know their precise nature, but that perception would indeed be dull, and that heart would be indeed flinty, that did not at once perceive that you are very very unhappy. Accept, madam, my deepest and most respectful sympathy.

MISS TREHERNE. You have guessed rightly, sir! I am indeed a most unhappy woman.

CHEVIOT. I am delighted to hear it—a—I mean I feel a pleasure, a melancholy and chastened pleasure, in reflecting that, if your distress is not of a pecuniary nature, it may perchance lie in my power to alleviate your sorrow.

MISS TREHERNE. Impossible, sir, though I thank you for your respectful sympathy.

CHEVIOT. How many women would forego twenty years of their lives to be as beautiful as yourself, little dreaming that extraordinary loveliness can co-exist with the most poignant anguish of mind! But so too often we find it, do we not, dear lady?

MISS TREHERNE. Sir! This tone of address, from a complete stranger!

CHEVIOT. Nay, be not unreasonably severe upon an impassionable and impulsive man, whose tongue is but the too faithful herald of his heart. We see the rose on the tree, and we say that it is fair; we see the bonnie brooks purling over the smooth stanes—I should say stones—in the burn, and we say that it is beautiful, and shall we close our eyes to the fairest of nature's works, a pure and beautiful woman? Why, it would be base ingratitude, indeed!

MISS TREHERNE. I cannot deny that there is much truth in the sentiments you so beautifully express, but I am, unhappily, too well aware that whatever advantages I may possess personal beauty is not among their number.

CHEVIOT. How exquisitely modest is this chaste insensibility to your own singular loveliness! How infinitely more winning than the bold-faced self-appreciation of under-bred country girls!

MISS TREHERNE. I am glad, sir, that you are pleased with my modesty. It has often been admired.

CHEVIOT. Pleased! I am more than pleased—that's a very weak word. I am enchanted. Madam, I am a man of quick impulse and energetic action. I feel and I speak—I cannot help it. Madam, be not surprised when I tell you that I cannot resist the conviction that you are the light of my future life, the essence of every hope, the tree upon which the fruit of my heart is growing—my Past, my Present, my Future, my own

To Come! Do not extinguish that light, do not disperse that essence, do not blight that tree! I am well off; I'm a bachelor; I'm thirty-two; and I love you, madam, humbly, truly, trust-fully, patiently. Paralyzed with admiration, I wait anxiously and yet hopefully for your reply.

MISS TREHERNE. Sir, that heart would indeed be cold that did not feel grateful for so much earnest, single-hearted devotion. I am deeply grieved to have to say one word to cause pain to one who expresses himself in such well-chosen terms of respectful esteem; but, alas, I have already yielded up my heart to one who, if I mistake not, is a dear personal friend of your own.

CHEVIOT. Am I to understand that you are the young lady of property whom Belvawney hopes to marry?

MISS TREHERNE. I am, indeed, that unhappy woman!

CHEVIOT. And is it possible that you love him?

MISS TREHERNE. With a rapture that thrills every fibre of my heart—with a devotion that enthralls my very soul! But there's some difficulty about his settlements.

CHEVIOT. A difficulty! I should think there was. Why, on my marrying, his entire income goes over to Symperson! I could reduce him to penury to-morrow. As it happens, I *am* engaged, I recollect, to Symperson's daughter; and if Belvawney dares to interpose between you and me, by George, I'll do it!

MISS TREHERNE. Oh, spare him, sir! [*Falls on her knees.*] You say that you love me? Then, for my sake, remain single for ever—it is all I ask; it is not much. Promise me that you will never, never marry, and we will both bless you with our latest breath!   [*Rises.*

CHEVIOT. There seems to be a special importance attached to a blessing conferred with one's latest breath that I entirely fail to grasp. It seems to me to convey no definite advantage of any kind whatever.

MISS TREHERNE. Cruel, cruel man!   [*Weeps.*

Enter BELVAWNEY, *in great alarm, over bridge.*

BELVAWNEY. We are lost! We are lost!

MISS TREHERNE. What do you mean?

CHEVIOT. Who has lost you?

BELVAWNEY. Major McGillicuddy discovered your flight, and followed in the next train. The line is blocked through our accident, and his train has pulled up within a few yards of our own. He is now making his way to this very cottage! What do you say to that?

MISS TREHERNE. I agree with you; we are lost!

CHEVIOT. I disagree with you; I should say you are found.

BELVAWNEY. This man is a reckless fire-eater; he is jealous of me. He will assuredly shoot us both if he sees us here together. I am no coward—but—I confess I am uneasy.

MISS TREHERNE. [*To* CHEVIOT.] Oh, sir, you have a ready wit; help us out of this difficulty, and we will both bless you——

BELVAWNEY. With our latest breath!

CHEVIOT. That decides me. Madam, remain here with me. Belvawney, withdraw. [BELVAWNEY *retires*.] I will deal with this maniac alone. All I ask is, that if I find it necessary to make a statement that is not consistent with strict truth, you, madam, will unhesitatingly endorse it?

MISS TREHERNE. I will stake my very existence on its veracity, whatever it may be.

CHEVIOT. Good. He is at hand. Belvawney, go.

[*Exit* BELVAWNEY.

Now, madam, repose upon my shoulders, place your arms around me so—is that comfortable?

MISS TREHERNE. It is luxurious.

CHEVIOT. Good.

MISS TREHERNE. You are sure it does not inconvenience you?

CHEVIOT. Not at all. Now we are ready for him.

Enter, over bridge, MCGILLICUDDY, *with two* FRIENDS *dressed as for a wedding, with white favours, and carrying a large wedding cake.* MCGILLICUDDY *has pistols. All greatly excited.*

MCGILLICUDDY. Where is the villain? I'll swear he is concealed somewhere. Search every tree, every bush, every geranium. [*Sees* CHEVIOT *and* MISS TREHERNE.] Ha! they are here. Perjured woman! I've found you at last.

MISS TREHERNE. [*To* CHEVIOT.] Save me!

Enter BELVAWNEY, *listening*.

MCGILLICUDDY. Who is the unsightly scoundrel with whom you have flown—the unpleasant-looking scamp whom you have dared to prefer to me? Uncurl yourself from around the plain villain at once, unless you would share his fate.

Enter MAGGIE *and* ANGUS.

MISS TREHERNE. Major, spare him!

CHEVIOT. Now, sir, perhaps you will be so good as to explain who the deuce you are, and what you want with this lady?

MCGILLICUDDY. I don't know who you may be, but I'm McGillicuddy. I am betrothed to this lady; we were to have been married this morning. I waited for her at the church from ten till four; then I began to get impatient.

CHEVIOT. I really think you must be labouring under some delusion.

MCGILLICUDDY. Delusion! Ha, ha! Here's the cake!

CHEVIOT. Still, I think there's a mistake somewhere. This lady is my wife.

MCGILLICUDDY. What! Belinda, oh, Belinda! Tell me that this unattractive man lies; tell me that you are mine and only mine, now and for ever!

MISS TREHERNE. I cannot say that. This gentleman is my husband!

[MCGILLICUDDY *falls sobbing on seat*; BELVAWNEY *tears his hair in despair*; MAGGIE *sobs on* ANGUS's *shoulder*.

ACT II

SCENE. *Double Drawing-room in* SYMPERSON'S *House in London. Door,* R.C., *open at back. Another door,* L. *Chair and stool,* R.C. *Piano,* R. *Sofa,* L.C. *Indications that a wedding is about to take place. A plate of tarts and a bottle of wine on table,* R., *against flat.*

Enter MINNIE SYMPERSON, *in wedding dress, followed by* PARKER, *her maid, holding her train.*

MINNIE. Take care, Parker—that's right. There! How do I look?

PARKER. Beautiful, miss; quite beautiful.

MINNIE. [*Earnestly.*] Oh, Parker, am I really beautiful? Really, *really* beautiful, you know?

PARKER. Oh, miss, there's no question about it. Oh, I do so hope you and Mr. Cheviot Hill will be happy.

MINNIE. Oh, I'm sure we shall, Parker. He has often told me that I am the tree upon which the fruit of his heart is growing; and one couldn't wish to be more than *that.* And he tells me that his greatest happiness is to see me happy. So it will be my duty—my *duty*, Parker—to devote my life, my whole life, to making myself as happy as I possibly can.

Enter SYMPERSON, *dressed for wedding.*

SYMPERSON. So, my little lamb is ready for the sacrifice. You can go, Parker. [*Exit* PARKER.] And I am to lose my pet at last; my little dickey-bird is to be married to-day! Well, well, it's for her good. I must try and bear it—I must try and bear it.

MINNIE. And as my dear old papa comes into £1000 a year by it, I hope he won't allow it to distress him too much. He must try and bear up. He mustn't fret.

SYMPERSON. My child, I will not deny that £1000 a year is a consolation. It's quite a fortune. I hardly know what I shall do with it.

MINNIE. I think, dear papa, you will spend a good deal of it on brandy, and a good deal more on billiards, and a good deal more on betting.

SYMPERSON. It may be so; I don't say it won't. We shall see, Minnie; we shall see. These simple pleasures would certainly tend to soothe your poor old father's declining years. And my darling has not done badly either, has she?

MINNIE. No, dear papa; only fancy! Cheviot has £2000 a year from shares in the Royal Indestructible Bank.

SYMPERSON. And don't spend £200. By-the-bye, I'm sorry that my little bird has not contrived to induce him to settle anything on her; that, I think, was remiss in my tom-tit.

MINNIE. Dear papa, Cheviot is the very soul of honour; he's a fine, noble, manly, spirited fellow, but if he *has* a fault, it is that he is very, oh very, *very* stingy. He would rather lose his heart's blood than part with a shilling unnecessarily. He's a noble fellow, but he's like that.

SYMPERSON. Still I can't help feeling that if my robin had worked him judiciously——

MINNIE. Papa, dear, Cheviot is an all but perfect character, the very type of knightly chivalry; but he *has* faults and among other things he's one of the worst tempered men I ever met in all my little life. Poor simple little Minnie thought the matter over very carefully in her silly childish way, and she came to the conclusion, in her foolish little noddle, that, on the whole, perhaps she could work it better after marriage, than before.

SYMPERSON. Well, well, perhaps my wren is right.

MINNIE. Don't laugh at my silly little thoughts, dear papa, when I say I'm sure she is.

SYMPERSON. Minnie, my dear daughter, take a father's advice, the last he will ever be entitled to give you. If you would be truly happy in the married state, be sure you have your own way in everything. Brook no contradictions. Never yield to outside pressure. Give in to no argument. Admit no appeal. However wrong you may be, maintain a firm, resolute, and determined front. These were your angel mother's principles through life, and she was a happy woman indeed. I neglected those principles, and while she lived I was a miserable wretch.

MINNIE. Papa, dear, I have thought over the matter very carefully in my little baby-noddle, and I have come to the conclusion—don't laugh at me, dear papa—that it is my duty—my *duty*—to fall in with Cheviot's views in everything *before* marriage, and Cheviot's duty to fall into my views in everything *after* marriage. I think that is only fair, don't you?

SYMPERSON. Yes, I dare say it will come to that.

MINNIE. Don't think me a very silly little goose when I say I'm sure it will. Quite, quite sure, dear papa. Quite. [*Exit.*

SYMPERSON. Dear child—dear child! I sometimes fancy I can see traces of her angel mother's disposition in her. Yes, I think—I *think* she will be happy. But poor Cheviot! Oh lor, poor Cheviot! Dear me, it won't bear thinking of!

Enter MISS TREHERNE, *unobserved. She is dressed in stately and funereal black.*

MISS TREHERNE. Come here, manservant. Approach. I'm not going to bite you. Can I see the fair young thing they call Minnie Symperson?

SYMPERSON. Well really, I can hardly say. There's nothing wrong, I hope?

MISS TREHERNE. Nothing wrong? Oh, thoughtless, frivolous, light-hearted creature! Oh, reckless old butterfly! Nothing wrong! You've eyes in your head, a nose on your face, ears on each side of it, a brain of some sort in your skull, haven't you, butler?

SYMPERSON. Undoubtedly, but I beg to observe I'm not the——

MISS TREHERNE. Have you or have you not the gift of simple apprehension? Can you or can you not draw conclusions? Go to, go to, you offend me.

SYMPERSON. [*Aside.*] There *is* something wrong, and it's *here*. [*Touching his forehead.*] I'll tell her you're here. Whom shall I say?

MISS TREHERNE. Say that one on whose devoted head the black sorrows of a long lifetime have fallen, even as a funeral pall, craves a minute's interview with a dear old friend. Do you think you can recollect that message, butler?

SYMPERSON. I'll try, but I beg, I *beg* to observe, I'm not the butler. [*Aside.*] This is a most surprising young person!

[*Exit.*

MISS TREHERNE. At last I'm in my darling's home, the home of the bright blythe carolling thing that lit, as with a ray of heaven's sunlight, the murky gloom of my miserable school-days. But what do I see? Tarts? Ginger wine? There are rejoicings of some kind afoot. Alas, I am out of place here. What have I in common with tarts? Oh, I am ill-attuned to scenes of revelry!   [*Takes a tart and eats it.*

Enter MINNIE.

MINNIE. Belinda!   [*They rush to each other's arms.*

MISS TREHERNE. Minnie! My own long-lost lamb! This is the first gleam of joy that has lighted my darksome course this many and many a day! And in spite of the change that time and misery have brought upon me, you knew me at once!

[*Eating the tart all this time.*

MINNIE. Oh, I felt sure it was you, from the message.

MISS TREHERNE. How wondrously fair you have grown! And this dress! Why, it is surely a bridal dress! Those tarts—that wine! Surely this is not your wedding-day?

MINNIE. Yes, dear, I shall be married in half an hour.

MISS TREHERNE. Oh, strange chance! Oh, unheard-of coincidence! Married! And to whom?

MINNIE. Oh, to the dearest love—my cousin, Mr. Cheviot Hill. Perhaps you know the name?

MISS TREHERNE. I have heard of the Cheviot Hills somewhere. Happy—strangely happy girl! You, at least, know your husband's name.

MINNIE. Oh yes, it's on all his pocket-handkerchiefs.

MISS TREHERNE. It is much to know. I do not know mine.

MINNIE. Have you forgotten it?

MISS TREHERNE. No; I never knew it. It is a dark mystery. It may not be fathomed. It is buried in the fathomless gulf of the Eternal Past. There let it lie.

MINNIE. Oh, tell me all about it, dear.

MISS TREHERNE. It is a lurid tale. Three months since I fled from a hated one who was to have married me. He pursued me. I confided my distress to a young and wealthy stranger. Acting on his advice, I declared myself to be his wife; he declared himself to be my husband. We were parted immediately afterwards, and we have never met since. But this took place in Scotland, and by the law of that remarkable country we are man and wife, though I didn't know it at the time.

MINNIE. What fun!

MISS TREHERNE. Fun! Say, rather, horror—distraction—chaos! I am rent with conflicting doubts! Perhaps he was already married; in that case I am a bigamist. Maybe he is dead; in that case I am a widow. Maybe he is alive; in that case I am a wife. What am I? Am I single? Am I married? Am I a widow? Can I marry? Have I married? May I marry? Who am I? Where am I? What am I? What is my name? What is my condition in life? If I am married, to whom am I married? If I am a widow, how came I to be a widow, and whose widow came I to be? Why am I his widow? What did he die of? Did he leave me anything? If anything, how much, and is it saddled with conditions? Can I marry again without forfeiting it? Have I a mother-in-law? Have I a family of step-children, and if so, how many, and what are their ages, sexes, sizes, names and dispositions? These are questions that rack me night and day, and until they are settled, peace and I are not on terms!

MINNIE. Poor dear thing!

MISS TREHERNE. But enough of my selfish sorrows. [*Goes up to table and takes a tart.* MINNIE *is annoyed at this.*] Tell me about the noble boy who is about to make you his. Has he any dross?

MINNIE. I don't know. [*Secretly removes tarts to another table.*] I never thought of asking—I'm such a goose. But papa knows.

MISS TREHERNE. Have those base and servile things called settlements been satisfactorily adjusted?   [*Eating.*

MINNIE. I don't know. It never occurred to me to inquire. But papa can tell you.

MISS TREHERNE. The same artless little soul!

MINNIE. [*Standing so as to conceal tarts from* BELINDA.] Yes, I am quite artless—quite, quite artless. But now that you *are* here you will stay and see me married.

MISS TREHERNE. I would willingly be a witness to my darling's joy, but this attire is, perhaps, scarcely in harmony with a scene of revelry.

MINNIE. Well, dear, you're not a cheerful object, and that's the truth.

MISS TREHERNE. And yet these charnel-house rags may serve to remind the thoughtless banqueters that they are but mortal.

MINNIE. I don't think it will be necessary to do that, dear. Papa's sherry will make *that* quite clear to them.

MISS TREHERNE. Then I will hie me home, and array me in garments of less sombre hue.

MINNIE. I think it would be better, dear. Those are the very things for a funeral, but this is a wedding.

MISS TREHERNE. I see very little difference between them. But it shall be as you wish, though I have worn nothing but black since my miserable marriage. There is breakfast, I suppose?

MINNIE. Yes, at dear Cheviot's house.

MISS TREHERNE. That is well. I shall return in time for it. Thank heaven I can still eat!

[*Takes a tart from table and exit, followed by* MINNIE.

Enter CHEVIOT HILL. *He is dressed as for a wedding.*

CHEVIOT. Here I am at last—quite flurried and hot after the usual row with the cabman, just when I wanted to be particularly calm and self-contained. I got the best of it though. Dear me, this is a great day for me—a great day. Where's Minnie, I wonder? Arraying herself for the sacrifice, no doubt. Pouf! This is a very nervous occasion. I wonder if I'm taking a prudent step. Marriage is a very risky thing; it's like Chancery: once in it you can't get out of it, and the costs are enormous. There you are—fixed. Fifty years hence, if we're both alive, there we shall both be—fixed. That's the devil of it. It's an unreasonably long time to be responsible for another person's expenses. I don't see the use of making it for as long as that. It seems greedy to take up half a century of another person's attention. Besides—one never knows—one might come across somebody else one liked better—that uncommonly nice girl I met in Scotland, for instance. No, no, I shall be true to my Minnie—quite true. I am quite determined that nothing shall shake my constancy to Minnie.

Enter PARKER.

What a devilish pretty girl!

PARKER. [*Aside.*] He's a mean young man, but he ought to be good for half-a-crown to-day.

CHEVIOT. Come here, my dear; a—how do I look?

PARKER. Very nice indeed, sir.

CHEVIOT. What, really?

PARKER. Really.

CHEVIOT. What, tempting, eh?

PARKER. Very tempting indeed.

CHEVIOT. Hah! The married state is an enviable state, Parker.

PARKER. *Is* it, sir? I hope it may be. It depends.

CHEVIOT. What do you mean by 'it depends?' You're a member of the Church of England, I trust? Then don't you know that in saying 'it depends' you are flying in the face of the marriage service? Don't go and throw cold water on the married state, Parker. I know what you're going to say—it's expensive. So it is, at first, very expensive, but with economy you soon retrench that. By a beautiful provision of Nature, what's enough for one is enough for two. This phenomenon points directly to the married state as our natural state.

PARKER. Oh, for that matter, sir, a tigress would get on with you. You're so liberal, so gentle, so—there's only one word for it—dove-like.

CHEVIOT. What, you've remarked that, eh? Ha, ha! But dove-like as I am, Parker, in some respects, yet [*Getting his arm round her.*] in other respects—[*Aside.*] deuced pretty girl!—in other respects I am a man, Parker, of a strangely impetuous and headstrong nature. I don't beat about the bush; I come quickly to the point. Shall I tell you a secret? There's something about you, I don't know what it is, that—in other words, you are the tree upon which—no, no, damn it, Cheviot —not to-day, not to-day.

PARKER. What a way you have with you, sir!

CHEVIOT. What, you've noticed that, have you? Ha, ha! Yes, I have a way, no doubt; it's been remarked before. Whenever I see a pretty girl—and you are a very pretty girl—I can't help putting my arm like that. [*Putting it round her waist.*] Now, pleasant as this sort of thing is—and you find it pleasant, don't you? [PARKER *nods.*] Yes, you find it pleasant—pleasant as it is, it is decidedly wrong.

PARKER. It is decidedly wrong in a married man.

CHEVIOT. It is decidedly wrong in a married man. In a married man it's abominable, and I shall be a married man in half an hour. So, Parker, it will become necessary to conquer this tendency, to struggle with it, and subdue it—in half an hour. [*Getting more affectionate.*] Not that there's any real harm in putting your arm round a girl's waist. Highly respectable people do it, when they waltz.

PARKER. Yes, sir, but then a band's playing.

CHEVIOT. True, and when a band's playing it don't matter, but when a band is *not* playing, why it's dangerous, you see. You begin with this, and you go on from one thing to another, getting more and more affectionate, until you reach *this* stage. [*Kissing her.*] Not that there's any real harm in kissing, either; for you see fathers and mothers, who ought to set a good example, kissing their children every day.

PARKER. Lor, sir, kissing's nothing; everybody does that.

CHEVIOT. That is your experience, is it? It tallies with my own. Take it that I am your father, you are my daughter—or take it even that I am merely your husband, and you my wife, and it would be expected of me.   [*Kissing her.*

PARKER. But I'm not your wife, sir.

CHEVIOT. No, not yet, that's very true, and of course makes a difference. That's why I say I must subdue this tendency; I must struggle with it; I must conquer it—in half an hour.

MINNIE. [*Without.*] Parker, where's Mr. Cheviot?

CHEVIOT. There is your mistress, my dear—she's coming. Will you excuse me? [*Releasing her.*] Thank you. Good day, Parker.

PARKER. [*Disgusted.*] Not so much as a shilling, and that man's worth thousands! [*Exit.*

Enter MINNIE.

CHEVIOT. My darling Minnie—my own, own To Come!
[*Kissing her.*

MINNIE. Oh, you mustn't crush me, Cheviot; you'll spoil my dress. How do you like it?

CHEVIOT. It's lovely. It's a beautiful material.

MINNIE. Yes; dear papa's been going it.

CHEVIOT. Oh, but you're indebted to me for that beautiful dress.

MINNIE. To you! Oh, thank you—thank you!

CHEVIOT. Yes. I said to your papa, 'Now do for once let the girl have a nice dress; be liberal; buy the very best that money will procure; you'll never miss it. So, thanks to me, he bought you a beauty. Seventeen and six a yard if it's a penny. Dear me! To think that in half an hour this magnificent dress will be *my* property!

MINNIE. Yes. Dear papa said that as you had offered to give the breakfast at your house, he would give me the best dress that money could procure.

CHEVIOT. Yes, I *did* offer to provide the breakfast in a reckless moment; that's so like me. It was a rash offer, but I've made it, and I've stuck to it. Oh, then there's the cake.

MINNIE. Oh, tell me all about the cake.

CHEVIOT. It's a very pretty cake. Very little cake is eaten at a wedding breakfast, so I've ordered what's known in the trade as the three-quarter article.

MINNIE. I see; three-quarters cake, and the rest wood.

CHEVIOT. No; three-quarters wood, the rest cake. Be sure, my dear, you don't cut into the wood, for it has to be returned to the pastrycook to be filled up with cake for another occasion. I thought at first of ordering a seven-eighths article; but one isn't married every day—it's only once a year—I mean it's only now and then. So I said, 'Hang the expense; let's do the thing well.' And so it's a three-quarters.

MINNIE. How good you are to me! We shall be very happy, shall we not?

CHEVIOT. I—I hope so—yes. I *hope* so. Playfully happy, like two little kittens.

MINNIE. That will be delightful.

CHEVIOT. Economically happy, like two sensible people.

MINNIE. Oh, we must be very economical.

CHEVIOT. No vulgar display; no pandering to a jaded appetite. A refined and economical elegance; that is what we must aim at. A simple mutton chop, nicely broiled, for you; and *two* simple mutton chops, *very* nicely broiled, for me—

MINNIE. And some flowery potatoes—

CHEVIOT. A loaf of nice household bread—

MINNIE. A stick of celery—

CHEVIOT. And a bit of cheese, and you've a dinner fit for a monarch.

MINNIE. Then how shall we spend our evenings?

CHEVIOT. We'll have pleasant little fireside games. Are you fond of fireside games?

MINNIE. Oh, they're great fun.

CHEVIOT. Then we'll play at tailoring.

MINNIE. Tailoring? I don't think I know that game.

CHEVIOT. It's a very good game. You shall be the clever little jobbing tailor, and I'll be the particular customer who brings his own materials to be made up. You shall take my measure, cut out the cloth (real cloth, you know), stitch it together, and try it on; and then I'll find fault like a real customer, and you shall alter it until it fits, and when it fits beautifully that counts one to you.

MINNIE. Delightful!

CHEVIOT. Then there's another little fireside game which is great fun. We each take a bit of paper and a pencil and try who can jot down the nicest dinner for ninepence, and the next day we have it.

MINNIE. Oh, Cheviot, what a paradise you hold open to me!

CHEVIOT. Yes. How's papa?

MINNIE. He's very well and very happy. He's going to increase his establishment on the strength of the £1000 a year, and keep a manservant.

CHEVIOT. I know. I've been looking after some servants for him; they'll be here in the course of the morning. A cook, a housemaid, and a footman. I found them through an advertisement. They're country people, and will come very cheap.

MINNIE. How kind and thoughtful you are! Oh, Cheviot, I'm a very lucky girl! 　　　　　　　　　　　　　　　　　[*Exit.*

CHEVIOT. Yes, I think so too, if I can only repress my tendency to think of that tall girl I met in Scotland. Cheviot, my boy, you must make an effort; you are going to be married, and the tall girl is nothing to you.

Enter PARKER.

PARKER. Please, sir, here's a gentleman to see you.

CHEVIOT. Oh, my solicitor, no doubt. Show him up.

PARKER. And please, some persons have called to see you about an advertisement.

CHEVIOT. Oh, Symperson's servants. To be sure. Show up the gentleman, and tell the others to wait. 　　　[*Exit* PARKER.

Enter BELVAWNEY. *He looks very miserable.*

CHEVIOT. [*Much confused.*] Belvawney! This is unexpected.

BELVAWNEY. Yes, Cheviot. At last we meet. Don't, oh don't frown upon a heartbroken wretch.

CHEVIOT. Belvawney; I don't want to hurt your feelings, but I will not disguise from you that, not having seen you for three months, I was in hopes that I had got rid of you for ever.

BELVAWNEY. Oh, Cheviot, don't say that; I am so unhappy. And you have it in your power to make me comfortable. Do this, and I will bless you with my latest breath.

CHEVIOT. It is a tempting offer; I am not proof against it. We all have our price, and that is mine. Proceed.

BELVAWNEY. Miss Treherne—Belinda, whom I love so dearly, won't have anything to say to me.

CHEVIOT. It does her credit. She's a very superior girl.

BELVAWNEY. It's all through you, Cheviot. She declares that the mutual declaration you made to protect her from McGillicuddy amounts to a Scotch marriage.

CHEVIOT. What!

BELVAWNEY. She declares she is your wife. She professes to love me as fondly as ever, but a stern sense of duty to you forbids her to hold any communication with me.

CHEVIOT. Oh, but this is absurd, you know!

BELVAWNEY. Of course it is, but what's to be done? You left with Symperson immediately after making the declaration. As soon as she found you were gone she implored me to tell her your name and address. Of course I refused, and she quitted me, telling me that she would devote her life to finding you out.

CHEVIOT. But this is simple madness. I can't have it! This day, too, of all others! [*Aside.*] If she'd claimed me last week, or even yesterday, I wouldn't have minded, for she's a devilish fine woman; but if she were to turn up now—! [*Aloud.*] Belvawney, my dear friend, tell me what to do—I'll do anything.

BELVAWNEY. It seems that there's some doubt whether this cottage, which is just on the border, is in England or Scotland. If it is in England, she has no case; if it is in Scotland, I'm afraid she has. I've written to the owner of the property to ascertain, and if, in the meantime, she claims you, you must absolutely decline to recognize this marriage for a moment.

CHEVIOT. Not for one moment!

BELVAWNEY. It was a mere artifice to enable her to escape from McGillicuddy.

CHEVIOT. Nothing more!

BELVAWNEY. It's monstrous—perfectly monstrous—that that should constitute a marriage. It's disgraceful—it's abominable. Damme, Cheviot, it's immoral.

CHEVIOT. So it is—it's immoral. That settles it in *my* mind. It's immoral.

BELVAWNEY. You're quite sure you'll be resolute, Cheviot?

CHEVIOT. Resolute? I should think so! Why, hang it all, man, I'm going to be married in twenty minutes to Minnie Symperson!

BELVAWNEY. What!

CHEVIOT. [*Confused at having let this out.*] Didn't I tell you? I believe you're right; I did *not* tell you. It escaped me. Oh, yes, this is my wedding-day.

BELVAWNEY. Cheviot, you're joking—you don't mean this! Why, I shall lose £1000 a year by it, every penny I have in the world! Oh, it can't be—it's nonsense!

CHEVIOT. What do you mean by nonsense? The married state is an honourable estate, I believe? A man is not looked upon as utterly lost to all sense of decency because he's got married, I'm given to understand. People have been married before this, and have not been irretrievably tabooed in consequence, unless I'm grossly misinformed? Then what the dickens do you mean by saying 'nonsense' when I tell you that I'm going to be married?

BELVAWNEY. Cheviot, be careful how you take this step. Beware how you involve an innocent and helpless girl in social destruction.

CHEVIOT. What do you mean, sir?

BELVAWNEY. You cannot marry; you are a married man.

CHEVIOT. Come, come, Belvawney, this is trifling.

BELVAWNEY. You are married to Miss Treherne. I was present, and can depose to the fact.

CHEVIOT. Oh, you're not serious.

BELVAWNEY. Never more serious in my life.

CHEVIOT. But as you very properly said just now, it was a mere artifice—we didn't mean anything. It would be monstrous to regard that as a marriage. Damme, Belvawney, it would be immoral!

BELVAWNEY. I may deplore the state of the law, but I cannot stand tamely by and see it deliberately violated before my eyes.

CHEVIOT. [*Wildly.*] But Belvawney, my dear friend, reflect; everything is prepared for my marriage, at a great expense. I love Minnie deeply, devotedly. She is the actual tree upon which the fruit of my heart is growing. There's no mistake about it. She is my own To Come. I love her madly—rapturously. [*Going on his knees to* BELVAWNEY.] I have prepared a wedding breakfast at a great expense to do her honour. I have ordered four flys for the wedding party. I have taken two second-class Cook's tourists' tickets for Ilfracombe, Devon, Exeter, Cornwall, Westward Ho! and Bideford Bay. The whole thing has cost me some twenty or twenty-five pounds, and all this will be wasted—utterly wasted—if you interfere. Oh, Belvawney, dear Belvawney, let the recollection of our long and dear friendship operate to prevent your shipwrecking my future life. [*Sobbing hysterically.*

BELVAWNEY. I have a duty to do. I must do it. [*Going.*

CHEVIOT. But reflect, dear Belvawney; if I am married to Miss Treherne, you lose your income as much as if I married Minnie Symperson.

BELVAWNEY. No doubt, if you could prove your marriage to Miss Treherne. But you can't——

[*With melodramatic intensity.*

CHEVIOT. Those eyes!

BELVAWNEY. You don't know where she is——

[*With fiendish exultation.*

CHEVIOT. Oh, those eyes!

BELVAWNEY. The cottage has been pulled down, and the cottagers have emigrated to Patagonia——

CHEVIOT. Oh, those eyes!

BELVAWNEY. I'm the only witness left. *I* can prove your marriage, if I like; but you can't. [CHEVIOT *falls sobbing into a chair*.] Ha, ha, ha, ha! [*With Satanic laugh.*] It's a most painful and unfortunate situation for you; and, believe me, dear Cheviot, you have my deepest and most respectful sympathy.   [*Exit.*

CHEVIOT. This is appalling, simply appalling! The cup of happiness dashed from my lips just as I was about to drink a life-long draught. The ladder kicked from under my feet just as I was about to pick the fruit of my heart from the tree upon which it has been growing so long. I'm a married man! More than that, my honeymoon's past, and I never knew it! Stop a moment, though. The bride can't be found; the cottage is pulled down, and the cottagers have emigrated. What proof is there that such a marriage ever took place? There's only Belvawney, and Belvawney isn't a proof. Corroborated by the three cottagers, his word might be worth something; uncorroborated, it is worthless. I'll risk it. He can do nothing; the bride is nowhere; the cottagers are in Patagonia, and——

At this moment enter MRS. MACFARLANE, MAGGIE, *and* ANGUS. *They stand bobbing and curtseying in rustic fashion to* CHEVIOT, *whom they do not recognize. He stares aghast at them for a moment, then staggers back to sofa.*

CHEVIOT. The man, the woman, and the girl, by all that's infernal!

MRS. MACFARLANE. Gude day, sir. We've just ca'd to see ye about the advertisement.   [*Producing paper.*

CHEVIOT. I don't know you—I don't know you. Go away.
    [CHEVIOT *buries his head in a newspaper, and pretends to read.*

MAGGIE. Ah, sir, ye said that we were to ca' on ye this day at eleven o'clock, and sae we've coom a' the way fra Dumfries to see ye.

CHEVIOT. I tell you I don't know you. Go away. I'm not at all well. I'm very ill, and it's infectious.

ANGUS. We fear no illness, sir. This is Mistress Macfarlane, the gude auld mither, who'll cook the brose and boil the parritch, and sit wi' ye, and nurse ye through your illness till the sad day ye dee!   [*Wiping his eye.*
    [CHEVIOT *pokes a hole with his finger through newspaper, and reconnoitres unobserved.*

MRS. MACFARLANE. And this is Meg, my ain lass Meg!

CHEVIOT. [*Aside*.] Attractive girl, very. I remember her perfectly.

MRS. MACFARLANE. And this is Angus Macalister, who's going to marry her, and who'll be mair than a son to me!

ANGUS. Oh, mither, mither, dinna say it, for ye bring the teardrop to my ee, and it's no canny for a strong man to be blithering and soughing like a poor weak lassie!

[*Wiping his eye.*
[MAGGIE *advances to hole in newspaper and peeps through.*

MAGGIE. Oh, mither, mither!

[*Staggers back into* ANGUS's *arms.*

MRS. MACFARLANE. What is it, Meg?

ANGUS. Meg, my weel lo'ed Meg, my wee wifie that is to be, tell me what's wrang wi' 'ee.

MAGGIE. Oh, mither, it's him, the noble gentleman I plighted my troth to three weary months agone! The gallant Englishman who gave Angus twa golden pound to give me up!

ANGUS. It's the coward Sassenach who well nigh broke our Meg's heart!

MRS. MACFARLANE. My lass, my lass, dinna greet; maybe he'll marry ye yet.

CHEVIOT. [*Desperately*.] Here's another! Does anybody else want to marry me? Don't be shy. You, ma'am, [*To* MRS. MACFARLANE.] you're a fine woman—perhaps *you* would like to try your luck?

MAGGIE. Ah, sir! I dinna ken your name, but your bonnie face has lived in my twa een, sleeping and waking, three weary, weary months! Oh, sir, ye should na ha' deceived a trusting, simple Lowland lassie. 'Twas na weel done—'twas na weel done!

[*Weeping on his shoulder*; *he puts his arm round her waist.*

CHEVIOT. [*Softening*.] My good girl, what do you wish me to do? I remember you now perfectly. I *did* admire you very much—in fact, I do still; you're a very charming girl. Let us talk this over, calmly and quietly. [MAGGIE *moves away*.] No, you needn't go; you can stop there if you like. There,

there, my dear, don't fret. [*Aside.*] She *is* a very charming girl,
I almost wish I—I really begin to think I—no, no, damn it,
Cheviot! not to-day.

MAGGIE. Oh, mither, he told me he loved me!

CHEVIOT. So I did. The fact is, when I fell in love with you—
don't go my pretty bird—I quite forgot that I was engaged.
There, there! I thought at the time that you were the tree
upon which the fruit of my heart was growing, but I was
mistaken. Don't go; you needn't go on that account. It was
another tree—

MAGGIE. Oh, mither, it was anither tree!

> [*Weeping on* CHEVIOT's *shoulder.*

MRS. MACFARLANE. Angus, it was anither tree!

> [*Weeping on* ANGUS's *shoulder.*

ANGUS. Dinna, mither, dinna; I canna bear it!　　　[*Weeps.*

CHEVIOT. Yes, it was another tree—you can remain there for
the present—in point of fact, it was growing on both trees.
I don't know how it is, but it seems to grow on a great many
trees—a perfect orchard—and you are one of them, my dear.
Come, come, don't fret, you are one of them!

Enter MINNIE *and* SYMPERSON.

MINNIE. Cheviot!

SYMPERSON. What is all this?

CHEVIOT. [*Rapidly referring to piece of paper given to him by*
MRS. MACFARLANE, *as if going over a washerwoman's bill.*]
'Twenty-four pairs socks, two shirts, thirty-seven collars, one
sheet, forty-four nightshirts, twenty-two flannel waistcoats,
one white tie.' Ridiculous—quite ridiculous—I won't pay it.

MINNIE. Cheviot, who is this person who is hanging on your
neck? Say she is somebody—for instance, your sister or your
aunt. Oh, Cheviot, say she is your aunt, I implore you!

> [*The three cottagers curtsey and bow to* MINNIE.

SYMPERSON. Cheviot, say she is your aunt, I command you.

CHEVIOT. Oh, I beg your pardon. I didn't see you. These
ladies are—are my washerwomen. Allow me to introduce
them. They have come—they have come for their small

account. [MAGGIE, *who has been sobbing through this, throws herself hysterically on to* CHEVIOT'*s bosom.*] There's a discrepancy in the items—twenty-two flannel waistcoats are ridiculous, and, in short, some washerwomen are like this when they're contradicted—they can't help it—it's something in the suds; it undermines their constitution.

SYMPERSON. [*Sternly.*] Cheviot, I should like to believe you, but it seems scarcely credible.

MAGGIE. Oh, sir, he's na telling ye truly. I'm the puir Lowland lassie that he stole the hairt out of three months ago, and promised to marry; and I love him sae weel—sae weel, and now he's married to anither!

CHEVIOT. Nothing of the kind. I—

SYMPERSON. You are mistaken, and so is your mith—mother. He is not yet married to anith—nother.

MAGGIE. Why, sir, it took place before my very ain eyes, before us a', to a beautiful lady, three months since.

MINNIE. Cheviot, say that this is not true. Say that the beautiful lady was somebody—for instance, your aunt. Oh, say she was your aunt, I implore you!

SYMPERSON. [*Sternly.*] Cheviot, say she was your aunt, I command you!

CHEVIOT. Minnie, Symperson, don't believe them—it was no marriage. I don't even know the lady's name—I never saw her before—I've never seen her since. It's ridiculous—I couldn't have married her without knowing it—it's out of the question!

SYMPERSON. Cheviot, let's know exactly where we are. I don't much care whom you marry, so that you marry someone—that's enough for me. But please be explicit, for this is business and mustn't be trifled with. Tell me all about it.

CHEVIOT. [*In despair.*] I cannot!

Enter BELVAWNEY.

BELVAWNEY. I can.

SYMPERSON. Belvawney!

BELVAWNEY. I was present when Cheviot and a certain lady declared themselves to be man and wife. This took place in a cottage on the border—in the presence of these worthy people.

SYMPERSON. That's enough for me. It's a Scotch marriage! Minnie, my child, we must find you someone else. Cheviot's married. Belvawney, I am sorry to say I deprive you of your income.

BELVAWNEY. I beg your pardon, not yet.

SYMPERSON. Why not?

BELVAWNEY. In the first place, it's not certain whether the cottage was in England or in Scotland; in the second place, the bride can't be found.

SYMPERSON. But she *shall* be found. What is her name?

BELVAWNEY. That I decline to state.

SYMPERSON. But you shall be made to state. I insist upon knowing the young lady's name.

Enter MISS TREHERNE, *in a light and cheerful dress.*

BELVAWNEY. [*Amazed.*] Belinda Treherne!

MISS TREHERNE. [*Rushing to* MINNIE.] Minnie, my own old friend!

CHEVIOT. 'Tis she!

MISS TREHERNE. [*Turns and recognizes* CHEVIOT.] My husband!

CHEVIOT. My wife!

[MISS TREHERNE *throws herself at* CHEVIOT'*s feet, kissing his hands rapturously.* BELVAWNEY *staggers back.* MINNIE *faints in her father's arms.* MAGGIE *sobs on* ANGUS'*s breast. Picture.*

ACT III

SCENE. *Same as Act II.* BELVAWNEY *discovered with* MISS
TREHERNE *and* MINNIE. *He is singing to them.* MISS TRE-
HERNE *is leaning romantically on piano.* MINNIE *is seated
picturesquely on a stool.*

BELVAWNEY. [*Sings.*]

> Says the old Obadiah to the young Obadiah,
>> I am drier, Obadiah, I am drier.
>>> I am drier.
>
> Says the young Obadiah to the old Obadiah,
>> I'm on fire, Obadiah, I'm on fire.
>>> I'm on fire.

MINNIE. Oh, thank you, Mr. Belvawney. How sweetly pretty that is. Where can I get it?

MISS TREHERNE. How marvellous is the power of melody over the soul that is fretted and harassed by anxiety and doubt. I can understand how valuable must have been the troubadours of old, in the troublous times of anarchy. Your song has soothed me, sir.

BELVAWNEY. I am indeed glad to think that I have comforted you a little, dear ladies.

MINNIE. Dear Mr. Belvawney, I don't know what we should have done without you. What with your sweet songs, your amusing riddles, and your clever conjuring tricks, the weary days of waiting have passed like a delightful dream.

MISS TREHERNE. It is impossible to be dull in the society of one who can charm the soul with plaintive ballads one moment, and the next roll a rabbit and a guinea-pig into one.

BELVAWNEY. You make me indeed happy, dear ladies. But my joy will be of brief duration, for Cheviot may return at any moment with the news that the fatal cottage was in Scotland, and then—oh, Belinda, what is to become of me?

MISS TREHERNE. How many issues depend on that momentous

question? Has Belvawney a thousand a year, or is he ruined? Has your father that convenient addition to his income, or has he not? May Maggie marry Angus, or will her claim on Cheviot be satisfied? Are you to be his cherished bride, or are you destined to a life of solitary maidenhood? Am I Cheviot's honoured wife, or am I but a broken-hearted and desolate spinster? Who can tell? Who can tell?

BELVAWNEY. [*Goes to window.*] Here is a cab with luggage—it is Cheviot! He has returned with the news! Ladies—one word before I go. One of you will be claimed by Cheviot; that is very clear. To that one (whichever it may be) I do not address myself—but to the other (whichever it may be), I say I love you (whichever you are) with a fervour which I cannot describe in words. If you (whichever you are) will consent to cast your lot with mine, I will devote my life to proving that I love you and you only (whichever it may be) with a single-hearted and devoted passion, which precludes the possibility of my ever entertaining the slightest regard for any other woman in the whole world. I thought I would just mention it. Good morning! [*Exit.*

MISS TREHERNE. How beautifully he expresses himself. He is indeed a rare and radiant being.

MINNIE. [*Nervously.*] Oh, Belinda, the terrible moment is at hand.

MISS TREHERNE. Minnie, if dear Cheviot should prove to be my husband, swear to me that that will not prevent your coming to stop with us—with dear Cheviot and me—whenever you can.

MINNIE. Indeed I will. And if it should turn out that dear Cheviot is at liberty to marry me, promise me that that will not prevent you looking on our house—on dear Cheviot's and mine—as your home.

MISS TREHERNE. I swear it. We will be like dear, dear sisters.

Enter CHEVIOT, *as from journey, with bag and rug.*

MISS TREHERNE. Cheviot, tell me at once—are you my own—husband?

MINNIE. Cheviot, speak—is poor, little, simple Minnie to be your bride?

CHEVIOT. Minnie, the hope of my heart, my pet fruit tree! Belinda, my Past, my Present, and my To Come! I have sorry news, sorry news.

MISS TREHERNE. [*Aside.*] Sorry news! Then I am *not* his wife.

MINNIE. [*Aside.*] Sorry news! Then she *is* his wife.

CHEVIOT. My dear girls—my very dear girls, my journey has been fruitless—I have no information.

MISS TREHERNE *and* MINNIE. No information!

CHEVIOT. None. The McQuibbigaskie has gone abroad!
                              [*Both ladies fall weeping into chairs.*

MISS TREHERNE. More weary waiting, more weary waiting!

MINNIE. Oh, my breaking heart; oh, my poor bruised and breaking heart!

CHEVIOT. We must be patient, dear Belinda. Minnie, my own, we must be patient. After all, is the situation so very terrible? Each of you has an even chance of becoming my wife, and in the mean time I look upon myself as engaged to both of you. I shall make no distinction. I shall love you both, fondly, and you shall both love me. My affection shall be divided equally between you, and we will be as happy as three little birds.

MISS TREHERNE. [*Wiping her eyes.*] You are very kind and thoughtful, dear Cheviot.

MINNIE. I believe, in my simple little way, that you are the very best man in the whole world.

CHEVIOT. [*Deprecatingly.*] No, no.

MINNIE. Ah, but do let me think so; it makes me so happy to think so!

CHEVIOT. Does it? Well, well, be it so. Perhaps I am. And now tell me, how has the time passed since I left? Have my darlings been dull?

MISS TREHERNE. We should have been dull indeed but for the airy Belvawney. The sprightly creature has done his best to make the lagging hours fly. He is an entertaining rattlesnake —I should say, rattletrap.

CHEVIOT. [*Jealous.*] Oh, *is* he so? Belvawney has been making the hours fly, has he? I'll make *him* fly, when I catch him!

MINNIE. His conjuring tricks are wonderful.

CHEVIOT. Confound his conjuring tricks!

MINNIE. Have you seen him bring a live hen, two hair brushes, and a pound and a half of fresh butter out of his pocket-handkerchief?

CHEVIOT. No, I have not had that advantage.

MISS TREHERNE. It is a thrilling sight.

CHEVIOT. So I should be disposed to imagine. Pretty goings on in my absence! You seem to forget that you two girls are engaged to be married to *me*!

MISS TREHERNE. Ah, Cheviot, do not judge us harshly. We love you with a reckless fervour that thrills us to the very marrow—don't we, darling? But the hours crept heavily without you, and when, to lighten the gloom in which we were plunged, the kindly creature swallowed a live rabbit and brought it out, smothered in onions, from his left boot, we could not choose but smile. The good soul has promised to teach *me* the trick.

CHEVIOT. Has he? That's his confounded impudence. Now, once for all, I'll have nothing of this kind. One of you will be my wife, and until I know which, I will permit no Belvawney-ing of any kind whatever, or anything approaching thereto. When that is settled, the other may Belvawney until she is black in the face.

MISS TREHERNE. And how long have we to wait before we shall know which of us may begin Belvawneying?

CHEVIOT. I can't say. It may be some time. The McQuibbi-gaskie has gone to Central Africa. No post can reach him, and he will not return for six years.

MISS TREHERNE. Six years! Oh, I cannot wait six years! Why, in six years I shall be eight-and-twenty!

MINNIE. Six years! Why, in six years the Statute of Limitations will come in, and he can renounce us both.

MISS TREHERNE. True; you are quite right. [*To* CHEVIOT.] Cheviot, I have loved you madly, desperately, as other woman never loved other man. This poor inexperienced child, [*Embracing* MINNIE.] who clings to me as the ivy clings to the oak, also loves you as woman never loved before. Even that poor cottage maiden, whose rustic heart you so recklessly enslaved, worships you with a devotion that has no parallel in the annals of the heart. In return for all this unalloyed affection, all we ask of you is that you will recommend us to a respectable solicitor.

CHEVIOT. But, my dear children, reflect—I can't marry all three. I am most willing to consider myself engaged to all three, and that's as much as the law will allow. You see I do all I can. I'd marry all three of you with pleasure if I might; but, as our laws stand at present, I'm sorry to say—I'm very sorry to say—it's out of the question.   [*Exit.*

MISS TREHERNE. Poor fellow. He has my tenderest sympathy; but we have no alternative but to place ourselves under the protecting ægis of a jury of our countrymen.

Enter SYMPERSON, *with two letters.*

SYMPERSON. Minnie—Miss Treherne—the post has just brought me two letters; one of them bears a Marseilles postmark, and is, I doubt not, from the McQuibbigaskie. He must have written just before starting for Central Africa.

MINNIE. From the McQuibbigaskie? Oh, read, read!

MISS TREHERNE. Oh, sir, how can you torture us by this delay? Have you no curiosity?

SYMPERSON. Well, my dear, very little on this point; you see it don't much matter to me whom Cheviot marries. So that he marries some one, that's enough for me. But, however, *your* anxiety is natural, and I will gratify it. [*Opens letter and reads.*] 'Sir—In reply to your letter, I have to inform you that Evan Cottage is certainly in England. The deeds relating to the property place this beyond all question.'

MINNIE. In England!

MISS TREHERNE. [*Sinking into chair.*] This blow is indeed a crusher. Against such a blow I cannot stand up!   [*Faints.*

MINNIE. [*On her knees.*] My poor Belinda—my darling sister—love—oh, forgive me—oh, forgive me! Don't look like that! Speak to me, dearest—oh, speak to me—speak to me.

MISS TREHERNE. [*Suddenly springing up.*] Speak to you? Yes, I'll speak to you! All is *not* yet lost! True, he is not married to me, but why should he not be? I am as young as you! I am as beautiful as you! I have more money than you! I will try— oh, how hard I will try!

MINNIE. Do, darling, and I wish—oh, how I wish you may get him!

MISS TREHERNE. Minnie, if you were not the dearest little friend I have in the world I could pinch you!   [*Exit.*

SYMPERSON. [*Who has been reading the other letter.*] Dear me— how terrible!

MINNIE. What is terrible, dear papa?

SYMPERSON. Belvawney writes to tell me the Indestructible Bank stopped payment yesterday, and Cheviot's shares are waste paper.

MINNIE. Well, upon my word. There's an end of *him*!

SYMPERSON. An end of him. What do you mean? You are not going to throw him over?

MINNIE. Dear papa, I am sorry to disappoint you, but unless your tom-tit is very much mistaken, the Indestructible was not registered under the Joint-Stock Companies Act of sixty-two, and in that case the shareholders are jointly and severally liable to the whole extent of their available capital. Poor little Minnie don't pretend to have a business head, but she's not *quite* such a little donkey as *that*, dear papa.

SYMPERSON. You decline to marry him? Do I hear rightly?

MINNIE. I don't know, papa, whether your hearing is as good as it was, but from your excited manner I should say you heard me perfectly.   [*Exit.*

SYMPERSON. This is a pretty business! Done out of a thousand a year, and by my own daughter! What a terrible thing is this incessant craving after money! Upon my word, some people seem to think that they're sent into the world for no other purpose but to acquire wealth; and, by Jove, they'll sacrifice their nearest and dearest relations to get it. It's most humiliating—most humiliating!

Enter CHEVIOT, *in low spirits.*

CHEVIOT. [*Throwing himself into a chair; sobs aloud.*] Oh, Uncle Symperson, have you heard the news?

SYMPERSON. [*Angrily.*] Yes, I *have* heard the news; and a pretty man of business *you* are to invest all your property in an unregistered company!

CHEVIOT. Uncle, don't *you* turn against me! Belinda is not my wife. I'm a ruined man; and my darlings—my three darlings, whom I love with a fidelity, which, in these easy-going days, is simply Quixotic—will have nothing to say to me. Minnie, your daughter, declines to accompany me to the altar. Belinda I feel sure will revert to Belvawney, and Maggie is at this present moment hanging round that Scotch idiot's neck, although she knows that in doing so she simply tortures me. Symperson, I never loved three girls as I loved those three—never! never! and now they'll all three slip through my fingers—I'm sure they will.

SYMPERSON. Pooh, pooh, sir. Do you think nobody loses but you? Why, I'm done out of a thousand a year by it.

CHEVIOT. [*Moodily.*] For that matter, Symperson, I've a very vivid idea that you won't have to wait long for the money.

SYMPERSON. What d'you mean? Oh—of course—I understand.

CHEVIOT. Eh?

SYMPERSON. Mrs. Macfarlane! I have thought of her myself. A very fine woman for her years; a majestic ruin, beautiful in decay. My dear boy, my very dear boy, I congratulate you.

CHEVIOT. Don't be absurd. I'm not going to marry anybody.

SYMPERSON. Eh? Why, then how—? I don't think I quite follow you.

CHEVIOT. There is another contingency on which you come into the money. My death.

SYMPERSON. [*Delighted.*] To be sure! I never thought of that! And, as you say, a man can die but once.

CHEVIOT. I beg your pardon. I didn't say anything of the kind —*you* said it; but it's true, for all that.

SYMPERSON. I'm very sorry, but of course, if you have made up your mind to it——

CHEVIOT. Why, when a man's lost everything, what has he to live for?

SYMPERSON. True, true. Nothing whatever. Still——

CHEVIOT. His money gone, his credit gone, the three girls he's engaged to gone.

SYMPERSON. I cannot deny it. It is a hopeless situation. Hopeless, quite hopeless.

CHEVIOT. His happiness wrecked, his hopes blighted; the three trees upon which the fruit of his heart was growing— all cut down. What is left but suicide?

SYMPERSON. True, true! You're quite right. Farewell.

[*Going.*

CHEVIOT. Symperson, you seem to think I *want* to kill myself. I don't want to do anything of the kind. I'd much rather live —upon my soul I would—if I could think of any reason for living. Symperson, can't you think of *something* to check the heroic impulse which is at this moment urging me to a tremendous act of self-destruction?

SYMPERSON. Something! Of course I can! Say that you throw yourself into the Serpentine—which is handy. Well, it's an easy way of going out of the world, I'm told—rather pleasant than otherwise, I believe—quite an agreeable sensation, I'm given to understand. But you—you get wet through, and your—your clothes are absolutely ruined.

CHEVIOT. [*Mournfully.*] For that matter, I could take off my clothes before I went in.

SYMPERSON. True, so you could. I never thought of that. You could take them off before you go in—there's no reason why you shouldn't, if you do it in the dark—and *that* objection falls to the ground. Cheviot, my lion-hearted boy, it's impossible to resist your arguments; they are absolutely convincing.

[*Shakes his hand. Exit.*

CHEVIOT. Good fellow, Symperson—I like a man who's open to conviction. But it's no use—all my attractions are gone— and I can *not* live unless I feel I'm fascinating. Still, there's one chance left—Belinda! I haven't tried her. Perhaps, after all, she loved me for myself alone. It isn't likely—but it's barely possible.

Enter BELVAWNEY, *who has overheard these words.*

BELVAWNEY. Out of the question; you are too late. I represented to her that you are never likely to induce any one to
marry you now that you are penniless. She felt that my income
was secure, and she gave me her hand and her heart.

CHEVIOT. Then all is lost; my last chance is gone, and the
irrevocable die is cast! Be happy with her, Belvawney; be
happy with her!

BELVAWNEY. Happy! You shall dine with us after our honeymoon and judge for yourself.

CHEVIOT. No, I shall not do that; long before you return I shall
be beyond the reach of dinners.

BELVAWNEY. I understand—you are going abroad. Well, I
don't think you could do better than try another country.

CHEVIOT. [*Tragically.*] Belvawney, I'm going to try another
world!   [*Drawing a pistol from his pocket.*

BELVAWNEY. [*Alarmed.*] What do you mean?

CHEVIOT. In two minutes I die!

BELVAWNEY. You're joking, of course?

CHEVIOT. Do I look like a man who jokes? Is my frame of mind
one in which a man indulges in trivialities?

BELVAWNEY. [*In great terror.*] But my dear Cheviot, reflect—

CHEVIOT. Why should it concern you? You will be happy with
Belinda. You will not be well off, but Symperson will, and I
dare say he will give you a meal now and then. It will not be
a nice meal, but still it will be a meal.

BELVAWNEY. Cheviot, you mustn't do this; pray reflect; there
are interests of magnitude depending on your existence.

CHEVIOT. My mind is made up.   [*Cocking the pistol.*

BELVAWNEY. [*Wildly.*] But I shall be ruined!

CHEVIOT. There is Belinda's fortune.

BELVAWNEY. She won't have me if I'm ruined! Dear Cheviot,
don't do it—it's culpable—it's wrong!

CHEVIOT. Life is valueless to me without Belinda.
                              [*Pointing the pistol to his head.*

BELVAWNEY. [*Desperately.*] You shall have Belinda; she is much—very much to me, but she is not everything. Your life is very dear to me, and when I think of our old friendship——— Cheviot, you shall have anything you like, if you'll only consent to live!

CHEVIOT. If I thought you were in earnest, but no—no.

[*Putting pistol to head.*

BELVAWNEY. In earnest? Of course I'm in earnest! Why, what's the use of Belinda to me if I'm ruined? Why, she wouldn't look at me.

CHEVIOT. But perhaps if I'm ruined, she wouldn't look at *me*.

BELVAWNEY. Cheviot, I'll confess all, if you'll only live. You— you are *not* ruined!

CHEVIOT. Not ruined?

BELVAWNEY. Not ruined. I—I invented the statement.

CHEVIOT. [*In great delight.*] You invented the statement? My dear friend! My very dear friend! I'm very much obliged to you! Oh, thank you, thank you a thousand times! Oh, Belvawney, you have made me very, very happy! [*Sobbing on his shoulder, then suddenly springing up.*] But what the devil did you mean by circulating such a report about me? How dare you do it, sir? Answer me that, sir.

BELVAWNEY. I did it to gain Belinda's love. I knew that the unselfish creature loved you for your wealth alone.

CHEVIOT. It was a liberty, sir; it was a liberty. To put it mildly, it was a liberty.

BELVAWNEY. It was. You're quite right—that's the word for it—it was a liberty. But I'll go and undeceive her at once.

[*Exit.*

CHEVIOT. Well, as I've recovered my fortune, and with it my tree, I'm about the happiest fellow in the world. My money, my mistress, and my mistress's money, all my own. I believe I could go mad with joy!

Enter SYMPERSON, *in deep black*; *he walks pensively, with a white handkerchief to his mouth.*

CHEVIOT. What's the matter?

SYMPERSON. [*Disappointed*]. Hallo! You're still alive?

CHEVIOT. Alive? Yes; why, [*Noticing his dress.*] is anything wrong?

SYMPERSON. No, no, my dear young friend, these clothes are symbolical; they represent my state of mind. After your terrible threat, which I cannot doubt you intend to put at once into execution——

CHEVIOT. My dear uncle, this is very touching; this unmans me. But, cheer up, dear old friend, I have good news for you.

SYMPERSON. [*Alarmed.*] Good news? What do you mean?

CHEVIOT. I am about to remove the weight of sorrow which hangs so heavily at your heart. Resume your fancy check trousers—I have consented to live.

SYMPERSON. Consented to live? Why, sir, this is confounded trifling. I don't understand this line of conduct at all. You threaten to commit suicide; your friends are dreadfully shocked at first, but eventually their minds become reconciled to the prospect of losing you; they become resigned, even cheerful; and when they have brought themselves to this Christian state of mind, you coolly inform them that you have changed your mind and mean to live. It's not business, sir— it's not business.

CHEVIOT. But my dear uncle, I've nothing to commit suicide for; I'm a rich man, and Belinda will, no doubt, accept me with joy and gratitude.

SYMPERSON. Belinda will do nothing of the kind. She has just left the house with Belvawney, in a cab, and under the most affectionate circumstances.

CHEVIOT. [*Alarmed.*] Left with Belvawney? Where have they gone?

SYMPERSON. I don't know. Very likely to get married.

CHEVIOT. Married?

SYMPERSON. Yes, before the registrar.

CHEVIOT. [*Excitedly.*] I've been sold! I see that now! Belvawney has done me! But I'm not the kind of man who stands such treatment quietly. Belvawney has found his match.

Symperson, they may get married, but they shall not be happy; I'll be revenged on them both before they're twenty-four hours older. She marries him because she thinks his income is secure. I'll show her she's wrong. I won't blow out my brains; I'll do worse.

SYMPERSON. What?

CHEVIOT. I'll marry.

SYMPERSON. Marry?

CHEVIOT. Anybody. I don't care who it is.

SYMPERSON. Will Minnie do?

CHEVIOT. Minnie will do; send her here.

SYMPERSON. In one moment, my dear boy—in one moment!
[*Exit hurriedly.*

CHEVIOT. Belinda alone in a cab with Belvawney! It's maddening to think of it! He's got his arm round her waist at this moment, if I know anything of human nature! I can't stand it —I cannot and I will not stand it! I'll write at once to the registrar and tell him she's married. [*Sits at writing table and prepares to write.*] Oh, why am I constant by disposition? Why is it that when I love a girl I can think of no other girl but that girl, whereas when a girl loves me she seems to entertain the same degree of affection for mankind at large? I'll never be constant again; henceforth I fascinate but to deceive!

Enter MINNIE.

MINNIE. Mr. Cheviot Hill, papa tells me that you wish to speak to me.

CHEVIOT. [*Hurriedly, writing at table.*] I do. Miss Symperson, I have no time to beat about the bush; I must come to the point at once. You rejected me a short time since—I will not pretend that I am pleased with you for rejecting me—on the contrary, I think it was in the worst taste. However, let bygones be bygones. Unforeseen circumstances render it necessary that I should marry at once, and you'll do. An early answer will be esteemed, as this is business.
[*Resumes his writing.*

MINNIE. Mr. Hill, dear papa assures me that the report about the loss of your money is incorrect. I hope this may be the case, but I cannot forget that the information comes from dear papa. Now dear papa is the best and dearest papa in the whole world, but he has a lively imagination, and when he wants to accomplish his purpose, he does not hesitate to invent—I am not quite sure of the word, but I think it is 'bouncers'.

CHEVIOT. [*Writing.*] You are quite right, the word is bouncers. Bouncers or bangers—either will do.

MINNIE. Then forgive my little silly fancies, Mr. Hill; but before I listen to your suggestion I must have the very clearest proof that your position is, in every way, fully assured.

CHEVIOT. Mercenary little donkey! I will not condescend to proof. I renounce her altogether.   [*Rings bell.*

Enter MAGGIE *with* ANGUS *and* MRS. MACFARLANE. ANGUS
has his arm round MAGGIE'S *waist.*

CHEVIOT. [*Suddenly seeing her.*] Maggie, come here. Angus, do take your arm from round that girl's waist. Stand back, and don't you listen. Maggie, three months ago I told you that I loved you passionately; to-day I tell you that I love you as passionately as ever; I may add that I am still a rich man. Can you oblige me with a postage-stamp? [MAGGIE *gives him a stamp from her pocket—he sticks it on to his letter.*] What do you say? I must trouble you for an immediate answer, as this is not pleasure—it's business.

MAGGIE. Oh sir, ye're ower late. Oh, Maister Cheviot, if I'd only ken'd it before! Oh sir, I love ye right weel; the bluid o' my hairt is nae sae dear to me as thou. [*Sobbing on his shoulder.*] Oh Cheviot, my ain auld love! My ain auld love!

ANGUS. [*Aside.*] Puir lassie, it just dra's the water from my ee to hear her. Oh, mither, mither! My hairt is just breaking.
    [*Sobs on* MRS. MACFARLANE'S *shoulder.*

CHEVIOT. But why is it too late? You say that you love me. I offer to marry you. My station in life is at least equal to your own. What is to prevent our union?

MAGGIE. [*Wiping her eyes.*] Oh, sir, ye're unco guid to puir little Maggie, but ye're too late; for she's placed the matter in her solicitor's hands, and he tells her that an action for breach will just bring damages to the tune of a thousand pound. There's a laddie waiting outside noo, to serve the bonnie writ on ye.

[Turns affectionately to ANGUS.

CHEVIOT. [*Falls sobbing on to sofa.*] No one will marry me. There is a curse upon me—a curse upon me. No one will marry me—no, not one!

MRS. MACFARLANE. Dinna say that, sir. There's mony a woman—nae young, soft, foolish lassie, neither, but grown women o' sober age who'd be mair a mither than a wife to ye; and that's what ye want, puir laddie, for ye're no equal to takin' care o' yersel'.

CHEVIOT. Mrs. Macfarlane, you are right. I am a man of quick impulse. I see, I feel, I speak. I—you are the tree upon which—that is to say—no, no, damn it, I can't, I can't! One must draw the line somewhere.

[Turning from her with disgust.

Enter MISS TREHERNE *and* BELVAWNEY. *They are followed by* SYMPERSON *and* MINNIE.

Belinda! Can I believe my eyes? You have returned to me; you have not gone off with Belvawney after all? Thank heaven, thank heaven!   *[Getting hysterical.*

MISS TREHERNE. I thought that as I came in I heard you say something about a tree.

CHEVIOT. You are right. As you entered I was remarking that I am a man of quick impulse. I see, I feel, I speak. I have two thousand a year, and I love you passionately. I lay my hand, my heart, and my income, all together, in one lot, at your feet!

MISS TREHERNE. Cheviot, I love you with an irresistible fervour that seems to parch my very existence. I love you as I never loved man before, and as I can never hope to love man again. But in the belief that you were ruined I went with my own adored Belvawney before the registrar, and that registrar has just made us one! *[Turns affectionately to* BELVAWNEY.

BELVAWNEY. [*Embraces* BELINDA.] Bless him for it—bless him for it!

CHEVIOT. [*Deadly calm.*] One word. I have not yet seen the

letter that blights my earthly hopes. For form's sake, I trust I may be permitted to cast my eye over that document? As a matter of business—that's all.

BELVAWNEY. Certainly. Here it is. You will find the situation of the cottage described in unmistakable terms.

[*Hands the letter to* CHEVIOT.]

CHEVIOT. [*Reads.*] 'In reply to your letter I have to inform you that Evan Cottage is certainly in England. The deeds relating to the property place this beyond all question.' Thank you; I am satisfied. [*Takes out pistol.*

BELVAWNEY. Now, sir, perhaps you will kindly release that young lady. She is my wife!

[CHEVIOT'*s arm has crept mechanically round* MISS TREHERNE'*s waist.*

MISS TREHERNE. Oh, Cheviot, kindly release me—I am his wife!

CHEVIOT. Crushed! Crushed! Crushed!

SYMPERSON. [*Looking over his shoulder at letter, reads.*] 'Turn over.'

CHEVIOT. [*Despairingly.*] Why should I? What good would it do? Oh, I see. I beg your pardon. [*Turns over the page.*] Hallo!

ALL. What?

CHEVIOT. [*Reads.*] 'P.S. I may add that the border line runs through the property. The cottage is undoubtedly in England, though the garden is in Scotland.'

MISS TREHERNE. And we were married in the garden!

CHEVIOT. [*Amorously.*] Belinda, we were married in the garden!

[BELINDA *leaves* BELVAWNEY, *and turns affectionately to* CHEVIOT, *who embraces her.*

BELVAWNEY. Belinda, stop a bit! Don't leave me like this!

MISS TREHERNE. Belvawney, I love you with an intensity of devotion that I firmly believe will last while I live. But dear Cheviot is my husband now; he has a claim upon me which it would be impossible—nay, criminal—to resist. Farewell, Belvawney; Minnie may yet be yours! [BELVAWNEY *turns sobbing to* MINNIE, *who comforts him.*] Cheviot—my husband —my own old love—if the devotion of a lifetime can atone for the misery of the last few days, it is yours, with every wifely sentiment of pride, gratitude, admiration, and love.

CHEVIOT. [*Embracing her.*] My own! My own! Tender blossom of my budding hopes! Star of my life! Essence of happiness! Tree upon which the fruit of my heart is growing! My Past, my Present, my To Come!

[*Picture.* CHEVIOT *is embracing* MISS TREHERNE. BELVAWNEY *is being comforted by* MINNIE. ANGUS *is solacing* MAGGIE, *and* MRS. MACFARLANE *is reposing on* SYMPERSON'S *bosom.*

THE MAGISTRATE

A FARCE IN THREE ACTS

BY

ARTHUR WING PINERO (1855–1934)

─────

*First performed at the Court Theatre
21 March 1885*

─────

CAST

MR. POSKET ⎫	magistrates of the	Mr. Arthur Cecil
MR. BULLAMY ⎭	Mulberry Street Police Court	Mr. Fred Cape
COLONEL LUKYN, from Bengal, retired		Mr. John Clayton
CAPTAIN HORACE VALE, Shropshire Fusiliers		Mr. F. Kerr
CIS FARRINGDON, Mrs. Posket's son by her first marriage		Mr. H. Eversfield
ACHILLE BLOND, proprietor of the Hôtel des Princes		Mr. Chevalier
ISIDORE, a waiter		Mr. Deane
MR. WORMINGTON, chief clerk at Mulberry Street		Mr. Gilbert Trent
INSPECTOR MESSITER ⎫		Mr. Albert Sims
SERGEANT LUGG ⎬ Metropolitan Police		Mr. Lugg
CONSTABLE HARRIS ⎭		Mr. Burnley
WYKE, servant at Mr. Posket's		Mr. Fayre
AGATHA POSKET, late Farringdon, *née* Verrinder		Mrs. John Wood
CHARLOTTE, her sister		Miss Marion Terry
BEATIE TOMLINSON, a young lady reduced to teaching music		Miss Norreys
POPHAM		Miss La Coste

ACT I

A well-furnished drawing-room in the house of MR. POSKET *in Bloomsbury.*

BEATIE TOMLINSON, *a pretty, simply dressed little girl of about sixteen, is playing the piano, as* CIS FARRINGDON, *a manly youth wearing an Eton jacket, enters the room.*

CIS. Beatie!

BEATIE. Cis dear! Dinner isn't over, surely?

CIS. Not quite. I had one of my convenient headaches and cleared out. [*Taking an apple and some cobnuts from his pocket and giving them to* BEATIE.] These are for you, dear, with my love. I sneaked 'em off the sideboard as I came out.

BEATIE. Oh, I mustn't take them!

CIS. Yes, you may—it's my share of dessert. Besides, it's a horrid shame you don't grub with us.

BEATIE. What, a poor little music mistress!

CIS. Yes. They're only going to give you four guineas a quarter. Fancy getting a girl like you for four guineas a quarter—why, an eighth of you is worth more than that! Now peg away at your apple. [*Produces a cigarette.*

BEATIE. There's company at dinner, isn't there?
[*Munching her apple.*

CIS. Well, hardly. Aunt Charlotte hasn't arrived yet, so there's only old Bullamy.

BEATIE. Isn't old Bullamy anybody?

CIS. Old Bullamy—well, he's only like the Guv'nor, a police magistrate at the Mulberry Street Police Court.

BEATIE. Oh, does each police court have two magistrates?

CIS. [*Proudly.*] All the best have two.

BEATIE. Don't they quarrel over getting the interesting cases? I should.

L

cis. I don't know how they manage—perhaps they toss up who's to hear the big sensations. There's a Mrs. Beldam, who is rather a bore sometimes; I know the Guv always lets old Bullamy attend to her. But, as a rule, I fancy they go half and half, in a friendly way. [*Lighting cigarette.*] For instance, if the Guv'nor wants to go to the Derby he lets old Bullamy have the Oaks—and so on, see?

[*He sits on the floor, comfortably reclining against* BEATIE, *and puffing his cigarette.*

BEATIE. Oh, I say, Cis, won't your mamma be angry when she finds I haven't gone home?

cis. Oh, put it on to your pupil. [*Kissing her.*] Say, I'm very backward.

BEATIE. I think you are extremely forward—in some ways. I do wish I could get you to concentrate your attention on your music lessons. But I wouldn't get you into a scrape.

cis. No fear of that. Ma is too proud of me.

BEATIE. But there's your step-father.

cis. The dear old Guv'nor! Why, he's too good-natured to say 'Bo!' to a goose. You know, Beatie, I was at a school at Brighton when ma got married—when she got married the second time, I mean—and the Guv'nor and I didn't make each other's acquaintance till after the honeymoon.

BEATIE. Oh, fancy your step-father blindly accepting such a responsibility!   [*Gives him a cobnut to crack for her.*

cis. Yes, wasn't the Guv'nor soft! I might have been a very indifferent sort of young fellow for all he knew.

[*Having cracked the nut with his teeth, he returns it to her.*

BEATIE. Thank you, dear.

cis. Well, when I heard the new dad was a police magistrate, I *was* scared. Said I to myself, 'If I don't mind my P's and Q's, the Guv'nor—from force of habit—will fine me all my pocket-money.' But it's quite the reverse—he's the mildest, meekest—
[*The door opens suddenly.*] Look out! Some one coming!

[*They both jump up,* BEATIE *scattering the nuts that are in her lap all over the floor.* CIS *throws his cigarette into the fireplace and sits at the piano, playing a simple exercise very badly.* BEATIE *stands behind him, counting.*

BEATIE. One—and two—and one—and two.

WYKE, *the butler, appears at the door, and mysteriously closes it after him.*

WYKE. [*In a whisper.*] Ssss! Master Cis! Master Cis!

CIS. Hallo—what is it, Wyke?

WYKE. [*Producing a decanter from under his coat.*] The port wine what you asked for, sir. I couldn't get it away before—the old gentlemen do hug port wine so.

CIS. Got a glass?

WYKE. Yes, sir. [*Producing wine-glass from his pocket, and pouring out wine.*] What ain't missed ain't mourned, eh, Master Cis?

CIS. [*Offering wine.*] Here you are, Beatie dear.

BEATIE. The idea of such a thing! I couldn't!

CIS. Why not?

BEATIE. If I merely sipped it I shouldn't be able to give you your music lesson properly. Drink it yourself, you dear thoughtful boy.

CIS. I shan't—it's for you.

BEATIE. I can't drink it!

CIS. You must.

BEATIE. I won't!

CIS. You're disagreeable!

BEATIE. Not half so disagreeable as you are. [*They wrangle.*

WYKE. [*To himself, watching them.*] What a young gentleman it is, and only fourteen! Fourteen—he behaves like forty! [CIS *chokes as he is drinking the wine;* BEATIE *pats him on the back.*] Why, even Cook has made a 'ash of everything since he's been in the house, and as for Popham——! [*Seeing some one approaching.*] Look out, Master Cis!

[CIS *returns to the piano,* BEATIE *counting as before.* WYKE *pretends to arrange the window curtains, concealing the decanter behind him.*

BEATIE. One and two—and one and two—and one, &c.

Enter POPHAM, *a smart-looking maid-servant.*

POPHAM. Wyke, where's the port?

WYKE. [*Vacantly.*] Port?

POPHAM. Port wine. Missus is furious.

WYKE. Port?

POPHAM. [*Pointing to the decanter.*] Why! There! You're carrying it about with you!

WYKE. Why, so I am! Carrying it about with me! Shows what a sharp eye I keep on the Guv'nor's wines. Carrying it about with me! Missus will be amused.   [*Goes out.*

POPHAM. [*Eyeing* CIS *and* BEATIE. *To herself.*] There's that boy with *her* again! Minx! Her two hours was up long ago. Why doesn't she go home? Master Cis, I've got a message for you.

CIS. For me, Popham?

POPHAM. Yes, sir. [*Quietly to him.*] The message is from a young lady who up to last Wednesday was all in all to you. Her name is Emma Popham.

CIS. [*Trying to get away.*] Oh, go along, Popham!

POPHAM. [*Holding his sleeve.*] Ah, it wasn't 'Go along, Popham' till that music girl came into the house. I will go along, but—cast your eye over this before you sleep tonight. [*She takes out of her pocket-handkerchief a piece of printed paper which she hands him between her finger and thumb.*] Part of a story in *Bow Bells* called 'Jilted; or, Could Blood Atone?' Wrap it in your handkerchief—it came round the butter.

          [*She goes out;* CIS *throws the paper into the grate.*

CIS. Bother the girl! Beatie, she's jealous of you!

BEATIE. A parlour-maid jealous of *me*—and with a bit of a child of fourteen!

CIS. I may be only fourteen, but I feel like a grown-up man! You're only sixteen—there's not much difference—and if you will only wait for me, I'll soon catch you up and be as much a man as you are a woman. [*Lovingly.*] Will you wait for me, Beatie?

BEATIE. I can't—I'm getting older every minute!

CIS. [*Desperately.*] Oh, I wish I could borrow five or six years from somebody!

BEATIE. Many a person would be glad to lend them. [*Lovingly.*] And oh, I wish you could!

CIS. [*Putting his arm round her.*] You do! Why?

BEATIE. Because I—because——

CIS. [*Listening.*] Look out! Here's the mater!
[*They run to the piano; he resumes playing, and she counting as before.*

BEATIE. One and two—and one—and two, &c.

Enter AGATHA POSKET, *a handsome, showy woman, of about thirty-six, looking perhaps younger.*

AGATHA. Why, Cis child, at your music again?

CIS. Yes, ma, always at it. You'll spoil my taste by forcing it if you're not careful.

AGATHA. We have no right to keep Miss Tomlinson so late.

BEATIE. [*Nervously.*] Oh, thank you, it doesn't matter. I—I—am afraid we're not making—very—great—progress.

CIS. [*Winking at* BEATIE.] Well, if I play that again, will you kiss me?

BEATIE. [*Demurely.*] I don't know, I'm sure. [*To* AGATHA.] May I promise that, ma'am?
[*Sits in the window recess.* CIS, *joining her, puts his arm round her waist.*

AGATHA. [*Sharply.*] No, certainly not. [*To herself, watching them.*] If I could only persuade Æneas to dismiss this *protégée* of his, and to engage a music-master, it would ease my conscience a little. If this girl knew the truth, how indignant she would be! And then there is the injustice to the boy himself, and to my husband's friends who are always petting and fondling and caressing what they call 'a fine little man of fourteen!' Fourteen! Oh, what an idiot I have been to conceal my child's real age! [*Looking at the clock.*] Charlotte is late; I wish she would come. It will be a relief to worry her with my troubles.

POSKET. [*Outside.*] We smoke all over the house, Bullamy, all over the house.

AGATHA. I will speak to Æneas about this little girl, at any rate.

Enter POSKET, *a mild gentleman of about fifty, smoking a cigarette, followed by* BULLAMY, *a fat, red-faced man with a bronchial cough and general huskiness.*

POSKET. Smoke anywhere, Bullamy—smoke anywhere.

BULLAMY. Not with my bronchitis, thank ye.

POSKET. [*Beaming at* AGATHA.] Ah, my darling!

BULLAMY. [*Producing a small box from his waistcoat pocket.*] All I take after dinner is a jujube—sometimes two. [*Offering the box.*] May I tempt Mrs. Posket?

AGATHA. No, thank you. [*Treading on one of the nuts which have been scattered over the room.*] How provoking—who brings nuts into the drawing-room?

POSKET. Miss Tomlinson still here? [*To* BEATIE.] Don't go, don't go. Glad to see Cis so fond of his music. Your sister Charlotte is behind her time, my darling.

AGATHA. Her train is delayed, I suppose.

POSKET. You must stay and see my sister-in-law, Bullamy.

BULLAMY. Pleasure—pleasure!

POSKET. *I* have never met her yet; we will share first impressions. In the interim, will Miss Tomlinson delight us with a little music?

BULLAMY. [*Bustling up to the piano.*] If this young lady is going to sing she might like one of my jujubes.

   [BEATIE *sits at the piano with* CIS *and* BULLAMY *on each side of her.* POSKET *treads on a nut as he walks over to his wife.*

POSKET. Dear me—how come nuts into the drawing-room? [*To* AGATHA.] Of what is my darling thinking so deeply? [*Treads on another nut.*] Another! My pet, there are nuts on the drawing-room carpet!

AGATHA. [*Rousing herself.*] Yes. I want to speak to you, Æneas.

POSKET. About the nuts?

AGATHA. No—about Miss Tomlinson—your little *protégée*.

POSKET. Ah, nice little thing.

AGATHA. Very. But not old enough to exert any decided influence over the boy's musical future. Why not engage a master?

POSKET. What, for a mere child?

AGATHA. A mere child—oh!

POSKET. A boy of fourteen!

AGATHA. [*To herself.*] Fourteen!

POSKET. A boy of fourteen, not yet out of Czerny's exercises.

AGATHA. [*To herself.*] If we were alone now, I might have the desperation to tell him all!

POSKET. Besides, my darling, you know the interest I take in Miss Tomlinson; she is one of the brightest little spots on my hobby-horse. Like all our servants, like everybody in my employ, she has been brought to my notice through the unhappy medium of the Police Court over which it is my destiny to preside. Our servant, Wyke, a man with a beautiful nature, is the son of a person I committed for trial for marrying three wives. To this day, Wyke is ignorant as to which of those three wives he is the son of! Cook was once a notorious dipsomaniac, and has even now not entirely freed herself from early influences. Popham is the unclaimed charge of a convicted baby-farmer. Even our milkman came before me as a man who had refused to submit specimens to the analytic inspector. And this poor child, what is she?

AGATHA. Yes, I know.

POSKET. The daughter of a superannuated General, who abstracted four silk umbrellas from the Army and Navy Stores—and on a fine day too!   [BEATIE *ceases playing.*

BULLAMY. Very good—very good!

POSKET. Thank you—thank you!

BULLAMY. [*To* POSKET, *coughing and laughing and popping a jujube into his mouth.*] My dear Posket, I really must congratulate you on that boy of yours—your step-son. A most wonderful lad. So confoundedly advanced too.

POSKET. Yes, isn't he? Eh!

BULLAMY. [*Confidentially.*] While the piano was going on just now, he told me one of the most humorous stories I've ever heard. [*Laughing heartily and panting, then taking another jujube.*] Ha, ha! Bless me, I don't know when I have taken so many jujubes!

POSKET. My dear Bullamy, my entire marriage is the greatest possible success. A little romantic too. [*Pointing to* AGATHA.] Beautiful woman!

BULLAMY. Very, very. [*Looking at her through eyeglass.*] I never committed a more stylish, elegant creature.

POSKET. [*Warmly.*] Thank you, Bullamy—we met abroad, at Spa, when I was on my holiday.

Enter WYKE, *with tea-tray, which he hands round.*

BULLAMY. I shall go there next year.

POSKET. She lost her first husband about twelve months ago in India. He was an army contractor.

BEATIE. [*To* CIS *at the piano.*] I must go now—there's no excuse for staying any longer.

CIS. [*To her disconsolately.*] What the deuce shall *I* do?

POSKET. [*Pouring out milk.*] Dear me, this milk seems very poor. When he died, she came to England, placed her boy at a school in Brighton, and then moved about quietly from place to place, drinking—— [*Sips tea.*

BULLAMY. [*With concern.*] Drinking?

POSKET. The waters—she's a little dyspeptic. [WYKE *goes out.*] We encountered each other at the *Tours des Fontaines*—by accident I trod upon her dress——

BEATIE. Good-night, Cis dear.

CIS. Oh!

POSKET. I apologised. We talked about the weather, we drank out of the same glass, discovered that we both suffered from the same ailment, and the result is complete happiness.
[*He bends over* AGATHA *gallantly.*

AGATHA. Æneas!

[*He kisses her; then* CIS *kisses* BEATIE, *loudly.* POSKET *and* BULLAMY *both listen puzzled.*

POSKET. Echo?

BULLAMY. Suppose so!

[*He kisses the back of his hand experimentally;* BEATIE *kisses* CIS.

Yes.

POSKET. Curious. [*To* BULLAMY.] Romantic story, isn't it?

BEATIE. Good-night, Mrs. Posket. I shall be here early to-morrow morning.

AGATHA. I am afraid you are neglecting your other pupils.

BEATIE. [*Confused.*] Oh, they're not so interesting as Cis—[*Correcting herself.*] Master Farringdon. Good-night.

AGATHA. Good-night, dear.   [BEATIE *goes out quietly.*

POSKET. [*To* BULLAMY.] We were married abroad without consulting friends or relations on either side. That's how it is I have never seen my sister-in-law, Miss Verrinder, who is coming from Shropshire to stay with us—she ought to——

Enter WYKE.

WYKE. Miss Verrinder has come, ma'am.

POSKET. Here she is.

AGATHA. Charlotte!

Enter CHARLOTTE, *a fine handsome girl, followed by* POPHAM *with hand luggage.*

AGATHA. [*Kissing her.*] My dear Charley.   [WYKE *goes out.*

CHARLOTTE. Aggy darling, aren't I late! There's a fog on the line—you could cut it with a knife. [*Seeing* CIS.] Is that your boy?

AGATHA. Yes.

CHARLOTTE. Good gracious! What is he doing in an Eton jacket at his age?

AGATHA. [*Softly to* CHARLOTTE.] Hush! Don't say a word about my boy's age yet awhile.

CHARLOTTE. Oh!

AGATHA. [*About to introduce* POSKET.] There is my husband.

CHARLOTTE. [*Mistaking* BULLAMY *for him.*] Oh, how could she! [*To* BULLAMY, *turning her cheek to him.*] I congratulate you—I suppose you ought to kiss me.

AGATHA. No, no!

POSKET. Welcome to my house, Miss Verrinder.

CHARLOTTE. Oh, I beg your pardon. How do you do?

BULLAMY. [*To himself.*] Mrs. Posket's an interfering woman.

POSKET. [*Pointing to* BULLAMY.] Mr. Bullamy.

[BULLAMY, *aggrieved, bows stiffly.*

AGATHA. Come upstairs, dear; will you have some tea?

CHARLOTTE. No, thank you, pet, but I should like a glass of soda water.

AGATHA. Soda water!

CHARLOTTE. Well, dear, you can put what you like at the bottom of it.

[AGATHA *and* CHARLOTTE *go out,* POPHAM *following.*

POPHAM. [*To* CIS.] Give me back my *Bow Bells* when you have read it, you imp.   [*Goes out.*

CIS. By Jove, Guv, isn't Aunt Charlotte a stunner?

POSKET. Seems a charming woman.

BULLAMY. [*To himself.*] Posket's got the wrong one! That comes of marrying without first seeing the lady's relations.

CIS. Come along, Guv—let's have a gamble—Mr. Bullamy will join us.   [*Opens the card-table, arranges chairs and candles.*

BULLAMY. A gamble?

POSKET. Yes—the boy has taught me a new game called 'Fireworks'; his mother isn't aware that we play for money, of course, but we do.

BULLAMY. Ha, ha, ha! Who wins?

POSKET. He does now—but he says I shall win when I know the game better.

BULLAMY. What a boy he is!

POSKET. [*Delighted.*] Isn't he a wonderful lad? And only fourteen, too. I'll tell you something else—perhaps you had better not mention it to his mother.

BULLAMY. No, no, certainly not.

POSKET. He's invested a little money for me.

BULLAMY. What in?

POSKET. Not *in*—*on*—on Sillikin for the Lincolnshire Handicap. Sillikin to win and Butterscotch one, two, three.

BULLAMY. Good Lord!

POSKET. Yes, the dear boy said, 'Guv, it isn't fair you should give me all the tips; I'll give you some'—and he did—he gave me Sillikin and Butterscotch. He'll manage it for you, if you like. 'Plank it down', he calls it.

BULLAMY. [*Chuckling and choking.*] Ha, ha! Ho, ho! [*Taking a jujube.*] This boy will ruin me in jujubes.

CIS. All ready. Look sharp! Guv, lend me a sov to start with?

POSKET. A sov to start with? [*They sit at the table upstage. AGATHA and CHARLOTTE come into the room.*] We didn't think you would return so soon, my darling.

AGATHA. Go on amusing yourselves, I insist; only don't teach my Cis to play cards.

BULLAMY. Ho, ho!

POSKET. [*To* BULLAMY.] Hush! Hush!

AGATHA. [*To* CHARLOTTE.] I'm glad of this—we can tell each other our miseries undisturbed. Will you begin?

CHARLOTTE. Well, at last I am engaged to Captain Horace Vale.

AGATHA. Oh! Charley, I'm so glad!

CHARLOTTE. Yes—so is he—he says. He proposed to me at the Hunt Ball—in the passage—Tuesday week.

AGATHA. What did he say?

CHARLOTTE. He said, 'By Jove, I love you awfully.'

AGATHA. Well—and what did you say?

CHARLOTTE. Oh, I said, 'Well, if you're going to be as eloquent as all that, by Jove, I can't stand out.' So we settled it in the passage. He bars flirting till after we're married. That's my misery. What's yours, Aggy?

AGATHA. Something awful!

CHARLOTTE. Cheer up, Aggy! What is it?

AGATHA. Well, Charley, you know I lost my poor dear first husband at a very delicate age.

CHARLOTTE. Well, you were five-and-thirty, dear.

AGATHA. Yes, that's what I mean. Five-and-thirty is a very delicate age to find yourself single. You're neither one thing nor the other. You're not exactly a two-year-old, and you don't care to pull a hansom. However, I soon met Mr. Posket at Spa—bless him!

CHARLOTTE. And you nominated yourself for the Matrimonial Stakes. Mr. Farringdon's The Widow, by Bereavement, out of Mourning, ten pounds extra.

AGATHA. Yes, Charley, and in less than a month I went triumphantly over the course. But, Charley dear, I didn't carry the fair weight for age—and that's my trouble.

CHARLOTTE. Oh, dear!

AGATHA. Undervaluing Æneas' love, in a moment of, I hope, not unjustifiable vanity, I took five years from my total, which made me thirty-one on my wedding morning.

CHARLOTTE. Well, dear, many a misguided woman has done that before you.

AGATHA. Yes, Charley, but don't you see the consequences? It has thrown everything out. As I am now thirty-one, instead of thirty-six as I ought to be, it stands to reason that I couldn't have been married twenty years ago, which I was. So I have had to fib in proportion.

CHARLOTTE. I see—making your first marriage occur only fifteen years ago.

AGATHA. Exactly.

CHARLOTTE. Well then, dear, why worry yourself further?

AGATHA. Well, dear, don't you see? If I am only thirty-one now, my boy couldn't have been born nineteen years ago, and if he could, he oughtn't to have been, because on my own showing I wasn't married till four years later. Now you see the result!

CHARLOTTE. Which is, that that fine strapping young gentleman over there is only fourteen.

AGATHA. Precisely. Isn't it awkward! And his moustache is becoming more and more obvious every day.

CHARLOTTE. What does the boy himself believe?

AGATHA. He believes his mother, of course, as a boy should. As a prudent woman, I always kept him in ignorance of his age—in case of necessity. But it is terribly hard on the poor child, because his aims, instincts, and ambitions are all so horribly in advance of his condition. His food, his books, his amusements are out of keeping with his palate, his brain, and his disposition; and with all this suffering—his wretched mother has the remorseful consciousness of having shortened her offspring's life.

CHARLOTTE. Oh, come, you haven't quite done that.

AGATHA. Yes, I have—because, if he lives to be a hundred, he must be buried at ninety-five.

CHARLOTTE. That's true.

AGATHA. Then there's another aspect. He's a great favourite with all our friends—women friends especially. Even his little music mistress and the girl-servants hug and kiss him because he's such an engaging boy, and I can't stop it. But it's very awful to see these innocent women fondling a young man of nineteen.

CHARLOTTE. The women don't know it.

AGATHA. But they'd like to know it. They ought to know it! The other day I found my poor boy sitting on Lady Jenkins's lap, and in the presence of Sir George. I have no right to compromise Lady Jenkins in that way. And now, Charley, you see the whirlpool in which I am struggling—if you can throw me a rope, pray do.

CHARLOTTE. What sort of a man is Mr. Posket, Aggy?

AGATHA. The best creature in the world. He's a practical philanthropist.

CHARLOTTE. Um—he's a police magistrate, too, isn't he?

AGATHA. Yes, but he pays out of his own pocket half the fines he inflicts. That's why he has had a reprimand from the Home Office for inflicting such light penalties. All our servants have graduated at Mulberry Street. Most of the pictures in the dining-room are genuine Constables.

CHARLOTTE. Take my advice—tell him the whole story.

AGATHA. I dare not!

CHARLOTTE. Why?

AGATHA. I should have to take such a back seat for the rest of my married life.   [*The party at the card-table breaks up.*

BULLAMY. [*Grumpily.*] No, thank ye, not another minute. What is the use of talking about revenge, my dear Posket, when I haven't a penny piece left to play with?

POSKET. [*Distressed.*] I'm in the same predicament! Cis will lend us some money, won't you, Cis?

CIS. Rather!

BULLAMY. No, thank ye, that boy is one too many for me. I've never met such a child. Good-night, Mrs. Posket. [*Treads on a nut.*] Confound the nuts!

AGATHA. Going so early?

CIS. I hate a bad loser, don't you, Guv?

AGATHA. Show Mr. Bullamy down stairs, Cis.

BULLAMY. Good-night, Posket. Oh! I haven't a shilling left for my cabman.

CIS. I'll pay the cab.

BULLAMY. No, thank ye! I'll walk. [*Opening jujube box.*] Bah! Not even a jujube left and on a foggy night, too! Ugh!
          [*Goes out.*

Enter WYKE, *with four letters on salver.*

CIS. Any for me?

WYKE. One, sir.

CIS. [*To himself.*] From Achille Blond; lucky the mater didn't see it.
          [*Goes out.* WYKE *hands letters to* AGATHA, *who takes two, then to* POSKET, *who takes one.*

AGATHA. This is for you, Charley—already. [WYKE *goes out.*

CHARLOTTE. Spare my blushes, dear—it's from Horace, Captain Vale. The dear wretch knew I was coming to you. Heigho! Will you excuse me?

POSKET. Certainly.

AGATHA. Excuse me, please?

CHARLOTTE. Certainly, my dear.

POSKET. Certainly, my darling. Excuse me, won't you?

CHARLOTTE. Oh, certainly.

AGATHA. Certainly, Æneas.
[*Simultaneously they all open their letters, and lean back and read.*

Lady Jenkins is not feeling very well.

CHARLOTTE. [*Angrily.*] If Captain Horace Vale stood before me at this moment, I'd slap his face!

AGATHA. Charlotte!

CHARLOTTE. [*Reading.*] 'Dear Miss Verrinder—Your desperate flirtation with Major Bristow at the Meet on Tuesday last, three days after our engagement, has just come to my knowledge. Your letters and gifts, including the gold-headed hair-pin given me at the Hunt Ball, shall be returned to-morrow. By Jove, all is over! Horace Vale.' Oh, dear!

AGATHA. Oh, Charley, I'm so sorry! However, you can deny it.

CHARLOTTE. [*Weeping.*] That's the worst of it; I can't.

POSKET. [*To* AGATHA.] My darling, you will be delighted. A note from Colonel Lukyn.

AGATHA. Lukyn—Lukyn? I seem to know the name.

POSKET. An old schoolfellow of mine who went to India many years ago. He has just come home. I met him at the club last night and asked him to name an evening to dine with us. He accepts for to-morrow.

AGATHA. Lukyn, Lukyn?

POSKET. Listen. [*Reading.*] 'It will be especially delightful to me, as I believe I am an old friend of your wife and of her first husband. You may recall me to her recollection by reminding her that I am the Captain Lukyn who stood sponsor to her boy when he was christened at Baroda.'

AGATHA. [*Giving a loud scream.*] Oh!

POSKET. My dear!

AGATHA. I—I've twisted my foot.

POSKET. How *do* nuts come into the drawing-room?
                    [*Picks up nut and puts it on the piano.*

CHARLOTTE. [*Quietly to* AGATHA.] Aggy?

AGATHA. [*To* CHARLOTTE.] The boy's godfather.

CHARLOTTE. When was the child christened?

AGATHA. A month after he was born. They always are.

POSKET. [*Reading the letter again.*] This is *very* pleasant.

AGATHA. Let—let me see the letter, I—I may recognize the handwriting.

POSKET. [*Handing her the letter.*] Certainly, my pet. [*To himself.*] Awakened memories of Number One. [*Sighing.*] That's the worst of marrying a widow; somebody is always proving her previous convictions.

AGATHA. [*To* CHARLOTTE.] 'No. 19a, Cork Street.' Charley, put on your things and come with me.

CHARLOTTE. Agatha, you're mad!

AGATHA. I'm going to shut this man's mouth before he comes into this house to-morrow.

CHARLOTTE. Wait *till* he comes.

AGATHA. Yes, till he stalks in here with his 'How d'ye do, Posket? Haven't seen your wife since the year '66, by Gad, sir!' Not I! Æneas!

POSKET. My dear.

AGATHA. Lady Jenkins—Adelaide—is very ill; she can't put her foot to the ground with neuralgia.
                    [*Taking the letter from her pocket, and giving it to him.*

POSKET. Bless me!

AGATHA. We have known each other for six long years.

POSKET. Only six weeks, my love.

AGATHA. Weeks *are* years in close friendship. My place is by her side.

POSKET. [*Reading the letter.*] 'Slightly indisposed, caught trifling cold at the Dog Show. Where do you buy your handkerchiefs?' There's nothing about neuralgia or putting her foot to the ground here, my darling.

AGATHA. No, but can't you read between the lines, Æneas? That is the letter of a woman who is not at all well.

POSKET. All right, my darling, if you are bent upon going I will accompany you.

AGATHA. Certainly not, Æneas—Charlotte insists on being my companion; we can keep each other warm in a closed cab.

POSKET. But can't I make a third?

AGATHA. Don't be so forgetful, Æneas—don't you know that in a four-wheeled cab, the fewer knees there are the better?

[AGATHA *and* CHARLOTTE *go out.*]

Enter CIS *hurriedly.*

CIS. What's the matter, Guv?

POSKET. Your mother and Miss Verrinder are going out.

CIS. Out of their minds? It's a horrid night.

POSKET. Yes, but Lady Jenkins is ill.

CIS. Oh! Is ma mentioned in the will?

POSKET. [*Shocked.*] Good gracious, what a boy! No, Cis, your mother is merely going to sit by Lady Jenkins's bedside, to hold her hand, and to tell her where one goes to—to buy pocket-handkerchiefs.

CIS. [*Struck with an idea.*] By Jove! The mater can't be home again till half-past twelve or one o'clock.

POSKET. Much later if Lady Jenkins's condition is alarming.

CIS. Hurray! [*He takes the watch out of* POSKET'S *pocket.*] Just half-past ten. Greenwich mean, eh Guv?

[*He puts the watch to his ear, pulling* POSKET *towards him by the chain.*]

POSKET. What an extraordinary lad!

CIS. [*Returning watch.*] Thanks. They have to get from here to

Campden Hill and back again. I'll tell Wyke to get them the worst horse on the rank.

POSKET. My dear child!

CIS. Three-quarters of an hour's journey from here at least. Twice three-quarters, one hour and a half. An hour with Lady Jenkins—when women get together, you know, Guv, they do talk—that's two hours and a half. Good. Guv, will you come with me?

POSKET. [*Horrified.*] Go with you! Where?

CIS. Hôtel des Princes, Meek Street. A sharp hansom does it in ten minutes.

POSKET. Meek Street, Hôtel des Princes! Child, do you know what you're talking about?

CIS. Rather. Look here, Guv, honour bright—no blab if I show you a letter.

POSKET. I won't promise anything.

CIS. You won't! Do you know, Guv, you are doing a very unwise thing to check the confidence of a lad like me?

POSKET. Cis, my boy!

CIS. Can you calculate the inestimable benefit it is to a youngster to have some one always at his elbow, some one older, wiser, and better off than himself?

POSKET. Of course, Cis, of course, I *want* you to make a companion of me.

CIS. Then how the deuce can I do that if you won't come with me to Meek Street?

POSKET. Yes, but deceiving your mother!

CIS. *Deceiving* the mater would be to tell her a crammer—a thing, I hope, we're both of us much above.

POSKET. Good boy, good boy.

CIS. *Concealing* the fact that we're going to have a bit of supper at the Hôtel des Princes is doing my mother a great kindness, because it would upset her considerably to know of the circumstances. You've been wrong, Guv, but we won't say anything more about that. Read the letter.

[*Gives* POSKET *the letter.*

POSKET. [*Reading in a dazed sort of a way.*] 'Hôtel des Princes, Meek Street, W. Dear Sir—Unless you drop in and settle your arrears, I really cannot keep your room for you any longer. Yours obediently, Achille Blond. Cecil Farringdon, Esq.' Good heavens! You have a room at the Hôtel des Princes!

CIS. A room! It's little better than a coop.

POSKET. You don't occupy it?

CIS. But my friends do. When I was at Brighton I was in with the best set—hope I always shall be. I left Brighton—nice hole I was in. You see, Guv, I didn't want my friends to make free with your house.

POSKET. [*Weakly.*] Oh, didn't you?

CIS. So I took a room at the Hôtel des Princes—when I want to put a man up he goes there. You see, Guv, it's *you* I've been considering more than myself.

POSKET. [*Beside himself.*] But you are a mere child!

CIS. A fellow is just as old as he feels. I feel no end of a man. Hush, they're coming down! I'm off to tell Wyke about the rickety four-wheeler.

POSKET. Cis, Cis! Your mother will discover I have been out.

CIS. Oh, I forgot, you're married, aren't you?

POSKET. Married!

CIS. Say you are going to the club.

POSKET. But that's not the truth, sir!

CIS. Yes it is. We'll pop in at the club on our way, and you can give me a bitters.　　　　　　　　　　　　　　　[*Goes out.*

POSKET. Good gracious, what a boy! Hôtel des Princes, Meek Street! What shall I do? Tell his mother? Why, it would turn her hair grey. If I could only get a quiet word with this Mr. Achille Blond, I could put a stop to everything. That is my best course, not to lose a moment in rescuing the child from his boyish indiscretion. Yes, I must go with Cis to Meek Street.

Enter AGATHA *and* CHARLOTTE, *elegantly dressed.*

AGATHA. Have you sent for a cab, Æneas?

POSKET. Cis is looking after that.

AGATHA. Poor Cis! How late we keep him up.

Enter CIS.

CIS. Wyke has gone for a cab, ma dear.

AGATHA. Thank you, Cis darling.

CIS. If you'll excuse me, I'll go to my room. I've another bad headache coming on.

AGATHA. [*Kissing him.*] Run along, my boy.

CIS. Good-night, ma. Good-night, Aunt Charlotte.

CHARLOTTE. Good-night, Cis.

AGATHA. [*To herself.*] I wish the cab would come.
          [AGATHA *and* CHARLOTTE *look out of the window.*

CIS. [*At the door.*] Ahem! Good-night, Guv.

POSKET. You've told a story—two, sir! You said you were going up to your room.

CIS. So I am—to dress.

POSKET. You said you had a bad headache coming on.

CIS. So I have, Guv. I always get a bad headache at the Hôtel des Princes.   [*Goes out.*

POSKET. Oh, what a boy!

AGATHA. [*To herself.*] When will that cab come?

POSKET. Ahem! My pet, the idea has struck me that as you are going out, it would not be a bad notion for me to pop into my club.

AGATHA. The club! You were there last night.

POSKET. I know, my darling. Many men look in at their clubs every night.

AGATHA. A nice example for Cis, truly! I particularly desire that you should remain at home to-night, Æneas.

POSKET. [*To himself.*] Oh, dear me!

CHARLOTTE. [*To* AGATHA.] Why not let him go to the club, Agatha?

AGATHA. He might meet Colonel Lukyn there.

CHARLOTTE. If Colonel Lukyn is there we shan't find him in Cork Street.

AGATHA. Then we follow him to the club.

CHARLOTTE. Ladies never call at a club.

AGATHA. Such things have been known.

Enter WYKE.

WYKE. [*Grinning behind his hand.*] The cab is coming, ma'am.

AGATHA. Coming? Why didn't you bring it with you?

WYKE. I walk quicker than the cab, ma'am. It's a good horse, slow, but very certain.

AGATHA. We will come down.

WYKE. [*To himself.*] Just what the horse has done. [*To* AGATHA.] Yes, ma'am.   [*Goes out.*

AGATHA. Good-night, Æneas.

POSKET. [*Nervously.*] I wish you would allow me to go to the club, my pet.

AGATHA. Æneas, I am surprised at your obstinacy. It is so very different from my first husband.

POSKET. [*Annoyed.*] Really, Agatha, I am shocked. I presume the late Mr. Farringdon occasionally used his clubs?

AGATHA. Indian clubs. Indian clubs are good for the liver; London clubs are not. Good-night!

POSKET. I'll see you to your cab, Agatha.

AGATHA. No, thank you.

POSKET. Upon my word!

CHARLOTTE. [*To* AGATHA.] Why not?

AGATHA. He would want to give the direction to the cabman!

CHARLOTTE. The first tiff. Good-night, Mr. Posket.

POSKET. Good-night, Miss Verrinder.

AGATHA. Have you any message for Lady Jenkins?

POSKET. Confound Lady Jenkins!

AGATHA. I will deliver your message in the presence of Sir

George, who, I may remind you, is the Permanent Secretary at the Home Office.

[AGATHA *and* CHARLOTTE *go out;* POSKET *paces up and down excitedly.*

POSKET. Gurrh! I'm not to go to the club! I set a bad example to Cis! Ha, ha! I am different from her first husband. Yes, I am—I'm alive for one thing. I—I—I—I—I'm dashed if I don't go out with the boy.

CIS. [*Putting his head in at the door.*] Coast clear, Guv? All right.

Enter CIS, *in fashionable evening dress, carrying* POSKET'S *overcoat and hat.*

Here are your hat and overcoat.

POSKET. [*Recoiling.*] Where on earth did you get that dress suit?

CIS. Mum's the word, Guv. Brighton tailor—six months' credit. He promised to send in the bill to you, so the mater won't know. [*Putting* POSKET'S *hat on his head.*] By Jove, Guv, don't my togs show you up?

POSKET. [*Faintly.*] I won't go, I won't go. I've never met such a boy before.

CIS. [*Proceeds to help him with his overcoat.*] Mind your arm, Guv. You've got your hand in a pocket. No, no—that's a tear in the lining. That's it.

POSKET. I forbid you to go out!

CIS. Yes, Guv. And I forbid you to eat any of those devilled oysters we shall get at the Hôtel des Princes. Now you're right!

POSKET. I am not right!

CIS. Oh, I forgot! [*He pulls out a handful of loose money.*] I found this money in your desk, Guv. You had better take it out with you; you may want it. Here you are—gold, silver, and coppers. [*He empties the money into* POSKET'S *overcoat pocket.*] One last precaution, and then we're off.

[*Goes to the writing-table, and writes on a half-sheet of note-paper.*

POSKET. I shall take a turn round the Square, and then come home again! I will not be influenced by a mere child! A man of my responsible position—a magistrate—supping slily at the Hôtel des Princes in Meek Street—it's horrible.

CIS. Now then—we'll creep downstairs quietly so as not to bring Wyke from his pantry. [*Giving* POSKET *a paper*.] You stick that up prominently, while I blow out the candles.

[CIS *blows out the candles on the piano*.

POSKET. [*Reading*.] 'Your master and Mr. Cecil Farringdon are going to bed. Don't disturb them.' I will not be a partner to any written document. This is untrue.

CIS. No, it isn't—we are going to bed when we come home. Make haste, Guv.

POSKET. Oh, what a boy!   [*Pinning the paper on to the curtain*.

CIS. [*Turning down the lamp, and watching* POSKET.] Hallo, Guv, hallo! You're an old hand at this sort of game, are you?

POSKET. How dare you!

CIS. [*Taking* POSKET's *arm*.] Now then, don't breathe.

POSKET. [*Quite demoralised*.] Cis! Cis! Wait a minute—wait a minute!

CIS. Hold up, Guv.

Enter WYKE.

Oh, bother!

WYKE. Going out, sir?

POSKET. [*Struggling to be articulate*.] No—yes—that is— partially—half round the Square, and possibly—er—um— back again. [*To* CIS.] Oh, you bad boy!

WYKE. [*Coolly going up to the paper on curtain*.] Shall I take this down now, sir?

POSKET. [*Quietly to* CIS.] I'm in an awful position! What am I to do?

CIS. Do as I do—tip him.

POSKET. What!

CIS. Tip him.

POSKET. Oh, yes—yes. Where's my money?
[CIS *takes two coins out of* POSKET's *pocket and gives them to him without looking at them.*

CIS. Give him that.

POSKET. Yes.

CIS. And say—'Wyke, you want a new umbrella—buy a very good one. Your mistress has a latch-key, so go to bed.'

POSKET. Wyke!

WYKE. Yes, sir.

POSKET. [*Giving him money.*] Go to bed—buy a very good one. Your mistress has a latch-key—so—so you want a new umbrella!

WYKE. [*Knowingly.*] All right, sir. You can depend on me. Are you well muffled up, sir? Mind you take care of him, Master Cis.

CIS. [*Supporting* POSKET, *who groans softly.*] Capital, Guv, capital. Are you hungry?

POSKET. Hungry! You're a wicked boy. I've told a falsehood.

CIS. No, you haven't, Guv—he really does want a new umbrella.

POSKET. Does he, Cis? Does he? Thank heaven! [*They go out.*

WYKE. [*Looking at money.*] Here! What, twopence! [*Throws the coins down in disgust.*] I'll tell the missus.   [*Curtain.*

ACT II

A supper-room at the Hôtel des Princes, Meek Street, with two doors—the one leading into an adjoining room, the other into a passage—and a window opening on to a balcony.

ISIDORE, a French waiter, is showing in CIS *and* POSKET, *who is still very nervous and reluctant.*

CIS. Come on, Guv—come on. How are you, Isidore?

ISIDORE. I beg your pardon—I am quite well, and so are you, zank you.

CIS. I want a pretty little light supper for myself and my friend, Mr. Skinner.

ISIDORE. Mr. Skinner.

POSKET. [*To* CIS.] Skinner! Is some one else coming?

CIS. No, no. You're Skinner.

POSKET. Oh!   [*Wanders round the room.*

CIS. Mr. Skinner, of the Stock Exchange. What have you ready?

ISIDORE. [*In an undertone to* CIS.] I beg your pardon—very good—but Monsieur Blond he say to me, 'Isidore, listen now; if Mr. Farringdon he come here, you say, I beg your pardon, you are a nice gentleman, but will you pay your little account when it is quite convenient, before you leave the house at once.'

CIS. Quite so; there's no difficulty about that. What's the bill?

ISIDORE. [*Gives the bill.*] I beg your pardon. Eight pounds four shillings.

CIS. Phew! Here go my winnings from old Bullamy and the Guv. [*Counting out money.*] Two pounds short. [*Turning to* POSKET, *who is carefully examining the scratches on the mirrors.*] Skinner! Skinner!

POSKET. Visitors evidently scratch their names on the mirrors. Dear me! Surely this is a spurious title—'Lottie, Duchess of Fulham!' How very curious!

CIS. Skinner, got any money with you?

POSKET. Yes, Cis, my boy.   [*Feels for his money.*

CIS. You always keep it in that pocket, Skinner.

POSKET. [*Taking out money.*] Oh, yes.
[CIS *takes two sovereigns from* POSKET *and gives the amount of his bill to* ISIDORE, *who goes to the sideboard to count out change.*

CIS. No putting the change to bed, Isidore.

POSKET. What's that?

CIS. Putting the change to bed! Isidore will show you. [*To* ISIDORE, *who comes to them with the change and the bill on a plate.*] Isidore, show Mr. Skinner how you put silver to bed.

ISIDORE. Oh, Mr. Farringdon, I beg your pardon—no, no!

POSKET. It would be most instructive.

ISIDORE. Very good. [*Goes to the table, upon which he puts plate.*] Say I have to give you change sixteen shillings.

POSKET. Certainly.

ISIDORE. Very good, Before I bring it to you I slip a little half-crown under the bill—so. Then I put what is left on the top of the bill, and I say, 'I beg your pardon, your change.' You take it, you give me two shillings for myself, and all is right.

POSKET. [*Counting the silver on the bill with the end of his glasses.*] Yes, but suppose I count the silver; it is half-a-crown short!

ISIDORE. Then I say, 'I beg your pardon, how dare you say that?' Then I do so. [*He pulls the bill from the plate.*] Then I say, 'The bill is eight pounds four shillings, [*handing the plate*] count again.'

POSKET. Ah, of course, it's all right now.

ISIDORE. Very good, then you give me five shillings for doubting me. Do it, do it.

POSKET. [*In a daze, giving him the five shillings.*] Like this?

ISIDORE. Yes, like that. [*Slipping the money into his pocket.*] I beg your pardon—thank you. [*Handing* CIS *the rest of the change.*] Your change, Mr. Farringdon.

CIS. Oh I say, Isidore!

Enter BLOND, *a fat, middle-aged French hotel-keeper, with a letter in his hand.*

ISIDORE. Monsieur Blond.

BLOND. Good evening, Mr. Farringdon.

ISIDORE. [*Quietly to* BLOND.] Ze bill is all right.

CIS. Good evening. [*Introducing* POSKET.] My friend, Mr. Harvey Skinner, of the Stock Exchange.

BLOND. Very pleased to see you. [*To* CIS.] Are you going to enjoy yourselves?

CIS. Rather.

BLOND. You usually eat in this room, but you don't mind giving it up for to-night—now, do you?

CIS. Oh, Achille!

BLOND. Come, come, to please me. A cab has just brought a letter from an old customer of mine, a gentleman I haven't seen for over twenty years, who wants to sup with a friend in this room to-night. It's quite true.   [*Giving* CIS *a letter.*

CIS. [*Reading to himself.*] '19A, Cork Street. Dear Blond— Fresh, or rather, stale from India—want to sup with my friend, Captain Vale, to-night, at my old table in my old room. Must do this for Auld Lang Syne. Yours, Alexander Lukyn.' Oh, let him have it. Where will you put us?

BLOND. You shall have the best room in the house, the one next to this. This room—pah! Come with me. [*To* POSKET.] Have you known Mr. Farringdon for a long time?

POSKET. No, no. Not very long.

BLOND. Ah, he is a fine fellow—Mr. Farringdon. Now, if you please. You can go through this door.
          [*Wheels sofa away from before door and unlocks it.*

CIS. [*To* POSKET.] You'll look better after a glass or two of Pommery, Guv.

POSKET. No, no, Cis—now, no champagne.

CIS. No champagne, not for my friend, Harvey Skinner! Come, Guv—dig me in the ribs—like this. [*Digging him in the ribs.*] Chuck!

POSKET. [*Shrinking.*] Oh, don't!

CIS. And say, 'Hey!' Go on, Guv.

POSKET. I can't—I can't. I don't know what it may mean.

CIS. [*Digging him in the ribs again.*] Go on—ch-uck!

POSKET. What, like this? [*Returning the dig.*] Ch-uck.

CIS. That's it, that's it. Ha, ha! You are going it, Guv.

POSKET. [*Getting excited.*] Am I, Cis? Am I? [*Waving his arm.*] Hey!

CIS *and* POSKET. Hey!

CIS. Ha, ha! Come on! Serve the supper, Achille.

BLOND. Ah, he is a grand fellow, Mr. Farringdon! [CIS *and* POSKET *go into the other room. To* ISIDORE.] Replace the canapé.
[*There is a sharp knock at the other door.* BLOND *follows* CIS *and* POSKET *into the other room, then locks the door on the inside.*

ISIDORE. Come in, please.

Enter COLONEL LUKYN *and* CAPTAIN VALE. LUKYN *is a portly, grey-haired, good-looking military man;* VALE *is pale-faced and heavy-eyed, while his manner is languid and dejected.*

LUKYN. This is the room. Come in, Vale. This is my old supper-room—I haven't set foot here for over twenty years. By George, I hope to sup here for another twenty.

VALE. [*Dejectedly.*] Do you? In less than that, unless I am lucky enough to fall in some foreign set-to, I shall be in Kensal Green.

LUKYN. [*Looking round the room sentimentally.*] Twenty years ago! Confound 'em, they've painted it.

VALE. My people have eight shelves in the Catacombs at Kensal Green.

LUKYN. Nonsense, man, nonsense. You're a little low. Waiter, take our coats.

VALE. Don't check me, Lukyn. My shelf is four from the bottom.

LUKYN. You'll forget the number of your shelf before you're half-way through your oysters.

VALE. [*Shaking his head.*] An oyster merely reminds me of my own particular shell. [ISIDORE *begins to remove* VALE'*s coat.*

LUKYN. Ha, ha! Ha, ha!

VALE. Don't, Lukyn, don't [*In an undertone to* LUKYN.] It's very good of you, but by Jove, my heart is broken. [*To* ISIDORE.] Mind my flower, waiter, confound you.
                    [*He adjusts flower in his button-hole.*

ISIDORE. You have ordered supper, sir?

LUKYN. Yes, on the back of my note to Mr. Blond. Serve it at once.

ISIDORE. I beg your pardon, sir, at once.   [*Goes out.*

LUKYN. So, you've been badly treated by a woman, eh, Vale?

VALE. Shockingly. Between man and man, a Miss Verrinder—Charlotte. [*Turning away.*] Excuse me, Lukyn.
    [*Produces a folded silk handkerchief, shakes it out, and gently blows his nose.*

LUKYN. [*Lighting a cigarette.*] Certainly—certainly—does you great credit. Pretty woman?

VALE. Oh, lovely! A most magnificent set of teeth. All real, as far as I can ascertain.

LUKYN. No!

VALE. Fact.

LUKYN. Great loss—have a cigarette.

VALE. [*Taking case from* LUKYN.] Parascho's?

LUKYN. Yes. Was she—full grown?

VALE. [*Lighting his cigarette.*] Just perfection. She rides eight stone fifteen, and I have lost her, Lukyn. Beautiful tobacco.

LUKYN. What finished it?

VALE. She gave a man a pair of worked slippers three days after our engagement.

LUKYN. No!

VALE. Fact. You remember Bristow—Gordon Bristow?

LUKYN. Perfectly. Best fellow in the world.

VALE. He wears them.

LUKYN. Villain! Will you begin with a light wine, or go right on to the champagne?

VALE. By Jove, it's broken my heart, old fellow. I'll go right on to the champagne, please. Lukyn, I shall make you my executor.

LUKYN. Pooh! You'll outlive me! Why don't they bring the supper? My heart has been broken like yours. It was broken first in Ireland in '55. It was broken again in London in '61, but in 1870 it was smashed in Calcutta, by a married lady that time.

VALE. A married lady?

LUKYN. Yes, my late wife. Talk about broken hearts, my boy, when you've won your lady, not when you've lost her.

Enter ISIDORE, *with a tray of supper things.*

The supper. [*To* VALE.] Hungry?

VALE. [*Mournfully.*] Very.

Enter BLOND, *with an envelope.*

BLOND. Colonel Lukyn.

LUKYN. Ah, Blond, how are you? Not a day older. What have you got there?

BLOND. [*Quietly to* LUKYN *in an undertone.*] Two ladies, Colonel, downstairs in a cab, must see you for a few minutes alone.

LUKYN. Good gracious! Excuse me, Vale. [*Takes the envelope from* BLOND *and opens it: reading the enclosed card.*] Mrs. Posket—Mrs. Posket! 'Mrs. Posket entreats Colonel Lukyn to see her for five minutes upon a matter of urgent necessity, and free from observation.' By George! Posket must be ill in bed—I thought he looked seedy last night. [*To* BLOND.] Of course—of course. Say I'll come down.

BLOND. It is raining outside. I had better ask them up.

LUKYN. Do—do. I'll get Captain Vale to step into another room. Be quick. Say I am quite alone.

BLOND. Yes, Colonel. *[Hurries out.*

CIS. [*In the next room, rattling glasses and calling.*] Waiter! Waiter! Waiter-r-r! Where the deuce are you?

ISIDORE. Coming, sir, coming. I beg your pardon. [*Bustles out.*

LUKYN. My dear Vale, I am dreadfully sorry to bother you. Two ladies, one the wife of a very old friend of mine, have followed me here and want half a dozen words with me alone. I am in your hands—how can I manage it?

VALE. My dear fellow, don't mention it. Let me go into another room.

LUKYN. Thank you very much. You're so hungry too. Where's the waiter? Confound him, he's gone!

VALE. All right. I'll pop in here.
[*He passes behind sofa and tries the door leading into the other room.*

CIS. [*Within.*] What do you want? Who's there?

VALE. Occupied—never mind—I'll find my way somewhere.
[*There is a knock;* VALE *draws back.*

BLOND. [*Without.*] Colonel, are you alone? The ladies.

LUKYN. One moment. Deuce take it, Vale! The ladies don't want to be seen. By George—I remember. There's a little balcony to that window; step out for a few moments—keep quiet—I shan't detain you—it's nothing important—husband must have had a fit or something.

VALE. Oh, certainly!

LUKYN. Good fellow—here's your hat.
[*In his haste he fetches his own hat.*

BLOND. [*Outside, knocking.*] Colonel, Colonel!

LUKYN. One moment. [*Giving his hat to* VALE.] Awfully sorry. You're so hungry too. [VALE *puts on the hat, which is much too large for him.*] Ah, that's my hat.

VALE. My dear Lukyn—don't mention it.
[*Opening the window and going out.*

LUKYN. [*Drawing the curtain over the recess.*] Just room for him to stand like a man in a sentry-box. Come in, Blond.

BLOND *shows in* AGATHA *and* CHARLOTTE,
both wearing veils.

AGATHA. [*Agitated.*] Oh, Colonel Lukyn!

LUKYN. Pray compose yourself, pray compose yourself!

AGATHA. What will you think?

LUKYN. [*Holding out his hand, gallantly.*] That I am perfectly enchanted.

AGATHA. Thank you. [*Pointing to* CHARLOTTE.] My sister.

[LUKYN *and* CHARLOTTE *bow.*

LUKYN. Be seated. Blond? [*Softly to him.*] Keep the waiter out till I ring—that's all.   [*The loud pattering of rain is heard.*

BLOND. Yes, Colonel.

LUKYN. Good gracious, Blond! What's that?

BLOND. The rain outside. It is cats and dogs.

LUKYN. [*Horrified.*] By George, is it? [*To himself, looking towards window.*] Poor devil! [*To* BLOND, *anxiously.*] There isn't any method of getting off that balcony, is there?

BLOND. No—unless by getting on to it.

LUKYN. What do you mean?

BLOND. It is not at all safe. Don't use it.

[LUKYN *stands horror-stricken;* BLOND *goes out. Heavy rain is heard.*

LUKYN. [*After some nervous glances at the window, wiping perspiration from his forehead.*] I am honoured, Mrs. Posket, by this visit—though for the moment I can't imagine——

AGATHA. Colonel Lukyn, we drove to Cork Street to your lodgings, and there your servant told us you were supping at the Hôtel des Princes with a friend. No one will be shown into this room while we are here?

LUKYN. No—we—ah—shall not be disturbed. [*To himself.*] Good heavens, suppose I never see him alive again!

AGATHA. [*Sighing wearily.*] Ah!

LUKYN. I'm afraid you've come to tell me Posket is ill.

AGATHA. I—no—my husband is at home.

[*A sharp gust of wind is heard with the rain.*

LUKYN. [*Starts.*] Lord forgive me! I've killed him.

AGATHA. [*With horror.*] Colonel Lukyn!

LUKYN. [*Confused.*] Madam!

AGATHA. Indeed, Mr. Posket is at home.

LUKYN. [*Glancing at the window.*] Is he? I wish we all were.

AGATHA. [*To herself.*] Sunstroke, evidently. Poor fellow! [*To LUKYN.*] I assure you my husband is at home, quite well, and by this time sleeping soundly.

[CIS *and* POSKET *are heard laughing in the next room.*

ISIDORE. [*Within.*] You are two funny gentlemen, I beg your pardon.

AGATHA. [*Startled.*] What is that?

LUKYN. In the next room. [*Raps at the door.*] Hush—hush, hush!

CHARLOTTE. Get it over Aggy, and let us go home. I am so awfully hungry.

LUKYN. [*Peering through the curtains.*] It is still bearing him. What's his weight? Surely he can't scale over ten stone. Lord, how wet he is!

AGATHA. Colonel Lukyn!

LUKYN. Madam, command me!

AGATHA. Colonel Lukyn, we knew each other at Baroda twenty years ago.

LUKYN. When I look at you, impossible.

AGATHA. Ah, then you mustn't look at me.

LUKYN. Equally impossible.

CHARLOTTE. [*To herself.*] Oh, I feel quite out of this.

AGATHA. You were at my little boy's christening?

LUKYN. [*Absently.*] Yes—yes—certainly.

AGATHA. You remember what a fine little fellow he was.

LUKYN. [*Thoughtfully*]. Not a pound over ten stone.

AGATHA. Colonel Lukyn!

LUKYN. [*Recovering himself.*] I beg your pardon, yes—I was at the christening of your boy.

AGATHA. [*To herself.*] One of the worst cases of sunstroke I have ever known.

M

LUKYN. I remember the child very well. Has he still got that absurd mug?

AGATHA. Colonel Lukyn!

LUKYN. Madam!

AGATHA. My child is, and always was—perfect.

LUKYN. You misunderstand me! I was his godfather; I gave him a silver cup.

AGATHA. Oh, do excuse me. [*Wiping her eyes.*] How did I become acquainted with such a vulgar expression? I don't know where I pick up my slang. It must be through loitering at shop windows. Oh, oh, oh!

LUKYN. Pray compose yourself. I'll leave you for a moment.
[*Going to the window.*

AGATHA. How shall I begin, Charley?

CHARLOTTE. Make a bold plunge, do! The odour of cooking here, to a hungry woman, is maddening.
[VALE *softly opens the window and comes into the recess, but remains concealed by the curtain from those on the stage.*

VALE. [*To himself.*] This is too bad of Lukyn! I'm wet to the skin and frightfully hungry! Who the deuce are these women?

AGATHA. Colonel Lukyn!

LUKYN. Madam. [*Listening.*] No crash yet.

AGATHA. [*Impulsively laying her hand upon his arm.*] Friend of twenty years! I will be quite candid with you. You are going to dine with us to-morrow?

LUKYN. Madam, I will repay your candour as it deserves. I am.

AGATHA. My husband knows of your acquaintance with the circumstances of my first marriage. I know what men are. When the women leave the dinner-table, men become retrospective. Now, to-morrow night, over dessert, I beg you not to give my husband dates.

LUKYN. [*Astonished.*] Eh?

AGATHA. Keep anything like dates from him.

LUKYN. [*Puzzled.*] Mustn't eat stone fruit?

AGATHA. No, I mean years, months, days—dates connected with my marriage with Mr. Farringdon.

LUKYN. Dear me, sore subject!

AGATHA. I will be more than candid with you. My present husband, having a very short vacation in the discharge of his public duties, wooed me but for three weeks; you, who have in your time courted and married, know the material of which that happy period is made up. The future is all-engrossing to the man; the presents—I mean the present, a joyous dream to the woman. But in dealing with my past I met with more than ordinary difficulties.

LUKYN. Don't see why—late husband died a natural death—wasn't stood on a balcony or anything.

AGATHA. Colonel Lukyn, you know I was six-and-thirty at the time of my recent marriage!

LUKYN. You surprise me!

AGATHA. You know it! Be frank, Lukyn! Am I not six-and-thirty?

LUKYN. You are.

AGATHA. Very well, then. In a three weeks' engagement how was it possible for me to deal with the various episodes of six-and-thirty years? The past may be pleasant, golden, beautiful—but one may have too much of a good thing.

LUKYN. [*To himself.*] I am in that position now.

AGATHA. The man who was courting me was seeking relaxation from the discharge of multifarious responsibilities. How could I tax an already wearied attention with the recital of the events of thirty-six years?

LUKYN. What did you do?

AGATHA. Out of consideration for the man I loved, I sacrificed five years of happy girlhood—told him I was but one-and-thirty—that I had been married only fifteen years previously—that my boy was but fourteen!

LUKYN. By George, madam, and am I to subscribe to all this?

AGATHA. I only ask you to avoid the question of dates.

LUKYN. But at a man's dinner-table——

AGATHA. You need not spoil a man's dinner. [*Appealingly.*] Not only a man's—but a woman's! Lukyn, Lukyn! Promise!

LUKYN. Give me a second to think.

[LUKYN, *turning away, discovers* CHARLOTTE *in the act of lifting the covers from the dishes and inspecting the contents.*

LUKYN. Ah, devilled oysters!

CHARLOTTE. Oh!

[*Drops dish-cover with a crash, and runs over to the table and speaks to* AGATHA.

LUKYN. Don't go—pray look at 'em again—wish I could persuade you to taste them. [*To himself.*] What am I to do? Shall I promise? Poor Posket! If I don't promise, she'll cry and won't go home. The oysters are nearly cold—cold! What must *he* be! [*Drawing aside the curtain and not seeing* VALE, *he staggers back.*] Gone—and without a cry—brave fellow, brave fellow!

AGATHA. Colonel Lukyn.

LUKYN. [*To himself.*] Decay of stamina in the army—pah! The young 'uns are worthy of our best days.

AGATHA. Colonel Lukyn, will you promise?

LUKYN. Promise? Anything, my dear madam, anything.

AGATHA. Ah, thank you! May I ask you to see us to our cab?

LUKYN. Certainly! Thank heaven, they're going!

AGATHA. [*To* CHARLOTTE.] It's all right; come along.

CHARLOTTE. [*To* AGATHA.] Oh, those oysters look so nice.

LUKYN. [*To himself.*] Stop! In my trouble, I am forgetting even the commonest courtesies to these ladies. [*To* AGATHA.] You have a long journey before you. I am sure your husband would not forgive me for letting you face such weather unprepared. Let me recommend an oyster or two and a thimbleful of champagne.

AGATHA. No thank you, Colonel Lukyn.

CHARLOTTE. [*To* AGATHA.] Say yes. I'm starving.

LUKYN. As you please. [*To himself.*] I knew they'd refuse. I've done my duty.

CHARLOTTE. [*To* AGATHA.] I was in the train till seven o'clock. Wait till you're a bona fide traveller—accept.

AGATHA. Ahem! Colonel, the fact is my poor sister has been travelling all day and is a little exhausted.

LUKYN. [*Horrified.*] You don't mean to say you're going to give me the inestimable pleasure. [CHARLOTTE *looks across at him, nodding and smiling.*] I am delighted.
[CHARLOTTE *sits hungrily at table;* LUKYN *fetches a bottle of champagne from the sideboard.*

AGATHA. Charlotte, I am surprised.

CHARLOTTE. Nonsense, the best people come here. Some of them have left their names on the mirrors.

VALE. [*Behind the curtain.*] This is much too bad of Lukyn. What are they doing now? [LUKYN *draws the cork.*] Confound it, they're having my supper! [LUKYN *pours out wine.*

CHARLOTTE. Why doesn't he give me something to eat?
[*There is a clatter of knives and forks heard from the other room, then a burst of laughter from* CIS.

AGATHA. [*Starting*]. Charley, hark! How strange!

CHARLOTTE. Very. This bread is beautiful.
[CIS *is heard singing the chorus of a comic song boisterously.*

AGATHA. Don't you recognise that voice?

CHARLOTTE. [*Munching.*] The only voice I recognise is the voice of hunger.

AGATHA. I am overwrought, I suppose.
[LUKYN, *with his head drooping, fetches the dish of oysters from the sideboard.*

VALE. [*Behind the curtain.*] He has taken the oysters. I've seen him do it.

LUKYN. The oysters.
[LUKYN *sinks into his chair at the table and leans his head upon his hand; the two women look at each other.*

CHARLOTTE. [*To* AGATHA.] Anything wrong?

AGATHA. [*Tapping her forehead.*] Sunstroke—bad case!

CHARLOTTE. Oh—poor fellow. [*She gently lifts the corner of the dish, sniffs, then replaces cover.*] No plates.

AGATHA. Ask for them.

CHARLOTTE. You ask.

AGATHA. You're hungry.

CHARLOTTE. You're married. Comes better from you.

VALE. [*Behind curtain.*] This silence is terrible.

AGATHA. [*To* LUKYN.] Ahem! Ahem!

LUKYN. [*Looking up suddenly.*] Eh?

AGATHA. [*Sweetly.*] There are no plates.

LUKYN. [*Rousing himself.*] No plates? No plates? It's my fault. Pardon me. Where are the plates?
> [VALE, *still invisible, stretches out his hand through the curtain, takes up the plates and presents them to* LUKYN, *who recoils.*

VALE. [*In a whisper.*] Here are the plates. Look sharp, Lukyn.

LUKYN. [*With emotion.*] Vale! Safe and sound! [*He takes the plates, then grasps* VALE'S *extended hand.*] Bless you, old fellow. I'm myself again. [*Going gaily to the table with the plates.*] My dear ladies, I blush—I positively blush—I am the worst host in the world.

VALE. [*To himself.*] By Jove, that's true.

AGATHA. Not at all—not at all.

LUKYN. [*Helping the ladies.*] I'll make amends, by George! You may have noticed I've been confoundedly out of sorts. That's my temperament—now up, now down. I've just taken a turn, ha, ha! Oysters.   [*Handing plate to* AGATHA.

AGATHA. Thank you.

LUKYN. Ah, I've passed many a happy hour in this room. The present is not the least happy.

CHARLOTTE. [*Trying to attract his attention.*] Ahem! Ahem!

LUKYN. [*Gazing up at the ceiling.*] My first visit to the Hôtel des Princes was in the year—the year—let me think.

CHARLOTTE. [*Tearfully whispering to* AGATHA.] Isn't he going to help me?

LUKYN. Was it in '55?

AGATHA. [*Quickly passing her plate over to* CHARLOTTE.] I'm not hungry.

CHARLOTTE. You're a dear.

LUKYN. [*Emphatically.*] It *was* in '55. I'm forgetful again—pardon me. [*He hands plate of oysters to* CHARLOTTE, *and is surprised to find her eating vigorously.*] Why, I thought I—— [*To* AGATHA.] My dear madam, a thousand apologies. [*He helps her and then himself.*] Pah! they're cold—icy—you could skate on 'em. There's a dish of something else over there.

    [*He goes to the sideboard;* VALE's *hand is again stretched forth with the other covered dish.*

VALE. I say, Lukyn.

LUKYN. [*Taking the dish*] Thanks, old fellow. [*He returns to the table and lifts the cover.*] Soles—they look tempting. If there are only some lemons! Surely they are not so brutal as to have forgotten the lemons. Where are they? [*He returns to the sideboard.*] Where are they? [*In an undertone to* VALE.] Have you seen any lemons?

AGATHA. Pray, think less of us, Colonel Lukyn. Let me take care of you.

LUKYN. You're very kind. I wish you would let me ring for some lemons.

    [VALE's *hand comes as before from behind the curtain to the sideboard, finds the dish of lemons, and holds it out at arm's length.*

VALE. [*In a whisper.*] Lemons.

    [AGATHA *is helping* LUKYN, *when suddenly* CHARLOTTE, *with her fork in the air, leans back open-mouthed, staring wildly at* VALE's *arm extended with the dish.*

CHARLOTTE. [*In terror.*] Agatha! Agatha!

AGATHA. Charlotte! What's the matter, Charley?

CHARLOTTE. Agatha!

AGATHA. You're ill, Charlotte! Surely you are not choking?

CHARLOTTE. [*Pointing to the curtain.*] Look, look!

                    [*They both scream.*

LUKYN. Don't be alarmed—I——

CHARLOTTE *and* AGATHA. [*Together.*] Who's that?

LUKYN. I can explain. Don't condemn till you've heard. I——I——. Damn it, sir, put those lemons down!

CHARLOTTE. He calls him 'Sir'—it must be a man.

LUKYN. It is a man. I am not in a position to deny that.

AGATHA. Really, Colonel Lukyn!

LUKYN. It is my friend. He—he—he's merely waiting for his supper.

AGATHA. [*Indignantly.*] Your friend! [*To* CHARLOTTE.] Come home, dear.

LUKYN. Do, do hear me! To avoid the embarrassment of your encountering a stranger, he retreated to the balcony.

AGATHA. [*Contemptuously.*] To the balcony? You have shamefully compromised two trusting women, Colonel Lukyn.

LUKYN. [*Energetically.*] I would have laid down my life rather than have done so. I did lay down my friend's life.

AGATHA. He has overheard every confidential word I have spoken to you.

LUKYN. Hear his explanation. [*To the curtain.*] Why the devil don't you corroborate me, sir?

VALE. [*From behind the curtain.*] Certainly. I assure you I heard next to nothing.

CHARLOTTE. [*Grasping* AGATHA'*s arm.*] Oh, Agatha!

VALE. I didn't come in till I was exceedingly wet.

LUKYN. [*To* AGATHA.] You hear that?

VALE. And when I did come in——

CHARLOTTE. [*Hysterically.*] Horace!

VALE. I beg your pardon.

CHARLOTTE. It's Horace, Captain Vale.

VALE. [*Coming from behind the curtain, looking terribly wet.*] Charlotte—Miss Verrinder.

CHARLOTTE. What are you doing here? What a fright you look.

VALE. What am I doing here, Miss Verrinder? Really, Lukyn, your conduct calls for some little explanation.

LUKYN. My conduct, sir?

VALE. You make some paltry excuse to turn me out in the rain while you entertain a lady who you know has very recently broken my heart.

LUKYN. I didn't know anything of the kind.

VALE. I told you, Colonel Lukyn—this isn't the conduct of an officer and a gentleman.

LUKYN. Whose isn't, yours or mine?

VALE. Mine. I mean yours.

LUKYN. You are in the presence of ladies, sir; take off my hat.

VALE. I beg your pardon. I didn't know I had it on.
[*He throws the hat away, and the two men exchange angry words.*

CHARLOTTE. He's a very good-looking fellow; you don't see a man at his best when he's wet through.

AGATHA. [*Impatiently.*] Colonel Lukyn, do you ever intend to send for a cab?

LUKYN. Certainly, madam.   [*Going.*

VALE. One moment. I have some personal explanation to exchange with Miss Verrinder.

CHARLOTTE. [*To* AGATHA.] The slippers. [*To* VALE.] I am quite ready, Captain Vale.

VALE. Thank you. Colonel Lukyn, will you oblige me by stepping out on to that balcony?

LUKYN. [*Hotly.*] Certainly not, sir.

VALE. You're afraid of the wet, Colonel Lukyn; you are no soldier.

LUKYN. You know better, sir. As a matter of fact, that balcony can't bear a man like me.

VALE. Which shows that inanimate objects have a great deal of common sense, sir.

LUKYN. You don't prove it in your own instance, Captain Vale.

VALE. That's a verbal quibble, sir.   [*They talk angrily.*

AGATHA. [*To* CHARLOTTE.] It's frightfully late. Tell him to write to you.

CHARLOTTE. I must speak to him to-night; life is too short for letters.

AGATHA. Then he can telegraph.

CHARLOTTE. Half-penny a word and he has nothing but his pay.

AGATHA. Very well, then, Lady Jenkins has a telephone. I'll take you there to tea to-morrow. If he loves you, tell him to ring up 1338091.

CHARLOTTE. You thoughtful angel!

LUKYN. Mrs. Posket—Miss Verrinder—ahem—we——

VALE. Colonel Lukyn and myself——

LUKYN. Captain Vale and I fear that we have been betrayed, in a moment of——

VALE. Natural irritation.

LUKYN. Natural irritation, into the atrocious impropriety of differing——

VALE. Before ladies.

LUKYN. Charming ladies——

VALE. We beg your pardon—Lukyn!

LUKYN. Vale! [*They grasp hands.*] Mrs. Posket, I am now going out to hail a cab.

AGATHA. Pray do.

LUKYN. Miss Verrinder, the process will occupy five minutes.

VALE. [*Giving his hat to* LUKYN.] Lukyn, I return your kindness—my hat.

LUKYN. Thank you, my boy.
[LUKYN *puts on* VALE's *hat, which is much too small for him. As he is going out there is a knock at the door; he opens it:* BLOND *is outside.*]

BLOND. Colonel, it is ten minutes past the time of closing; may I ask you to dismiss your party?

LUKYN. Pooh! Isn't this a free country?   [*Goes out.*

BLOND. Yes, you are free to go home, Colonel. I shall get into trouble.   [*Following him out.*

CHARLOTTE. [*To* AGATHA.] I'll have the first word. Really, Captain Vale, I'm surprised at you.

VALE. There was a happy time, Miss Verrinder, when I might have been surprised at you.

CHARLOTTE. A few hours ago it was—'By Jove, all is over.' Now I find you with a bosom friend enjoying devilled oysters.

VALE. I beg your pardon; I find you enjoying devilled oysters.

CHARLOTTE. [*Haughtily.*] Horace Vale, you forget you have forfeited the right to exercise any control over my diet.

VALE. One would think I had broken off our engagement.

CHARLOTTE. If you have not, who has? I have your letter saying all is over between us. [*Putting her handkerchief to her eyes.*] That letter will be stamped tomorrow at Somerset House. [*With sobs.*] I know how to protect myself.

VALE. Charlotte, can you explain your conduct with Gordon Bristow?

CHARLOTTE. I could if I chose; a young lady can explain anything.

VALE. But he is showing your gift to our fellows all over the place.

CHARLOTTE. It was a debt of honour. He laid me a box of gloves to a pair of slippers about 'Forked Lightning' for the Regimental Cup, and 'Forked Lightning' went tender at the heel. I couldn't come to you with debts hanging over me. [*Crying.*] I'm too conscientious.

VALE. By Jove, I've been a brute.

CHARLOTTE. Y-y-yes.

VALE. Can you forget I ever wrote that letter?

CHARLOTTE. That must be a question of time. [*She lays her head on his shoulder and then removes it.*] How damp you are! [*She puts her handkerchief upon his shoulder, and replaces her head. She moves his arm gradually up and arranges it round her shoulder.*] If you went on anyhow every time I discharged an obligation, we should be most unhappy.

VALE. I promise you I won't mention Bristow's slippers again. By Jove, I won't—there.

CHARLOTTE. Very well, then, if you do that I'll give you my word I won't pay any more debts before our marriage.

VALE. My darling!

CHARLOTTE. [*About to embrace him, but remembering that he is wet.*] No—no—you are too damp.

ISIDORE. [*Outside.*] I beg your pardon; it is a quarter of an hour over our time.

[AGATHA *has been sitting on the sofa; suddenly she starts, listening intently.*]

POSKET. [*Outside.*] I know—I know. I'm going directly I can get the boy away.

AGATHA. [*To herself.*] Æneas!

CIS. [*Outside.*] All right, Guv, you finish your bottle.

AGATHA. My boy!

ISIDORE. [*Outside.*] Gentlemen, come—come.

AGATHA. [*To herself.*] Miserable deceiver! This, then, is the club, and the wretched man conspires to drag my boy down to his own awful level. What shall I do? I daren't make myself known here. I know; I'll hurry home, and if I reach there before Æneas, which I shall do, [*Clenching her fist.*] I'll sit up for him.

Enter LUKYN.

AGATHA. [*Excitedly.*] Is the cab at the door?

LUKYN. It is.

AGATHA. Charlotte! Charlotte!   [*Drawing her veil down.*

CHARLOTTE. I'm ready dear. [*To* VALE.] Married sisters are always a little thoughtless.

VALE. [*Offering his arm.*] Permit me.

LUKYN. [*Offering his arm to* AGATHA.] My dear madam.

They are all four about to leave when BLOND *enters hurriedly.*

BLOND. [*Holding up his hand for silence.*] Hush! Hush!

LUKYN. What's the matter?

BLOND. The police!

ALL. [*In a whisper.*] The police!

BLOND. [*Quietly.*] The police are downstairs at the door. I told you so.

CHARLOTTE. [*Clinging to* VALE.] Oh, dear! Oh, dear!

AGATHA. Gracious powers!

BLOND. Keep quiet, please. They may be satisfied with Madame Blond's assurances. I must put you in darkness; they can see the light here if they go round to the back.

[*Blows out candles, and turns down the other lights.*

AGATHA *and* CHARLOTTE. Oh!

BLOND. Keep quiet, please! My licence is once marked already. Colonel Lukyn, thank you for this. [*He goes out.*

AGATHA. [*Whimpering.*] Miserable men! What have you done? Are you criminals?

CHARLOTTE. You haven't deserted or anything on my account, have you, Horace?

LUKYN. Hush! Don't be alarmed. Our time has passed so agreeably that we have overstepped the prescribed hour for closing the hotel. That's all.

AGATHA. What can they do to us?

LUKYN. At the worst, take our names and addresses, and summon us for being here during prohibited hours.

AGATHA. [*Faintly.*] Oh!

CHARLOTTE. Horace, can't you speak?

VALE. By Jove, I very much regret this.

Enter ISIDORE.

LUKYN. Well, well?

ISIDORE. I beg your pardon; the police have come in.

LUKYN. The devil! [*To* AGATHA.] My dear lady, don't faint at such a moment.

Enter BLOND *quickly, carrying a rug.*

BLOND. They are going over the house! Hide!

AGATHA *and* CHARLOTTE. Oh!

[*There is a general commotion.*

BLOND. They have put a man at the back. Keep away from the window. [*They are all bustling, and everybody is talking in whispers;* LUKYN *places* AGATHA *under the table, where she is concealed by the cover; he gets behind the overcoats hanging from the pegs;* VALE *and* CHARLOTTE *crouch down behind sofa.*] Thank you very much. I am going to put Isidore to bed on the sofa. That will explain the light which has just gone out. [ISIDORE *quietly places himself upon the sofa;* BLOND *covers him with the rug.*] Thank you very much.   [*He goes out.*

AGATHA. [*In a stifled voice.*] Charley! Charley!

CHARLOTTE. Yes.

AGATHA. Where are you?

CHARLOTTE. Here.

AGATHA. Oh, where is Captain Vale?

CHARLOTTE. I think he's near me.

VALE. By Jove, Charlotte, I am!

AGATHA. Colonel Lukyn!

LUKYN. [*From behind the coats.*] Here, madam!

AGATHA. Don't leave us.

LUKYN. Madam, I am a soldier.

CHARLOTTE. Oh, Horace, at such a moment what a comfort we must be to each other.

VALE. My dear Charlotte, it's incalculable.
          [ISIDORE *gently raises himself and looks over the back of sofa.*

CHARLOTTE. [*In terror.*] What's that?

ISIDORE. [*Softly.*] I beg your pardon.   [*He sinks back.*

Enter BLOND *quietly, followed by* CIS *and* POSKET *on tip-toe,*
          POSKET *holding on to* CIS.

BLOND. This way; be quick. Excuse me, the police are just entering the room in which these gentlemen were having supper. One of them is anxious not to be asked any questions. Please to hide him and his friend somewhere. They are both very nice gentlemen. [*He goes out, leaving* CIS *and* POSKET.

POSKET. Cis, Cis! Advise me, my boy, advise me.

CIS. It's all right, Guv, it's all right. Get behind something.

AGATHA. [*Peeps from under the tablecloth.*] Æneas, and my child!
          [POSKET *and* CIS *wander about, looking for hiding-places.*

VALE. [*To* CIS.] Go away.

CIS. Oh!

LUKYN. [*To* POSKET, *who is fumbling at the coats.*] No, no.

BLOND. [*Popping his head in.*] The police—coming!
    [CIS *disappears behind the window-curtain.* POSKET *dives under the table.*

AGATHA. Oh!

POSKET. [*To* AGATHA *in a whisper.*] I beg your pardon. I think I am addressing a lady. I am entirely the victim of circumstances. Accept my apologies for this apparent intrusion. [*No answer.*] Madam, I applaud your reticence, though any statement made under the present circumstances would not be used against you. [*Looking out.*] Where is that boy? [*Disappearing suddenly.*] Oh! Madam, it may be acute nervousness on your part, but you are certainly pinching my arm.

There is the sound of heavy feet outside, then enter MESSITER, *a gruff matter-of-fact Inspector of Police, followed by* HARRIS, *a constable, and* BLOND.

BLOND. You need not trouble yourself—take my word for it.

MESSITER. No trouble, Mr. Blond, thank you. [*Sniffing.*] Candles—blown out—lately. This is where the light was.

BLOND. Perhaps. My servant, Isidore, sleeps here; he has only just gone to bed.

MESSITER. Oh! [*Taking a bull's-eye lantern from* HARRIS *and throwing the light on* ISIDORE, *who is apparently sleeping soundly.*] Dead tired, I suppose?

BLOND. I suppose so.

MESSITER. [*Slightly turning down the covering.*] He sleeps in his clothes?

BLOND. Oh, yes.

MESSITER. Always?

BLOND. Always—it is a rule of the hotel.

MESSITER. Oh—why's that?

BLOND. To be ready for the morning.

MESSITER. All right—all right. [*Throwing the rug and blanket aside.*] Isidore, go downstairs and give your full name and particulars to Sergeant Jarvis.

ISIDORE. [*Rising instantly.*] Yes, sir—very good.

BLOND. [*To* ISIDORE.] Why do you wake up so soon? Devil
take you!

ISIDORE. I beg your pardon.   [*Goes out.*

MESSITER. What is underneath that window, Mr. Blond?

BLOND. The skylight over the kitchen—devil take it!

MESSITER. Thank you—*you* can go down to the sergeant now,
Mr. Blond.

BLOND. With pleasure—devil take me!   [*Goes out.*

MESSITER. Now then, Harris.

HARRIS. Yes, sir.

MESSITER. Keep perfectly still and hold your breath as long as
you can.

HARRIS. Hold my breath, Sir?

MESSITER. Yes—I want to hear how many people are breathing
in this room. Are you ready?

HARRIS. Yes, sir.

MESSITER. Go! [HARRIS *stands still, tightly compressing his
lips;* MESSITER *quickly examines his face by the light of the
lantern, then walks round the room, listening, and nodding his
head with satisfaction as he passes the various hiding-places.*
HARRIS *writhes in agony; in the end he gives it up and breathes
heavily.*] Harris!

HARRIS. [*Exhausted.*] Yes, sir!

MESSITER. You're breathing.

HARRIS. Oh lor', yes, sir!

MESSITER. You'll report yourself to-night!

HARRIS. I held on till I nearly went off, sir.

MESSITER. [*Giving him the bull's-eye.*] Don't argue, but light
up. There are half a dozen people concealed in this room.
[*There is a cry from the women.* CHARLOTTE *and* VALE *rise;*
LUKYN *steps from behind the coats.*] I thought so.

[*As* MESSITER *turns,* AGATHA *and* POSKET *rise,* CIS *comes
quickly, catches hold of* POSKET, *and drags him across to the
window.*

CIS. Come on, Guv, Come on!

> [*They disappear through the curtain as* HARRIS *turns up the lights. Then there is a cry and the sound of a crash.*

AGATHA [*Sinking into chair.*] They're killed!

MESSITER. [*Looks through the window.*] No, they're not; they've gone into the kitchen and the balcony with them. Look sharp, Harris.   [HARRIS *goes out quickly.*

LUKYN. [*To* MESSITER.] I shall report you for this, sir.

MESSITER. [*Taking out his note-book.*] Very sorry, sir; it's my duty.

LUKYN. Duty, sir! Coming your confounded detective tricks on ladies and gentlemen! How dare you make ladies and gentlemen suspend their breathing till they nearly have apoplexy? Do you know I'm a short-necked man, sir?

MESSITER. I didn't want you to leave off breathing, sir. I wanted you to breathe louder. Your name and address, sir.

LUKYN. Gur-r-r-h!

MESSITER. [*Coaxingly.*] Army gentleman, sir?

LUKYN. How do you know that?

MESSITER. Short style of speaking, sir. Army gentlemen run a bit brusquish when on in years.

LUKYN. Oh! [*Conquering himself.*] Alexander Lukyn—Colonel— Her Majesty's Cheshire Light Infantry, late 41st Foot, 3rd Battalion—Bengal—Retired.

MESSITER. [*Writing.*] Hotel or club, Colonel?

LUKYN. Neither. 19A, Cork Street—lodgings.

MESSITER. [*Writing.*] Very nice part, Colonel. Thank you.

LUKYN. Bah!

MESSITER. Other gentleman?

VALE. [*With languid hauteur.*] Horace Edmund Cholmeley Clive Napier Vale—Captain—Shropshire Fusiliers—Stark's Hotel, Conduit Street.

MESSITER. [*Writing.*] Retired, sir?

VALE. No, confound you—active!

MESSITER. Thank you, Captain. Ahem! Beg pardon. The—
the ladies.

      [CHARLOTTE *clings to* VALE, AGATHA *to* LUKYN.

AGATHA *and* CHARLOTTE. No—no! No—no!

LUKYN. [*To* AGATHA.] All right—all right—trust to me! [*To*
MESSITER.] Well, sir?

MESSITER. Names and addresses, please.

LUKYN. [*Pacifically*.] Officer—my good fellow—tell me now—
er—um—at the present moment, [*putting his hand in his
pocket*] what are you most in want of?

MESSITER. These two ladies' names and addresses, please. Be
quick, Colonel. [*Pointing to* AGATHA.] That lady first.

LUKYN. [*With an effort*.] Christian names—er—ah—er—Alice
Emmeline.

MESSITER. [*Writing*.] Alice Emmeline. Surname?

LUKYN. Er—um—Fitzgerald—101, Wilton Street, Picca-
dilly.

MESSITER. Single lady?

LUKYN. Quite.

MESSITER. Very good, sir.

AGATHA. [*To* LUKYN, *tearfully*.] Oh, thank you, such a nice
address too.

MESSITER. [*To* VALE.] Now Captain, please—that lady.

VALE. [*Who has been reassuring* CHARLOTTE.] Haw—ah—this
lady is—ah—um—the other lady's sister.

MESSITER. Single lady, sir?

VALE. Certainly.

MESSITER. [*Writing*.] Christian name, Captain?

VALE. Ah—um—Harriet.

MESSITER. [*Writing*.] Surname?

VALE. Er—Macnamara.

MESSITER. [*With a grim smile*.] Quite so. Lives with her sister,
of course, sir?

VALE. Of course.

MESSITER. Where at, sir?

VALE. Albert Mansions, Victoria Street.

CHARLOTTE. [*To* VALE.] Oh, thank you, I always fancied that spot.

MESSITER. Very much obliged, gentlemen.

LUKYN. [*Who has listened to* VALE's *answers in helpless horror.*] By George, well out of it!

[*The two ladies give a cry of relief.* CHARLOTTE *totters across to* AGATHA, *who embraces her. Taking down the overcoats and throwing one to* VALE.
Vale, your coat.

Enter HARRIS.

HARRIS. [*To* MESSITER.] Very sorry, sir; the two other gentlemen got clean off, through the back scullery door—old hands, to all appearance.

[MESSITER *stamps his foot, with an exclamation.*

AGATHA. [*To herself.*] My boy—saved!

LUKYN. [*To* HARRIS, *who stands before the door.*] Constable, get out of the way.

MESSITER. [*Sharply.*] Harris!

HARRIS. [*Without moving.*] Yes, sir.

MESSITER. You will leave the hotel with these ladies, and not lose sight of them till you've ascertained what their names *are*, and where they *do* live.

LUKYN *and* VALE. What!

AGATHA *and* CHARLOTTE. Oh!

MESSITER. Your own fault, gentlemen; it's my duty.

LUKYN. [*Violently.*] And it is *my* duty to save these helpless women from the protecting laws of my confounded country! Vale!

VALE. [*Putting his coat on the sofa.*] Active!

LUKYN. [*To* HARRIS.] Let these ladies pass! [*He takes* HARRIS *by the collar and flings him over to* VALE, *who throws him over towards the ladies, who push him away.* MESSITER *puts a whistle to his mouth and blows; there is an immediate answer from without.*] More of your fellows outside?

MESSITER. Yes, sir, at your service. Very sorry, gentlemen, but you and your party are in my custody.

LUKYN *and* VALE. What?

AGATHA *and* CHARLOTTE. Oh!

MESSITER. For assaulting this man in the execution of his duty.

LUKYN. You'll dare to lock us up all night?

MESSITER. It's one o'clock now, Colonel—you'll come on first thing in the morning.

LUKYN. Come on? At what Court?

MESSITER. Mulberry Street.

AGATHA. [*With a scream.*] Ah! The magistrate?

MESSITER. Mr. Posket, mum.

[AGATHA *sinks into a chair,* CHARLOTTE *at her feet;* LUKYN, *overcome, falls on* VALE's *shoulders. Curtain.*

ACT III

SCENE I. *The Magistrate's room at Mulberry Street Police Court, with a doorway covered by curtains leading directly into the Court, and a door opening into a passage. It is the morning after the events of the last Act.*

POLICE SERGEANT LUGG, *a middle-aged man with a slight country dialect, enters with 'The Times' newspaper, and proceeds to cut it and glance at its contents while he hums a song.*

Enter MR. WORMINGTON, *an elderly, trim and precise man.*

WORMINGTON. Good morning, Lugg.

LUGG. Morning, Mr. Wormington.

WORMINGTON. Mr. Posket not arrived yet?

LUGG. Not yet, sir. Hullo! [*Reading.*] 'Raid on a West End Hotel. At an early hour this morning——'

WORMINGTON. Yes, I've read that—a case of assault upon the police.

LUGG. Why, these must be the folks who've been so precious rampageous all night.

WORMINGTON. Very likely.

LUGG. Yes, sir, protestin' and protestin' till they protested everybody's sleep away. Nice-looking women, too, though as I tell Mrs. Lugg, now-a-days there's no telling who's the lady and who isn't. Who's got this job, sir?

WORMINGTON. Inspector Messiter.

LUGG. [*With contempt.*] Messiter! That's luck! Why he's the worst elocutionist in the force, sir.* [*As he arranges the news-paper upon the table, he catches sight of* WORMINGTON'S *necktie, which is bright red.*] Well, I—excuse me, Mr.

---

* A City magistrate, censuring a constable for the indistinctness of his utter-ances in the witness-box, suggested that the police should be instructed in a method of delivering evidence articulately. AUTHOR'S NOTE.

Wormington, but all the years I've had the honour of knowin' you, sir, I've never seen you wear a necktie with, so to speak, a dash of colour in it.

WORMINGTON. [*Uneasily.*] Well, Lugg, no, that's true, but to-day is an exceptional occasion with me. It is, in fact, the twenty-fifth anniversary of my marriage, and I thought it due to Mrs. Wormington to vary, in some slight degree, the sombreness of my attire. I confess I am a little uneasy in case Mr. Posket should consider it at all disrespectful to the Court.

LUGG. Not he, sir.

WORMINGTON. I don't know. Mr. Posket is punctiliousness itself in dress, and his cravat's invariably black. However, it is not every man who has a silver wedding-day.

LUGG. It's not every man as wants one, sir.

[WORMINGTON *goes out.*

At the same moment POSKET *enters quickly, and leans on his chair as if exhausted. His appearance is extremely wretched; he is still in evening dress, but his clothes are muddy, and his linen soiled and crumpled, while across the bridge of his nose he has a small strip of black plaster.*

POSKET. [*Faintly.*] Good morning, Lugg.

LUGG. Good morning to you, sir. Regretting the liberty I'm taking, sir—I've seen you look more strong and hearty.

POSKET. I am fairly well, thank you, Lugg. My night was rather—rather disturbed. Lugg!

LUGG. Sir?

POSKET. [*Nervously.*] Have any inquiries been made about me this morning—any messenger from Mrs. Posket, for instance, to ask how I am?

LUGG. No, sir.

POSKET. Oh. My child, my stepson, young Mr. Farringdon has not called, has he?

LUGG. No, sir.

POSKET. [*To himself.*] Where can that boy be? [*To* LUGG.] Thank you, that's all.

LUGG. [*Who has been eyeing* POSKET *with astonishment, goes to the door, and then touches the bridge of his nose. Sympathetically.*] Nasty cut while shavin', sir?   [*Goes out.*

POSKET. Where can that boy have got to? If I could only remember how, when, and where we parted! I think it was at Kilburn. Let me think—first, the kitchen. [*Putting his hand to his side as if severely bruised.*] Oh! Cis was all right, because I fell underneath; I felt it was my duty to do so. Then what occurred? A dark room, redolent of onions and cabbages and paraffin oil, and Cis dragging me over the stone floor, saying, 'We're in the scullery, Guv; let's try and find the tradesmen's door.' Next, the night air—oh, how refreshing! 'Cis, my boy, we will both learn a lesson from to-night—never deceive.' Where are we? In Argyll Street. 'Look out, Guv, they're after us.' Then—then, as Cis remarked when· we were getting over the railings of Portman Square—then the fun began. We over into the Square—they after us. Over again, into Baker Street. Down Baker Street. Curious recollections, whilst running, of my first visit, as a happy child, to Madame Tussaud's, and wondering whether her removal had affected my fortunes. 'Come on, Guv—you're getting blown.' Where are we? Park Road. What am I doing? Getting up out of a puddle.·St. John's Wood. The cricket-ground. 'I say, Guv, what a run this would be at Lord's, wouldn't it? And no fear of being run out either, more fear of being run in.' 'What road is this, Cis?' Maida Vale. Good gracious! A pious aunt of mine once lived in Hamilton Terrace; she never thought I should come to this. 'Guv?' 'Yes, my boy.' 'Let's get this kind-hearted coffee-stall keeper to hide us.' We apply. 'Will you assist two unfortunate gentlemen?' 'No, blowed if I will,' 'Why not?' 'Cos I'm a goin' to join in the chase after you.' Ah! Off again, along Maida Vale! On, on, heaven knows how or where, 'till at last no sound of pursuit, no Cis, no breath, and the early Kilburn buses starting to town. Then I came back again, and not much too soon for the Court. [*Going up to the washstand and looking into the little mirror, with a low groan.*] Oh, how shockingly awful I look, and how stiff and sore I feel! [*Taking off his coat and hanging it on a peg, then washing his hands*.] What a weak and double-faced creature to be a magistrate! I really ought to get some member of Parliament to ask a question about me in the House. Where's the soap? I shall put five pounds and costs into the poor's box to-morrow. But I deserve a most severe caution. Ah, perhaps I shall get that from Agatha. [*He takes off his white tie, rolls it up and crams it into his pocket.*] When Wormington arrives I will borrow some money and send out for a black cravat. All my pocket money is in my overcoat at the Hôtel des Princes. If the police seize it there is some consolation in knowing that that money will never be returned to me. [*There is a knock at the door.*] Come in!

Enter LUGG.

LUGG. Your servant, Mr. Wyke, wants to see you, sir.

POSKET. [*Testily.*] Bring him in. [LUGG *goes out.*] Wyke! From Agatha! From Agatha!

Re-enter LUGG, *with* WYKE.

WYKE. Ahem! Good morning, sir.

POSKET. Good morning, Wyke. Ahem! Is Master Farringdon quite well?

WYKE. He hadn't arrived home when I left, sir.

POSKET. Oh! Where is that boy? [*To* WYKE.] How is your mistress this morning, Wyke?

WYKE. Very well, I hope, sir; *she* 'ain't come home yet, either.

POSKET. Not returned—nor Miss Verrinder?

WYKE. No, sir—neither of them.

POSKET. [*To himself.*] Lady Jenkins is worse; they are still nursing her! Good women, true women!

WYKE. [*To himself.*] That's eased his deceivin' old mind.

POSKET. [*To himself.*] Now if the servants don't betray me and Cis returns safely, the worst is over. To what a depth I have fallen when I rejoice at Lady Jenkins's indisposition!

WYKE. Cook thought you ought to know that the mistress hadn't come home, sir.

POSKET. Certainly. Take a cab at once to Campden Hill and

bring me back word how poor Lady Jenkins is. Tell Mrs. Posket I will come on the moment the Court rises.

WYKE. Yes, sir.

POSKET. And Wyke. It is not at all necessary that Mrs. Posket should know of my absence with Master Farringdon from home last night. Mrs. Posket's present anxieties are more than sufficient. Inform Cook and Popham and the other servants that I shall recognise their discretion in the same spirit I have already displayed towards you.

WYKE. [*With sarcasm.*] Thank you, sir. I will. [*He produces from his waistcoat-pocket a small packet of money done up in newspaper, which he throws down upon the table.*] Meanwhile, sir, I thought you would like to count up the little present of money you gave me last night, and in case you thought you'd been over-liberal, sir, you might halve the amount. It isn't no good spoiling of us all, sir.

Enter LUGG.

POSKET. You are an excellent servant, Wyke; I am very pleased. I will see you when you return from Lady Jenkins's. Be quick.

WYKE. Yes, sir. [*To himself.*] He won't give me twopence again in a hurry.   [*He goes out;* LUGG *is about to follow.*]

POSKET. Oh, Lugg, I want you to go to the nearest hosier's and purchase me a neat cravat.

LUGG. [*Looking inquisitively at* POSKET.] A necktie, sir?

POSKET. Yes. [*Rather irritably, turning up his coat collar to shield himself from* LUGG's *gaze.*] A necktie—a necktie.

LUGG. What sort of a kind of one, sir?

POSKET. Oh, one like Mr. Wormington's.

LUGG. One like he's wearing this morning, sir?

POSKET. Of course, of course, of course.

LUGG. [*To himself.*] Fancy him being jealous of Mr. Wormington, now. Very good, sir—what price, sir?

POSKET. The best. [*To himself.*] There now, I've no money. [*Seeing the packet on table.*] Oh, pay for i with this, Lugg.

LUGG. Yes, sir.

POSKET. And keep the change for your trouble.

LUGG. [*Delighted.*] Thank you, sir; thank you, sir—very much obliged to you, sir. [*To himself.*] That's like a liberal gentle- man.   [*Goes out.*

At the same moment WORMINGTON *enters through the curtains with the charge sheet in his hand.* WORMINGTON, *on seeing* POSKET, *uneasily tucks his pocket-handkerchief in his collar so as to hide his necktie.*

WORMINGTON. H'm! Good morning.

POSKET. Good morning, Wormington.

WORMINGTON. The charge sheet.

POSKET. Sit down.
      [WORMINGTON *puts on his spectacles;* POSKET *also attempts to put on his spectacles, but hurts the bridge of his nose, winces, and desists.*

POSKET. [*To himself.*] My nose is extremely painful. [*To* WORMINGTON.] You have a bad cold I am afraid, Wor- mington—bronchial?

WORMINGTON. Ahem! Well—ah—the fact is—you may have noticed how very chilly the nights are.

POSKET. [*Thoughtfully.*] Very, very.

WORMINGTON. The only way to maintain the circulation is to run as fast as one can.

POSKET. To run—as fast as one can—yes—quite so.

WORMINGTON. [*To himself, looking at* POSKET'*s shirt front.*] How very extraordinary—he is wearing no cravat whatever!

POSKET. [*Buttoning up his coat to avoid* WORMINGTON'*s gaze.*] Anything important this morning?

WORMINGTON. Nothing particular after the first charge, a serious business arising out of the raid on the Hôtel des Princes.

POSKET. [*Starting.*] Hôtel des Princes?

WORMINGTON. Inspector Messiter found six persons supping there at one o'clock this morning. Two contrived to escape.

POSKET. Dear me—I am surprised—I mean, did they?

WORMINGTON. But they left their overcoats behind them, and it is believed they will be traced.

POSKET. Oh, do you—do you think it is worth while? The police have a great deal to occupy them just now.

WORMINGTON. But surely if the police see their way to capture anybody we had better raise no obstacle.

POSKET. No—no—quite so—never struck me.

WORMINGTON. [*Referring to charge sheet.*] The remaining four it was found necessary to take into custody.

POSKET. Good gracious! What a good job the other two didn't wait! I beg your pardon—I mean —you say we have four?

WORMINGTON. Yes, on the charge of obstructing the police. The first assault occurred in the supper-room—the second in the four-wheeled cab on the way to the station. There were five persons in the cab at the time—the two women, the two men, and the Inspector.

POSKET. Dear me, it must have been a very complicated assault. Who are the unfortunate people?

WORMINGTON. The men are of some position. [*Reading.*] 'Alexander Lukyn, Colonel——'

POSKET. Lukyn! I—I—know Colonel Lukyn; we are old schoolfellows.

WORMINGTON. Very sad! [*Reading.*] The other is 'Horace, &c. &c. Vale—Captain—Shropshire Fusiliers'.

POSKET. And the ladies?

WORMINGTON. Call themselves 'Alice Emmeline Fitzgerald and Harriet Macnamara'.

POSKET. [*To himself.*] Which is the lady who was under the table with me?

WORMINGTON. They are not recognised by the police at present, but they furnish incorrect addresses, and their demeanour is generally violent and unsatisfactory.

POSKET. [*To himself.*] Who pinched me—Alice or Harriet?

WORMINGTON. I mention this case because it seems to be one calling for most stringent measures.

POSKET. Wouldn't a fine, and a severe warning from the Bench to the two persons who have got away——

WORMINGTON. I think not. Consider, Mr. Posket, not only defying the licensing laws, but obstructing the police!

POSKET. [*Reflectively.*] That's true—it is hard, when the police are doing anything, that they should be obstructed.

Enter LUGG.

LUGG. [*Attempting to conceal some annoyance.*] Your necktie, sir.

POSKET. [*Sharply.*] S-ssh!

WORMINGTON. [*To himself.*] Then he *came* without one—dear me!

LUGG. [*Clapping down a paper parcel on the table.*] As near like Mr. Wormington's as possible—brighter if anything.

POSKET. [*Opening the parcel, and finding a very common, gaudy neckerchief.*] Good gracious! What a horrible affair!

LUGG. [*Stolidly.*] According to my information, sir—like Mr. Wormington's.

POSKET. Mr. Wormington would never be seen in such an abominable colour.

WORMINGTON. [*In distress.*] Well—really—I—[*Removing the handkerchief from his throat.*] I am extremely sorry.

POSKET. My dear Wormington!

WORMINGTON. I happen to be wearing something similar— the first time for five-and-twenty years.

POSKET. Oh, I beg your pardon. [*To himself.*] Everything seems against me.

LUGG. One-and-nine it come to, sir. [*Producing the paper packet of money and laying it upon the table.*] And I brought back all the money you give me, thinking you'd like to look over it quietly. Really, sir, I never showed up smaller in any shop in all my life!

POSKET. [*Out of patience.*] Upon my word. First one and then another! What *is* wrong with the money? [*Opens the packet.*] Twopence! [*To himself, aghast.*] That man Wyke will tell all to Agatha! Oh, everything is against me!

[LUGG *has opened the door, taken a card from some one outside, and handed it to* WORMINGTON.

WORMINGTON. From cell No. 3. [*Handing the card to* POSKET.

POSKET. [*Reading.*] 'Dear Posket, for the love of goodness see me before the sitting of the Court. Alexander Lukyn.' Poor dear Lukyn! What on earth shall I do?

WORMINGTON. Such a course would be most unusual.

POSKET. [*Despairingly.*] Everything is unusual. Your cravat is unusual. This prisoner is invited to dine at my house to-day—that's peculiar. He is my wife's first husband's only child's godfather—that's a little out of the ordinary.

WORMINGTON. The charge is so serious!

POSKET. But I am a man as well as a magistrate; advise me, Wormington, advise me!

WORMINGTON. Well—you can apply to yourself for permission to grant Colonel Lukyn's request.

POSKET. [*Hastily scribbling on* LUKYN'*s card.*] I do—I do—and after much conflicting argument I consent to see Colonel Lukyn here immediately. [*Handing the card to* WORMINGTON, *who passes it to* LUGG, *who then goes out.*] Don't leave me, Wormington—you must stand by me to see that I remain calm, firm, and judicial. [*He hastily puts on the red necktie in an untidy manner; it sticks out grotesquely.*] Poor Lukyn! I must sink the friend in the magistrate, and in dealing with his errors apply the scourge to myself. Wormington, tap me on the shoulder when I am inclined to be more than usually unusual.   [WORMINGTON *stands behind him.*

LUGG *enters with* LUKYN. LUKYN'*s dressclothes are much soiled and disordered, and he too has a small strip of plaster upon the bridge of his nose. There is a constrained pause;* LUKYN *and* POSKET *both cough uneasily.*

LUKYN. [*To himself.*] Poor Posket!

POSKET. [*To himself.*] Poor Lukyn!

LUKYN. [*To himself.*] I suppose he has been sitting up for his wife all night, poor devil! Ahem! How are you, Posket?
          [WORMINGTON *touches* POSKET'*s shoulder.*

POSKET. [*Pulling himself together.*] I regret to see you in this terrible position, Colonel Lukyn.

LUKYN. By George, old fellow, I regret to find myself in it. [*Sitting, and taking up newspaper.*] I suppose they've got us in *The Times*, confound 'em!

[*While* LUKYN *is reading the paper,* POSKET *and* WORMING- TON *hold a hurried consultation respecting* LUKYN'*s behaviour.*

POSKET. [*With dignity.*] Hem! Sergeant, I think Colonel Lukyn may be accommodated with a chair.

LUGG. He's in it sir.

LUKYN. [*Rising and putting down paper.*] Beg your pardon; forgot where I was. I suppose everything must be formal in this confounded place?

POSKET. I am afraid, Colonel Lukyn, it will be necessary even here to preserve strictly our unfortunate relative positions. [LUKYN *bows.*] Sit down. [LUKYN *sits again.*] POSKET *takes up the charge sheet.*] Colonel Lukyn! In addressing you now, I am speaking, not as a man, but as an instrument of the law. As a man I may or may not be a weak, vicious, despicable creature.

LUKYN. Certainly—of course.

POSKET. But as a magistrate I am bound to say you fill me with pain and astonishment.

LUKYN. Quite right—every man to his trade; go on, Posket.

POSKET. [*Turning his chair to face* LUKYN.] Alexander Lukyn— when I look at you—when I look at you——. [*He attempts to put on his spectacles, but hurts his nose again. To himself.*] Ah— my nose. [*To* LUKYN, *holding his spectacles a little way from his nose.*] I say, when I look at you, Alexander Lukyn, I con- front a most mournful spectacle. A military officer, trained in the ways of discipline and smartness, now, in consequence of his own misdoings, lamentably bruised and battered, shamefully disfigured by plaster, with his apparel soiled and damaged—all terrible evidence of a conflict with that power of which I am the representative.

LUKYN. [*Turning his chair to face* POSKET.] Well, Posket, if it comes to that, when I look at you, when I look at you—[*He attempts to fix his glass in his eye, and hurts his nose. To himself.*] confound my nose! [*To* POSKET.] When I look at you, *you* are not a very imposing object this morning.

POSKET. [*Uneasily.*] Lukyn!

LUKYN. You look quite as shaky as I do—and you're not quite innocent of court plaster.

POSKET. [*Rising.*] Lukyn! Really!

LUKYN. And as for our attire, we neither of us look as if we had slipped out of a bandbox.

POSKET. [*In agony.*] Don't, Lukyn, don't! Pray respect my legal status! [WORMINGTON *leads* POSKET *back to his seat.*] Thank you, Wormington. Alexander Lukyn, I have spoken. It remains for you to state your motive in seeking this painful interview.

LUKYN. Certainly! Hem! You know, of course, that I am not alone in this affair?

POSKET. [*Referring to charge sheet.*] Three persons appear to be charged with you.

LUKYN. Yes. Two others got away. Cowards! If ever I find them, I'll destroy them!

POSKET. [*Wiping his brow.*] Lukyn!

LUKYN. I will! Another job for you, Posket.

POSKET. [*With dignity.*] I beg your pardon; in the event of such a deplorable occurrence, I should not occupy my present position. Go on, sir.

LUKYN. Horace Vale and I are prepared to stand the brunt of our misdeeds. [*Seriously*]. But Posket, there are ladies in the case.

POSKET. In the annals of the Mulberry Street Police Court such a circumstance is not unprecedented.

LUKYN. Two helpless, forlorn ladies.

POSKET. [*Referring to charge sheet.*] Alice Emmeline Fitzgerald and Harriet Macnamara. [*Gravely shaking his head.*] Oh, Lukyn, Lukyn!

LUKYN. Pooh! I ask no favour for myself or Vale, but I come to you, Posket, to beg you to use your power to release these two ladies without a moment's delay.

[WORMINGTON *touches* POSKET's *shoulder.*

POSKET. Upon my word, Lukyn! Do you think I am to be under-mined?

LUKYN. [*Hotly.*] Undermine the devil, sir! Don't talk to me! Let these ladies go, I say! Don't bring them into Court, don't see their faces—don't hear their voices—if you do, you'll regret it!

POSKET. Colonel Lukyn!

LUKYN. [*Leaning across the table and gripping* POSKET *by the shoulder.*] Posket, do you know that one of these ladies is a married lady?

POSKET. Of course I don't sir. I blush to hear it.

LUKYN. And do you know that from the moment this married lady steps into your confounded Court, the happiness, the contentment of a doting husband become a confounded wreck and ruin?

POSKET. [*Rising.*] Then, sir, let it be my harrowing task to open the eyes of this foolish doting man to the treachery, the perfidy, which nestles upon his very hearthrug!

LUKYN. [*Sinking back.*] Oh, lor'! Be careful, Posket! By George, be careful!

POSKET. Alexander Lukyn, you are my friend. Amongst the personal property taken from you when you entered these precincts may have been found a memorandum of an engage-ment to dine at my house to-night at a quarter to eight o'clock. But Lukyn, I solemnly prepare you, you stand in danger of being late for dinner! I go further—I am not sure, after this morning's proceedings, that Mrs. Posket will be ready to receive you.

LUKYN. I'm confoundedly certain she *won't*!

POSKET. Therefore, Lukyn, as an English husband and father it will be my duty to teach you and your disreputable com-panions, [*referring to charge-sheet*] Alice Emmeline Fitz-gerald and Harriet Macnamara, some rudimentary notions of propriety and decorum.

LUKYN. [*Rising.*] Confound you, Posket—listen!

POSKET. [*Grandly.*] I am listening, sir, to the guiding voice of Mrs. Posket—that newly-made wife still blushing from the embarrassment of her second marriage, and that voice says, 'Strike for the sanctity of hearth and home, for the credit of the wives of England—no mercy!'

WORMINGTON. It is time to go into Court, sir. The charge against Colonel Lukyn is first on the list.

LUKYN. Posket, I'll give you one last chance! If I write upon a scrap of paper the real names of these two unfortunate ladies, will you shut yourself up for a moment, away from observation, and read these names before you go into Court?

POSKET. Certainly not, Colonel Lukyn! I cannot be influenced by private information in dealing with an offence which is, in my opinion, as black as—as my cravat! Ahem!

[WORMINGTON *and* POSKET *look at each other's necktie and turn up their collars hastily.*

LUKYN. [*To himself.*] There's no help for it. Then, Posket, you must have the plain truth where you stand, by George! The two ladies who are my companions in this affair are——

POSKET. Sergeant! Colonel Lukyn will now join his party.

[LUGG *steps up to* LUKYN *sharply.*

LUKYN. [*Boiling with indignation.*] What, sir? What?

POSKET. Lukyn, I think we both have engagements—will you excuse me?

LUKYN. [*Choking.*] Posket! You've gone too far! If you went down on your knees—which you appear to have been recently doing—and begged the names of these two ladies, you shouldn't have 'em! No sir, by George, you shouldn't.

POSKET. Good morning, Colonel Lukyn.

LUKYN. You've lectured me, pooh-poohed me, snubbed me— a soldier, sir—a soldier! But when I think of your dinner-party to-night, with my empty chair—like Banquo, by George, sir—and the chief dish composed of a well-browned, well-basted, family skeleton, served up under the best silver cover, I pity you, Posket! Good morning!

[*He marches out with* LUGG.

POSKET. Ah! Thank goodness that ordeal is passed. Now, Wormington, I think I am ready to face the duties of the day. Shall we go into Court?

WORMINGTON. Certainly, sir.

[WORMINGTON *gathers up papers from the table.* POSKET *with a shaking hand pours out water from carafe and drinks.*

POSKET. [*To himself.*] My breakfast. [*To* WORMINGTON.] I hope I defended the sanctity of the Englishman's hearth, Wormington?

WORMINGTON. You did, indeed. As a married man, I thank you.

POSKET. [*Unsteadily.*] Give me your arm, Wormington. I am not very well this morning, and this interview with Colonel Lukyn has shaken me. I think your coat-collar is turned up, Wormington.

WORMINGTON. So is yours, I fancy, sir.

POSKET. Ahem!

[*They turn their collars down;* POSKET *takes* WORMINGTON'S *arm. They are going towards the curtains when* WYKE *enters hurriedly at the door.*

WYKE. [*Panting.*] Excuse me, sir.

WORMINGTON. Hush, hush! Mr. Posket is just going into Court.

WYKE. Lady Jenkins has sent me back to tell you that she hasn't seen the missis for the last week or more.

POSKET. Mrs. Posket went to Campden Hill with Miss Verrinder last night!

WYKE. They haven't arrived there, sir.

POSKET. Haven't arrived!

WYKE. No sir—and even a slow four-wheeler won't account for that.

POSKET. Wormington, there's something wrong! Mrs. Posket quitted a fairly happy home last night and has not been seen or heard of since!

WORMINGTON. [*Taking his arm again.*] Pray don't be anxious, sir, the Court is waiting.

POSKET. [*In a frenzy, shaking him off.*] But I am anxious! Tell Sergeant Lugg to look over the Accident-Book, this morning's Hospital Returns, List of Missing Children,

Suspicious Pledges, People left Chargeable to the Parish, Attend to your Window Fastenings——! I—I—Wormington, Mrs. Posket and I disagreed last night!

WORMINGTON. [*Soothingly.*] Don't think of it, sir; you should hear me and Mrs. Wormington. Pray do come into Court.

POSKET. [*Hysterically.*] Court! I'm totally unfit for business, totally unfit for business!

> [WORMINGTON *hurries him off through the curtains.*

Enter LUGG, *almost breathless.*

LUGG. We've got charge one in the Dock—all four of 'em. [*Seeing* WYKE.] Hallo, you back again!

WYKE. Yes—seems so. [*They stand facing each other, dabbing their foreheads with their handkerchiefs.*] Phew! You seem warm.

LUGG. Phew! You don't seem so cool.

WYKE. I've been lookin' after two ladies.

LUGG. So have I.

WYKE. I haven't found 'em.

LUGG. If I'd known, I'd 'a been pleased to lend you our two. [*From the other side of the curtains there is the sound of a shriek from* AGATHA *and* CHARLOTTE.

WYKE. Lor', what's that!

LUGG. That *is* our two. Don't notice them—they're hystericals. They're mild now to what they have been. I say, old fellow—is your Guv'nor all right in his head?

WYKE. I suppose so—why?

LUGG. I've a partickler reason for asking. Does he ever tell you to buy him anything and keep the change?

WYKE. What d'yer mean?

LUGG. Well, does he ever come down handsome for your extry exertion—do you ever get any tips?

WYKE. Rather. What do you think he made me a present of last night?

LUGG. Don't know.

WYKE. Twopence—to buy a new umbrella.

LUGG. Well, I'm blessed! And he gave me the same sum to get him a silk necktie. It's my opinion he's got a softenin' of the brain. [*Another shriek from the two women, a cry from* POSKET, *and then a hubbub are heard. Running up to the curtains and looking through.*] Hallo, what's wrong? Here! I told you so—he's broken out, he's broken out.

WYKE. Who's broken out?

LUGG. The lunatic. Keep back, I'm wanted. [*He goes through the curtains.*]

WYKE. [*Looking after him.*] Look at the Guv'nor waving his arms and going on anyhow at the prisoners! Prisoners! Gracious goodness—it's the missis!

Amid a confused sound of voices POSKET *is brought in through the curtains by* WORMINGTON. LUGG *follows.* POSKET *is placed in a chair.* WORMINGTON *holds a glass of water to his lips.*

POSKET. [*Wildly.*] Wormington, Wormington! The two ladies, the two ladies! I know them!

WORMINGTON. [*Soothingly.*] It's all right, sir, it's all right— don't be upset, sir!

POSKET. I'm not well; what shall I do?

WORMINGTON. Nothing further, sir. What you have done is quite in form.

POSKET. What I *have* done?

WORMINGTON. Yes, sir—you did precisely what I suggested— took the words from me. They pleaded guilty.

POSKET. Guilty!

WORMINGTON. Yes, sir—and you sentenced them.

POSKET. [*Starting up.*] Sentenced them! The ladies!

WORMINGTON. Yes, sir. You've given them seven days, without the option of a fine.

[POSKET *collapses into* WORMINGTON'*s arms.*

SCENE II. POSKET's *drawing-room, as in the first act.*

Enter BEATIE *timidly, dressed in simple walking-costume.*

BEATIE. How dreadfully early! Eleven o'clock, and I'm not supposed to come till four. I wonder why I want to instruct Cis all day. I'm not nearly so enthusiastic about the two little girls I teach in Russell Square.

Enter POPHAM. *Her eyes are red as if from crying.*

POPHAM. [*Drawing back on seeing* BEATIE.] That music person again. I beg your pardon—I ain't got no instructions to prepare no drawing-room for no lessons till four o'clock.

BEATIE. [*Haughtily.*] I wish to see Mrs. Posket.

POPHAM. She hasn't come home.

BEATIE. Oh, then—er—um—Master Farringdon will do.

POPHAM. [*In tears.*] He haven't come home either!

BEATIE. Oh, where is he?

POPHAM. No one knows! His wicked old stepfather took him out late last night and hasn't returned him. Such a night as it was, too, and him still wearing his summer under-vests.

BEATIE. Mr. Posket?

POPHAM. Mr. Posket—no, my Cis!

BEATIE. How dare you speak of Master Farringdon in that familar way?

POPHAM. How dare I? Because me and him formed an attachment before ever you darkened our doors. [*Taking a folded printed paper from her pocket.*] You may put down the iron 'eel too heavy, Miss Tomlinson. I refer you to *Bow Bells*— 'First Love is Best Love; or, The Earl's Choice.' [*Offers paper.*

Enter CIS, *looking very pale, wornout, and dishevelled.*

POPHAM *and* BEATIE. Oh!

CIS. [*Staggering to a chair.*] Where's the mater?

POPHAM. Not home yet.

CIS. [*Faintly.*] Thank giminy!

BEATIE. He's ill!

POPHAM. Oh!

> [BEATIE, *assisted by* POPHAM, *quickly wheels the large arm-chair forward. They catch hold of* CIS *and place him in it; he submits limply.*

BEATIE. [*Taking* CIS's *hand.*] What is the matter, Cis dear? Tell Beatie.

POPHAM. [*Taking his other hand, indignantly.*] Well, I'm sure! Who's given you raisins and ketchup from the store cupboard? Come back to Emma!

> [CIS, *with his eyes closed, gives a murmur.*

BEATIE. He's whispering!

> [*They both bob their heads down to listen.*

POPHAM. He says his head's a-whirling.

BEATIE. Put him on the sofa.

> [*They take off his boots, loosen his necktie, and dab his forehead with water out of a flower-vase.*

CIS. [*Indistinctly.*] I—I—I wish you two girls would leave off.

> [*They bob their heads down as before.*

BEATIE. He's speaking again. He hasn't had any breakfast! He's hungry!

POPHAM. Hungry! I thought he looked thin. Wait a minute, dear. Emma Popham knows what her boy fancies!

> [*She runs out of the room.*

CIS. Oh, Beatie, hold my head while I ask you something.

BEATIE. Yes, darling?

CIS. No lady would marry a gentleman who had been a convict, would she?

BEATIE. No; certainly not!

CIS. I thought not. Well, Beatie, I've been run after by a policeman.

BEATIE. [*Leaving him.*] Oh!

CIS. [*Rising unsteadily.*] Not caught, you know, only run after; and walking home from Hendon this morning I came to the conclusion that I ought to settle down in life. Beatie—could I write out a paper promising to marry you when I'm one-and twenty?

BEATIE. Don't be a silly boy—of course you could.

CIS. Then I shall; and when I feel inclined to have a spree I shall think of that paper and say, 'Cis Farringdon, if you ever get locked up, you'll lose the most beautiful girl in the world.'

BEATIE. And so you will.

CIS. I'd better write it now, before my head gets well again.

[*He writes; she bends over him.*

BEATIE. [*Tenderly.*] You simple, foolish Cis! If your head is so queer, shall I tell you what to say?

Enter POPHAM, *carrying a tray with breakfast dishes.*

POPHAM. [*To herself.*] He won't think so much of *her* now. His breakfast is my triumph. [*To* CIS.] Coffee, bacon, and a tea-cake.

BEATIE. Hush! Master Farringdon is writing something very important.

POPHAM. [*Going to the window.*] That's a cab at our door.

CIS. It must be the mater—I'm off!

[*He picks up his boots and goes out quickly.*

BEATIE. [*Following him with the paper and inkstand.*] Cis, Cis! You haven't finished the promise! You haven't finished the promise!

LUGG. [*Outside.*] All right, sir—I've got you—I've got you.

[POPHAM *opens the door.*

POPHAM. The master and a policeman!

Enter LUGG, *supporting* POSKET, *who sinks into an armchair with a groan.*

Oh, what's the matter?

LUGG. All right, my good girl, you run downstairs and fetch a drop of brandy and water.   [POPHAM *hurries out.*

POSKET. [*Groaning again.*] Oh!

LUGG. Now don't take on so, sir. It's what might happen to any married gentleman. Now, you're all right now, sir. And I'll hurry back to the Court to see whether they've sent for Mr. Bullamy.

POSKET. My wife! My wife!

LUGG. [*Soothingly.*] Oh, come now, sir, what *is* seven days! Why, many a married gentleman in your position, sir, would have been glad to have made it fourteen.

POSKET. Go away—leave me.

LUGG. Certainly sir.

Re-enter POPHAM *with a small tumbler of brandy and water; he takes it from her and drinks it.*

It's not wanted. I'm thankful to say he's better.

POPHAM. [*To* LUGG.] If you please, Cook presents her compliments, and she would be glad of the pleasure of your company downstairs, before leavin'.   [*They go out.*

POSKET. Agatha and Lukyn! Agatha and Lukyn supping together at the Hôtel des Princes, while I was at home and asleep—while I ought to have been at home and asleep! It's awful!

CIS. [*Looking in at the door.*] Hallo, Guv!

POSKET. [*Starting up.*] Cis!

Enter CIS.

CIS. Where did you fetch, Guv?

POSKET. Where did I fetch! You wretched boy! I fetched Kilburn, and I'll fetch you a sound whipping when I recover my composure.

CIS. What for?

POSKET. For leading me astray, sir. Yours is the first bad companionship I have ever formed! Evil communication with you, sir, has corrupted me! [*Taking* CIS *by the collar and shaking him.*] Why did you abandon me at Kilburn?

CIS. Because you were quite done, and I branched off to draw the crowd away from you after me.

POSKET. Did you, Cis, did you? *Putting his hand on* CIS's *shoulder.*] My boy—my boy! Oh Cis, we're in such trouble!

CIS. You weren't caught, Guv?

POSKET. No—but do you know who the ladies are who were supping at the Hôtel des Princes?

CIS. No—do you?

POSKET. Do I? They were your mother and Aunt Charlotte.

CIS. The mater and Aunt Charlotte! Ha, ha, ha! [*Laughing and dancing with delight.*] Ha, ha! Oh, I say, Guv, what a lark!

POSKET. A lark! They were taken to the police station!

CIS. [*Changing his tone.*] My mother?

POSKET. They were brought before the magistrate and sentenced.

CIS. Sentenced?

POSKET. To seven days' imprisonment.

CIS. Oh!   [*He puts his hat on fiercely.*

POSKET. [*Alarmed.*] What are you going to do?

CIS. Get my mother out first, and then break every bone in that magistrate's body.

POSKET. Cis, Cis! He's an unhappy wretch and he did his duty.

CIS. His duty! To send another magistrate's wife to prison! Guv, I'm only a boy, but I know what professional etiquette is. Come along! Which is the police station?

POSKET. [*In agony.*] Mulberry Street.

CIS. [*Recoiling.*] Who's the magistrate?

POSKET. I am!

CIS. You! [*Seizing* POSKET *by the collar and shaking him.*] You dare to lock up my mother! Come with me and get her out!

He is dragging POSKET *towards the door, when* BULLAMY *enters breathlessly.*

BULLAMY. My dear Posket!

CIS. [*Seizing* BULLAMY *and dragging him with* POSKET *to the door.*] Come with me and get my mother out!

BULLAMY. Leave me alone, sir! She *is* out! [*Panting.*] I managed it.

CIS *and* POSKET. [*Together.*] How?

BULLAMY. Wormington sent to me when you were taken ill. When I arrived at the Court, he had discovered from your man-servant Mrs. Posket's awful position.

CIS. [*Warmly.*] You leave my mother alone! Go on!

BULLAMY. Said I to myself, 'This won't do; I must extricate these people somehow!' I'm not so damned conscientious as you are, Posket.

CIS. Bravo! Go on!

BULLAMY. [*Producing his jujube box.*] The first thing I did was to take a jujube.

CIS. [*Snatching the jujube box from him.*] Will you make haste?

BULLAMY. Then said I to Wormington, 'Posket was *non compos mentis* when he heard this case—I'm going to reopen the matter!'

CIS. Hurrah!

BULLAMY. And I did. And what do you think I found out from the proprietor of the hotel?

POSKET *and* CIS. What?

BULLAMY. That this young scamp, Mr. Cecil Farringdon, hires a room at the Hôtel des Princes.

CIS. I know that.

BULLAMY. And that Mr. Farringdon was there last night with some low stockbroker of the name of Skinner.

CIS. Go on—go on! [*Offering him the jujube box.*] Take a jujube.

BULLAMY. [*Taking a jujube.*] Now the law, which seems to me quite perfect, allows a man who rents a little apartment at an inn to eat and drink with his friends all night long.

CIS. Well?

BULLAMY. So said I from the bench, 'These ladies and gentlemen appear to be friends or relatives of a certain lodger in the Hôtel des Princes.'

CIS. So they are!

BULLAMY. 'They were all discovered in one room.'

POSKET. So we were—I mean, so they were!

BULLAMY. 'And I shall adjourn the case for a week to give Mr. Farringdon an opportunity of claiming these people as his guests.'

CIS. Three cheers for Bullamy!

BULLAMY. So I censured the police for their interference and released the ladies on their own recognisances.

POSKET. [*Taking* BULLAMY'*s hand.*] And the men?

BULLAMY. Well, unfortunately, Wormington took upon himself to despatch the men to the House of Correction before I arrived.

POSKET. [*Violently.*] I'm glad of it! They are dissolute villains! I'm glad of it.

Enter POPHAM, *scared.*

POPHAM. Oh, sir! Here's the missis and Miss Verrinder! In such a plight!

CIS. The mater! Guv, you explain! [*He hurries out.* POSKET *rapidly retires into the window recess.*

Enter AGATHA *and* CHARLOTTE, *pale, red-eyed, and agitated. They carry their hats, or bonnets, which are much crushed.*
POPHAM *goes out.*

AGATHA *and* CHARLOTTE. [*Falling on to* BULLAMY'*s shoulders.*] O—o—h—h!

BULLAMY. My dear ladies!   [*They seize* BULLAMY'*s hands.*

AGATHA. Preserver!

CHARLOTTE. Friend!

AGATHA. How is my boy?

BULLAMY. Never better.

AGATHA. [*Fiercely.*] And the man who condemned his wife and sister-in-law to the miseries of a jail?

BULLAMY. Ahem! Posket—oh—he——

AGATHA. Is he well enough to be told what that wife thinks of him?

BULLAMY. It might cause a relapse.

AGATHA. It is my duty to risk that.

CHARLOTTE. [*Raising the covers of the dishes on the table. With an hysterical cry.*] Food!

AGATHA. Ah!

[AGATHA *and* CHARLOTTE *begin to devour a teacake voraciously.*]

POSKET. [*Advancing with an attempt at dignity.*] Agatha Posket!

AGATHA. [*Rising, with her mouth full and a piece of teacake in her hand.*] Sir!

[CHARLOTTE *takes the tray and everything on it from the table and goes towards the door.*]

BULLAMY. [*Going to the door.*] There's going to be an explanation.

CHARLOTTE. [*At the door.*] There's going to be an explanation.

[CHARLOTTE *and* BULLAMY *go out quietly.*]

POSKET. How dare you look me in the face, madam?

AGATHA. How dare you look at anybody in any position, sir? You send your wife to prison for pushing a mere policeman.

POSKET. I didn't know what I was doing.

AGATHA. Not when you requested two ladies to raise their veils and show their faces in the dock? We shouldn't have been discovered but for that.

POSKET. It was my duty.

AGATHA. Duty! You don't go to the Police Court again alone! I guess now, Æneas Posket, why you clung to a single life so long. *You liked it*!

POSKET. I wish I had.

AGATHA. Why didn't you marry till you were fifty?

POSKET. Perhaps I hadn't met a widow, madam.

AGATHA. Paltry excuse. You revelled in a dissolute bachelorhood!

POSKET. Hah! Whist every evening!

AGATHA. You can't play whist *alone*. You're an expert at hiding, too!

POSKET. If I were I should thrash your boy!

AGATHA. When you wished to conceal yourself last night, you selected a table with a lady under it.

POSKET. [*Rubbing his arm.*] Ah, did you pinch me, or did Charlotte?

AGATHA. I did—Charlotte's a single girl.

POSKET. I fancy, madam, you found my conduct under that table perfectly respectful?

AGATHA. I don't know—I was too agitated to notice.

POSKET. Evasion—you're like all the women.

AGATHA. Profligate! You oughtn't to know that.

POSKET. No wife of mine sups unknown to me, with dissolute military men; we will have a judicial separation, Mrs. Posket.

AGATHA. Certainly—I suppose you'll manage that at your Police Court, too?

POSKET. I shall send for my solicitor at once.

AGATHA. Æneas! Mr. Posket! Whatever happens, you shall not have the custody of my boy.

POSKET. Your boy! *I* take charge of *him*? Agatha Posket, he has been my evil genius! He has made me a gambler at an atrocious game called 'Fireworks'—he has tortured my mind with abstruse speculations concerning 'Sillikin' and 'Butterscotch' for the St. Leger—he has caused me to cower before servants, and to fly before the police.

AGATHA. He! My Cis?

Enter CIS, *having changed his clothes.*

CIS. [*Breezily.*] Hallo, mater—got back?

AGATHA. You wicked boy! You dare to have apartments at the Hôtel des Princes!

POSKET. Yes—and it was to put a stop to that which induced me to go to Meek Street last night.

CIS. Don't be angry mater! I've got you out of your difficulties.

POSKET. But you got me into mine!

CIS. Well, I know I did—one can't be always doing the right thing. It isn't Guv's fault—there!

POSKET. Swear it!

AGATHA. No, he doesn't know the nature of an oath. I believe him. Æneas, I see now this is all the result of a lack of candour on my part. Tell me, have you ever particularly observed this child?

POSKET. [*Weakly.*] Oh!

AGATHA. Has it ever struck you he is a little forward?

POSKET. Sometimes.

AGATHA. You are wrong; he is awfully backward. [*Taking* POSKET's *hand*.] Æneas, men always think they are marrying angels, and women would be angels if they never had to grow old. That warps their dispositions. I have deceived you, Æneas.

POSKET. [*Clenching his fists.*] Ah! Lukyn!

AGATHA. No—no—you don't understand! Lukyn was my boy's godfather in 1866.

POSKET. [*Starting.*] 1866?

CIS. 1866?

CIS *and* POSKET. [*Reckoning rapidly upon their fingers.*] 1866.

AGATHA. [*Quickly.*] S-s-s-h! Don't count! Cis, go away! [*To* POSKET.] When you proposed to me in the Pantheon at Spa, you particularly remarked, 'Mrs. Farringdon, I love you for yourself *alone*'.

POSKET. I know I did.

AGATHA. Those were terrible words to address to a widow with a son of nineteen. [CIS *and* POSKET *again reckon rapidly upon their fingers.*] Don't count, Æneas, don't count! Those words tempted me. I glanced at my face in a neighbouring mirror, and I said 'Æneas is fifty—why should I—a mere woman, compete with him on the question of age? He has already the advantage—I will be generous—I will add to it!' I led you to believe I had been married only fifteen years ago; I deceived you and my boy as to his real age, and I told you I was but one-and-thirty.

POSKET. It wasn't the truth?

AGATHA. Ah! I merely lacked woman's commonest fault, exaggeration.

POSKET. But—Lukyn?

AGATHA. Knows the real facts. I went to him last night to beg him not to disturb an arrangement which had brought happiness to all parties. Look. In place of a wayward, troublesome child, I now present you with a youth old enough to be a joy, comfort and support!

CIS. Oh, I say, mater, this is a frightful sell for a fellow.

AGATHA. Go to your room, sir.

CIS. I always thought there was something wrong with me. Blessed if I'm not behind the age! [CIS *goes out.*

AGATHA. Forgive me, Æneas. Look at my bonnet! A night in Mulberry Street, without even a powder-puff, is an awful expiation.

POSKET. Agatha! How do I know Cis won't be five-and-twenty to-morrow?

AGATHA. No—no—you know the worst, and as long as I live, I'll never deceive you again—except in little things.

Enter LUKYN *and* VALE.

LUKYN. [*Boiling with rage.*] By George, Posket!

POSKET. My dear Lukyn!

LUKYN. Do you know I am a confounded jail-bird, sir?

POSKET. An accident!

LUKYN. And do you know what has happened to me in jail—a soldier, sir—an officer?

POSKET. No.

LUKYN. I have been washed by the authorities!

POSKET. Lukyn, no!

Enter CHARLOTTE; *she rushes across to* VALE.

CHARLOTTE. Horace! Horace! Not you, too?

VALE. By Jove, Charlotte, I would have died first.

Enter BULLAMY, *quickly.*

BULLAMY. Mr. Posket, I shall choke, sir! Inspector Messiter is downstairs and says that Isidore the waiter swears that you are the man who escaped from Meek Street last night.

LUKYN. What?

BULLAMY. This is a public scandal, sir!

LUKYN. Your game is up, sir!

BULLAMY. You have brought a stain upon a spotless Police Court.

LUKYN. And lectured me upon propriety and decorum.

POSKET. Gentlemen, gentlemen, when you have heard my story you will pity me.

LUKYN *and* BULLAMY. [*Laughing ironically.*] Ha, ha!

POSKET. You will find your old friend a Man, a Martyr, and a Magistrate!

Enter CIS, *pulling* BEATIE *after him.*

CIS. Come on, Beatie! Guv—mater! Here's news! Beatie and I have made up our minds to be married.

AGATHA. Oh!

Enter POPHAM, *with champagne and glasses.*

POSKET. What's this?

CIS. Bollinger—'74—extra dry—to drink our health and happiness.

CHARLOTTE. Champagne! It may save my life!

AGATHA. Miss Tomlinson, go home!

POSKET. [*Grimly.*] Stop! Cis Farringdon, my dear boy, you are but nineteen at present, but you were only fourteen yesterday, so you are a growing lad; on the day you marry and start for Canada, I will give you a thousand pounds!

POPHAM. [*Putting her apron to her eyes.*] Oh!

CIS. [*Embracing* BEATIE.] Hurrah! We'll be married directly.

AGATHA. He's an infant! I forbid it!

POSKET. I am his legal guardian. Gentlemen, bear witness. I solemnly consent to that little wretch's marriage!

[AGATHA *sinks into a chair as the curtain falls.*

MRS. DANE'S DEFENCE

A PLAY IN FOUR ACTS

BY

HENRY ARTHUR JONES (1851–1929)

═══════

First performed at Wyndham's Theatre, 9 October 1900

═══════

CAST

SIR DANIEL (MR. JUSTICE) CARTERET	Mr. Charles Wyndham
LIONEL CARTERET, his adopted son	Mr. Alfred Kendrick
CANON BONSEY	Mr. Alfred Bishop
MR. BULSOM-PORTER	Mr. E. W. Garden
MR. JAMES RISBY	Mr. Charles Thursby
FENDICK, a private inquiry agent	Mr. Stanley Pringle
ADAMS, butler to Lady Eastney	Mr. Reginald Walter
WILSON, butler to Sir Daniel	Mr. Charles Terric
MRS. DANE	Miss Lena Ashwell
MRS. BULSOM-PORTER	Miss Marie Illington
JANET COLQUHOUN, niece to Lady Eastney	Miss Beatrice Irwin
LADY EASTNEY	Miss Mary Moore

═══════

The whole of the action takes place at Sunningwater, about twenty-five miles from London, in the present day.

ACT I

The blue drawing-room at LADY EASTNEY'S, *Sunningwater.
A very brightly furnished room in a country house about twenty
miles from London. At back are doors opening into a conservatory
which is lighted up. On the right side are French windows opening
upon a lawn. On the left side up stage is a door opening off into the
large drawing-room. This door is curtained. When it is opened a
buzz of conversation, as from a reception, is heard. Down stage on
the left side is a fire-place. Time: after dinner on an evening in
July. The doors are all open. A violin is played off left as if it were
two rooms away.* MRS. BULSOM-PORTER, *a lady of forty-five,
enters showing great irritation. She seats herself on sofa and fans
herself. A moment or two later,* MR. BULSOM-PORTER *enters by
the same door. He is a flabby, affable, easy-going English gentleman
about fifty. He looks round cautiously to see that he is not followed,
then closes the door softly and comes up to his wife.*

BULSOM-PORTER [*a quiet drawling, good-humoured utterance*].
It's a mystery to me, Henrietta, that we can't arrange to
celebrate these little domestic battles on our own domestic
hearth.

MRS. BULSOM-PORTER. I warn you that if you continue to
pay such marked attention to that woman, I shall tell the
whole neighbourhood her history.

BULSOM-PORTER. You will please hold your tongue about
Mrs. Dane. Jim says that he is mistaken, and that she is not
the lady he knew in Vienna.

MRS. BULSOM-PORTER. He is only saying that to shelter her.
The fact is, she is leading Jim by the nose, the same as she is
leading you and young Carteret; and it only remains to be
seen which of the three will be her victim.

BULSOM-PORTER. Well, I trust I shall be the lucky fellow, but
I'm afraid the odds are on Lionel Carteret, and I shall come
in a bad third.

MRS. BULSOM-PORTER. At least you might have the good taste to try and hide your infidelities!

BULSOM-PORTER. My dear, you may depend, when I have any, I shall. Now, suppose we get back to the others?

MRS. BULSOM-PORTER. You wish to get back to that woman?

BULSOM-PORTER. I wish to get back to Lady Eastney and the other guests.

MRS. BULSOM-PORTER. You admire this Mrs. Dane?

BULSOM-PORTER [*cordially, going off*]. Very much indeed.

MRS. BULSOM-PORTER [*stopping him*]. Why do you admire her?

BULSOM-PORTER. Because she has a pretty face, a soft voice, and a charming manner.

MRS. BULSOM-PORTER. Of course! Mere physical charms! What horribly disgusting minds men must have!

BULSOM-PORTER. We have! Give us up! Wash your hands of us, and let us go our own wicked ways! [*Going.*

MRS. BULSOM-PORTER [*still stopping him*]. To what extent do you admire her?

BULSOM-PORTER. To the extent of very much preferring her company to yours when you're in one of these unreasonable jealous fits. Now, will you oblige me by returning to the drawing-room?

He opens the drawing room door. Enter by it MR. JAMES RISBY, *an ordinary Englishman about thirty-five.*

MRS. BULSOM-PORTER. I shall not speak to that woman—

BULSOM-PORTER. Hush! [*Closes door sharply after* RISBY.

RISBY. My dear aunt, I'm leaving for Paris to-morrow morning, and before I go I want to put you right on a little matter.

MRS. BULSOM-PORTER. You mean Mrs. Dane?

RISBY. Exactly. When I first saw her at Sir Daniel Carteret's a fortnight ago, I thought I recognized her—

MRS. BULSOM-PORTER. You did recognize her.

RISBY. I was mistaken.

MRS. BULSOM-PORTER. You told me she was the Miss Hindemarsh who was connected with a disgraceful scandal in Vienna five years ago. I particularly watched your manner, and I'm sure you were speaking the truth.

RISBY. I was speaking the truth—as I supposed. And therefore my manner carried conviction. But I am now speaking the truth when I tell you I was mistaken. I trust my manner carries equal conviction.   [*Looking at her very fixedly.*

MRS. BULSOM-PORTER [*looks at him very fixedly for a few moments*]. No, Jim; I do not and cannot believe you.

RISBY. I'm sorry. However, the fact remains, my dear aunt, that I have inadvertently injured a very charming woman—

MRS. BULSOM-PORTER. Of course! A very charming woman! That's the reason you withdraw your accusation.

RISBY. I made no accusation. And if you have repeated what I told you in the strictest confidence about Mrs. Dane, I must beg you to put the matter right at once. For if you give me as your authority I shall have to explain that I was mistaken, that consequently you were mistaken, and further, that from this moment, you are fully aware that you are mistaken.

MRS. BULSOM-PORTER. I'm not fully aware that I'm mistaken.

BULSOM-PORTER. What does it matter whether you're mistaken or no? Suppose Mrs. Dane is Miss Hindemarsh, what then?

MRS. BULSOM-PORTER. What then?! Do you consider her fit to mix in the society of your wife?

BULSOM-PORTER. I daresay she's as fit as nine out of ten of the women you meet if the truth were only known. [*To* RISBY.] What was the exact story of this Miss Hindemarsh?

RISBY. Oh, the eternal trio! *Dramatis personae*, Mr. Horace Trent, charming, devoted, middle-aged husband; Mrs. Horace Trent, charming, devoted, middle-aged wife; Felicia Hindemarsh, charming, devoted, youthful governess to their children and companion to Mrs. Trent; the whole forming a truly happy family, who passed the autumn at the Italian lakes, and returned by Vienna at the time I was an *attaché* there five years ago. During their stay in Vienna, charming, middle-aged wife discovers a *liaison* between charming, middle-aged husband and charming, youthful governess; and instead of sensibly packing off missy with a month's salary and saying no more about it, charming, middle-aged wife, being a neurotic creature, commits suicide. Charming, middle-aged husband is naturally horrified, and also refrains from doing the sensible thing—in fact, goes out of his mind, and is at present in an asylum in the north of England. Missy does the sensible thing and disappears. The story is hushed up as far as possible, but the moral remains: 'Upon the verge of such a tragedy may any one of us poor innocents be treading at this moment.' [*Takes out watch.*] Adieu, auntie. I have to catch an early train to town to-morrow morning.

MRS. BULSOM-PORTER. You are sure Mrs. Dane is not Miss Hindemarsh?

RISBY. Quite sure.

[*The violin ceases and there is some applause.*

MRS. BULSOM-PORTER. She doesn't resemble Miss Hindemarsh?

RISBY [*after a pause*]. There is a slight resemblance. Perhaps I should say a considerable resemblance.

MRS. BULSOM-PORTER [*after looking at him fixedly for a moment*]. Jim, I shall fully inquire into this Mrs. Dane's antecedents—

BULSOM-PORTER. What for? What business is it of yours to rake up old scandals? It's five years ago, and—

RISBY. Sh—!

Enter MRS. DANE, *a pretty, soft-voiced, dark little woman about twenty-eight. They show some embarrassment at her entrance. With some little hesitation* MRS. DANE *comes up to* MRS. BULSOM-PORTER.

MRS. DANE. Lady Eastney has a great find in her new violinist, don't you think?

MRS. BULSOM-PORTER [*coldly*]. Really, I didn't hear her. Ah, I see she is going to play again. Alfred, I very much want you to hear this. Alfred! Come and listen! I want to decide whether we shall engage this lady for our garden party.

[*She waits at door till he comes up, then goes off.* BULSOM-PORTER *follows reluctantly, exchanging a little shrug and grin with* RISBY. *After they have gone off there is a little pause. The violin begins again and the buzz of conversation in the next room ceases.* RISBY *goes to door, left, closes it.* MRS. DANE *has been watching him a little furtively. Having closed the door he comes up to her.*

RISBY. My dear Mrs. Dane, when one has inadvertently made a mistake, the best way is to own up at once.

MRS. DANE. Yes? Who has made a mistake?

RISBY. I have—a stupid, ill-natured, idiotic mistake. You remember when I first met you?

MRS. DANE [*glances at him very quickly*]. At Sir Daniel Carteret's, a fortnight ago.

RISBY [*after a slight pause*]. Yes. Do you know I thought then that we had met before?

MRS. DANE. Indeed? Where?

RISBY. In Vienna five years ago.

MRS. DANE. I have never been in Vienna.

RISBY. No. The second time I saw you I was convinced I was mistaken. But in the meantime—I scarcely know how to confess my folly—I had thoughtlessly told my aunt, Mrs. Bulsom-Porter, that I recognized you.

MRS. DANE. I've noticed that Mrs. Bulsom-Porter seems to avoid me. You must have told her I was some very wicked person. Whom does she suppose me to be?

RISBY. You have some resemblance to a Miss Felicia Hinde-marsh—

MRS. DANE. Who is she?

RISBY. She was connected with an unfortunate affair in Vienna five years ago.   [*Pause.*

MRS. DANE. And does Mrs. Bulsom-Porter really think I am this—this Miss what's-her-name?

RISBY. I have assured her you are not.

MRS. DANE. Thank you. What would you advise me to do?

RISBY. I am obliged to leave for Paris to-morrow morning on my way to Switzerland. If you find yourself in any difficulty, write to me and I will reply in such a way that there can be no doubt.

MRS. DANE. Thank you. You're very good.

RISBY. Not at all. I can't tell you how vexed I am to have made such a horrible mistake. But having made it, I thought it better to put you on your guard. Good-bye. [*Offering hand.*

MRS. DANE. Good-bye.

[*He goes a few steps, then returns.*

RISBY. Mrs. Dane, if you think of passing the winter away from Sunningwater, I have the most delightful little villa near Mentone—untenanted—I should be pleased to place it at your disposal.

MRS. DANE. No, thank you. Why should I leave Sunningwater?

RISBY. Is there anything I can do for you before I start?

MRS. DANE. Will you tell Sir Daniel and Mr. Carteret that I am not this lady?

RISBY [*after a moment or two's deliberation*]. Believe me, it will be better to let the matter drop entirely, unless it is raised by others. Lady Eastney is busy. I'll slip round by the conservatory and send her a little note of adieu. Again, good-bye.

MRS. DANE. Good-bye. I may always reckon you my friend?

RISBY [*shakes her hand warmly*]. Rely on me.

[*Exit by conservatory. She watches him off; then in anxious deliberation walks up and down the room for a few moments.*

Enter LIONEL CARTERET, *a fresh, bright, enthusiastic, clear-complexioned English lad of twenty-four. He closes the door after him.*

LAL. Mrs. Dane, if I ask you a question will you answer me truthfully instead of telling me a polite fib?

MRS. DANE [*after showing a little alarm*]. Ask me the question.

LAL. You seem to be keeping out of my way, trying not to give me a chance of speaking to you alone. [*She shows delight when she sees his drift.*] And the other night at our place you were so different; you seemed to like my company. Have I offended you?

MRS. DANE. No.

LAL. Then why have you changed? For you have changed.

MRS. DANE. Perhaps I was a little foolish last Wednesday.

LAL. No, no! You don't know what I felt that night! I waited outside your window till past midnight; then I tramped about the country till three; then the birds began to wake and sing and I whistled back their songs to them; then I went down to the river and had a swim; then I came back to the house and plundered the larder and ate up everything in it; then I went to the stables and saddled Moon Daisy, and galloped her all round the park; then I came back and had another breakfast, and then I kept just mad with happiness all the rest of the day!

MRS. DANE [*she has listened with great delight, keeping her face away from him*]. I see I was very foolish.

LAL. No. Why?

MRS. DANE. Believe me, a friendship between us wouldn't be for your good.

LAL. It isn't friendship I want.

MRS. DANE [*delighted*]. What else can it be? You're twenty-four. I'm twenty-seven. That means many years between us, and there will be more as we grow older.

LAL [*shaking his head*]. You will always be the same age that I am—the very same day, the very same hour.

MRS. DANE [*she smiles and shakes her head*]. But you know nothing of me.

LAL. I know you as you know yourself.

MRS. DANE [*a little cautiously*]. Do you? How?

LAL. My heart has told me all.

MRS. DANE. Perhaps your heart has spoken falsely.

LAL. You shan't persuade me that you aren't exactly what I want you to be.

MRS. DANE [*shows great delight*]. Perhaps my best self isn't very far from that. But then we have so many different selves.

LAL. You have but your own self, and that is the one I know.

MRS. DANE. Then that is the particular self you must always believe me to be. It will do no harm when we are parted.

LAL. Parted?

MRS. DANE. Did you notice Sir Daniel looking at us down the table at dinner? He was thinking, 'I must get Lionel away from Mrs. Dane.' And he has made up his mind to do it.

LAL. He won't wish to part us when he knows how much I love you.

MRS. DANE. You haven't told him?

LAL. No. The truth is, a year ago I thought I was in love with Miss Colquhoun. But Lady Eastney and my father said she was too young.

MRS. DANE. So it was broken off?

LAL. We were to wait a year, and then if we were both of the same mind, we were to be formally engaged.

MRS. DANE. And is Miss Colquhoun of the same mind?

LAL. Janet? I don't know. I only know it would be a sin to be engaged to her while I love you as I do.

MRS. DANE. I'm afraid of Sir Daniel.

LAL. Why?

MRS. DANE. I suppose his reputation frightens me.

LAL. They say he's the pleasantest judge that ever hanged a man.

MRS. DANE. Mr. Risby was telling us about some famous cross-examination—something about a forger.

LAL. Oh, Kettleby, the forger-murderer. On the morning of his execution Kettleby said that to have heard my father's cross-examination of his witnesses was very well worth being hanged for.

MRS. DANE. Then do you wonder I'm rather afraid of Sir Daniel?

LAL. You needn't be. In private he's the dearest, kindest-hearted man. And when he knows that the happiness of my whole life depends upon you, I'm sure he won't withhold his consent.

MRS. DANE. He isn't your own father?

LAL. No, but if he were I couldn't love him more than I do.

MRS. DANE. But if he doesn't think me suitable; if after consideration he says 'No'?

LAL. Then I'll disobey him and marry you.

MRS. DANE. Are you sure of yourself?

LAL. Try me.

MRS. DANE [*after some consideration*]. No. I'm very proud and happy to be loved as you love me. But I won't come between you and your father.

LAL. But if I can get his consent?

Enter SIR DANIEL (MR. JUSTICE) CARTERET, *about fifty-five. A pause of embarrassment.* SIR DANIEL *is sauntering off at back.*

MRS. DANE. We are missing all the music—

SIR DANIEL. It's worth hearing. Mademoiselle Lemonier is just going to play.

MRS. DANE. Thank you. I want to hear her—

               [*Exit* MRS. DANE. LAL *is following her.*

SIR DANIEL. Lal! [LAL *stops.* SIR DANIEL *closes the door. Piano faintly heard through following scene.*] I've spoken to Sir Robert Jennings to take you out as assistant to him on this new Egyptian railway.

LAL. I'd rather not leave England just now, sir.

SIR DANIEL [*very firmly*]. I wish it.

LAL. Why, sir?

SIR DANIEL [*very affectionately putting his hand on* LAL'*s shoulder*]. My dear Lal, to stop you from making an unhappy fool of yourself.

LAL. In what way, sir?

SIR DANIEL. When I came up to London to read for the bar, I fell very desperately in love with my landlady's sister, a lady some six years older and some two stone heavier than myself. She was in the mantle business and wore a large crinoline. I used to call her my Bonnie Louisa. My father got wind of it, came up to town and promptly shattered our applecart; sent Bonnie Louisa flying to Paris, and packed me off on a judicial commission to India.

LAL. I don't see the point of the story, sir.

SIR DANIEL. Twelve years after, I happened to be coming down the Edgware Road on a Sunday morning, and I met Bonnie Louisa with a husband and five children, sailing along the pavement, all in their Sunday best.

LAL. Still, I don't see the point, sir.

SIR DANIEL. I did! I hurried to church and devoutly thanked Heaven that my father had had the sense and the courage to do for me what I'm trying to do for you to-night. [*Very firmly.*] Now, my boy, you'll take this post under Sir Robert Jennings.

LAL. I can't leave her, sir. I love her so much.

SIR DANIEL. But a year ago you loved Janet Colquhoun.

LAL. I *thought* I loved Janet. I'm *sure* I love Mrs. Dane.

SIR DANIEL. And in a year you'll be sure you love somebody else, and you'll think you loved Mrs. Dane. [LAL *shakes his head.* SIR DANIEL *shakes his more vigorously still.*] Yes, yes. Bonnie Louisa, Janet Colquhoun, Juliet Capulet—the divine illusion is always the same—and it always ends unhappily.

LAL. It always ends unhappily?

SIR DANIEL. Or in bathos, which is far worse. Rather than that let us be thankful when the red-hot ploughshare is driven right through our hearts, or when we have the pluck to drive it through ourselves. Now Lal, I want you to leave England at once.

LAL. I'm very sorry. I can't, unless—unless Mrs. Dane goes with me. [SIR DANIEL *looks astonished and indignant.*] I've asked her to be my wife.

SIR DANIEL. You might have told me first, Lal.

LAL. Forgive me, sir. I meant to, but my heart was so full and the words slipped out. You're angry with me?

SIR DANIEL [*very kindly*]. No. [*Pause.*] Has she accepted you?

LAL. She will—if you consent.

SIR DANIEL. How long have you cared for her?

LAL. From the very first day I met her.

SIR DANIEL. Two months ago. Has she told you anything of her people?

LAL. No.

SIR DANIEL. Circumstances? Position?

LAL. No.

SIR DANIEL. Where she has lived all her life?

LAL. She happened to say that she had spent some years in Canada.

SIR DANIEL. Canada? Come, that's something. There was a Mr. Dane—who was he?

LAL. I don't know.

SIR DANIEL. Hasn't she mentioned him?

LAL. Naturally not.

SIR DANIEL. Naturally not. Still, there was a Mr. Dane, and he remains a factor in the situation. Has she told you her age?

LAL. Twenty-seven.

SIR DANIEL. Twenty-seven? Dear, dear, I should have said a year or so older.

LAL. She wouldn't tell me a lie.

SIR DANIEL. No?

LAL. A woman doesn't tell a lie to the man she loves. Why do you laugh?

SIR DANIEL. My dear Lal, fifty women out of a hundred have no notion of what truth means, and don't bother about it. The other fifty have the rudiments of a truth-sense in various stages of development, and will generally tell the truth where their own interests don't clash. But in matters of love, there isn't one woman in a hundred—there isn't one woman in a thousand, that, when she's put to it, won't lie right and left, up and down, backwards and forwards, *to* the man she loves, *for* the man she loves, *with* the man she loves, *about* the man she loves, to gain her ends, and *keep* the man she loves.

LAL. You have a very low opinion of women, sir.

SIR DANIEL. I have a very high opinion of them—in matters of strategy.

LAL. You won't stand in my way, sir? Think, sir, has there never been a time in your life when you would have thrown up everything, just for the right of calling one woman your own?

SIR DANIEL [*is moved by his appeal; takes the hand he is holding out; shakes it warmly*]. I won't stand in your way, Lal.

LAL. Thank you, sir. You've always been better than a dozen fathers to me.

SIR DANIEL. I won't stand in your way—unless there's some good reason why you shouldn't marry her.

LAL. What reason can there be? You don't know anything against her?

SIR DANIEL. No. Still, it's a little strange that she has lived in Sunningwater some months and nobody seems to know anything about her. Have you said anything to Janet?

LAL. No. I thought it better to let her guess—from my manner. You know, sir, there was no engagement between us.

SIR DANIEL. I'm sorry. I hope this business won't twist poor little Janet's heartstrings.

Enter LADY EASTNEY, *about thirty, bright, fashionable, handsomely dressed.* LAL *goes up to back.*

LADY EASTNEY. Sir Daniel! Playing truant here! Everybody will be putting the worst interpretation upon it.

SIR DANIEL. What interpretation?

LADY EASTNEY. That I've accepted you at last, and that you've come in here to repent and think of the best way of getting out of it. Lionel! The young people are getting up a dance! Janet is posing against a pillar in an attitude of maiden-meditation fancy-free. Go and ask her to dance with you.

LAL [*confused*]. I'm very sorry, Lady Eastney—will you tell her, sir? And will you tell Miss Colquhoun?

[*Exit hurriedly.* LADY EASTNEY *looks at* SIR DANIEL *for an explanation.*

SIR DANIEL. It seems that Lal didn't know his own mind last year.

LADY EASTNEY. He's going to throw over my Janet for Mrs. Dane?

SIR DANIEL. I'm very sorry. I think you should tell Janet.

LADY EASTNEY. Help me.

Enter JANET COLQUHOUN, *about eighteen, with a slight Scotch accent; she saunters towards right.*

LADY EASTNEY. Aren't you going to dance, Janet?

JANET. I'm thinking I won't to-night.

LADY EASTNEY. But what are all the young men doing? Hasn't anybody asked you?

JANET. Oh, I'm not standing out for want of partners, but I thought there were plenty of them in there to tumble over each other, so I'd just get a breath of cool air outside.

    [*Going up to conservatory.* LIONEL CARTERET *passes in conservatory and takes no notice of her. She flushes up, shows for a moment that she is very much hurt, then conquers her feelings, and with great effort controls herself during the remainder of the scene.*

LADY EASTNEY. Janet darling, go and have a dance, and don't think anything more about him.

JANET. Him?! Him?! Which him? [*Pointing off to where* LIONEL CARTERET *has just gone by. Very contemptuously.*] *That* him? Oh, there are plenty of other 'hims' in the world, and I'll have a good conceit of myself and not trouble about any of them.

LADY EASTNEY [*very tenderly*]. Then you've forgotten all about your little flirtation a year ago?

JANET. Flirtation?

LADY EASTNEY. With Mr. Carteret.

JANET. A year's a long time, isn't it? [*To* SIR DANIEL.] I suppose Mr. Carteret has forgotten all about it too. Has he?

SIR DANIEL. I'm afraid Lal is very much like many other young men.

JANET. You mean he makes love to every girl he meets and then breaks his word to all of them?

SIR DANIEL. No! No! But perhaps he was a little too hasty a year ago.

JANET. Is there any harm done?

SIR DANIEL. Not unless you have taken it too seriously.

JANET. Didn't he wish me to take it seriously?

SIR DANIEL. He did at the time.

JANET. But now he doesn't?

SIR DANIEL. He's grieving to think that he has caused you pain.

JANET. Poor fellow! Poor fellow! Do call him in and tell him that I'll try and not break my heart over him. Mr. Carteret! [LAL enters.] Sir Daniel and Auntie have just reminded me that we were very foolish a year ago. I've seen so little of you lately that I'd forgotten all about it. Perhaps you've been grieving about it—

LAL. Janet!

JANET. Ah, you have! You won't take it too much to heart if I ask you not to think anything more of our—our flirtation? I was only seventeen. At seventeen one may change one's mind. I've changed my mind, Mr. Carteret.

LAL. If I've caused you any pain you'll forgive me?

JANET. Forgive you? And I thought you'd be just breaking your heart for me! Aren't you breaking your heart?

LAL. Miss Colquhoun, I know I've behaved badly.

JANET [mocking a Scotch peasant's dialect]. Dinna fash yourself. Ye're a braw laddie, but I'll just mak up my mind to do without ye. [A little contemptuous curtsey to him.] Now! Will you dance with me just once for auld lang syne, and then I'll not trifle with your feelings any longer, Mr. Carteret?

LAL. If you wish.   [Gives her his arm. Exeunt.

LADY EASTNEY. I'm very angry with Lionel.

SIR DANIEL. Why?

LADY EASTNEY. For not seeing where his happiness lies after I'd planned it out so carefully for him.

SIR DANIEL. Is there any knowing where married happiness lies for other people, or even for ourselves?

LADY EASTNEY. Apparently not. The happiest marriage I've ever known was between my old governess of forty-six and a young piano-tuner of twenty-two. We all went down on our knees, and begged her to see the monstrous unsuitability of it, but she wouldn't! She would marry the man, and the result is she has lived happily ever afterwards!

SIR DANIEL. Give me your advice. Lal wants to marry this Mrs. Dane—

LADY EASTNEY. I can't quite forgive her for taking him away from Janet, and I can't quite forgive Lionel.

SIR DANIEL. Don't be hard on him. Help me to do the best for the young fellow. I don't want him to make a mess of his life as I've done of mine.

LADY EASTNEY. Have you made a mess of your life?

SIR DANIEL. Yes, so far as women are concerned.

LADY EASTNEY. H'm. [*Looks at him very critically.*] You seem to have thrived very well on it. It can't have been a very unpleasant process. I wonder how many poor women have been sacrificed in the—scrimmage?

SIR DANIEL. None, I hope. At least—[*Deep sigh.*] I've had one great love story in my life. Shall I tell you about it?

LADY EASTNEY. I should love to hear, if it isn't too sad and too sacred.

SIR DANIEL. I've never told this to anyone. I wouldn't tell it to you except—except that you know I would gladly give you the right to ask me for some knowledge of my past attachments.

LADY EASTNEY. I have already the right to ask you, the right of friendship and the right of a woman's curiosity. [*Goes to door, looks off.*] I think I can leave them for five minutes, and I've really done my duty to them to-night. [*Closes door.*] Now, begin! Don't spare yourself. Don't shock me, and skip nothing of vital interest.

SIR DANIEL. We'll skip the first thirty-five years of my life.

LADY EASTNEY. Were they all barren of love stories?

SIR DANIEL. None of them, after fifteen. But what's a boy's love?

LADY EASTNEY. That's what poor Janet is thinking.

SIR DANIEL. When I was just getting into comfortable practice I was thrown very much into the company of the wife of one of my clients. We grew to love each other deeply, passionately, almost before we were aware of it. We owned our love, recognized its hopelessness, and resolved to part. We parted, and endured some months of banishment worse than death; then we met again, and after a few mad weeks we determined to make our own happiness in our own world. She arranged to leave her home and to meet me at Liverpool by a certain train. I had our passages taken, and I remember waiting for her, waiting, waiting, waiting. She never came. I went back to town and found a letter from her. Her boy, her only child, was dangerously ill and she had stayed to nurse him. She was a deeply religious woman, though she loved me, and she had vowed to God that if her child's life was spared she would never see me again. I was heart-broken, but I sent her a message that she had done right. The boy's life was spared. I never saw her again. In a few months she was dead. I had a big bout or two of dissipation, then I pulled myself together and worked hammer and tongs, day and night, at my profession. I became successful, and met other women; had my affairs with them—I won't call them love-affairs—some of them graceful, some of them romantic, none of them quite degrading, but all of them empty and heartless. And so I frittered away what affections I had left in cheap and facile amours; and all the while her tender ghost was standing beside me, whispering, 'This isn't love! This isn't love! You'll never love again as you loved me!' I've been successful and happy after a fashion; but there has never been a moment since I lost her when I wouldn't have cheerfully bartered every farthing, every honour, every triumph I've scored in my profession, to stand again on that platform at Liverpool and know that she was coming to me.

LADY EASTNEY. My poor friend!

SIR DANIEL. Her husband died, rather badly off, fifteen years ago. I took the boy, gave him my name, and made him my

own. I've been a better man for having him, and I love him—
I've never allowed Lal to see how much I love him—I don't
think I quite know myself, but the young fellow is very dear
to me, very, very dear.

LADY EASTNEY. I should like to have been that woman.
You've made me very jealous of her.

SIR DANIEL. Why?

LADY EASTNEY. We all long to be the object of an undying
love, and it so seldom comes off.

SIR DANIEL. Curious I should be telling you all this, and at the
same time asking you to be my wife.

LADY EASTNEY. My dear friend, I've never been so near
accepting you as I am at this moment.

SIR DANIEL. Will you?

LADY EASTNEY. Now, if you had that same love to offer me—

SIR DANIEL. I haven't, and I care for you too much to deceive
you. But I can give you a very genuine attachment and
perfect fidelity. If I were to pretend to offer you more I
should be wronging you. Well?

LADY EASTNEY. Will you keep the offer open?

SIR DANIEL. As long as you please.

LADY EASTNEY. You shouldn't say that. You should make me
fear I'm going to lose you if I don't say 'Yes' this moment.

SIR DANIEL. I'm past fifty. You're not thirty. There's no
chance of your losing me. Well?

LADY EASTNEY. Well, we'll let the matter stay over again, if
you don't mind?

SIR DANIEL. I can wait. Meantime, you understand now why
I want the boy to make a happy marriage. Will you help me?

LADY EASTNEY. Yes, with all my heart. What have you done
so far?

SIR DANIEL. Tried to laugh him out of it. When I found that
was impossible I promised him he should marry her if we
found she was suitable. What do you know of her?

LADY EASTNEY. Nothing. I met her at the Canon's.

Enter very cautiously CANON BONSEY, *a rather jovial, good-natured clergyman about sixty, shrewd, plausible, worldly. He closes the door behind him.*

CANON BONSEY. Dear Lady Eastney, may I intrude for one moment. [*He comes up rather slowly and mysteriously.*] Do you know, I'm rather afraid we are going to have another scandal?

LADY EASTNEY [*quickly*]. I don't know anything about it, Canon. I won't know anything about it. And above all, I decline to give a certificate of injured innocence to any young person who misses her last train. Now, [*Inclining her ear to him.*] gently breathe the name of the minx and her victim, and do, please, keep me out of it this time.

CANON BONSEY. Dear Lady Eastney, you may rely I shall do my best to keep everybody out of it—especially myself. You haven't heard any whisper about one of your guests this evening?

LADY EASTNEY. No—whom?

CANON BONSEY. Mrs. Dane.

[SIR DANIEL *and* LADY EASTNEY *exchange looks.*

LADY EASTNEY. What of her?

CANON BONSEY. Ask Mrs. Bulsom-Porter.

LADY EASTNEY. Mrs. Bulsom-Porter! How is it that everything horrid in this neighbourhood radiates to and from that woman! What is she saying, and how does she know?

CANON BONSEY. It seems her nephew, Mr. Risby, told her that Mrs. Dane was connected with a very ugly scandal in Vienna some years ago.

LADY EASTNEY. Where is Mr. Risby? Will you ask him to come to me?

Enter ADAMS, *with letter on tray which he brings to* LADY EASTNEY.

ADAMS. From Mr. Risby, my lady. He has just gone.

[LADY EASTNEY *takes letter, reads it. Exit* ADAMS.

SIR DANIEL. Canon, you introduced Mrs. Dane to us all.

CANON BONSEY [*a little uncomfortable*]. Yes. She came to church. Of course I called on her. I found she played the piano divinely, and had been living in Winchester for some months, and knew some very nice people there whom I knew; and above all was a very delightful lady. And when a delightful lady comes to church, and subscribes regularly to all the parish charities, and has a perfect mastery of the piano, and is evidently a very dear sweet creature in every way, and a gentlewoman, I don't think it's the duty of a clergyman to ask her for references as if she were a housemaid, eh?

SIR DANIEL [*to* LADY EASTNEY]. Does Risby mention anything of this?

LADY EASTNEY [*who has been reading* RISBY's *letter*]. No. He only sends me a word of adieu. He has gone to town to-night on his way to Switzerland.

SIR DANIEL [*to* CANON BONSEY]. Then you have no knowledge of Mrs. Dane, whether she is a desirable acquaintance?

CANON BONSEY. A woman with such a face, and such a figure, and such a divine musician, cannot be an undesirable acquaintance. At the same time, as she is to take a stall at the bazaar, and the duchess is to open it, I should like to get this little matter cleared up. Our dear duchess is not a latitudinarian in these matters. What had we better do?

SIR DANIEL. You are the clergyman of the parish, and responsible for her introduction here. Oughtn't you to call on her and get to know her history?

CANON BONSEY. My dear Sir Daniel, what would happen? If there is anything shady in her past life she would omit to mention it. With my easy, ingenuous nature I should be a mere baby in her hands. No, I think this is a case where your legal experience might be of service, eh?

SIR DANIEL. If she were in the witness-box it might; but she isn't.

CANON BONSEY. Or, as it is essentially a woman's question, and as she is your guest, Lady Eastney, perhaps you might venture to gently—gently—

LADY EASTNEY. Invite a lady to dinner, and then ask her whether she is fit to mix with my guests?

CANON BONSEY. H'm! It's very awkward. What is to be done?

LAL *enters quickly. At the same moment* MRS. DANE *appears in conservatory behind a shrub, and gently moves towards centre, apparently much engaged with the plants.*

LAL [*quick, indignant*]. Lady Eastney, Mrs. Bulsom-Porter is circulating a most malicious story about Mrs. Dane. I beg you to inquire into the matter. [*To* SIR DANIEL.] Sir, you will help us?

SIR DANIEL [*in a hurried whisper*]. Not here, not now. We mustn't have a scene here. Hush!

[*Pointing to* MRS. DANE *in conservatory. She comes to centre door, enters, and comes down to them.* CANON BONSEY *goes off very quietly at the window.*

SIR DANIEL [*looking off*]. Ah, Lal, there is Sir Robert. Now we can get a word with him about the railway.

LAL. But sir—

SIR DANIEL [*in a low tone, very peremptory, and taking* LAL'*s arm*]. If you please, Lal. If you please.   [*Takes* LAL *off.*

LADY EASTNEY. They are serving a little supper for the late guests. Won't you come and have some?

MRS. DANE. No, thank you. I'm a little faint. I'll stay here.

[LADY EASTNEY *goes to drawing-room door, looks back, returns to* MRS. DANE.

LADY EASTNEY. Is anything the matter?

MRS. DANE. No! No! What should there be?

LADY EASTNEY [*with meaning*]. Can I be of any service to you?

MRS. DANE. In what way? [*Pause—the two women look at each other.*] I'm only a little faint. Please don't wait.

LADY EASTNEY. I'll send my maid to you. Let me know if there is anything further I can do.

[*Exit.* MRS. DANE *watches her off furtively; then, after a second or two, rises, creeps round at back to behind the curtain hanging over the door, peeps through, watching, listening, with drawn, frightened face. Laughter, buzz and hum of conversation strains of distant dance music.*

QUICK CURTAIN.

(*Nearly three weeks pass between Acts I and II.*)

ACT II

SCENE. *The same. Afternoon. Discover* JANET *seated on sofa at fancy work. She throws down the work, bursts into tears, then dries them, goes up to looking-glass on wall, stands looking at herself.*

JANET [*to herself in the glass*]. Ah, you poor coward! Aren't you ashamed of yourself? To be troubling about a man who has had the bad taste to throw you over? Have a better opinion of yourself, my poor Janet! There are as good fish in the sea as ever came out of it! And a better man than Lionel Carteret will come and take a fancy to your bonnie, bonnie face! So dry your eyes and bide a wee bit, my lassie.

Enter LADY EASTNEY. *She comes up to* JANET *and looks in her face.*

LADY EASTNEY. Janet.

JANET [*faces her, picks up her work*]. Auntie, I'm just sick of staying in England, and wasting my life in such trumpery as this, [*Shaking her work ferociously.*] so I'm going straight out to India!

LADY EASTNEY. India?

JANET. The Indian women are fearfully demoralized and ignorant; they don't know how to treat their babies, and when the poor wee mites come into the world they just perish by the score for the want of a sensible body to teach the mothers how to use them.

LADY EASTNEY. My dear Janet, if Providence has neglected to endow the Indian women with the common instincts of maternity, I question if you're quite qualified to supply the deficiency.

JANET. Mrs. Patterson is organizing a mission to go out there to doctor and civilize the poor creatures, so I'll just go out and help her to do for them.

LADY EASTNEY. Janet, I knew you were fretting—

JANET. What will I be fretting about?

LADY EASTNEY. Lionel Carteret.

JANET [*bursts into laughter*]. Oh, my poor little Auntie, [*Kissing her.*] I'd clean forgotten all about the man.

LADY EASTNEY. Janet, tell me the truth—

JANET. The truth is, Auntie, that if Mr. Lionel Carteret were lying down there on the floor and begging me to pick him up, I wouldn't take the trouble to stoop down to him, or to any other man-body in the world! There!

Enter ADAMS, *announcing* SIR DANIEL *and* MR. LIONEL CARTERET. *Enter* SIR DANIEL *and* LAL. *Exit* ADAMS.

SIR DANIEL [*to* JANET]. How d'ye-do, dear?

JANET. How-d'ye-do, Sir Daniel? How-d'ye-do, Mr. Carteret?

LAL [*confused*]. How-dy'e-do?

[JANET *takes up her hat which is lying on the settee, and goes off at back, swinging it with an affectation of carelessness.* LADY EASTNEY *has shaken hands with* SIR DANIEL *and* LAL.

SIR DANIEL. Well, how do we stand now?

LADY EASTNEY. The Bulsom-Porters are coming over to meet you, and I've asked the Canon to look in. They'll be here directly.   [*Taking out watch.*

SIR DANIEL. And then what are we to do?

LADY EASTNEY. Talk it over.

SIR DANIEL. Don't you think there's been quite enough talking it over the last fortnight?

LADY EASTNEY. We haven't had your assistance. Candidly, what is your opinion?

SIR DANIEL. I have none. I'm waiting for facts. Have you heard from Risby?

LADY EASTNEY. Not a word.

SIR DANIEL. What did you say to him?

LADY EASTNEY. I asked him to tell me in the strictest confidence all he knew about Mrs. Dane.

SIR DANIEL. And he hasn't replied?

LADY EASTNEY. It's only five days ago that I wrote. Perhaps my letter hasn't reached him.

SIR DANIEL. Rather strange, isn't it?

LAL [*indignantly*]. It's much more strange that everybody should be saying and believing the worst of an innocent woman without a shadow of proof.

SIR DANIEL. Without a shadow of proof that she is innocent.

LAL. I thought, sir, that English law assumed everybody to be innocent until he is proved to be guilty.

SIR DANIEL. I do not assume Mrs. Dane is guilty—or innocent. I only say I don't know.

LAL. Mrs. Dane has done exactly what an innocent woman naturally would do.

SIR DANIEL. Ah, pardon my inexperience, my dear Lal. What does an innocent woman naturally do?

LAL. She treats all slander with silent contempt. She knows her life will stand the test of inquiry, and therefore she doesn't stoop to answer calumny.

SIR DANIEL. Meantime everybody cuts her.

LAL. Lady Eastney, if you were in Mrs. Dane's place how would you have acted?

SIR DANIEL. Supposing you were innocent?

LADY EASTNEY [*after a little pause*]. I think I should have acted exactly as Mrs. Dane has done.

SIR DANIEL. Supposing you were guilty?

LADY EASTNEY. I don't know.

SIR DANIEL. If you were guilty don't you think you would try to act exactly in the same way? And whether you succeeded would depend, not so much upon your guilt or your innocence, as upon your self-control, and how far you had cultivated the woman's gift for acting. Guilt is the natural and necessary mimic of innocence as hypocrisy is the natural and necessary mimic of virtue; and just as nature is always ready to lend a mimic-skin of protection to any beast or bird or insect that needs its shelter, so she is always ready to lend the sheepskin of innocence to any criminal that's clever enough to draw it over him.

LAL. Criminal! You are speaking, sir, of the lady whom I have asked to be my wife.

SIR DANIEL. Not at all. I am speaking generally. For all I know, Mrs. Dane is the most innocent and virtuous lady in the world.

LAL. But you don't believe she is!

SIR DANIEL. I have no means of judging. The lady knows that her reputation is being torn to rags. She doesn't put the matter in her lawyer's hands. She avoids, or seems to avoid, meeting me; she gives you a few very vague details of her past life, and then wraps herself in a mantle of injured innocence—

LAL [very indignantly]. Injured innocence! I asked you for your help to clear the woman who is dearer to me than my life from a lying slander, and you insinuate that she is a criminal and a hypocrite! [Seizes his hat.] I will never again ask you for the smallest favour as long as I live. I give you back your name, and I take my own to offer it to her. Good-day, Sir Daniel Carteret.   [Going off.

LADY EASTNEY. Lionel! [He doesn't stop.] Lionel! [He half stops.] Lionel! [He stops.] You want Mrs. Dane's reputation to be cleared. Don't you think Sir Daniel is the best man in England to help you? For her sake don't quarrel with him. Don't throw over the best of fathers and the best of friends in a moment of temper. [Takes his hat from him.] Sir Daniel, I think you are a little hard on Mrs. Dane. Lionel doesn't want a legal machine to grind out the evidence. He wants a friend to stand by him and the woman he loves. Come, shake hands with him and promise you'll help him.

[She joins their hands.

SIR DANIEL. Forgive me, my dear boy. I didn't mean to wound you.

LAL. Forgive me, sir. I can't bear that anyone should speak ill of her.

LADY EASTNEY. And now let us put our heads together and set to work to do our best to clear her.

SIR DANIEL. Ah! How can we do that?

LAL. You soon cleared that poor governess who was accused of stealing the bracelet!

SIR DANIEL. Because she came to me and told me a plain, simple story which I was able to verify.

LADY EASTNEY. I'll write a note to Mrs. Dane and ask her to step over; then I'll advise her to tell her story to you and put herself entirely in your hands.

SIR DANIEL. That may be very unkind to her.

LADY EASTNEY. Why?

SIR DANIEL. For the past fortnight I have kept away from Mrs. Dane, I have tried to keep Lal away from her, because we have not a single fact to go upon. Risby, who is responsible for this story, doesn't answer your letter. Mrs. Dane herself keeps silence. Now suppose this story is true—[*Indignant gesture from* LAL.] My dear Lal, have patience! If it's false, we shall soon be able to demolish it and put Mrs. Dane right with the world. But suppose it's true; you force her hand, you make it impossible for her to hide it, and you give Mrs. Bulsom-Porter a public triumph over her. Don't you think it might be kinder to Mrs. Dane to wait?

LAL. No. Lady Eastney, will you write to Mrs. Dane and say that we all think she should stop these stories at once by coming over here and giving Sir Daniel the means of proving them false.

LADY EASTNEY [*seats herself at writing-table*]. After all, we only want to know the truth.

SIR DANIEL. You'll get it that way. Lal, if I take this story to pieces and find it false, you shall marry Mrs. Dane as soon as you please.

LAL. Thank you, sir.

SIR DANIEL. But—don't be angry with me—if I find it true, of course there's an end to everything between you and her?

LAL. Of course, sir.

Enter ADAMS, *announcing* CANON BONSEY. *Enter* CANON BONSEY. *He shakes hands with* SIR DANIEL *and* LAL. LADY EASTNEY *smiles and nods to* CANON *from writing-table.*

LADY EASTNEY. Adams, will you send this note to Mrs. Dane at once?

LAL. I'll take it myself, Lady Eastney.

[LAL *takes letter and goes off. Exit* ADAMS.

LADY EASTNEY [*shaking hands with* CANON]. I'm delighted you've come. Is there anything fresh?

CANON BONSEY. I met Bulsom-Porter this morning; he is most anxious to withdraw, or apologize, or do anything to smooth the matter over.

LADY EASTNEY. I saw Mrs. Bulsom-Porter yesterday, and I'm quite sure she will never withdraw anything that can damage the reputation of another woman. It would be a concession to immorality.

SIR DANIEL. You've not seen Mrs. Dane again, I suppose, Canon?

CANON BONSEY. No. I called ten days ago and dropped a hint that under the circumstances it would be advisable for her not to take a stall at the bazaar.

SIR DANIEL. Did she take the hint?

CANON BONSEY. No; somehow or other she managed to convince me that she was a very much ill-used woman, and I left her with the understanding that she should take the stall at the bazaar.

LADY EASTNEY. Then she will?

CANON BONSEY. Well, this morning I understand our dear duchess has got wind of the story, and is going to send for me, and mercilessly haul me over the coals; in fact, I hear she refuses to open the bazaar unless Mrs. Dane retires; so between these two dear ladies my peace of mind is likely to be rudely shaken, if not rent in twain. Such is my reward for twenty-five years' management of this parish on the principle of the widest toleration for everybody's views in doctrine, and everybody's practices in morals.

LADY EASTNEY. But you say Mrs. Dane convinced you that she was a very ill-used woman.

CANON BONSEY. She did. But then I was very willing to be convinced.

LADY EASTNEY. Did you think her manner was that of an innocent woman?

CANON BONSEY. So far as I could judge. But, dear Lady Eastney, I am the veriest amateur in dealing with your sex; and so far as your manner goes I wouldn't presume to say that any one of you could ever be guilty of anything. Eh, Sir Daniel?

SIR DANIEL. I never judge from manner alone. There is the confusion of guilt and the confusion of innocence; the brazen self-confidence of guilt and the serene self-confidence of innocence—I won't pretend I know which is which—except that sometimes a look, a gesture, a word, will give you a peep into the very soul of a man or woman, and you cry at once, 'This is certain guilt', or 'This is certain innocence'.

LADY EASTNEY. I wonder if we shall get such a peep to-day?

CANON BONSEY. How?

LADY EASTNEY. I've just written to ask Mrs. Dane to come on here and meet Sir Daniel and you and Mrs. Bulsom-Porter.

Enter ADAMS *announcing* MR. *and* MRS. BULSOM-PORTER. *Enter* MR. *and* MRS. BULSOM-PORTER. *Exit* ADAMS. *Handshakes and how-d'ye-dos exchanged.* SIR DANIEL *retires to a corner and watches.*

LADY EASTNEY [*cordially to* MRS. BULSOM-PORTER]. Now this is very charming of you. We shall be able to talk this little matter over before Mrs. Dane comes.

MRS. BULSOM-PORTER. I didn't understand that Mrs. Dane was to be present. [*Glancing sharply at* BULSOM-PORTER.] Of course Mr. Bulsom-Porter is pleased. He sees nothing objectionable in his wife meeting her.

BULSOM-PORTER. My dear, if you consider Mrs. Dane's company objectionable, pray don't stay. I don't think I shall come to much harm, so I'll risk it.

[MRS. BULSOM-PORTER *looks very indignantly at* BULSOM-PORTER.

LADY EASTNEY [*hurriedly*]. Of course you know that Mrs. Dane denies this story?

MRS. BULSOM-PORTER. Naturally she would. But I'm hourly expecting some very important information.

LADY EASTNEY. About Mrs. Dane?

MRS. BULSOM-PORTER. Yes. The messenger is now on his way from town, and I've directed him to be sent over from my house the moment he arrives, if you don't mind.

LADY EASTNEY. Certainly not. We only wish to get at the truth.

BULSOM-PORTER. I've heard nothing about this messenger. Who is he?

MRS. BULSOM-PORTER. That's my business for the present. I have taken this affair entirely into my own hands.

BULSOM-PORTER. The last time you took an affair into your own hands you involved me in a law-suit which cost me a thousand pounds.

MRS. BULSOM-PORTER. The hussy was guilty, but she made eyes at the jury. Of course they were men. What could you expect? They gave her damages.

BULSOM-PORTER. So would I, if it hadn't been coming out of my own pocket.

MRS. BULSOM-PORTER. On the whole the money was well spent. The matter was thoroughly ventilated, as I intend this shall be.

LADY EASTNEY. But my dear Mrs. Bulsom-Porter, you surely wish to find yourself mistaken in this story?

MRS. BULSOM-PORTER. Of course I should be very pleased to find myself mistaken, but my instincts tell me that I'm not; and my instincts in these cases are invariably right.

LADY EASTNEY. But have you nothing better than mere instincts to guide you?

MRS. BULSOM-PORTER. Yes. There is a curious expression on Mrs. Dane's face which exactly corresponds with that of a Miss Spooner—[*Glances sternly at* BULSOM-PORTER.] I need not pursue the story.

BULSOM-PORTER. There was no story, [*Sighs deeply.*] I regret to say.

MRS. BULSOM-PORTER [*very severely*]. You might have the good taste to leave your flippancies at home. If this woman is guilty, as I am convinced she is, I'm sure Canon Bonsey, as a clergyman, will own that I have rendered a very great service to Sunningwater society in not allowing the matter to rest.

CANON BONSEY. Quite true. Whenever it is necessary that any disagreeable scandal should be stirred up for the good of society, I'm very much obliged to those dear, good people who will kindly stir it up for me, and save me the trouble. And with regard to the present case, I hope you'll ask Sir Daniel to give you the benefit of his vast legal experience, and then—then it won't be necessary to stir it up any further, will it?

LADY EASTNEY. Sir Daniel will be only too pleased to give us his advice. Sir Daniel, why don't you come and help us?

SIR DANIEL [*rising, coming forward*]. Help you talk it over? Will you please give me one single fact, one single scrap of evidence to go upon, and I'll then join the fray on one side or the other, as the case may be? Mrs. Bulsom-Porter, didn't I hear you say that you had a messenger now on his way from town with some important information? Who is he?

MRS. BULSOM-PORTER. I'd rather not say.

SIR DANIEL. Where does he get the information?

MRS. BULSOM-PORTER. He has been over to Vienna on purpose.

SIR DANIEL. That sounds hopeful. What means has he of getting at the truth?

MRS. BULSOM-PORTER. Every means.

SIR DANIEL. Better and better! Surely you might tell us who this omniscient person is?

MRS. BULSOM-PORTER. When I saw that my husband was determined to shelter this woman, and prevent the truth from coming to light, I sent up to town for Mr. Fendick, the private detective—

BULSOM-PORTER [*startled*]. What!

MRS. BULSOM-PORTER. And instructed him to make all inquiries, no matter at what expense.

BULSOM-PORTER. What! Now please understand I entirely dissociate myself from your action.

MRS. BULSOM-PORTER. It's of no consequence. I can proceed alone.

Enter LAL.

BULSOM-PORTER. But my dear Henrietta—

LAL. Mrs. Dane is here. Shall I ask her to come in?

LADY EASTNEY. One moment, Lionel.

BULSOM-PORTER [*to* LAL]. Will you please ask Mrs. Dane if she will spare me a few minutes? I have an explanation to make to her.

[*Exit* LAL.

MRS. BULSOM-PORTER. If you have any explanation to make to that lady you will please make it in my presence.

LADY EASTNEY. Aren't we getting a little heated? I want to have a few words with Mrs. Dane alone—Ah!—

Enter MRS. DANE. *She is dressed very simply, is very quiet and self-possessed, and is followed by* LAL, *who stands at door. She bows all round.* SIR DANIEL *and* BULSOM-PORTER *return her bow cordially.*

MRS. DANE. I didn't quite understand your note, Lady Eastney, but you see I'm here.

LADY EASTNEY [*going to her, cordially shaking hands*]. I'm very glad you've come. I wanted a few minutes' talk with you. Won't you sit down? It's fearfully hot indoors. Suppose you all go down to the summer-house and I'll send you some cooling drinks, and come to you in a little while. Canon, will you see that Mrs. Bulsom-Porter is made comfortable?

CANON BONSEY. Delighted. How d'ye-do, my dear Mrs. Dane? [*Shaking hands.*] Then we'll await you in the summer-house. [*Going to* MRS. BULSOM-PORTER.] Allow me.

[SIR DANIEL *and* MRS. DANE *are watching each other furtively—he very searchingly, she quiet, self-possessed.* MRS. BULSOM-PORTER *waits a moment to see that her husband does not speak to* MRS. DANE, *then goes off with the* CANON.

BULSOM-PORTER [*confidentially to* SIR DANIEL]. I say, [*Draws him aside.*] how am I to stop my wife from dragging me into another confounded lawsuit?

SIR DANIEL. Ah! Come and talk it over.

[*Exeunt* SIR DANIEL *and* BULSOM-PORTER, SIR DANIEL *turning to glance slightly at* MRS. DANE *as he goes off.*

LADY EASTNEY. Lionel, will you find Adams and ask him to take tea and iced drinks to the summer-house?

[LAL *shakes hands with* LADY EASTNEY *in thankfulness for her consideration for* MRS. DANE *and goes off.*

LADY EASTNEY. Now, my dear Mrs. Dane, you know that I am your friend and Lionel's friend.

MRS. DANE. Yes.

LADY EASTNEY. And between ourselves I hate Mrs. Bulsom-Porter with the most ungodly, unchristian hatred. I'm only waiting for some tolerable excuse to get everybody in Sunningwater to cut her. Lionel has told you what she says of you?

MRS. DANE. He says that she is spreading some story about my being a Miss Hindemarsh. What is the use of taking any notice of such a tale?

LADY EASTNEY. You must take notice of it.

MRS. DANE. I have denied it.

LADY EASTNEY. You must do more than that. Lionel is waiting to make you his wife—

MRS. DANE. If he doesn't believe me I do not wish to bind him. [*Triumphantly.*] But he does believe me.

LADY EASTNEY. Yes, but Sir Daniel—

MRS. DANE. If Sir Daniel doesn't believe me what happiness can there be for me if I marry Mr. Carteret?

LADY EASTNEY. Then you mean to give him up? Is that right? Is it wise? Is it kind to Lionel? Then there are your other friends; we are all waiting to give this woman the lie and show her the door. If you don't defend yourself what are we to think?

MRS. DANE. You think I am an impostor.

LADY EASTNEY. No. I said to Sir Daniel a few minutes ago that I should have acted throughout as you have done—

MRS. DANE [*very gratefully*]. Thank you! Thank you!

LADY EASTNEY. Up to the present moment. There is a point at which it is prudent to neglect slander—if it's false. There is a point at which it is imprudent, impossible to neglect slander—unless it is true. You have reached that point. This story is being repeated everywhere. Why won't you trust yourself to Sir Daniel?

MRS. DANE. What does Sir Daniel propose to do?

LADY EASTNEY. To hear the story of your life, obtain the evidence for it, and then get Mrs. Bulsom-Porter to make you an ample apology.

MRS. DANE [*cunningly*]. I suppose Sir Daniel has no doubt he would be able to prove the story?

LADY EASTNEY. My dear Mrs. Dane, the cleverest lawyer of our generation! And he is only waiting one word from you to undertake your defence. If you refuse, what inference will everybody draw?

Enter LAL *hastily.*

LAL. Lady Eastney, what do you suppose Mrs. Bulsom-Porter has done? She has gone to Fendick, the private detective. [*A spasm of fright passes over* MRS. DANE'*s face, which is hidden from them.*] Did you know of it?

LADY EASTNEY. She said she was expecting some information this afternoon. I've told Mrs. Dane that she must meet this slander.

[MRS. DANE *has recovered from her fright and regained her self-assurance. After a moment's deliberation she takes an opened telegram from her pocket and gives it to* LADY EASTNEY.

MRS. DANE [*very quietly*]. Read that, Lady Eastney.

LADY EASTNEY. From whom?

MRS. DANE. From Mr. Risby.

LADY EASTNEY [*takes a telegram from envelope—it is on two sheets; reads*]. 'Lady Eastney writes me that Mrs. Bulsom-Porter repeats some absurd story about you. Am writing

Lady Eastney this post that I was quite mistaken in recognizing you. If any further trouble, let me know and will immediately set matter right. James Risby, Schweizerhof, Lucerne.' When did you get this?

MRS. DANE. Yesterday.

LADY EASTNEY. But this explains everything. Why didn't you show it us at once?   [*Rings bell.*

MRS. DANE. Why should I? You forget that you and all Sunningwater are very much concerned to know whether I'm this Miss Somebody. I have told you that I'm not, and you don't believe me. Why should I trouble any further?

Enter ADAMS.

LADY EASTNEY. Is the afternoon post in, Adams?

ADAMS. Not yet, my lady.

LADY EASTNEY. Bring my letters to me the moment they arrive.

ADAMS. Yes, my lady.   [*Exit.*

LAL. The thing is quite clear. Risby has made a mistake. May I show that telegram to my father?

MRS. DANE. No. Let Mrs. Bulsom-Porter repeat her slanders, and pay her detectives to repeat them. I shall not take the least notice of her.

LADY EASTNEY. You must! You owe it to Lionel to prove this story false. Let me show this telegram to Sir Daniel.

MRS. DANE [*after a pause*]. Very well. As you please.

LADY EASTNEY. We will very soon settle Mrs. Bulsom-Porter.   [*Exit.*

LAL [*lingering*]. My father has been asking for evidence. Now he has got it.

MRS. DANE. Yes. But suppose Sir Daniel cannot prove my innocence, suppose this story is still believed and we are parted after all, you will remember that I shall love you till my last breath, with all the love of my heart, with all that is best and truest in me?

LAL. Yes, but we shan't be parted. Come and tell my father everything.

MRS. DANE. That woman is there. I hate scenes of any kind.

LAL. Then I'll bring him to you.

[*She shows him a radiant, smiling face. He runs off. The moment he has gone she utters a sharp cry, followed by a long groan of despair, sits down on sofa with a white, drawn, haggard face, wringing her hands, staring in front of her. A pause. The door opening into drawing-room has been left open. Voices heard off.*]

ADAMS. What name did you say?

FENDICK. Fendick.

ADAMS. You say Mrs. Bulsom-Porter does expect you?

FENDICK. Yes. She left word at home I was to come on here to her.

ADAMS. I'll let her know you're here.

Enter ADAMS; *he crosses the room and goes off at window.* MRS. DANE *creeps up to door, looks through it, utters a little cry of alarm, and comes away. Enter* FENDICK, *an ordinary-looking, middle-class man about forty, clean-shaven.*

FENDICK. I beg pardon—[*Stops, seeing her.*] Oh!

MRS. DANE. Fendick! You, Fendick! You gave me some other name. Why did you come to my house a fortnight ago?

FENDICK. Well, you see, the fact is, I wanted to get a photograph of you in the way of business, and so I adopted the slight ruse of saying I was taking photographic views of the neighbourhood, and I asked you to give me an opportunity of taking a view from your garden.

MRS. DANE. Did you get a photograph of me?

FENDICK. My partner took two whilst I was chatting with you and taking off your attention. [*She shows great fright.*] I know it was rather shabby, but my profession has its shabby side.

MRS. DANE. What use have you made of the photograph?

FENDICK. Well, of course that's my business. There! [*Looks all round.*] You treated me very well that day—if it's any use to you to know, I've been over to Vienna for Mrs. Bulsom-Porter, and after a good deal of trouble I found a man over there that remembers Miss Hindemarsh, and can recognize her if necessary. I mustn't say any more.

MRS. DANE. Yes! You're a detective. I'll employ you. Name your own sum. I'll give you double, treble, ten times what she gives. You'll find some one that knows that I'm not this Miss Hindemarsh—not the least like her?

FENDICK. No, ma'am, I can't. Thank you all the same.

MRS. DANE [getting more frantic]. Yes! Yes! You must! I say you must! Don't ruin me! This man in Vienna? He doesn't know who and where I am now?

FENDICK. Not unless I bring him over.

MRS. DANE. But you won't! He won't recognize me. You've been to Vienna. Listen! Please understand from this time I employ you, and you shall be handsomely paid. There's nobody who recognizes me. I'm not in the least like that lady. You understand?

FENDICK. I can't do it. I can't, indeed. It might be found out.

MRS. DANE. It shan't be. How can it? Oh, how can I move you? I'll give you every farthing I have. Don't betray me! Don't betray me! It's everything to me—my happiness, my life, my all. Oh, don't ruin me! Hush! [She looks off at window, points him off, whispering as he goes.] You won't betray me?

[She comes back, with an immense effort regains her self-possession, takes a novel, and sits on sofa.

Enter LAL, followed by ADAMS, who crosses and goes off into drawing-room, leaving door open.

LAL. My father's coming. I made him promise to take up your case and fight it through.

MRS. DANE. How kind of him.

ADAMS [heard off. MRS. DANE listens, with great apprehension]. Mrs. Bulsom-Porter will be here in a minute if you will wait.

Enter SIR DANIEL and LADY EASTNEY.

LADY EASTNEY. Here is your champion. Tell him everything.

SIR DANIEL. If I can be of any service I shall be delighted.

ADAMS *re-enters and brings letter on tray to* LADY EASTNEY. *She takes it, reads it. Exit* ADAMS, *closing the door after him.*

MRS. DANE [*to* SIR DANIEL]. When I heard this story was being circulated I thought it would be better to take no notice and let it die a natural death. Don't you think I was wise?

SIR DANIEL. Very wise, if it had died a natural death. But you see it hasn't. So suppose we set to work and crush the life out of it, shall we?

MRS. DANE. Shan't I be trespassing upon you? Won't it be wasting your valuable time?

SIR DANIEL. I've no hobby but my profession, so it won't be a waste of time to spend a few hours in my long vacation to free you from an unjust suspicion. [LAL *comes up to them.*] I said I had no hobby but my profession. That isn't true. This young fellow [*Taking* LAL's *arm affectionately.*] is another very dear hobby of mine. You, too, are concerned for his happiness?

[*Watching her very closely.*

MRS. DANE. Yes, indeed.

SIR DANIEL [*watching her keenly*]. And therefore you wish me to sift this affair thoroughly? [*She is going to speak.*] Knowing that the happiness of his whole life is staked on the result?

MRS. DANE. I only wish for his happiness—not my own. Do just as you please.

SIR DANIEL. Then you place yourself entirely in my hands?

MRS. DANE. Yes; most willingly. How can I thank you?

SIR DANIEL. Wait till I deserve your thanks.

LADY EASTNEY [*who has been reading the letter*]. Really, the whole affair is too absurdly simple.

Enter MRS. BULSOM-PORTER *at window, followed by* BULSOM-PORTER *and* CANON BONSEY.

MRS. BULSOM-PORTER. Lady Eastney, there's a man waiting to see me. Will you allow me?

LADY EASTNEY. Certainly. I believe he is in the next room, but [*Stopping her.*] I think you should hear this letter first. It is from your nephew, Mr. Risby. 'Dear Lady Eastney, I have received your letter. It is quite true that at the first glance I thought I recognized in Mrs. Dane a lady whom I had previously met, and I casually mentioned the fact to my aunt, Mrs. Bulsom-Porter. But on seeing Mrs. Dane a second time I discovered my mistake, and I told Mrs. Bulsom-Porter of my error. Will you express my sincere regrets to Mrs. Dane, and will you assure anyone who may revive the story that it is utterly false.' What more do we want? [*Hands the letter to* SIR DANIEL, *who reads it carefully.* LADY EASTNEY *then turns to* MRS. BULSOM-PORTER.] Surely that is enough, and you will be only too glad to own to Mrs. Dane that you're mistaken.

MRS. BULSOM-PORTER [*a little taken aback*]. I don't know. I should like to hear what Fendick has to say.

SIR DANIEL [*suddenly, as if struck with an idea*]. One moment. Mrs. Dane has already placed herself in my hands. Mrs. Bulsom-Porter, may I offer you my services?

MRS. BULSOM-PORTER. For what purpose?

SIR DANIEL. To get at the truth. You have circulated a story which from this letter seems to be quite false. Your husband has asked me to use my influence to prevent the very disagreeable consequences which are likely to follow. Will you allow me to call in Mr. Fendick and ask him a few questions?

MRS. BULSOM-PORTER. Well, I—

BULSOM-PORTER. Yes, if you please, Sir Daniel. I shall be guided entirely by you.

SIR DANIEL. Lady Eastney, you will permit me. [LADY EASTNEY *nods assent.* SIR DANIEL *goes to door.*] Mr. Fendick!

FENDICK *enters.*

SIR DANIEL. You've been to Vienna lately?

FENDICK. Yes, sir.

SIR DANIEL. To ask certain questions about a lady who formerly lived there, a Miss Hindemarsh?

FENDICK. Yes, sir.

SIR DANIEL. What are the results of your inquiries?

FENDICK. Well, sir, I'm not at liberty to say, as you're not employing me.

SIR DANIEL. Mrs. Bulsom-Porter wishes you to speak.

MRS. BULSOM-PORTER. Will you please tell us all that you've found out in Vienna?

FENDICK. In respect of what, ma'am?

SIR DANIEL. Perhaps I'd better put a direct question. Is Miss Hindemarsh identical with a lady who is now living in this neighbourhood?

FENDICK. This neighbourhood?

SIR DANIEL. Is Miss Hindemarsh identical with a lady who is now in this room? [*Turning to* MRS. DANE.] Is this lady Miss Hindemarsh?

FENDICK. No, sir.

SIR DANIEL [*very searchingly*]. You're quite sure?

FENDICK. Quite sure, sir.

SIR DANIEL. You have trustworthy evidence that she is not Miss Hindemarsh?

FENDICK. Yes, sir.

SIR DANIEL. What evidence have you?

FENDICK [*producing photograph*]. I took this portrait of Mrs. Dane over to Vienna, and the parties over there that remember Miss Hindemarsh say distinctly that this isn't the lady.

SIR DANIEL. She doesn't resemble Miss Hindemarsh?

FENDICK. No, sir. Not in the least like her.

SIR DANIEL. Thank you. We shall want fuller information, but that will do for the present. [*Exit* FENDICK. *To* MRS. BULSOM-PORTER.] I'm afraid you've committed yourself very deeply. On Mrs. Dane's behalf I shall have to insist that you withdraw this story without the least reserve.

MRS. BULSOM-PORTER. In what way?

SIR DANIEL. May I suggest a form? If you will allow me I will draw it out and you can sign it before leaving the room.

[SIR DANIEL *sits down to write.*

CANON BONSEY [*coming up to* MRS. DANE]. I congratulate you. [*Shaking hands, looking round.*] I think we are all to be congratulated. You upon the pleasant termination to this very unpleasant affair; myself upon the restoration of peace to this idyllic neighbourhood; and Mrs. Bulsom-Porter for having stirred up this matter so vigorously, and to an issue which, I am sure, must be as gratifying to her as it was evidently unexpected. [*Smiling on* MRS. BULSOM-PORTER.

BULSOM-PORTER. I hope Mrs. Dane will allow me to offer her my sincere regrets.

MRS. DANE. Thank you. I was so sorry that I was not at home the other day when you called. You will forgive me for not answering your note?

MRS. BULSOM-PORTER. Your note? You've been making calls and leaving notes on—

BULSOM-PORTER. For heaven's sake keep your hysterics till you get home.

SIR DANIEL [*having written, comes to* MRS. BULSOM-PORTER]. Will you kindly read it over and sign it?

MRS. BULSOM-PORTER [*glancing at note*]. But this is a public apology!

SIR DANIEL. I have made it as agreeable as I could.

MRS. BULSOM-PORTER. A public apology! [*Again looks at it.*] No. I'm quite sure from my nephew's manner that he was concealing something. I shall not apologize or withdraw anything until I've made further inquiries.

[*She is about to tear up the paper.*

SIR DANIEL [*stops her very quietly*]. Pardon me. Don't tear that. [*To* LADY EASTNEY.] Where is Mr. Risby now?

LADY EASTNEY. At the Schweizerhof, Lucerne.

SIR DANIEL. To-day is Saturday. We can get him back next week. [*To* MRS. BULSOM-PORTER.] You have slandered an innocent lady without the least justification. Take that paper home, think the matter over, and—will you accept a piece of advice from an old lawyer?—gratis—let me have it signed and witnessed by next Saturday. The alternative will be very troublesome, very humiliating to you, and terribly expensive —to your husband. [*Gesture of despair from* BULSOM-PORTER.] Take it home. Let me have it signed and witnessed by next Saturday.

MRS. DANE. How good of you!

> LADY EASTNEY *has rung the bell.* ADAMS *enters.*

LADY EASTNEY. The door, Adams.

> [MRS. BULSOM-PORTER, *much ruffled, rises and goes off, giving* MRS. DANE *an indignant look as she passes.* MR. BULSOM-PORTER *follows his wife off.*

CURTAIN.

Four days pass between Acts II and III.

ACT III

SCENE. *Library at* SIR DANIEL CARTERET's, *Sunningwater.
A cosy room in a modern Queen Anne red-brick house. At the back is
a fireplace with a looking-glass in the overmantel. On the right a
door leading into a passage. On the left windows opening upon a
garden. A large flat-topped writing-table down stage on the right
side. A sofa down stage left. Book-shelves all round the room.*

Time: The following Wednesday afternoon. Discover SIR DANIEL,
looking in the glass on book-case L., *arranging a flower in his
button-hole, regarding himself critically.*

Enter WILSON *announcing* LADY EASTNEY. *Enter* LADY
EASTNEY. *Exit* WILSON.

LADY EASTNEY [*shaking hands*]. You're busy?

SIR DANIEL. Yes; trying to persuade myself I am forty—solely
on your account.

LADY EASTNEY. That's not necessary. I like you well enough
as you are.

SIR DANIEL [*tenderly*]. Give me the best proof of that.

LADY EASTNEY. I have. I'm here a quarter of an hour before
my time.

SIR DANIEL. You couldn't be that in my house.

LADY EASTNEY. How are matters going with Mrs. Dane?

SIR DANIEL. Splendidly. [*Going up to writing-table; taking up
two sheets of foolscap, closely written over in a lady's hand.*] She
has given me a detailed history of her whole life. She accounts
for every moment from her childhood.

LADY EASTNEY. Has Mr. Fendick sent his evidence?

SIR DANIEL. Yes, it came this morning. That's quite satisfactory too.   [*Taking up another paper from table.*

LADY EASTNEY. And Mr. Risby?

SIR DANIEL. He's coming specially from Lucerne to put
matters right. I expect him almost every moment, and

Fendick is also running down from town for a little conference, so to-night I shall have all the threads of the case in my hands, and then—

LADY EASTNEY. Then?

SIR DANIEL. Then I shall be able to talk to Mrs. Bulsom-Porter.

LADY EASTNEY. I'm delighted. The whole neighbourhood is still in a perfect fever over the affair. Nothing else is talked about.

SIR DANIEL. I wish there wasn't quite so much gossip about it.

LADY EASTNEY. My dear Sir Daniel, we live in a residential neighbourhood in a wicked world, and what possible occupation is there for us poor women except to discuss scandal, or—to create it? The duchess is going to make an important call on you this afternoon.

SIR DANIEL. Why?

LADY EASTNEY. She's very much interested in Mrs. Dane's affair, and wants to know all about it. We shall find the duchess a useful ally.

SIR DANIEL [handling the foolscap]. We shall need no ally, except the truth.

LADY EASTNEY [smiling]. Won't you? The truth is all very well, Sir Daniel, but if I had to live down a scandal, I'd rather have a duchess on my side.

LAL enters at window.

LAL. How d'ye do, Lady Eastney?

LADY EASTNEY. How d'ye do?   [Shaking hands.

LAL. Risby hasn't turned up yet?

SIR DANIEL. No, I expect him very soon. You haven't brought Mrs. Dane?

LAL. No. She has thought of some more particulars of her history, and is writing them out for you.

SIR DANIEL. Go back and tell her not to trouble any further, and ask her to be here to meet Risby in [Taking out watch.] ten minutes.

LAL. All right. Lady Eastney, I can't thank you enough.

LADY EASTNEY. What for?

LAL. For helping us to beat down these horrible lies.

LADY EASTNEY. My dear Lal, I feel very strongly about it, and I shan't rest till I've worked the whole neighbourhood into a frenzy of virtuous sympathy for Mrs. Dane, and a frenzy of virtuous indignation against Mrs. Bulsom-Porter. Give my love to Mrs. Dane, and tell her that, will you?

LAL. God bless you! Then I'll go and fetch Lucy, sir?

SIR DANIEL [*who has been studying* MRS. DANE*'s foolscap paper*]. Yes. Bring her at once.

[*Exit* LAL *at window with a bright look of gratitude to* LADY EASTNEY.

LADY EASTNEY. You're quite reconciled to their engagement?

SIR DANIEL. Yes. I find I'm beginning to like her very much. I think the boy will be happy with her.

LADY EASTNEY. You seem to take a greater interest in Lionel's love-affairs than you do in your own.

SIR DANIEL. Ah no! You shouldn't say that. But you have discouraged me so often—

LADY EASTNEY. I, discouraged you? Why, I've encouraged you to propose to me I don't know how many times.

SIR DANIEL. Give me a little encouragement now.

LADY EASTNEY. I am a woman. I am twenty-eight. My first essay in marriage was not a conspicuous success. On the other hand, it was not a disastrous failure. Altogether I'm quite willing to make a fresh experiment. But, on the other hand, I'm quite happy in my present state. It has very great advantages. I shall need a very great deal of wooing before I am induced to change it. Indeed, on second thoughts why should I change it at all?

SIR DANIEL. I wouldn't have you change it, except for a happier one.

LADY EASTNEY. I won't, if I can help it. But there's the rub. I like you very much, but, honestly, I don't love you. At least, [*Looking him up and down critically.*] I don't think I do. But there again, I'm open to persuasion.

SIR DANIEL. Give me the benefit of the doubt.

LADY EASTNEY. I will—and say 'No'.

SIR DANIEL. 'No'?

LADY EASTNEY. If I say 'Yes' how can I be sure that Mr. Somebody else won't come along and make me sorry all my life that I didn't say 'No'?

SIR DANIEL. Is Mr. Somebody else likely to come?

LADY EASTNEY. How can I tell? He's always hanging about just round the corner, and if I married you, and you neglected me, or were unkind, I'm sure he'd turn up, and I do believe I should listen to the wretch, and then—heigho!

SIR DANIEL. Be my wife and if Mr. Somebody else ever wins a word, or a look, or a thought from you, I'll own it's my fault and I'll forgive him and you too.

LADY EASTNEY [*looks up at him*]. You know I shall end by accepting you.

SIR DANIEL. I'm sure you will.

LADY EASTNEY. Then I'm sure I won't. At least not until—

SIR DANIEL. Not until when?

LADY EASTNEY. Not until I've made up my mind. I want to be persuaded, I want to be wooed. I want you to see in me a thousand more perfections than ever a woman had, and value me a thousand times more than ever a woman was valued.

SIR DANIEL. I couldn't value you more than I do.

LADY EASTNEY [*shakes her head and smiles*]. It won't do! It won't do! With every wish in the world to oblige you, I really cannot sell my liberty at your present quotations.

Enter WILSON *announcing* MISS COLQUHOUN. *Enter* JANET. *Exit* WILSON.

JANET. How d'ye do, Sir Daniel?

SIR DANIEL [*shakes hands*]. How are you, dear?

JANET. Auntie, Mrs. Patterson has just come over to see you about her mission to the Indian women. Can you spare her just a few minutes?

LADY EASTNEY. A few minutes? My dear child, Mrs. Patterson is a woman with a mission, and it takes years to persuade people out of that folly.

Enter LAL *at window.*

LAL. I've brought Lucy, sir. She's here—

[*Stops, seeing* JANET.

JANET. Auntie, you will let Mrs. Patterson take me away from England?

LADY EASTNEY. I'll come and talk it over with her, dear. [*Puts* JANET *off at door, which has been left open. To* SIR DANIEL.] I'll come back by-and-by to see how everything goes with Mrs. Dane.

[*Exit* LADY EASTNEY. *He closes the door after her, and goes up to writing-table, takes up* MRS. DANE'*s and* FENDICK'*s notes. Enter* MRS. DANE *and* LAL *at window. She has a large blue envelope in her hand, partly written over.*

MRS. DANE. How d'ye do, Sir Daniel?

SIR DANIEL [*shaking hands very cordially*]. How d'ye do?

MRS. DANE. Have you read my statement?

SIR DANIEL. Every word. I congratulate you.

MRS. DANE. On what?

SIR DANIEL. On having told a perfectly plain, straightforward story, in a perfectly plain, straightforward way.

MRS. DANE. I only put down what I knew and felt, just as it came to me. I've jotted down a few more notes.

[*Taking out of the envelope another sheet of foolscap, which is partly written over.*

SIR DANIEL [*taking sheet*]. You've already given me all I want.

MRS. DANE. Tell me what else I can do.

SIR DANIEL [*takes her hands, very quietly and tenderly*]. Leave yourself in my hands, and await the result with perfect confidence.

Enter WILSON, *announcing* MR. RISBY. *Enter* RISBY. *Exit*
WILSON.

MRS. DANE [*rather quickly and eagerly*]. Oh, Mr. Risby, how
d'ye do?

> [RISBY *is a little taken aback; she gives him a significant
> glance.*

RISBY. Ah, my dear Mrs. Dane! [*Shakes hands very cordially
with her, then goes to* SIR DANIEL.] Sir Daniel!

> [*Shakes hands with* SIR DANIEL.

SIR DANIEL. How are you?

RISBY. Lionel!   [*Shaking hands with* LAL.

LAL. How d'ye do?

RISBY [*to* SIR DANIEL]. You got my wire?

SIR DANIEL. Yes. I'm really sorry to drag you half across
Europe—

RISBY. Half across Europe? Mrs. Dane may be quite sure that
I would willingly be dragged half across the celestial spaces,
if I can only repair my absurd mistake. [*Glancing at* LAL.] I
suppose I may speak quite freely—

SIR DANIEL. Oh, yes. Lionel is to marry Mrs. Dane when we
have cleared this up.

RISBY. Indeed! [*Goes to* LAL.] My congratulations—and to
Mrs. Dane. That makes it all the more necessary that I
should put matters right. Now tell me what can I do?

SIR DANIEL. You told Mrs. Bulsom-Porter that Mrs. Dane
was in reality Miss Felicia Hindemarsh?

RISBY. Yes. I was misled by a certain general resemblance on
seeing Mrs. Dane at some distance. When I got quite close
to her I saw that I had made a horrible blunder.

SIR DANIEL. Of course you withdraw the statement?

RISBY. Utterly and entirely, with a thousand apologies.

SIR DANIEL. And suppose we have to bring the matter into
court?

> [MRS. DANE *watches* RISBY *anxiously*.

RISBY. Will that be necessary?

SIR DANIEL. I hope not. I think not. But we must be prepared. We should need your evidence.

RISBY. Of course—if I'm in England. But I expect to make a very extended tour, and might be absent for a year or two.

SIR DANIEL. Then we must take your evidence before you start.

RISBY. Certainly. But you'll keep it out of court, won't you?

SIR DANIEL. I shall do my best. But we shall want you to say that this lady is not Felicia Hindemarsh, whom you knew in Vienna.

RISBY. By all means. But before I leave Sunningwater I'll go over to Auntie and try again to drive that fact into her comprehension.

SIR DANIEL. That might help us.

RISBY. I'll go at once.   [*Takes up his hat.*

Enter WILSON.

WILSON. Her Grace has called, Sir Daniel. I've shown her into the drawing-room.

SIR DANIEL. Very well, Wilson. Tell Her Grace I'll be there in a moment.

[*Exit* WILSON.

RISBY. Is there anything further that you wish to know?

SIR DANIEL. I think not. When do you leave England?

RISBY. In a day or two—as soon as I can get away.

SIR DANIEL. I've given Mrs. Bulsom-Porter till Saturday to choose between a lawsuit and an apology. Can you stay till after then?

RISBY. Certainly. I'll hold myself at your disposal till Monday night. The Senior Varsity will find me till then.

SIR DANIEL. Very well.

RISBY. Good-bye, if all goes well and I don't see you again.

SIR DANIEL. Good-bye. [*Shakes hands with* RISBY—*turns to* MRS. DANE.] You'll wait here, won't you? I expect Fendick every moment. I must go and get rid of this bothering old woman—

MRS. DANE. I understand she has come to make inquiries about me?

P

SIR DANIEL. Yes, I believe. I shall be able to set her mind at rest.   [*Exit.*

MRS. DANE [*to* RISBY]. It was so good of you to come and help us—

RISBY. Surely I could do no less.

MRS. DANE. Thank you so much. [*Suddenly.*] Lionel—

LAL. Yes?

MRS. DANE. I've left my keys in my escritoire. And it's open. There are some letters of yours—I wouldn't like them to be read. Would you mind running across and locking it, and bringing me the keys?

LAL. Yes, if you wish. I shall see you again, Risby?

RISBY. Yes, I daresay.

> [*Exit* LAL *at window. They both watch him off. She then turns to* RISBY *in a burst of gratitude, wrings his hands.*

MRS. DANE. Thank you, with all my heart!

RISBY. Hush! Take care!   [*Looks round warningly.*

MRS. DANE. Sir Daniel seems to be quite satisfied—

RISBY. Yes, I think I've pulled you through so far, but I've gone as far as it's safe to go—perhaps farther. But [*Very emphatically.*] whatever you do, you must keep Sir Daniel from bringing it into court.

MRS. DANE. You think everything would come out?

RISBY. I fear so. This history of your life that you've given to Sir Daniel?

MRS. DANE. Yes?

RISBY. He has read it?

MRS. DANE. Yes, and he's quite satisfied. He says it's perfectly plain and straightforward. Naturally it would be, as I knew Lucy's life almost as well as I know my own.

RISBY. And she was really Mrs. Dane?

MRS. DANE. Yes; when she died I took her name and became her.

RISBY. And you think you can carry it out to the end?

MRS. DANE. Yes; I think I can now I've begun. I must! I must!
Why do you look at me like that? You think I'm a horrid
creature—you despise me?

RISBY. No, no—

MRS. DANE. Yes, you do, I can see you do! Don't you think
I despise myself? Do you think I'd do all this, if I could help
myself, if there were any other way out of it? But I don't
want you to despise me—

RISBY. Believe me, I am only sorry, deeply sorry for you. May
I say one word—Lionel?

MRS. DANE. Well?

RISBY. Don't you think it would be better to tell him—safer?

MRS. DANE. I can't now. He loves me and believes in me.

RISBY. Good-bye. [*Offers hand.*

MRS. DANE [*again seizes his hand—wrings it with gratitude*].
Thanks! Thanks! This has shown me how good and true a
friend a man can be to a woman!

RISBY [*retaining her hand*]. I've been awfully puzzled what to do.
When I called on you this morning I came to tell you to face
the worst, that it would be impossible for me to hide the
truth from Sir Daniel—

MRS. DANE. But you did!

RISBY. Yes. I'm not a very soft-hearted chap, but when I saw
that tear, I felt I couldn't round on you. I hope I've played
the game fairly.

MRS. DANE. Fairly? Most generously, to me.

RISBY. And I hope not unfairly to Lionel.

MRS. DANE. I'll make him the best and truest wife that ever
lived. You believe that?

RISBY. Yes, I believe you will. Good-bye. [*Kisses her hand, drops
it, looks at her.*] After all, it isn't always the good women who
are the best for us rascals.

Enter WILSON, *showing in* FENDICK. MRS. DANE *shows very
slight confusion, and a look is exchanged between her and* FENDICK,
which RISBY *notices.*

WILSON. Sir Daniel is engaged for a minute, but he told me to
tell you to wait.

FENDICK. All right. 'No hurry', tell Sir Daniel.

[*Exit* WILSON.

RISBY. Good-bye.

[*She shakes his hand warmly. Exit* RISBY.

MRS. DANE. Good morning.

FENDICK. Good morning.

MRS. DANE. Anything new since I saw you last night?

FENDICK. No. You're sure you can pull this cousin business off? Got all your dates and facts at your finger's ends?

MRS. DANE. Yes. We lived together all our lives except when I was a governess.

FENDICK. That's the time as you've got to be careful about. As I told you last night, I rummaged about pretty well amongst the yokels at Tawhampton, and so far as I can gather I don't think there's the requisite intelligence in Tawhampton to say that you aren't Lucy Allen. Especially as there was a likeness between you and your cousin.

MRS. DANE. Yes; we were the same height, and the same complexion.

FENDICK. Then you went as pupil teacher to Eastbourne?

MRS. DANE. Yes.

FENDICK. Ware off Eastbourne. The old dowager at the school would spot you at once. And I've got to mind my p's and q's about the concierge at Vienna—

MRS. DANE. But you say there isn't a concierge.

FENDICK. I fancy I can lay my hands on an old Italian friend, who'll pass at a pinch. But I tell you this, if I get out of this business with clean boots I'll take good care I don't land myself in a dirty mess like this a second time.

MRS. DANE. I'm sorry you should call it that. You know that I'm quite willing you should make any charge—

FENDICK. It isn't the money. If I'd known what I was letting myself in for I wouldn't have done it for a thousand pounds. But you worked on my feelings, so that before I knew what I was saying I'd said you weren't the woman, and being a bit short-sighted I didn't recognize Sir Daniel in his private get-up. Hush!

[*They compose themselves.*

SIR DANIEL *enters.*

SIR DANIEL. Ah, Mr. Fendick, how d'ye do?

[*Goes up to writing-table and takes up* FENDICK'*s notes.*

FENDICK. How d'ye do, Sir Daniel? I wasn't aware when I met you at Lady Eastney's the other day that I had the pleasure and honour of addressing the famous judge, Sir Daniel Carteret.

SIR DANIEL. No, Mr. Fendick? There I had the advantage of you, for I was aware I was addressing Mr. Fendick, the famous detective.

FENDICK. Well, our professions are, in a manner of speaking, somewhat similar, aren't they?

SIR DANIEL. Not similar, Mr. Fendick. Say co-operative, mutually assistant and necessary to each other. You elicit the truth, I deal with it—when I get it. You catch the hare—I cook him.

FENDICK. Him or her as the case may be.

SIR DANIEL. Him or her as the case may be. Well, I don't think it will take long to hunt this hare down, eh?

FENDICK. No, Sir Daniel, I think not. You received my copy of the evidence I obtained in Vienna?

SIR DANIEL [*handling* FENDICK'*s notes*]. Yes, it came this morning. It seems very satisfactory.

FENDICK. Most satisfactory, I thought, Sir Daniel.

SIR DANIEL. You rely chiefly upon the evidence of this concierge, I see. He is perfectly clear in his remembrance of Miss Hindemarsh?

FENDICK. Perfectly clear.

SIR DANIEL [*taking up a photograph*]. And from this photograph of Mrs. Dane that you gave me the other day, which, by the way, is a very good one—

FENDICK. Taken by my partner, Burton.

SIR DANIEL. The concierge is prepared to swear that Mrs. Dane is not Miss Hindemarsh?

FENDICK. Yes, Sir Daniel.

SIR DANIEL. Have you sent Mrs. Bulsom-Porter a copy of this evidence?

FENDICK. No, Sir Daniel. When I called on her the other day, after seeing you at Lady Eastney's, she rowed me like a pickpocket—

SIR DANIEL. What for?

FENDICK. She said she'd sent me to Vienna to procure evidence of Mrs. Dane's guilt, instead of which I'd gone and proved her innocence, with other remarks quite *infra dig.* to me and my character.

SIR DANIEL. The woman must be mad!

FENDICK. That's what I say—mad on the rampage for social purity.

SIR DANIEL. I'll see Mr. Bulsom-Porter and explain to him how the matter stands.

FENDICK. Then I may consider the job concluded so far as I am concerned?

SIR DANIEL. Yes, I think so. We know where to find you.

FENDICK. Fifty-four Buckingham Street. Telegraphic address, Sharpshot, London. Good-day to you, Sir Daniel. Good-day to you, ma'am. Glad this little affair has ended so pleasantly for all parties.

MRS. DANE. Good-day, Mr. Fendick. Thank you for the trouble you have taken.

FENDICK. Don't name it, ma'am. I congratulate you heartily, I assure you.   [*Exit.*

SIR DANIEL. You must let me congratulate you too.

MRS. DANE. You think it is all ended? I'm free from this scandal at last?

SIR DANIEL. Yes. I have something to say to you.

MRS. DANE. Yes?

SIR DANIEL. Now that we may consider it over, I don't mind owning that at first I thought Mrs. Bulsom-Porter's tale was true.

MRS. DANE. But you don't now? You believe in me? You think that I am worthy of Lionel?

SIR DANIEL. Yes, and it gives me the greatest pleasure, my dear Lucy, to welcome you into my family as my daughter.

[*He kisses her forehead. She bursts into a little fit of tears.*

MRS. DANE. Oh! I can't help it! Don't look at me please.

SIR DANIEL. Cry away! Cry away! I'll go into the next room and send a little note to Bulsom-Porter. Between us I daresay we can put it all straight.   [*Exit.*

MRS. DANE [*left alone, she clasps her hands in gratitude and breathes out*]. I thank Thee! I thank Thee! All my life shall show my gratitude!

[*She continues sobbing. After some moments* SIR DANIEL *re-enters with an open sheet of note-paper on which he has begun to write a letter.*

SIR DANIEL. By the way, my dear Lucy, I've been thinking—

[*She turns around and he sees she is still crying.*

MRS. DANE. Isn't it foolish of me? This horrible thing has been hanging over me for weeks, and the relief seems too great. There! It's all over now! [*Looks up at him radiantly.*] Yes— you've been thinking—what?

SIR DANIEL. I've been thinking what you should do. Taw-hampton is only six hours by rail—

MRS. DANE. Well?

SIR DANIEL. You lived there, you say, till you were fifteen?

MRS. DANE. Yes, and then my father and mother took me to Canada.

SIR DANIEL. You had no other home in your childhood?

MRS. DANE. No.

SIR DANIEL. Have you been there since your return to England?

MRS. DANE. No. It's an out-of-the-way place, and I've had no occasion to go.

SIR DANIEL. Some of your childhood's friends must be living there still?

MRS. DANE. Yes, I daresay.

SIR DANIEL. You shall go down there to-morrow and hunt up some of your old friends who remember you as Lucy Allen.

MRS. DANE. Yes, that's a splendid idea. I hadn't thought of that. [*Cunningly.*] But suppose I'm not able to find anybody at Tawhampton who can positively identify me, you have still sufficient evidence to prove who I am?

SIR DANIEL. I have no evidence whatever to prove who you are. I have Risby's and Fendick's evidence to prove that you are not Felicia Hindemarsh.

MRS. DANE. Isn't that enough?

SIR DANIEL. Not if the matter comes into court. We shall then need evidence to prove that you are Lucy Dane, *née* Allen, with a history that can be traced.

MRS. DANE. I see. This doesn't mean that I'm to be dragged all through this horrible scandal again?

SIR DANIEL. No. I think not. Bulsom-Porter is sure to meet the matter with an apology. Still, I think you should go to Tawhampton.

MRS. DANE. I'm quite willing.

SIR DANIEL. Did you keep up any correspondence with anyone there after you left?

MRS. DANE. Yes, for a little while, but it soon ceased.

SIR DANIEL. Whom did you write to?

MRS. DANE. Mrs. Garton was one—

SIR DANIEL. You don't know if she is living there still?

MRS. DANE. No. She was over sixty then—

SIR DANIEL. Do you remember anybody else? [*No reply.*] I have a topographical dictionary somewhere. [*Looking along bookshelves.*] That might help us, if I can put my hands on it. [*Going along the bookshelves; she watches him furtively and with great anxiety.*] It used to be somewhere on these shelves. I wonder what has become of it. Who was the parson of the place?

MRS. DANE. There were several curates. Mr. Inskip; he was a very stout little man with spectacles; he would remember me, and Mr. Charlesworth—

SIR DANIEL. Have you any idea where either of them is to be found?

MRS. DANE. No.

SIR DANIEL. Who taught you? Did you go to school?

MRS. DANE. No. We had governesses.

SIR DANIEL. 'We'? You say you were an only child. Who's 'we'?

MRS. DANE. My cousin and I.

SIR DANIEL. Your cousin? [*Turns over the foolscap sheets.*] Your cousin? A girl?

MRS. DANE. Yes.

SIR DANIEL [*running hastily over the sheets*]. You haven't mentioned her. Where is she now?

MRS. DANE. I don't know. She left Tawhampton before I did.

SIR DANIEL. Where did she go?

MRS. DANE. She took a situation as governess, I think.

SIR DANIEL. Did she live with you in Tawhampton?

MRS. DANE. No. Her father lived in the village, and she used to come to our house to be taught.

SIR DANIEL [*running over the notes*]. You haven't mentioned her father?

MRS. DANE. No. I didn't see what he had to do with my story. He died before I left the village.

SIR DANIEL. What was your cousin's name?

MRS. DANE [*after a slight pause*]. Annie.

SIR DANIEL. Annie what?

MRS. DANE. Annie Allen.

SIR DANIEL. And you have completely lost sight of her?

MRS. DANE. Yes. Are there any other questions you wish to ask me?

SIR DANIEL. No. I think not.

Q

MRS. DANE. Then I'll go back home and rest. My head is ready to split. Thank you for believing in me. You know Lionel will be happy with me?

SIR DANIEL. I feel sure he will. [*Going with her to the window. As he comes up to the book-case his eye lights on volumes of the topographical dictionary.*] Ah! Here's the very thing.

MRS. DANE. What?

SIR DANIEL [*taking a volume out of the shelf*]. Topographical dictionary of England and Wales. [*Looking along the volumes.*] Volume one, Devonshire. Let's see what it has to say about Tawhampton. [*Taking the volume to table and turning over the leaves—she watches him with great anxiety.*] Devonshire— Devonshire—Tawhampton—[*Reading from the book.*] Tawhampton is a parish and village—picturesquely situated— mid-division of the county—Wonford hundred—rural deanery of Crockenwell—Archdeaconry of Okestock. The church of Saint Andrew is a building in the Perpendicular style. The living is a vicarage, net yearly value £376, and has been held since eighteen-seventy-five by—[*Turns round to her, she shows great fright.*] by the Reverend Francis Hindemarsh! Hindemarsh?

MRS. DANE. He was my uncle.

SIR DANIEL. Your uncle?

MRS. DANE. Sir Daniel, I've done wrong, very wrong to hide from you that Felicia Hindemarsh was my cousin.

SIR DANIEL. Felicia Hindemarsh was your cousin!

MRS. DANE. Can't you understand why I have hidden it? The whole affair was so terrible! I can't tell you how keenly I felt the disgrace, how keenly I feel it still.

SIR DANIEL. But she was only your cousin. Surely there was no reason for you to hide it from Lionel and me.

MRS. DANE. I didn't intend to hide it from you. But I had always concealed it from everybody. And having once begun I was obliged to go on. Can't you understand?

[*He doesn't reply. His face shows very grave concern, and he again walks up and down as if in perplexity as to what course he should take.*]

MRS. DANE [*after a considerable pause*]. You're angry with me?

SIR DANIEL. Not angry. But grieved, deeply grieved that you hadn't the courage to tell me the truth.

MRS. DANE. I will now—the whole truth—indeed, I will.

SIR DANIEL [*drily*]. Yes. Perhaps it would be advisable.

[*He is still evidently distressed and annoyed; at length goes up to writing-table, takes up the foolscap sheets, glances through them.*

SIR DANIEL. Of course this puts the matter in a new light.

MRS. DANE. How? I'll tell Lionel. Promise me it shan't part us!

SIR DANIEL. There is no reason you should be parted because you happen to be the cousin of Felicia Hindemarsh. But—

MRS. DANE. But what?

SIR DANIEL. Why didn't you deal openly with us? See how Lionel loves you! How he believes in you! And I too had grown to like you. I felt glad that you were going to be my daughter. Ah, why didn't you trust us?

MRS. DANE. Oh, I've done wrong, very wrong! Say that it shan't part us. You forgive me?

SIR DANIEL [*after a pause offers his hand which she takes eagerly*]. I forgive you. But you wish me to clear you thoroughly from this slander?

MRS. DANE. Yes, indeed. And you will?

SIR DANIEL. Yes. But understand, my dear Lucy, from this moment there must not be the faintest suspicion of trifling with the truth. Understand that most clearly.

MRS. DANE. I do.

SIR DANIEL. Then we'll consider that episode closed, and we'll make a fresh start.

MRS. DANE. Yes, ask me anything you please. I'm only too anxious to help you in getting at the truth.

SIR DANIEL. That ought not to be very difficult. [*Seats himself in revolving chair at writing-table, takes a pen, and occasionally makes notes of her answers.*] Now, Felicia Hindemarsh was your cousin?

MRS. DANE. Yes.

SIR DANIEL. Her father was the vicar of Tawhampton?

MRS. DANE. Yes.

SIR DANIEL. And your other cousin—Annie Allen?

MRS. DANE. I had no other cousin. When you asked what my cousin's name was I couldn't say 'Felicia Hindemarsh', so I gave the first name I could think of.

SIR DANIEL. Had you any other relatives in or near Tawhampton?

MRS. DANE. No.

SIR DANIEL. You were the only child of—[*Consulting foolscap sheets.*] of Robert and Sophia Allen?

MRS. DANE. Yes, my mother and her mother were sisters.

SIR DANIEL [*reading from foolscap*]. Robert Allen, woollen manufacturer, Tawhampton. In eighty-seven, being in difficulties, he sold his business and went to Montreal. You, his only child, went with him, and five years later you married Charles Lewis Dane, surgeon, Montreal. You lived there till two years ago when your husband died, and a year ago you came back to England and took up your residence at Winchester.

MRS. DANE. Yes.

SIR DANIEL. There are, of course, people in Montreal who knew you intimately as Mrs. Dane and can identify you.

MRS. DANE. Oh yes, of course.

SIR DANIEL. Will you please make me out a list of their names and addresses?

MRS. DANE. Yes, certainly. Shall I do it now?

[*Half rising to go.*

SIR DANIEL. No, by-and-by will do. Now to go back to your cousin, Felicia Hindemarsh. You have no idea where she is now?

MRS. DANE. Not the least.

SIR DANIEL. When was the last time you saw her?

MRS. DANE. When I left Tawhampton.

SIR DANIEL. When you left Tawhampton. [*Refers back to her statement.*] You haven't seen her since?

MRS. DANE. No. Sir Daniel, I feel I could collect my thoughts much better if I were alone and had time to remember. I feel so confused—

SIR DANIEL. I'll try not to tax you, if you'll answer one or two simple questions.

MRS. DANE. Very well.

SIR DANIEL. Felicia Hindemarsh was younger or older than you?

MRS. DANE. A year younger.

SIR DANIEL. Have you any portrait of her?

MRS. DANE. No.

SIR DANIEL. You kept up a correspondence with her when you left England?

MRS. DANE [*after a little pause*]. Yes.

SIR DANIEL. For how long?

MRS. DANE. For some years, I think.

SIR DANIEL. Have you any letter of hers?

MRS. DANE. No. After the dreadful affair in Vienna I destroyed everything.

SIR DANIEL. There would doubtless be persons in Tawhampton who would remember her as well as you?

MRS. DANE. Oh, yes, I should think. We only lived there as girls, and perhaps people might not recollect sufficiently to be sure—

SIR DANIEL. When Felicia Hindemarsh left Tawhampton, where did she go?

MRS. DANE. I don't quite know.

SIR DANIEL. But you had letters from her. Where did they come from?

MRS. DANE. Let me think—it was some seaside place, I think.

[*Pause.*

SIR DANIEL. You don't remember?

MRS. DANE. No. I'm getting so terribly muddled, I don't know what I'm saying. I—I—you frighten me!

SIR DANIEL. I frighten you?

[*His manner throughout has been calm and kind but very firm.*

MRS. DANE. Yes. I know you're very kind, and that I've nothing to fear, but I feel—I feel as if I were being thumb-screwed, and if you ask me one more question I must shriek out for help. [*A little pause.*] I'm sure it would be better for me to go and write it all out when I'm alone. [*Making a movement to go.*] Don't you think so?

SIR DANIEL [*arresting her with a gesture*]. No.

MRS. DANE. I'm in such a state that I can't be sure I'm giving you the right answers.

SIR DANIEL [*calm, stern*]. You must be sure you are giving me the right answers. Come now, sit down, and [*Very kindly.*] remember that I have not a single interest at stake except what is yours and Lionel's. Remember that I have no hope or desire in this matter, except to clear you triumphantly in the eyes of the world, and give you to Lionel for his wife. Now don't get anxious or excited. We'll soon get this tiresome business over!

MRS. DANE. Oh, I know I'm foolish, and you have been so patient and kind.

SIR DANIEL. This seaside place that Felicia Hindemarsh wrote from. Was it north, south, east, or west?

MRS. DANE. South, I think.

SIR DANIEL. Portsmouth, Brighton, Hastings, Eastbourne?

MRS. DANE. Brighton, I think.

SIR DANIEL. What was she doing there? [*No reply.*] You said your cousin was a governess?

MRS. DANE. I think she was pupil teacher at a school.

SIR DANIEL. Good. That's a clue.

MRS. DANE. A clue to what?

SIR DANIEL. If Felicia Hindemarsh was a pupil teacher at a school on the south coast, we shall doubtless be able to find out where it was, and some one who remembers her.

MRS. DANE. Yes. Yes. But I hope I shall find somebody at Tawhampton to-morrow—

SIR DANIEL. Yes. By the way, I'm free to-morrow; I think I'll run down to Tawhampton with you.

MRS. DANE [*feigning delight*]. Will you? That will be such a help to me. You can tell me exactly what kind of evidence you want, and you can be sure whether people are telling the truth.

SIR DANIEL. Can I?   [*Looking at her*.

MRS. DANE [*looking at him with the utmost frankness*]. I know that I shouldn't like to tell you what was false. I should feel that you would very soon drag the truth out of me. See how quickly you forced me to tell you that Felicia Hindemarsh was my cousin. And I'm glad you did! I should never have been happy or comfortable till I had told you and Lionel. Then you will go down to Tawhampton with me?

SIR DANIEL [*who has been keenly watching her*]. If you don't mind.

MRS. DANE. I shall be delighted. I hope my head will be better, and that I shall be well enough to go.

SIR DANIEL. I hope so. If not, I'll take a little journey there by myself.

MRS. DANE. Ye-es—

SIR DANIEL. Was your cousin anything like you?

MRS. DANE. I think there was a likeness. I daresay it was that which made Mr. Risby mistake me for her.

SIR DANIEL. Possibly. But Mr. Fendick said the other day that you were not in the least like Felicia Hindemarsh.

MRS. DANE. Did he? But often one person sees a likeness where another sees none. What time shall we start for Tawhampton to-morrow?

SIR DANIEL. I'll look out the trains by-and-by. . . . Then you never saw your cousin after childhood?

MRS. DANE. No—I—I—[*Suddenly breaks down.*] I can't bear it! I can't bear it!

SIR DANIEL. What?

MRS. DANE. Your questioning me as if I was guilty! I feel you suspect me still. Tell me, do you trust me thoroughly? [*He does not reply.*] Ah, you see you do not answer! So be it. Make me out a list of the questions you want answered and I'll answer them. But I can endure this torture no longer.

[*Going to window.*

SIR DANIEL. Stop. Come, my dear Lucy, this won't do. We are here to get at the truth, aren't we?

MRS. DANE. Yes, and you must see how ready and willing I am to answer your questions—I'm very faint—

SIR DANIEL. I'll only keep you a moment. Now I am going to ask you one question. Think well before you reply, because all your happiness and Lionel's depend upon my receiving a correct answer.

MRS. DANE. Well?!

SIR DANIEL. When was the last time you saw your cousin Felicia Hindemarsh?   [*A long pause.*

MRS. DANE. I'll tell you everything.

SIR DANIEL. Go on.

MRS. DANE. I don't know what you'll think of me. I don't care. I'd almost rather everybody believed me guilty than suffer what I have done the last few weeks. It's horrible!

SIR DANIEL. When was the last time you saw Felicia Hindemarsh?

MRS. DANE. After the fearful scandal in Vienna she wrote to me in Montreal. She was desperate and begged us to shelter her. We had been like sisters, and I wrote to her to come out to us, and we would give her a home.

SIR DANIEL. And you did?

MRS. DANE. Yes, till her death.

SIR DANIEL. When was that?

MRS. DANE. About a year ago.

SIR DANIEL. Where?   [*Pause.*

MRS. DANE. At Montreal.

SIR DANIEL. She lived with you in Montreal—as Felicia Hindemarsh?

MRS. DANE. No; we called her Mrs. Allen.

SIR DANIEL. Give me the names and addresses of those people who knew you in Montreal as Mrs. Dane and her as Mrs. Allen.

MRS. DANE. I'll write them out. Let me bring it to you this evening. What are you going to do with it?

SIR DANIEL. I'm going to prove that you are Lucy Dane—*if you are Lucy Dane*. [*She looks at him.* [Does Risby know who you are?

MRS. DANE. What do you mean?

SIR DANIEL. Does Risby know who you are?

MRS. DANE. Yes—he knows that I am Mrs. Dane.

SIR DANIEL. The cousin of Felicia Hindemarsh.

MRS. DANE [*after a pause*]. Yes.

SIR DANIEL. You told Risby, a mere acquaintance, that Felicia Hindemarsh was your cousin, and you didn't tell Lionel, you didn't tell me?

MRS. DANE. I—I—[*She looks at him.*] I—oh—I'll answer you no more. Believe what you please of me! I want no more of your help! Let me go!

SIR DANIEL [*stopping her*]. How much does Risby know?

MRS. DANE. Don't I tell you he knows I am Mrs. Dane?

SIR DANIEL. Woman, you're lying!

MRS. DANE [*flashes out on him*]. How dare you? How dare you?

SIR DANIEL. I say you're lying! You are Felicia Hindemarsh!

[*He looks at her steadily. Her eyes drop. She sinks on her knees before him, seizes his hand in supplication, looks at him appealingly; he angrily withdraws his hand.*

MRS. DANE. Don't tell Lionel!

SIR DANIEL [*with a little laugh*]. Not tell Lionel?

MRS. DANE [*in a dry, quiet voice*]. I'm not a bad woman. You don't know. You wouldn't condemn me if you knew all.

SIR DANIEL. Tell me.

MRS. DANE. I'd been brought up in a village. I was a child in knowledge. I knew nothing of life, nothing of the world. Mr.

Trent was very kind to me. He was rich and distinguished and flattered me by his notice. And I—oh, why didn't somebody warn me? Why did they keep me ignorant? I didn't even love him, not in that way—not as I love Lionel. I tell you I knew nothing! Nothing! Till it was too late! You believe me, don't you?

SIR DANIEL. Tell me all.

MRS. DANE. I hated myself. I should have hated him but he was very kind. It went on till all was discovered. His wife killed herself. He was frantic with grief and went out of his mind. I thought I'd kill myself—I did buy the poison—but I hadn't the courage. My cousin Lucy was living in Montreal. She was an angel—she took me into her home and gave out that I was a widow. My child was born there.

SIR DANIEL. There was a child?

MRS. DANE. Yes.

SIR DANIEL. Is it living?

MRS. DANE. Yes.

SIR DANIEL. Where is it?

MRS. DANE. In North Devon, with an old servant of ours. I see him every month. He is the sweetest boy, and I love him so much—next to Lionel. He'll never be any trouble—or disgrace. Now you know everything. I'm not a bad woman.

SIR DANIEL. I'm sorry for you, believe me, very sorry. But why did you wade through all that morass of lies and deceit? Why didn't you have the courage to tell me the truth?

MRS. DANE. Because I felt that you would part me from Lionel. If you loved a woman as I love him, wouldn't you tell lies, wouldn't you dare anything to keep her? You know you would! You know you would! And so did I, and I would do it again. You won't tell Lionel?

SIR DANIEL. He must be told. And this marriage must be broken off.

MRS. DANE. Why? Nobody need know. Mr. Risby won't betray me. The detective can't. I've paid him and he daren't. You won't tell Lionel?

SIR DANIEL. He must be told.

MRS. DANE. It can be hushed up. I'll make him such a good wife. Give me this one chance—don't tell him. Give me this one chance!

SIR DANIEL. He must be told.

Enter LAL *at window, excited.*

LAL. Lucy, I went for the keys; they weren't there. The escritoire was locked. Just as I was coming away Risby came up with a note for you. While he was talking at the door with the maid, she said something about his having called upon you this morning before lunch. Was that so? You met him here as if you hadn't seen him. I couldn't understand it—I've been questioning him all this time, but he only puts me off. He says I must ask you—

MRS. DANE [*to* SIR DANIEL]. Tell him.

Enter LADY EASTNEY.

LADY EASTNEY. Well, how is it going? Have you got all the evidence you want?

MRS. DANE. Will you come home with me? I wish to speak to you.

LADY EASTNEY. What's the matter?

MRS. DANE. Come home with me.

LADY EASTNEY. What has happened?

MRS. DANE. I want a friend. Don't be hard on me! Don't be hard on me!

[*Exit* MRS. DANE, *followed by* LADY EASTNEY. LAL *is going after them.*

SIR DANIEL [*holds up his hand, stops him*]. Lal!

CURTAIN.

ACT IV

SCENE. *The same as Act III. Time: the following Saturday evening. Windows open. Discover* LAL, *very haggard and restless, walking up and down. Enter* WILSON *at door, goes over to window, stops.*

WILSON. Sir Daniel has finished dinner, sir. [*No reply. Exit* WILSON *at window, returns in a few moments bringing in a rug and a light garden chair, which he leaves in the window; he folds the rug and places it on the arm of sofa.*] Shall I keep any dinner for you, sir?

LAL. Eh—no thank you, Wilson.

> [*Exit* WILSON *at door.* LAL *comes down to sofa and sits in a despairing attitude.*

Enter JANET *at door in evening dress—at first she does not see him.*

JANET. I beg pardon.

LAL. [*rises*] Janet—you wish to see my father?

JANET. No, I've just left him. Auntie and I have been dining here.

LAL. Oh yes. I'd forgotten.

JANET. We wondered what had become of you. Why didn't you come in to dinner?

LAL. I'm not fit for any company but my own.

JANET. Sir Daniel and Auntie are taking coffee in the veranda. Won't you come and join them?

LAL. I'd rather not. Please don't take any notice of me.

> [*She is going off at door—he sits down again in despair—she suddenly stops; comes back to him.*

JANET. Mr. Carteret, I don't know what has happened. But I can see there's something the matter with you. Perhaps you've had a great sorrow. Well, you'll pull yourself together and be a man. It'll tak you all your time, I've nae doubt, but you've just got to do it, d'ye understand?

LAL. I'll try.

JANET. And you needn't think that you're the only poor body on earth that's badly used. For if ye did but know, there's many a man, and many a wee bit of a woman that has just as thankless a lot as yours. So I'd not be wasting too much pity on myself if I were you.

LAL. I won't, Janet.

JANET. And if you've lost one friend, perhaps that may be the very means of showing you the value of them that are left.

Enter LADY EASTNEY, *at door, in dinner dress.*

JANET. I've just been giving him the very best advice in the world.

LADY EASTNEY. How d'ye do, Lionel?

LAL. How d'ye do, Lady Eastney?

LADY EASTNEY [*comes very tenderly and sympathetically to him, takes both hands of his in hers, looks at him, shakes her head at him*]. No sleep again? No appetite?

LAL [*withdraws his hands*]. I can't eat. And I feel I shall never sleep again.

LADY EASTNEY. Your father is grieving very much about you.

LAL. I'm sorry, for there never was anybody less worth grieving about than I am.

LADY EASTNEY. Go to him. Try and eat something just to please him.

LAL. It would choke me. Don't bother any more about me, Lady Eastney. I daresay I shall get over it by the time I'm dead.   [*Going off at window.*

LADY EASTNEY. Lionel! [*He stops. In a low tone.*] You've not seen her since—

LAL. No, I've kept my word, and broken my heart. I heard the clock chime every quarter of an hour last night. I feel I should like to lie at the bottom of the river to-night where I couldn't hear it.

LADY EASTNEY. Lionel, where are you going?

LAL. Does it matter where I go or what becomes of me?

JANET [*trying to stop him*]. Mr. Carteret—

LAL. Let me be, Janet!

LADY EASTNEY. Lionel! you won't do anything rash?

LAL. You needn't fear I shall kill myself. I'm too much of a coward. But—tell my father I can keep my promise no longer. I'm going across to her.   [*Exit.*]

JANET [*bursts into tears and throws her arms round* LADY EASTNEY's *neck*]. Auntie, I can just bear it no longer! My heart will break! Let Mrs. Patterson take me away—anything—anything—so that I can be at work and forget!

LADY EASTNEY. Hush, hush! You mustn't be a coward!

Enter SIR DANIEL *at door.* JANET *controls herself.*

LADY EASTNEY. There! There's a brave Janet.

JANET. I'm just a poor silly body that ought to know better!

LADY EASTNEY. Janet, would you go home and look in my dressing-table. You'll find a sleeping powder in the second drawer—

JANET. Yes, I know.

LADY EASTNEY. Bring it to me here.

JANET. Yes, Auntie.   [*Exit.*

LADY EASTNEY. We must manage to give Lionel a little sleep tonight. He's nearly distracted for want of it.

SIR DANIEL. Poor fellow! I'm rather glad he has taken it so violently.

LADY EASTNEY. Why?

SIR DANIEL. It means that in six months it will be out of his system.

LADY EASTNEY. It's a genuine love. Don't you think it will last?

SIR DANIEL. A few months. But even if it goes deeper than I think it does, it must be broken off.

LADY EASTNEY. Why? Nobody except ourselves need know that this story is true.

SIR DANIEL. The Bulsom-Porters know it—the whole neighbourhood must know it before long.

LADY EASTNEY. The Bulsom-Porters think that Mr. Risby was really mistaken. The Canon has them to dinner tonight, and he's doing his best to get her to sign the apology you drew up.

SIR DANIEL. We can't ask Mrs. Bulsom-Porter for an apology now!

LADY EASTNEY. Indeed we can. Whatever happens to Mrs. Dane, I'm quite determined Mrs. Bulsom-Porter shall make a handsome apology, and everybody shall know it; then I don't think the story will ever be repeated.

SIR DANIEL. And will Mrs. Dane continue to live in Sunning-water?

LADY EASTNEY. She's quite willing to do whatever you and Lionel wish. I've been with her all the afternoon. Oh, the pearls of wisdom and good advice that dropped from this small mouth! And I felt myself such a transcendent humbug all the while!

SIR DANIEL. Why?

LADY EASTNEY. Aren't we all humbugs? Isn't it all a sham? Don't we all have one code on our lips and another in our hearts, one set of rules to admonish our neighbours, and another to guide our own conduct? Why should I lecture that poor woman on her duty to Society? Why should I take her name off my visiting list and pretend that I can't know her?

SIR DANIEL. Because you're a virtuous woman, and she isn't.

LADY EASTNEY. That's true—as it happens—and so far as it goes. Small credit to me! I wasn't in her place—I didn't meet with her temptations—and if I had I should have been cold-hearted enough, or cunning enough to resist.

SIR DANIEL. Very well. That's all a man can ask; the temperament—call it virtue or cunning—that resists.

LADY EASTNEY. Not a pretty kind of cunning, that! And sometimes the man gets the other kind of cunning—the cunning that conceals!

SIR DANIEL. Very well. We can't help ourselves. But at any rate the outside of the platter must be clean.

LADY EASTNEY. Oh, aren't you Pharisees and tyrants, all of you? And don't you make cowards and hypocrites of all of us? Don't you lead us into sin and then condemn us for it? Aren't you first our partners and then our judges?

SIR DANIEL. The rules of the game are severe. If you don't like them, leave the sport alone. They will never be altered.

LADY EASTNEY. But where's the justice of the whole business? Here is this poor woman whom Lionel loves, and who loves Lionel with all her heart—why shouldn't he marry her?

SIR DANIEL. If he were your son would you wish him to marry her? Would you wish all his after-life to be poisoned by the thought that she had deceived him, that she had belonged to another man, and that man and his child still living? Do, for heaven's sake, let us get rid of all this sentimental cant and sophistry about this woman business. [*Unconsciously getting very heated.*] A man demands the treasure of a woman's purest love. It's what he buys and pays for with the strength of his arm and the sweat of his brow. It's the condition on which he makes her his wife and fights the world for her and his children. It's his fiercest instinct, and he does well to guard it; for it's the very mainspring of a nation's health and soundness. And whatever I've done, whatever I've been myself, I'm quite resolved my son shan't marry another man's mistress. There's the plain sense of the whole matter, so let us have no more talk about patching up things that ought not to be patched up, that can't be patched up, and that shan't be patched up if I can stop them from being patched up!

LADY EASTNEY [*looks at him very much amused*]. I wouldn't get into a temper about it if I were you.

SIR DANIEL. Am I in a temper? Pray forgive me.

LADY EASTNEY. I rather like you in a temper. It shows me that if I marry you, you'd be my master.

SIR DANIEL. Let me assure you I'd try. Will you take me?

LADY EASTNEY. Couldn't you manage to put a little of the fervour you waste on social ethics into your love-making?

SIR DANIEL. I'll try. Will you take me?

LADY EASTNEY [*pauses, looks at him merrily*]. I'm really half inclined—

Enter WILSON *at door*.

WILSON. Canon Bonsey would like to speak to you for a moment, Sir Daniel.

SIR DANIEL. Show him in.   [*Exit* WILSON.

LADY EASTNEY. He has come from the Bulsom-Porters. Now remember that we can't go back from the position we have taken up—the fullest apology.

Enter WILSON *showing in* CANON BONSEY.

WILSON. Canon Bonsey.

Enter CANON BONSEY. *Exit* WILSON.

CANON BONSEY. How d'ye do, Sir Daniel? How d'ye do, Lady Eastney?

LADY EASTNEY [*shaking hands*]. How d'ye do, Canon?

CANON BONSEY [*making a wry face*]. I've had the Bulsom-Porters to dinner. And seeing that Bulsom-Porter knows a glass of good wine I felt bound to bring out my elegant eighty-nine Ayala and my sixty-three port. I cannot imagine a more unworthy office for either vintage than that of assisting Mrs. Bulsom-Porter's digestion. However, I've persuaded her to go home and fetch the apology you drew up last Saturday. They're coming on here, and I think, with a little judicious handling, we shall persuade the lady to sign it. Don't I hear voices? [*Goes to the window*.] They're coming. Eh? [*Looks very grave and shocked*.] They're quarrelling in the lane. I heard an ejaculation from Bulsom-Porter which ill accords with the sylvan beauty of the scene. What!

[*Exit quickly at window*.

SIR DANIEL. Take care how you work this apology business. Suppose Mrs. Bulsom-Porter finds out that we know Mrs. Dane is an impostor?

LADY EASTNEY. We don't know it. Mr. Risby and the detective say she isn't. I intend that Mrs. Dane shall leave this place, if she does leave it, without a stain on her character. And I intend that Mrs. Bulsom-Porter shall stay in it, if she does stay in it, as a self-confessed scandal-monger.

SIR DANIEL. But I can't exact an apology—

LADY EASTNEY [*very firmly*]. I can! Hush!

CANON BONSEY *enters at window leading in* MRS. BULSOM-PORTER *very carefully.* BULSOM-PORTER *follows.* BULSOM-PORTER *and* MRS. BULSOM-PORTER *are evidently in a bad temper with each other.*

CANON BONSEY. Take care of the window-threshold. Perhaps Sir Daniel will excuse us entering this way?

SIR DANIEL. Certainly. [*To* MRS. BULSOM-PORTER, *shaking hands.*] How d'ye do?

MRS. BULSOM-PORTER. How d'ye do, Sir Daniel?

SIR DANIEL. How d'ye do?

[*To* BULSOM-PORTER. BULSOM-PORTER *says nothing, but shakes hands, glances at* MRS. BULSOM-PORTER. SIR DANIEL *gives a sympathetic handshake behind the back of* MRS. BULSOM-PORTER, *who is exchanging a constrained bow with* LADY EASTNEY.

CANON BONSEY [*to* MRS. BULSOM-PORTER]. Did you bring the paper?

MRS. BULSOM-PORTER [*produces the paper that* SIR DANIEL *has given her at the end of Act II*]. I shall not sign this.

CANON BONSEY [*taken aback*]. But, my dear lady, I understood you at dinner to say that you would sign it.

MRS. BULSOM-PORTER. Yes. But since dinner Mr. Bulsom-Porter has chosen to use such dreadful language to me, that I must first of all insist upon an apology from him.

[CANON *turns helplessly to* BULSOM-PORTER.

BULSOM-PORTER. Tell her to kindly send in a form of an apology to Rawlinson, my lawyer, and I'll sign it.

CANON BONSEY. Hush! [*Turns to* MRS. BULSOM-PORTER.] Mr. Bulsom-Porter is only too anxious to withdraw his language to you, as I am sure you are only too anxious to withdraw your allegations against Mrs. Dane.

MRS. BULSOM-PORTER. I object to the word 'allegations'. I made certain statements—

CANON BONSEY. 'Statements', by all means. Which you are anxious to withdraw.

MRS. BULSOM-PORTER. I object to the word 'withdraw'.

CANON BONSEY. Which you will not repeat.

MRS. BULSOM-PORTER. Which will not be repeated. The word 'apologize' is used in this paper. I cannot apologize to Mrs. Dane. I would rather go to gaol.

[CANON BONSEY *goes to* BULSOM-PORTER.

BULSOM-PORTER [*in a low tone, but sufficiently loud for his wife to hear*]. Kindly arrange a settlement on that basis.

CANON BONSEY [*tries to soothe him*]. Hush! [*To* MRS. BULSOM-PORTER.] You will not apologize. I suppose you would not mind expressing your regret?

MRS. BULSOM-PORTER. I do not mind some slight expression of regret, but I will never apologize.

CANON BONSEY [*helpless*]. Sir Daniel, what do you advise under the circumstances?

SIR DANIEL [*looks at* LADY EASTNEY]. Well, I—a—

LADY EASTNEY. Mrs. Bulsom-Porter, will you please allow me to look at that paper? [MRS. BULSOM-PORTER *gives paper to* LADY EASTNEY, *who reads it*.] I'm surprised!

MRS. BULSOM-PORTER. At what?

LADY EASTNEY. At Sir Daniel's moderation. [SIR DANIEL *makes a face*.] I don't think you quite realize the very awkward position you are in.

MRS. BULSOM-PORTER. How?

LADY EASTNEY [*to* BULSOM-PORTER]. You thoroughly approve of this?

BULSOM-PORTER. Most certainly.

LADY EASTNEY. Sir Daniel, what would happen if Mr. Bulsom-Porter were to instruct his lawyer to offer his own apologies to Mrs. Dane, at the same time declaring that he wouldn't hold himself responsible for what Mrs. Bulsom-Porter does or says?

SIR DANIEL. Well, a—I scarcely know.

MRS. BULSOM-PORTER. I shall not be bound by my husband's actions.

LADY EASTNEY. Isn't it whether he will be bound by yours? The only question is as to how far Mr. Bulsom-Porter is prepared to go—

BULSOM-PORTER. My dear Lady Eastney, I am prepared to go to any lengths. I will offer Mrs. Dane the most abject apology on my knees, and I will allow her lawyer to dictate it in any terms and make any use of it that he pleases.

LADY EASTNEY. I think that will meet our views, Sir Daniel?

SIR DANIEL. Yes, yes. I think so—

LADY EASTNEY. Mrs. Dane will then bring her action against Mrs. Bulsom-Porter?

SIR DANIEL. Yes, I suppose so—

MRS. BULSOM-PORTER. Action against me?

LADY EASTNEY. And call Mr. Bulsom-Porter for a witness—

MRS. BULSOM-PORTER. What? My husband will not dare—

BULSOM-PORTER [*very sympathetic*]. My dear, I shall!

LADY EASTNEY. I suppose there is no doubt whatever of the effect upon the jury, Sir Daniel?

SIR DANIEL. None whatever, I should say—or upon the judge.

LADY EASTNEY [*to* MRS. BULSOM-PORTER]. Don't you see what a very awkward position you are in? Mr. Bulsom-Porter, will you step across to Mrs. Dane with me at once?

BULSOM-PORTER. Delighted.

LADY EASTNEY [*to* BULSOM-PORTER]. My cloak is in the next room.   [*Going off at door.*

MRS. BULSOM-PORTER. One moment! I do not object to sign this if Sir Daniel will remove the word 'apology'.

LADY EASTNEY. It must be signed exactly as it stands.

MRS. BULSOM-PORTER. No! I will do anything that Sir Daniel may require, but I will not apologize.

LADY EASTNEY. Now, Mr. Bulsom-Porter—

MRS. BULSOM-PORTER. One moment please. [*Very long pause.*] Sir Daniel, if I had to sign this—agreement, where should I have to put my name?

SIR DANIEL [*pointing*]. There.

LADY EASTNEY [*takes up a pen from writing-table*]. Do you like a broad nib? Or a quill?

MRS. BULSOM-PORTER. Neither.

LADY EASTNEY [*takes up another*]. This seems a nice one.

[MRS. BULSOM-PORTER *takes it after great hesitation, at last dashes off the signature and bursts into a fit of hysterical tears.*

LADY EASTNEY [*offering pen*]. Canon, will you sign as witness?

CANON BONSEY. Certainly.   [*Signs.*

LADY EASTNEY. And I will put my autograph, and then the interesting document will be complete.   [*Signs.*

CANON BONSEY. And peace will be restored to my distracted parish.

MRS. BULSOM-PORTER [*getting more and more hysterical*]. If any future question arises, I wish it to be distinctly understood that my signature was forced from me, against my will, and under threats from my husband—and—I'm quite sure Jim Risby knows something dreadful about that woman—and if my husband had the least sense of what was due to his wife—I—understand—I do not apologize. I have not, and I never will apologize, and, oh—[*To* BULSOM-PORTER.] Let me pass, sir! Let me pass!   [*Exit in hysterics at window. Pause.*

BULSOM-PORTER [*very quietly*]. It's my silver wedding on the twentieth of next month.

CANON BONSEY [*to* BULSOM-PORTER]. Mrs. Bulsom-Porter seemed very much upset. Oughtn't one of us attend her home?

BULSOM-PORTER. Well, perhaps you will.

[CANON BONSEY *goes up to window—stops, comes back.*

CANON BONSEY. Perhaps we had better both go. Are you ready?

BULSOM-PORTER [*shrugs his shoulders*]. I shall be there before Mrs. Bulsom-Porter has recovered. Good-night, Sir Daniel. My very best thanks. Good-night, my dear Lady Eastney; you have saved me from a lawsuit and a thousand pounds damages.

LADY EASTNEY. Don't mention it. Good-night.

BULSOM-PORTER. Now, Canon!

> [*Goes to window, takes out cigar and lights it.*

CANON BONSEY. Good-night, Sir Daniel.

SIR DANIEL. Good-night, my dear Canon.

CANON BONSEY. Good-night, dear Lady Eastney.

LADY EASTNEY [*shaking hands*]. Good-night, Canon.

CANON BONSEY. Give my kindest regards to Mrs. Dane. Of course she will take the stall at the bazaar. And I'll bring the duchess to call upon her one day next week.

> [*Exit after* BULSOM-PORTER *at window.*

SIR DANIEL. Did you hear that?

LADY EASTNEY. Yes. I must persuade Mrs. Dane to go away for a few months.

SIR DANIEL. And then?

LADY EASTNEY. I do want to save Mrs. Dane. How can I?

SIR DANIEL. Impossible. The thing can't be patched up. It ought not to be patched up.

LADY EASTNEY. What is to be done?

SIR DANIEL. We must get Lal away from her; take him out to Egypt; give him some work; throw him into young society, and trust to time and his healthy instincts to bring him round.

LADY EASTNEY. I suppose you are right. But in any case I'll give Mrs. Dane this certificate of character from Mrs. Bulsom-Porter.

> [*Taking up the paper which* MRS. BULSOM-PORTER *has signed.*

Enter JANET *at door with evening cloak over her dress.*

JANET. Here is the sleeping powder, Auntie. Will you be coming home now?

LADY EASTNEY. In a little while, darling. [*Passing her hand caressingly over* JANET'*s forehead.*] Why, how hot and feverish your forehead is. Go and sit under the cedars till I'm ready.

> [*Taking* JANET *towards window; they both stop.* JANET *hides her head on* LADY EASTNEY'*s shoulders;* LADY EASTNEY *takes her off at door as* LAL *enters at window.*

LAL. I've broken my word. I've seen her. I've asked her to come over here and see you. You won't refuse to receive her?

SIR DANIEL. No. I wish to see her.

LAL. I'll fetch her.   [*Going off.*

SIR DANIEL. Stay. Lal, this must end. You must give her up.

LAL. I can't. I won't! Why should I? She was sinned against, not sinning. She was ignorant! She knew no better!

SIR DANIEL. Get rid of that sorry cant, my lad. Every girl of fifteen knows black from white, knows her right hand from her left, knows that if she lets some plausible scoundrel rob her of her jewel, she'll by-and-by come a beggared bride to a cheated bride-groom!

LAL. I don't care! I love her! And I shall never be happy with anybody else.

SIR DANIEL. Do you think you'll be happy with her when the first burst of passion is over? Don't you think you'll begin to remember that she has deceived you, hoodwinked you, that her lover is now living, that his child is now living? Remember! You haven't had all her love! She loved and gave herself away before she knew you—

[LAL, *mad with resentment, raises both arms as if he would strike* SIR DANIEL.

SIR DANIEL. Ah! that stabs you, does it? Don't you think that same thought will come and stab you continually? Say in a few years some good-looking friend comes along and is civil to her. She's civil to him. You'll begin to wonder how far it has gone; you'll remember that she can deceive; you won't be sure; you'll question her; she'll reassure you, she'll swear and re-swear and swear again, but you'll never be certain; you may be wronging her but—she may be wronging you. You'll never know. All that you'll know is, 'She can lie; she lied to me; she lied to my father; she lied to all of us; she lied, and lied, and lied—is she lying to me now?' And you'll never know. Your life will be a very hell to you.

LAL. So be it! Hell with her, rather than heaven with any other woman!

SIR DANIEL. Nonsense! Pull yourself together! Put all your heart and soul into your work. You'll have an awful three months, an awful six months perhaps. But you'll conquer yourself. You'll be a better and stronger and braver man all your life for it. Love isn't the only thing on earth. It oughtn't always to be the first—

LAL. What's the use of your preaching to me? You've never been in love.

SIR DANIEL. You think that?

LAL. You've never loved a woman as I love her and then had to give her up.

SIR DANIEL [*very tenderly and impressively*]. My boy, I loved one woman when you were a child—ah, I did love her—you don't know what love is, if you compare your hot boyish passion of a few weeks with my deep love of years. I gave her up; we gave each other up; it broke our hearts but we did it— her son doesn't blush when he remembers her—you and I have stood by her grave together—

LAL [*startled*]. Sir!   [*Looks at* SIR DANIEL.

SIR DANIEL Do you think I'd deny her son anything? Don't you think I'd give all I have in the world to make him happy? And when I ask him to renounce an unworthy love, a love that will by-and-by bring him to misery—[*A cry of anguish from* LAL.] You'll do it, Lal! I'm not asking you to do what I haven't done myself! You'll do it?

LAL. Yes, sir.

> [*A warm handshake.* MRS. DANE *comes to window with a face of despair. She is unseen by* LAL, *but* SIR DANIEL *sees her and makes her a motion; she withdraws.*

SIR DANIEL. Let me say good-bye for you.

LAL. Mustn't I see her?

SIR DANIEL. It will be better not.

LAL. You'll be very kind to her?

SIR DANIEL. She will find me the truest and best of friends to her and her child. Go into the other room—Lady Eastney is there. I think she has something for you.

LAL. Be very gentle to her——

> [SIR DANIEL *reassures him with a look and a grasp of the hand. Exit* LAL *at door.*

MRS. DANE *enters.*

SIR DANIEL. What have you heard?

MRS. DANE. Enough. You mean to part us then?

SIR DANIEL. It is not I who will part you.

MRS. DANE. Who will, then?

SIR DANIEL. Yourself. You wish him to be happy?

MRS. DANE. I have no other wish in the world.

SIR DANIEL. I believe that if you hold up your finger and beckon him he will come to you from the end of the world and marry you.

MRS. DANE [*delighted*]. Ah!

SIR DANIEL. What does that mean? He is on the threshold of a fine career; devoted to his work, with a large circle of friends. If you become his wife, will you tell them your history? They will all fall away from you. Will you hide it? That's impossible. He loves you now, but in a few years' time—dare you put his love to such a test? Dare you marry him knowing that day by day he must help you deceive till disclosure comes; and then, day by day, he must endure social isolation *with* you, disorder and failure in his career *for* you—dare you marry him? Will it be for your own happiness?

MRS. DANE. My happiness! What does that matter? Tell me what is best for him?

SIR DANIEL. Don't you know what is best for him?

[*A long pause.*

MRS. DANE. So be it! Say 'Good-bye' to him for me.

Enter LADY EASTNEY *at door, bringing cloak on her arm.*

LADY EASTNEY. I've something for you.

[*Taking the paper from her pocket, and giving it to* MRS. DANE.

MRS. DANE [*takes the paper, reads it, smiles very bitterly*]. Thank you.

LADY EASTNEY. What have you decided to do?

MRS. DANE. I'm going to Devonshire tomorrow. I shall make a long stay there. I shan't let him know where I am. How is he now?

LADY EASTNEY. He's quieter. I've persuaded him to take a mouthful of food and some wine. I put a strong sleeping powder in the wine, so he'll sleep to-night, poor fellow.

MRS. DANE. He'll sleep to-night, poor fellow. Tell him about my going away when you think he can bear it. I needn't stay, need I? Thank you for this—[*Referring to paper.*] but what's the use of it?

LADY EASTNEY. Mrs. Bulsom-Porter daren't attack your reputation now.

MRS. DANE. Reputation? Reputation isn't much, is it, when love has gone. Don't think I'm ungrateful to you—[*Tearing it.*] but I shan't trouble to defend my reputation. Good-bye, Sir Daniel. Don't you think the world is very hard on a woman?

SIR DANIEL. It isn't the world that's hard. It isn't men and women. Am I hard? Call on me at any time, and you shall find me the truest friend to you and yours. Is Lady Eastney hard? She has been fighting all the week to save you.

MRS. DANE. Then who is it, what is it, drives me out?

SIR DANIEL. The law, the hard law that we didn't make, that we would break if we could, for we are all sinners at heart— the law that is above us all, made for us all, that we can't escape from, that we must keep or perish.

MRS. DANE. Won't it do if we pretend to keep it, and force our neighbours to keep it instead?

SIR DANIEL. Even that shows that we own the law.

MRS. DANE. Only we mustn't get found out. I'm afraid I've broken that part of the law. Good-bye, Sir Daniel.

SIR DANIEL. I'll see you across to your home.

MRS. DANE. No, I would rather you didn't. Just put me outside your palings and then I'll find my way. Good-bye, Lady Eastney.

LADY EASTNEY. Good-bye. [*Shaking hands warmly.*] Write to me. Tell me how you are. Will you? I shall be pleased to hear.

MRS. DANE. If ever I come here again, will you receive me?

LADY EASTNEY [*after a pause*]. If you call, I shall be at home.

MRS. DANE. God bless you! Now, Sir Daniel, you shall see me outside the palings—no further. I shall see my boy tomorrow.

[*Exit at window followed by* SIR DANIEL. LADY EASTNEY *goes up to window. Enter* LAL *at door looking very much quieter but rather bewildered as if under the influence of a sleeping draught.*

LAL. Well?

LADY EASTNEY. How tired you look!   [*Takes him to sofa.*

LAL. Well? [*Sits on sofa.*] I shall get over this, you know.

LADY EASTNEY. I'm sure you will.

LAL. Father is right. I shall go out to Sir Robert and get on with this railway—and then I—

[*He shows symptoms of sleepiness.* LADY EASTNEY *watches him a moment and then goes to window. He lies on sofa, a distant church clock chimes, and strikes eleven.* SIR DANIEL *re-enters at window, and they come to* LAL. *They stand watching him.*

SIR DANIEL. We'll take him off to Egypt—you'll come and bring Janet?

LADY EASTNEY [*nods*]. It's getting late. Where is Janet? [*Calls indoors.*] Janet! Janet! Janet! I suppose she has gone, poor child. Will you take me home?

SIR DANIEL. Say that in a little while I shall not have to take you home.

LADY EASTNEY. I think I could feel at home with you.

SIR DANIEL. Say that you *are* at home now.

LADY EASTNEY [*takes his arm*]. I am at home now.

[SIR DANIEL *turns off the electric light. Exeunt at window. A little pause.* JANET *enters at door, comes up to* LAL, *who is lying on the sofa in the moonlight; she looks at him, bends over him, and kisses him. Curtain falls as she goes off at window.*

A NOTE ON THE TEXTS

John Bull. There are many texts of *John Bull,* both acting and reading editions; the one printed here is a conflation of the authorized London edition of 1805 (there was a pirated Dublin edition of 1803) with the earliest acting edition, *Cumberland's British Theatre,* v. 36, and two Drury Lane prompt-books of 1812 and 1818. The earlier acting editions preserve the original five acts with some cuts; the later versions reduce the number of acts to three and make further cuts. The Lord Chamberlain's manuscript and the text in v. 21 of Inchbald's *British Theatre* (1808) are useful in correcting occasional misprints in the 1805.

The Miller and His Men. The text is based primarily on the earliest acting edition, in *Cumberland* v. 26, collated with the 1813 second edition. *Lacy's Acting Edition of Plays,* supp. v. 1, is a record of the Haymarket revival of 1861, but is useful for correcting misprints in *Cumberland.* A later acting edition still, *Dicks' Standard Plays* no. 28, is identical with *Cumberland.*

The Factory Lad. The text is a collation of *Duncombe's British Theatre,* v. 11, and *Dicks'* no. 230, which although much later is virtually a reprint of *Duncombe.* As *The Factory Lad* was performed at the Surrey Theatre, outside the Lord Chamberlain's pre-1843 jurisdiction, no copy was submitted to his Examiner of Plays for licensing.

How to Settle Accounts with Your Laundress. The authoritative text is the *National Acting Drama,* v. 14; the much later *Dicks'* no. 1006 is almost identical. The acting editions amplify the Lord Chamberlain's manuscript considerably.

Box and Cox. Four acting editions were collated to establish the present text: *Lacy* v. 5, *Duncombe* v. 60, *Dicks'* no. 1059, and *Heywood's Original Dramas, Farces, Operettas,* no. 190. Of these the earlier *Lacy* and *Duncombe* are more authoritative; actually the four texts are virtually the same. The *Lacy* text turns up again in the American *French's Minor Drama,* v. 21. The Lord Chamberlain's copy is slightly shorter than the printed texts, but there are no changes of substance.

The Corsican Brothers. The only printed text of the play is that published by Chapman in 1852. This has been collated with Charles Kean's prompt copy in the Harvard Theatre Collection (with which it is virtually identical) and the Lord Chamberlain's copy, which is a little fuller than the other texts.

A NOTE ON THE TEXTS

Engaged. The text is that in the Chatto and Windus *Original Plays*, Second Series (1881) collated with the privately printed 1877 edition, the *French's Acting Edition*, v. 117, which is virtually identical with the 1877, and the Lord Chamberlain's copy. The stage directions in the 1877 are somewhat fuller than in other texts and have been incorporated here.

The Magistrate. The text here is the Heinemann first edition of 1892, collated with the *French* acting edition of 1936 and the Lord Chamberlain's copy; stage directions from the *French*, much the same as those in the licenser's copy, have been included. Corruptions in the 1892 can be remedied from the licenser's text, which is slightly longer than the printed texts.

Mrs. Dane's Defence. The text is a conflation of the privately printed Chiswick Press edition of 1900, the Macmillan first edition of 1905, the *French* acting edition of 1908, and the text edited by Clayton Hamilton in v. 3 of Jones's *Representative Plays* (1926).